SWEATS ARE GETTING OLD! THESE ARE THE DAYS OF SAMUE!!
LET'S MAKE EVERYONE HAPPY BY INCREASING MY APPEARANCES! ♡
BOOYAH!

和月伸宏

NOBUHIRO WATSUKI

SAMUE

I ACQUIRED A *SAMUE* (MONK WORK CLOTHES) AS MY EVERYDAY WORK OUTFIT. CONGRATULATIONS!!

A *SAMUE* HAS BEEN, FOR A LONG TIME, SOMETHING I ASSOCIATED WITH THE PROFESSIONAL WORLD. I HAVE SECRETLY ADMIRED THE OUTFIT THINKING, "MAYBE I WILL BE ABLE TO BECOME A CREATOR FULL OF PROFESSIONAL SPIRIT..." AND NOW, MY LONGTIME WISH HAS COME TRUE... HUH!!

COULD IT BE THAT I AM JUST COSPLAYING, WANTING TO "BECOME" A PROFESSIONAL!?

Rurouni Kenshin, which has found fans not only in Japan but around the world, first made its appearance in 1992, as an original short story in ***Weekly Shonen Jump Special***. Later rewritten and published as a regular, continuing ***Jump*** series in 1994, ***Rurouni Kenshin*** ended serialization in 1999 but continued in popularity, as evidenced by the 2000 publication of ***Yahiko no Sakabatô*** ("Yahiko's Reversed-Edge Sword") in ***Weekly Shonen Jump***. His most current work, ***Busô Renkin*** ("Armored Alchemist"), began publication in June 2003, also in ***Jump***.

RUROUNI KENSHIN
VOL. 23: SIN, JUDGMENT, ACCEPTANCE
The SHONEN JUMP Manga Edition

STORY AND ART BY
NOBUHIRO WATSUKI

English Adaptation/Pancha Diaz
Translation/Kenichiro Yagi
Touch-Up Art & Lettering/Steve Dutro
Design/Matt Hinrichs
Editor/Kit Fox

VP, Production/Alvin Lu
VP, Publishing Licensing/Rika Inouye
VP, Sales & Product Marketing/Gonzalo Ferreyra
VP, Creative/Linda Espinosa
Publisher/Hyoe Narita

Printed in the U.S.A.

Published by VIZ Media, LLC
P.O. Box 77010
San Francisco, CA 94107

SHONEN JUMP Manga Edition
10 9 8 7 6 5 4 3 2
First printing, January 2006
Second printing, February 2009

www.viz.com

PARENTAL ADVISORY
RUROUNI KENSHIN is rated T+ for Older Teen and is recommended for ages 16 and up. This volume contains realistic violence and tobacco use.
ratings.viz.com

THE WORLD'S
MOST POPULAR MANGA

www.shonenjump.com

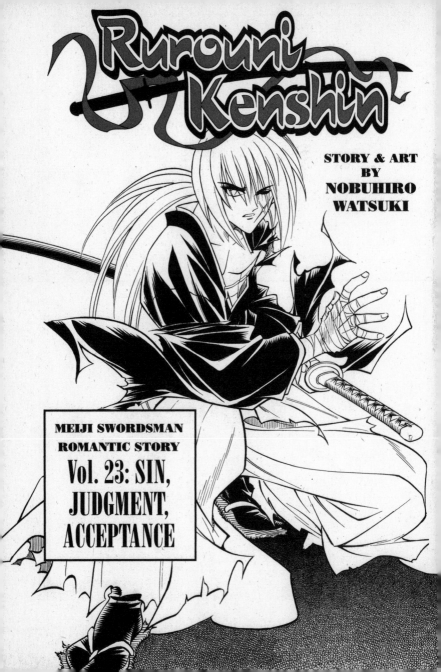

Rurouni Kenshin

STORY & ART
BY
NOBUHIRO
WATSUKI

MEIJI SWORDSMAN
ROMANTIC STORY
Vol. 23: SIN, JUDGMENT, ACCEPTANCE

CAST

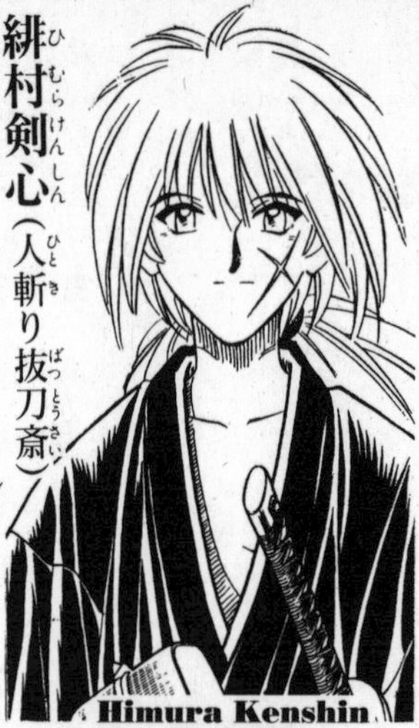

緋村剣心（人斬り抜刀斎）

Himura Kenshin (Hitokiri Battōsai)

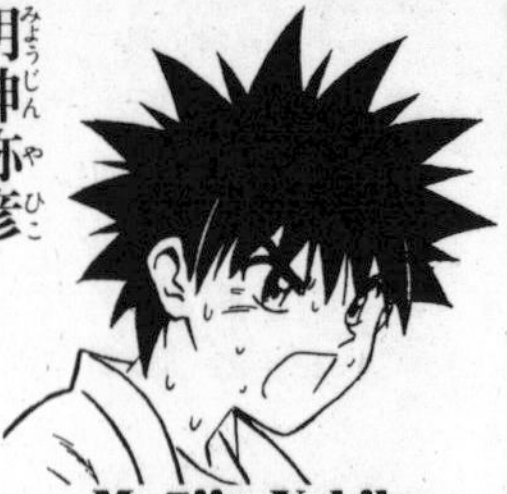

明神弥彦

Myōjin Yahiko

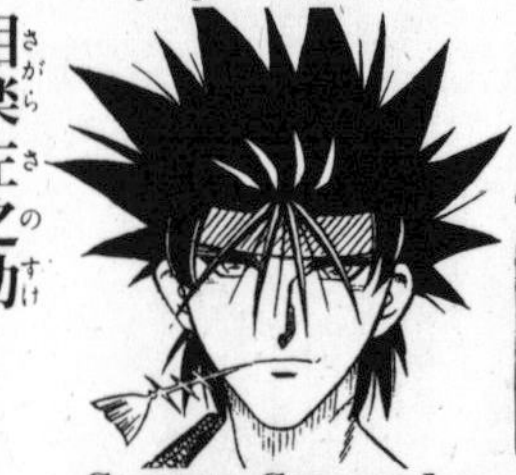

相楽左之助

Sagara Sanosuke

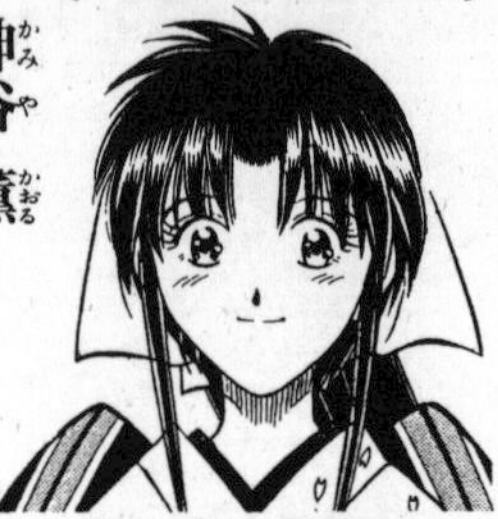

神谷 薫

Kamiya Kaoru

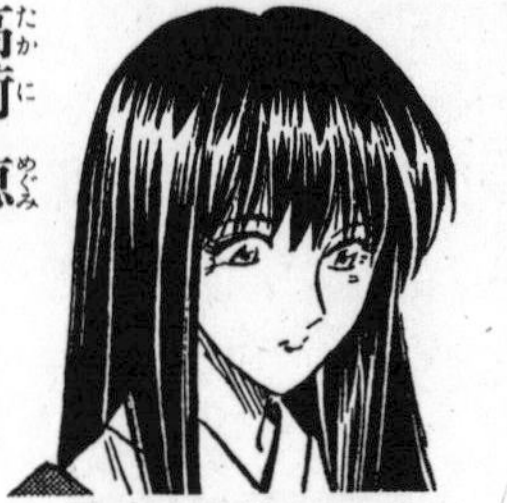

高荷 恵

Takani Megumi

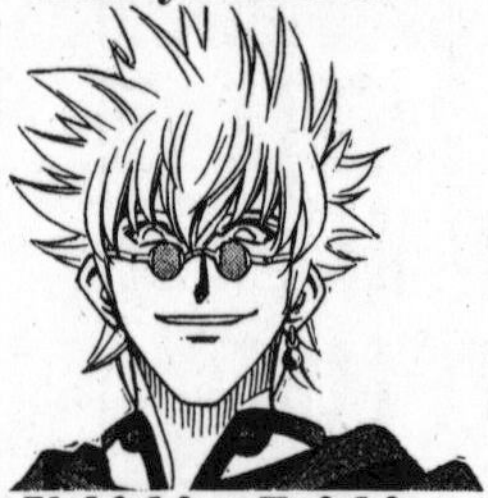

雪代 縁

Yukishiro Enishi

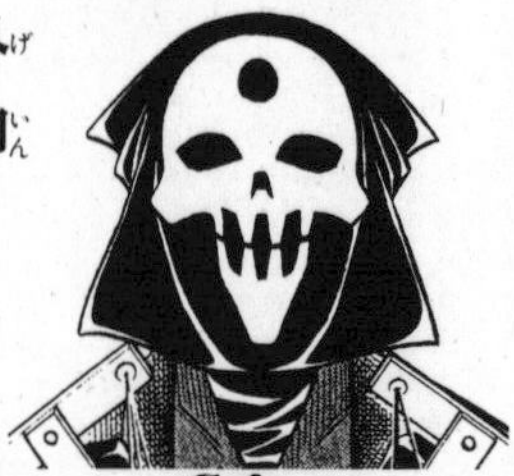

外印

Gein

るろうに剣心

和月伸宏

Once he was *hitokiri*, an assassin, called Battōsai. His name was legend among the pro-Imperialist or "patriot" warriors who launched the Meiji Era. Now, Himura Kenshin is *rurouni*, a wanderer, and carries a reversed-edge *sakabatō* to prohibit himself from killing.

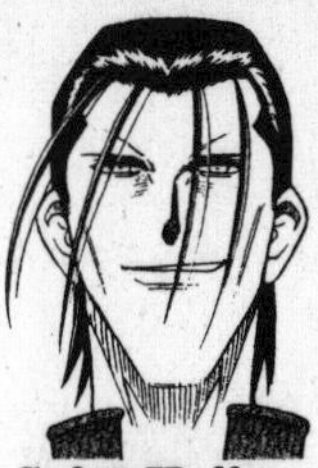

斎藤一（さいとう はじめ）

Saitō Hajime

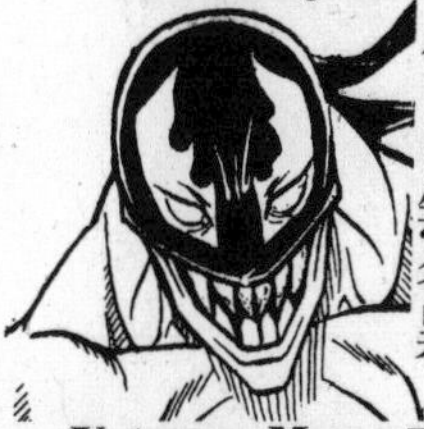

八ツ目無名異（やつめむみょうい）

Yatsume Mumyōi

THUS FAR

Kenshin and his friends return to Tokyo after a deadly battle to defeat Shishio Makoto and his ambitions of conquering Japan. However, their peace is short lived as those with grudges against Battōsai gather for revenge, attacking Akabeko, Maekawa Dojo, and police chief Uramura's house. To make matters worse, Kenshin finds out that the mastermind of this new attack is Enishi, the brother of Kenshin's deceased wife Tomoe—who died at Kenshin's own hand. Enishi confronts Kenshin and declares that he will lead an assault on Kamiya Dojo in ten days. Kenshin decides that although he can never fully atone for the crimes of his past, he will fight to protect the present, and begins by telling his friends his history. Ten days later, Enishi and his crew appear mid-air above Kamiya Dojo in hot air balloons. Kujiranami attacks first with the Armstrong Cannon attached to his right arm. With a well-timed combination of offense and defense, Kenshin and Sanosuke are able to render Kujiranami temporarily immobile. Inui, Otowa, and Gein break the standstill with a three point second attack—Kenshin against Gein and his Iwanbō version three, Sanosuke against Inui, and Yahiko against Otowa! But the attack fails as Kenshin defeats Iwanbō with *Amakakeru Ryū no Hirameki*, Sanosuke trounces Inui with the "Mastery of Two Layers," and Yahiko uses Kamiya Kasshin-ryū's secret move *Hawatari*—Blade Crossing—to overcome Otowa. Yatume uses Team Kenshin's relief at Yahiko's safety to ambush Kenshin and his friends...and then Saitō Hajime appears!

CONTENTS

RUROUNI KENSHIN
Meiji Swordsman Romantic Story
BOOK TWENTY-THREE: SIN, JUDGMENT, ACCEPTANCE

Act 197
The Wolf Returns

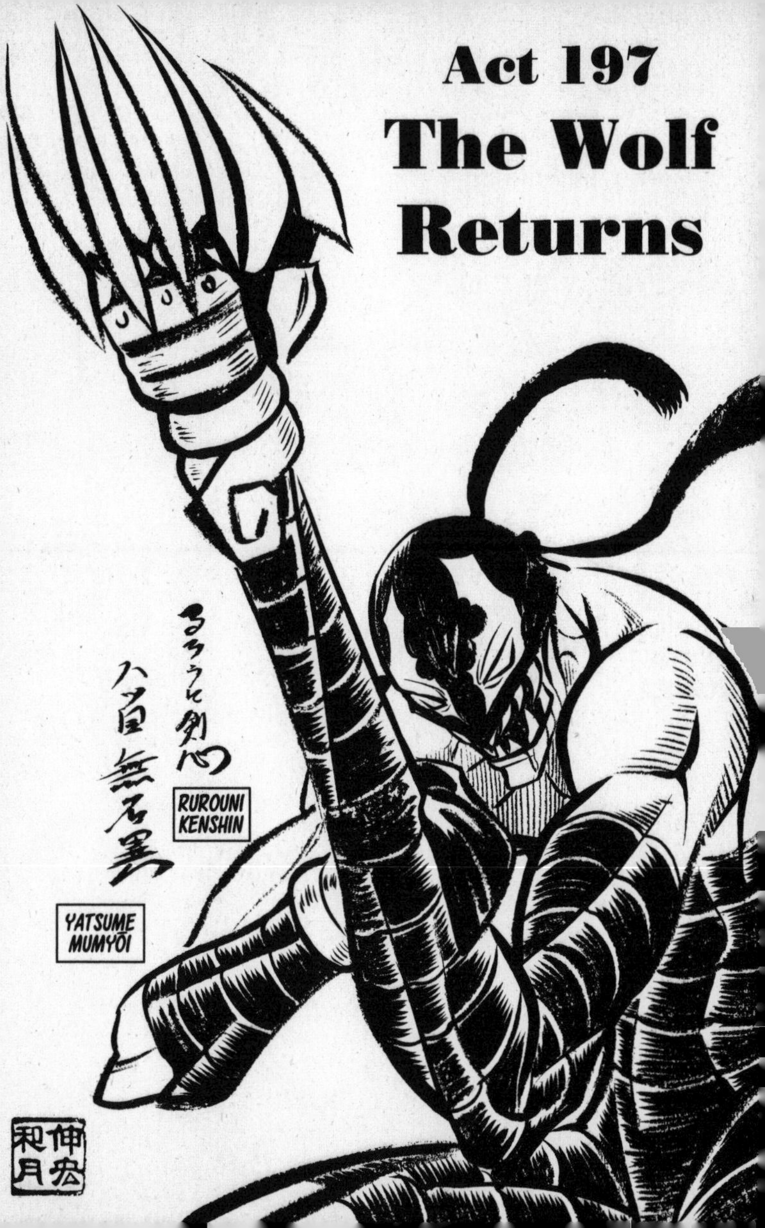
るろうに剣心
八ツ目無名異
RUROUNI KENSHIN
YATSUME MUMYŌI

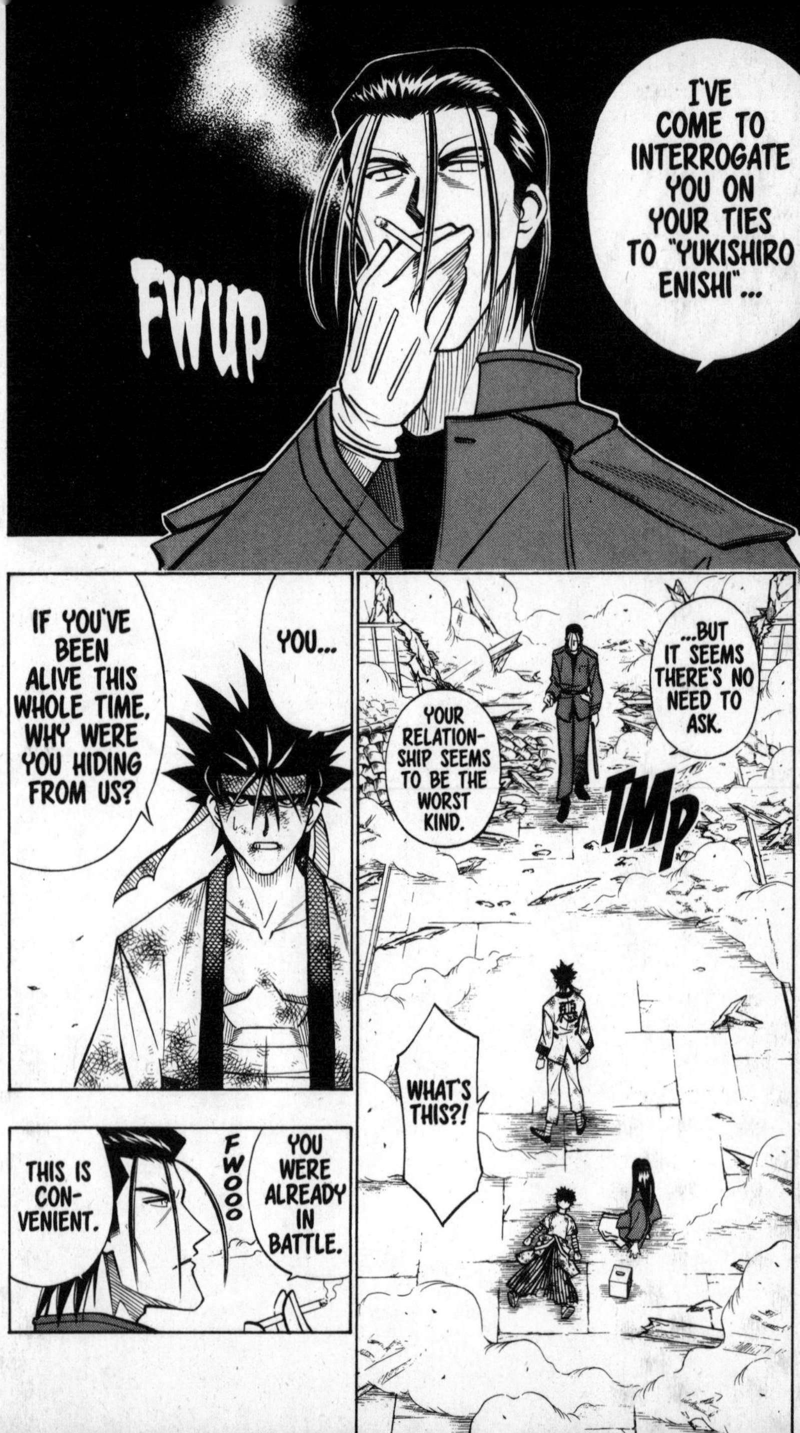
I'VE COME TO INTERROGATE YOU ON YOUR TIES TO "YUKISHIRO ENISHI"...
FWUP
...BUT IT SEEMS THERE'S NO NEED TO ASK.
YOUR RELATION-SHIP SEEMS TO BE THE WORST KIND.
TMP
WHAT'S THIS?!
YOU...
IF YOU'VE BEEN ALIVE THIS WHOLE TIME, WHY WERE YOU HIDING FROM US?
YOU WERE ALREADY IN BATTLE.
FWOOO
THIS IS CON-VENIENT.

READ THIS WAY

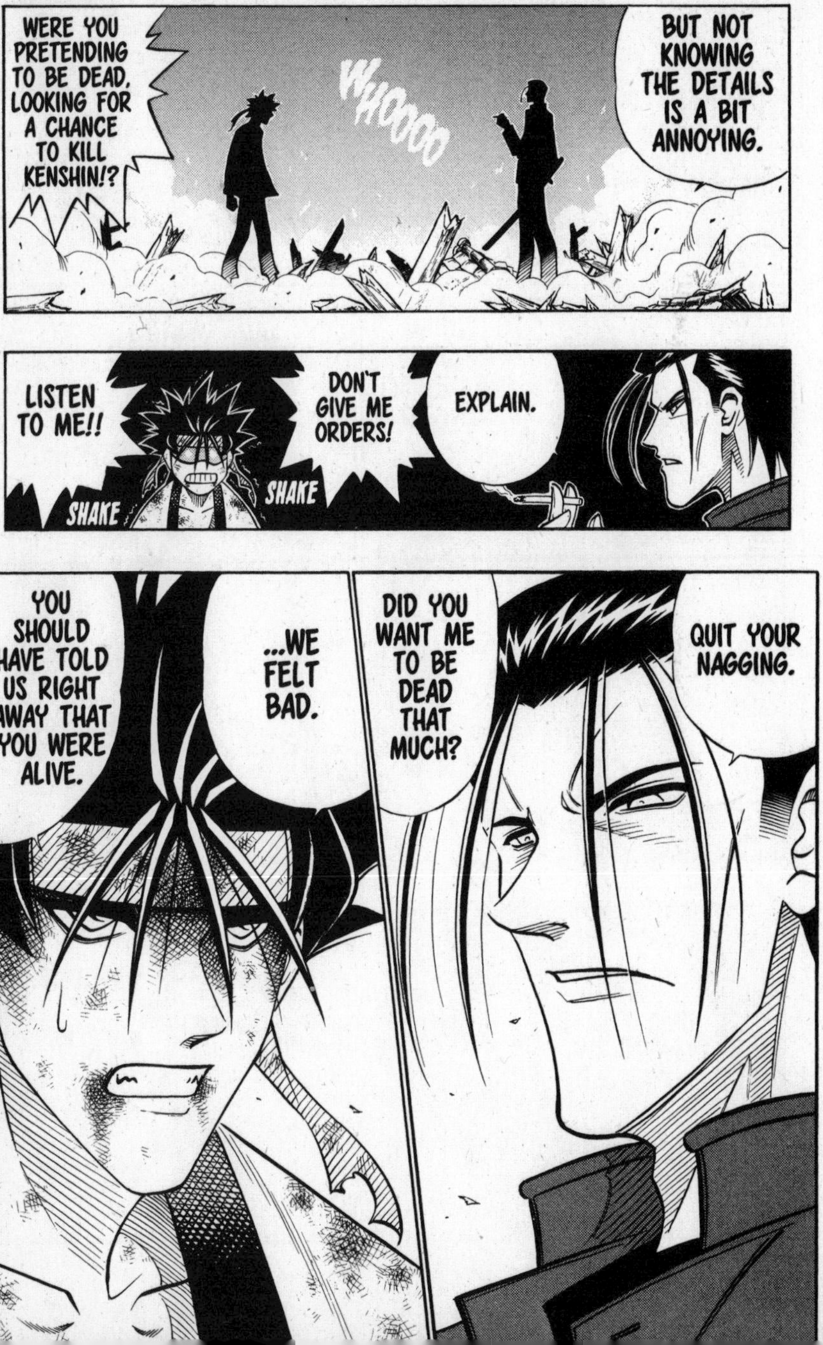
BUT NOT KNOWING THE DETAILS IS A BIT ANNOYING.
WHOOOO
WERE YOU PRETENDING TO BE DEAD, LOOKING FOR A CHANCE TO KILL KENSHIN!?
EXPLAIN.
DON'T GIVE ME ORDERS!
SHAKE
SHAKE
LISTEN TO ME!!
QUIT YOUR NAGGING.
DID YOU WANT ME TO BE DEAD THAT MUCH?
...WE FELT BAD.
YOU SHOULD HAVE TOLD US RIGHT AWAY THAT YOU WERE ALIVE.

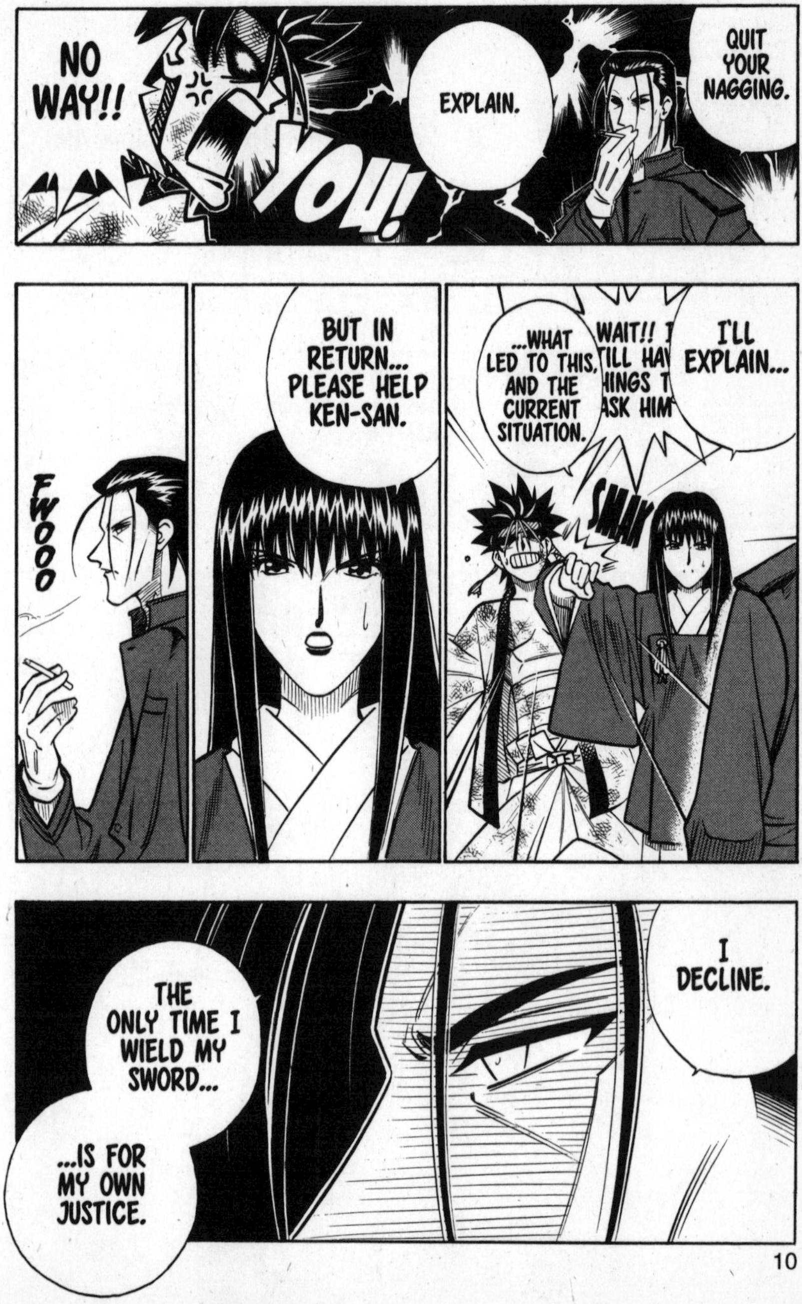
QUIT YOUR NAGGING.
EXPLAIN.
YOU!
NO WAY!!
I'LL EXPLAIN...
WAIT!! I TILL HAV HINGS T ASK HIM
...WHAT LED TO THIS, AND THE CURRENT SITUATION.
SMAK
BUT IN RETURN... PLEASE HELP KEN-SAN.
FWOOO
I DECLINE.
THE ONLY TIME I WIELD MY SWORD...
...IS FOR MY OWN JUSTICE.

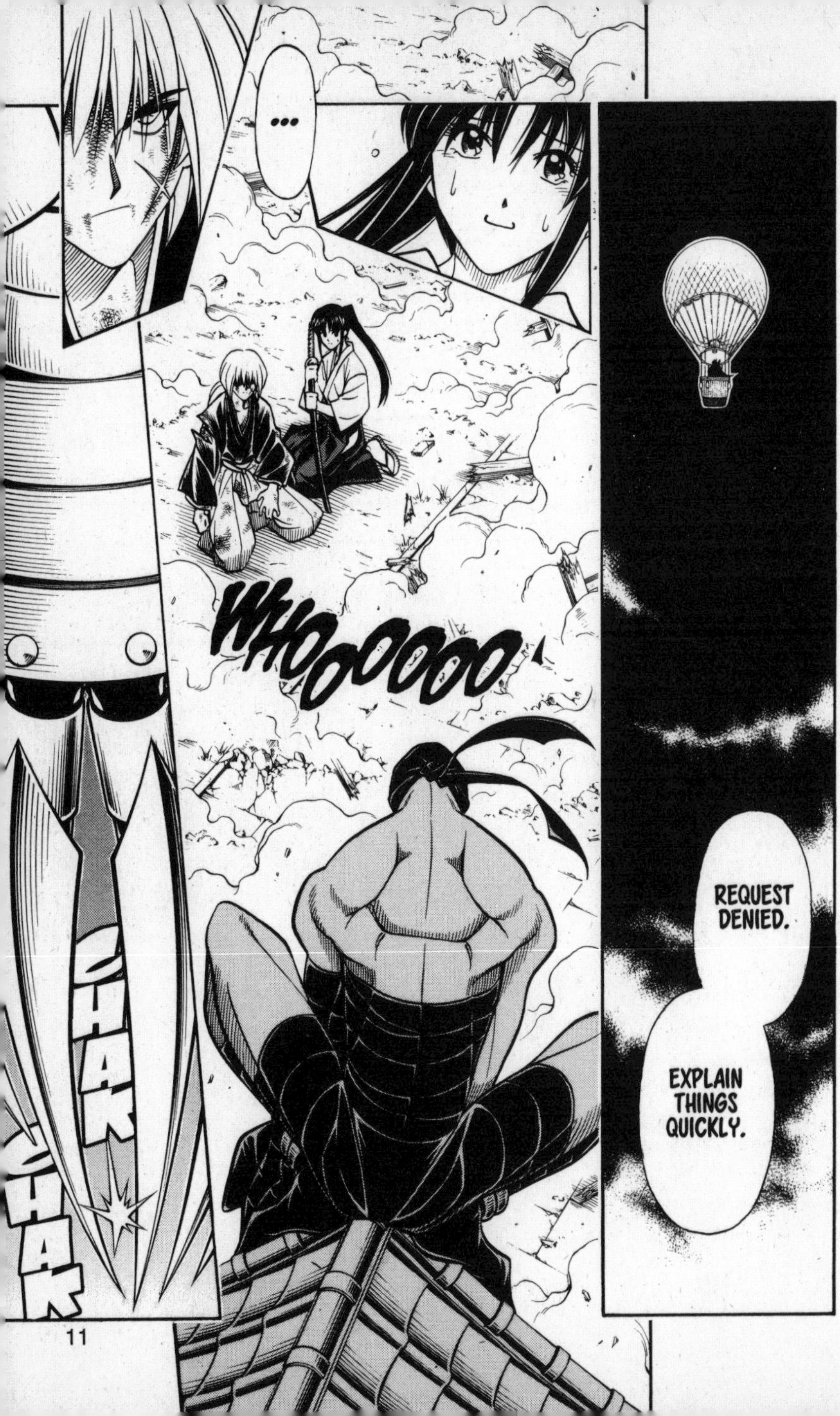
REQUEST DENIED.
EXPLAIN THINGS QUICKLY.
...
WHOOOOOOO
CHAK
CHAK

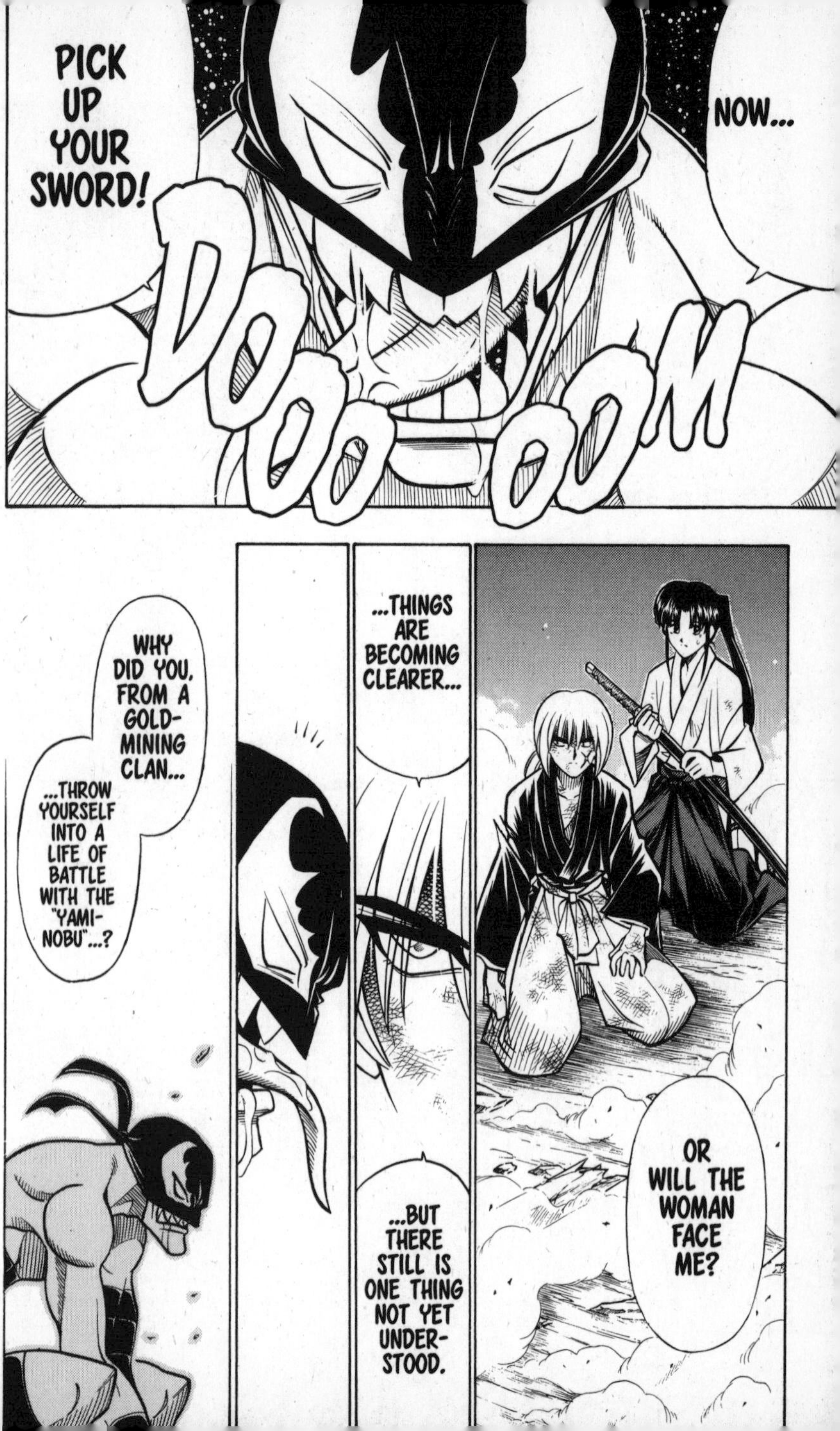
NOW...
DOOO-OOM
PICK UP YOUR SWORD!
OR WILL THE WOMAN FACE ME?
...THINGS ARE BECOMING CLEARER...
...BUT THERE STILL IS ONE THING NOT YET UNDERSTOOD.
WHY DID YOU, FROM A GOLD-MINING CLAN...
...THROW YOURSELF INTO A LIFE OF BATTLE WITH THE "YAMI-NOBU"...?

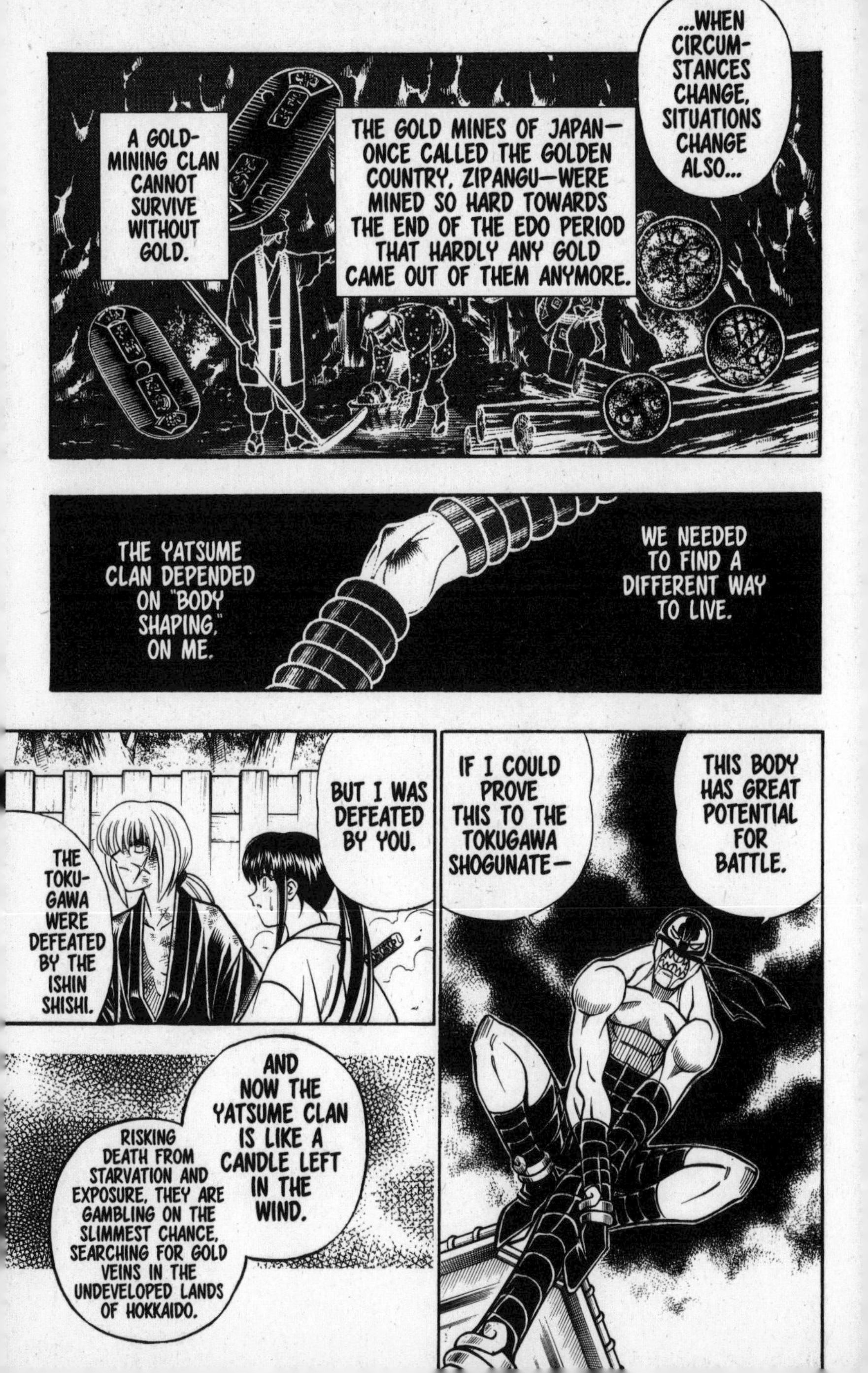
...WHEN CIRCUMSTANCES CHANGE, SITUATIONS CHANGE ALSO...
THE GOLD MINES OF JAPAN—ONCE CALLED THE GOLDEN COUNTRY, ZIPANGU—WERE MINED SO HARD TOWARDS THE END OF THE EDO PERIOD THAT HARDLY ANY GOLD CAME OUT OF THEM ANYMORE.
A GOLD-MINING CLAN CANNOT SURVIVE WITHOUT GOLD.
WE NEEDED TO FIND A DIFFERENT WAY TO LIVE.
THE YATSUME CLAN DEPENDED ON "BODY SHAPING," ON ME.
THIS BODY HAS GREAT POTENTIAL FOR BATTLE.
IF I COULD PROVE THIS TO THE TOKUGAWA SHOGUNATE—
BUT I WAS DEFEATED BY YOU.
THE TOKUGAWA WERE DEFEATED BY THE ISHIN SHISHI.
AND NOW THE YATSUME CLAN IS LIKE A CANDLE LEFT IN THE WIND.
RISKING DEATH FROM STARVATION AND EXPOSURE, THEY ARE GAMBLING ON THE SLIMMEST CHANCE, SEARCHING FOR GOLD VEINS IN THE UNDEVELOPED LANDS OF HOKKAIDO.

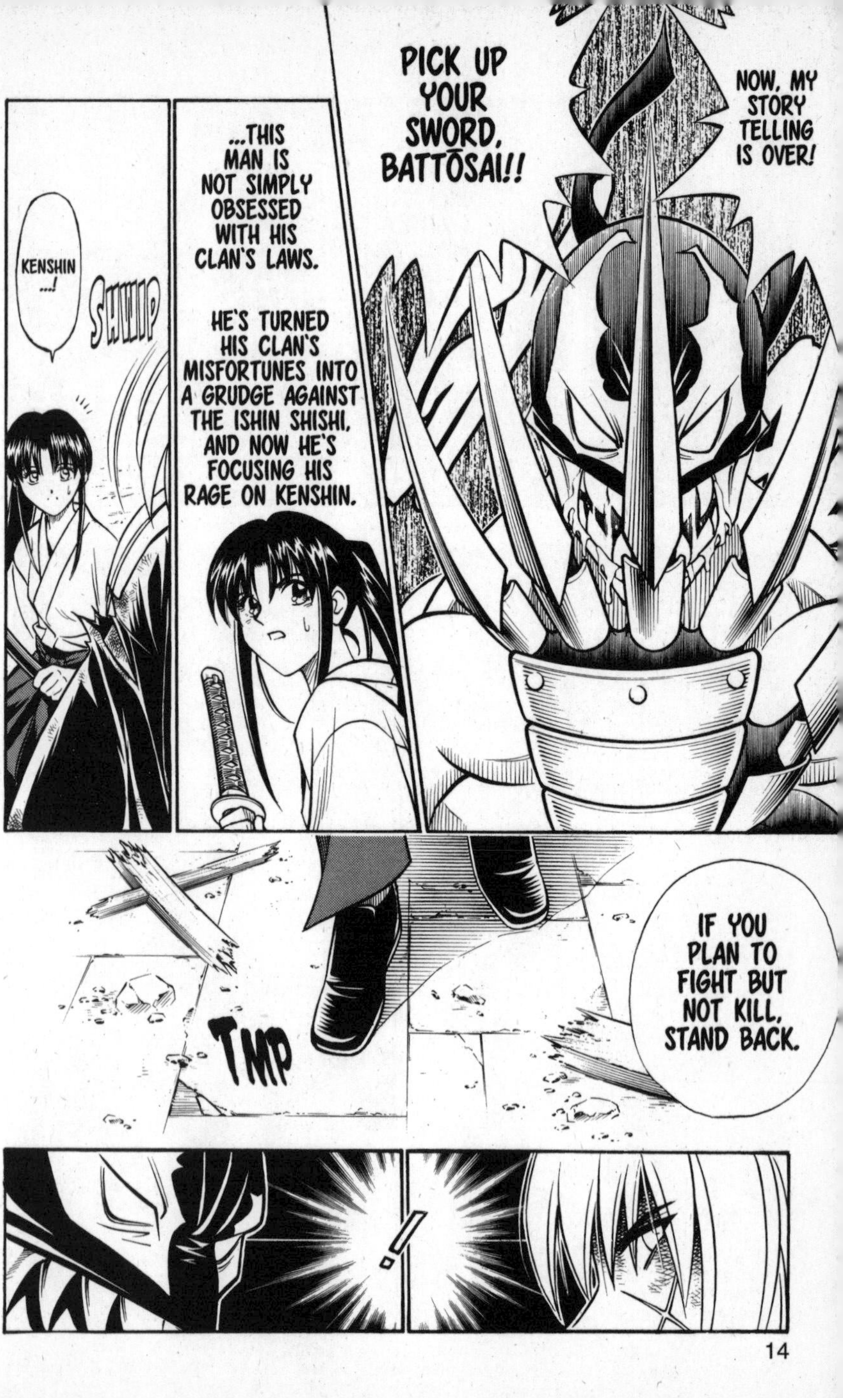
NOW, MY STORY TELLING IS OVER!
PICK UP YOUR SWORD, BATTŌSAI!!
...THIS MAN IS NOT SIMPLY OBSESSED WITH HIS CLAN'S LAWS.
HE'S TURNED HIS CLAN'S MISFORTUNES INTO A GRUDGE AGAINST THE ISHIN SHISHI, AND NOW HE'S FOCUSING HIS RAGE ON KENSHIN.
KENSHIN ...!
SHWIP
IF YOU PLAN TO FIGHT BUT NOT KILL, STAND BACK.
TMP
!

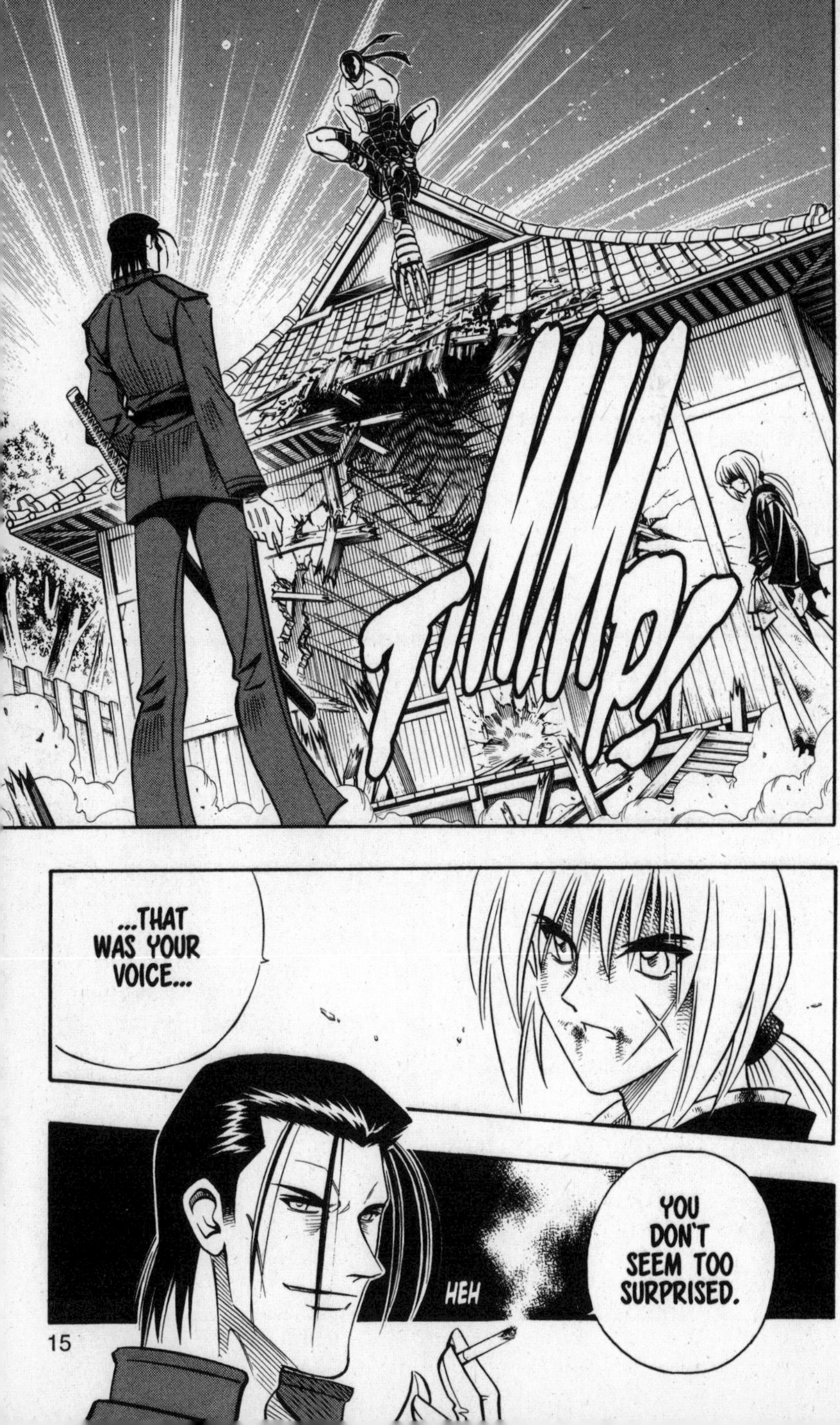
...THAT WAS YOUR VOICE...
YOU DON'T SEEM TOO SURPRISED.
HEH

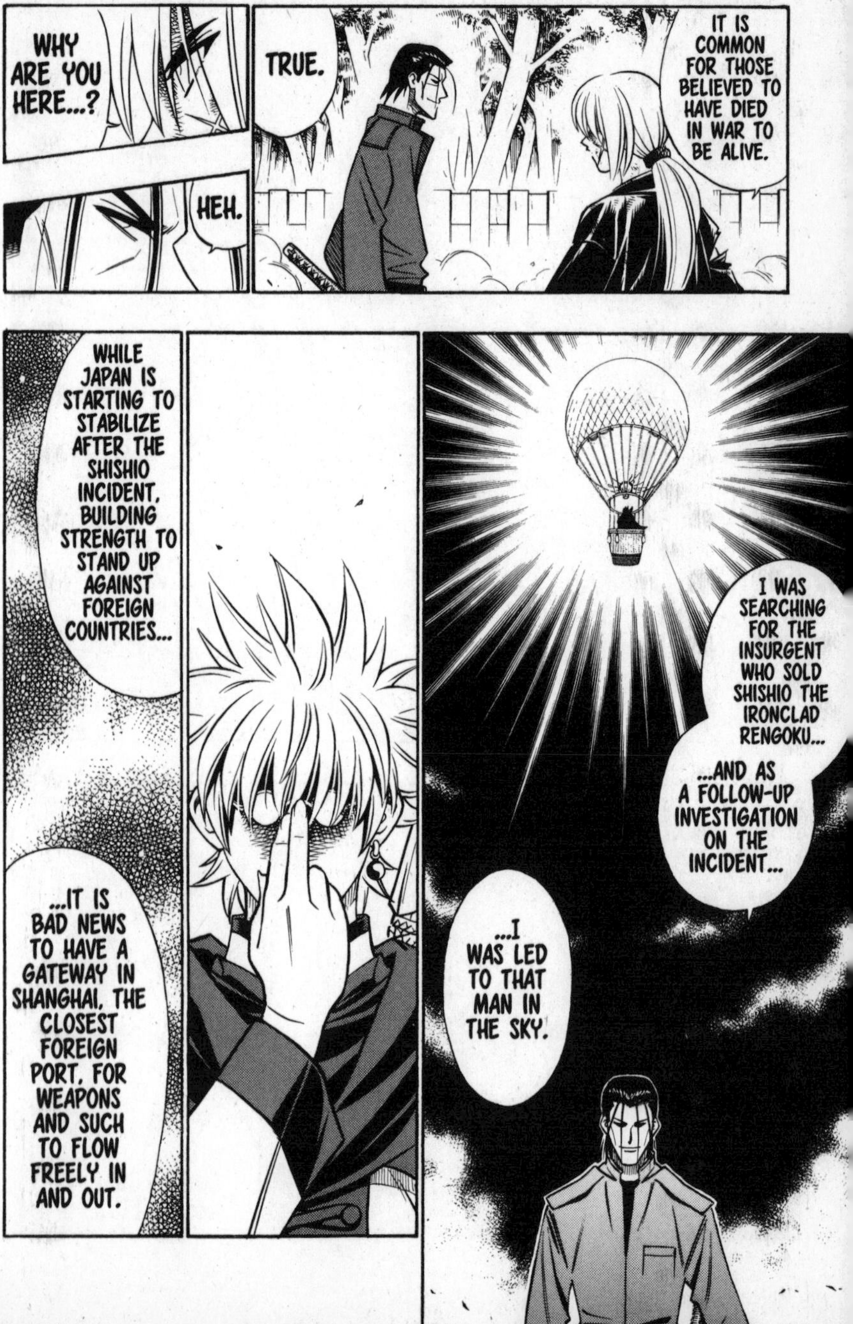
IT IS COMMON FOR THOSE BELIEVED TO HAVE DIED IN WAR TO BE ALIVE.
TRUE.
WHY ARE YOU HERE...?
HEH.
I WAS SEARCHING FOR THE INSURGENT WHO SOLD SHISHIO THE IRONCLAD RENGOKU...
...AND AS A FOLLOW-UP INVESTIGATION ON THE INCIDENT...
...I WAS LED TO THAT MAN IN THE SKY.
WHILE JAPAN IS STARTING TO STABILIZE AFTER THE SHISHIO INCIDENT, BUILDING STRENGTH TO STAND UP AGAINST FOREIGN COUNTRIES...
...IT IS BAD NEWS TO HAVE A GATEWAY IN SHANGHAI, THE CLOSEST FOREIGN PORT, FOR WEAPONS AND SUCH TO FLOW FREELY IN AND OUT.

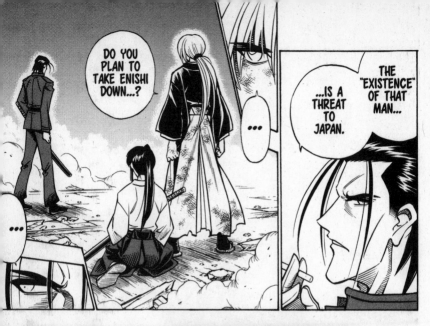

THE "EXISTENCE" OF THAT MAN...
...IS A THREAT TO JAPAN.
...
DO YOU PLAN TO TAKE ENISHI DOWN...?
...
TAKING HIM DOWN...
...ARRESTING HIM...
WHOOOO
...OR EXILING HIM...
WE'LL HAVE TO DRAG HIM TO THE GROUND FIRST.
HE'S GOING TO COME DOWN ONCE EVERYONE HERE IS DEFEATED, RIGHT?
...
AND...
...THAT FREAK IS ALL THAT REMAINS.

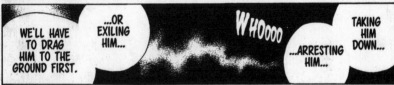

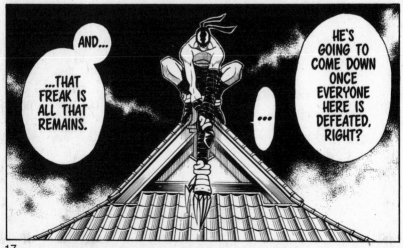

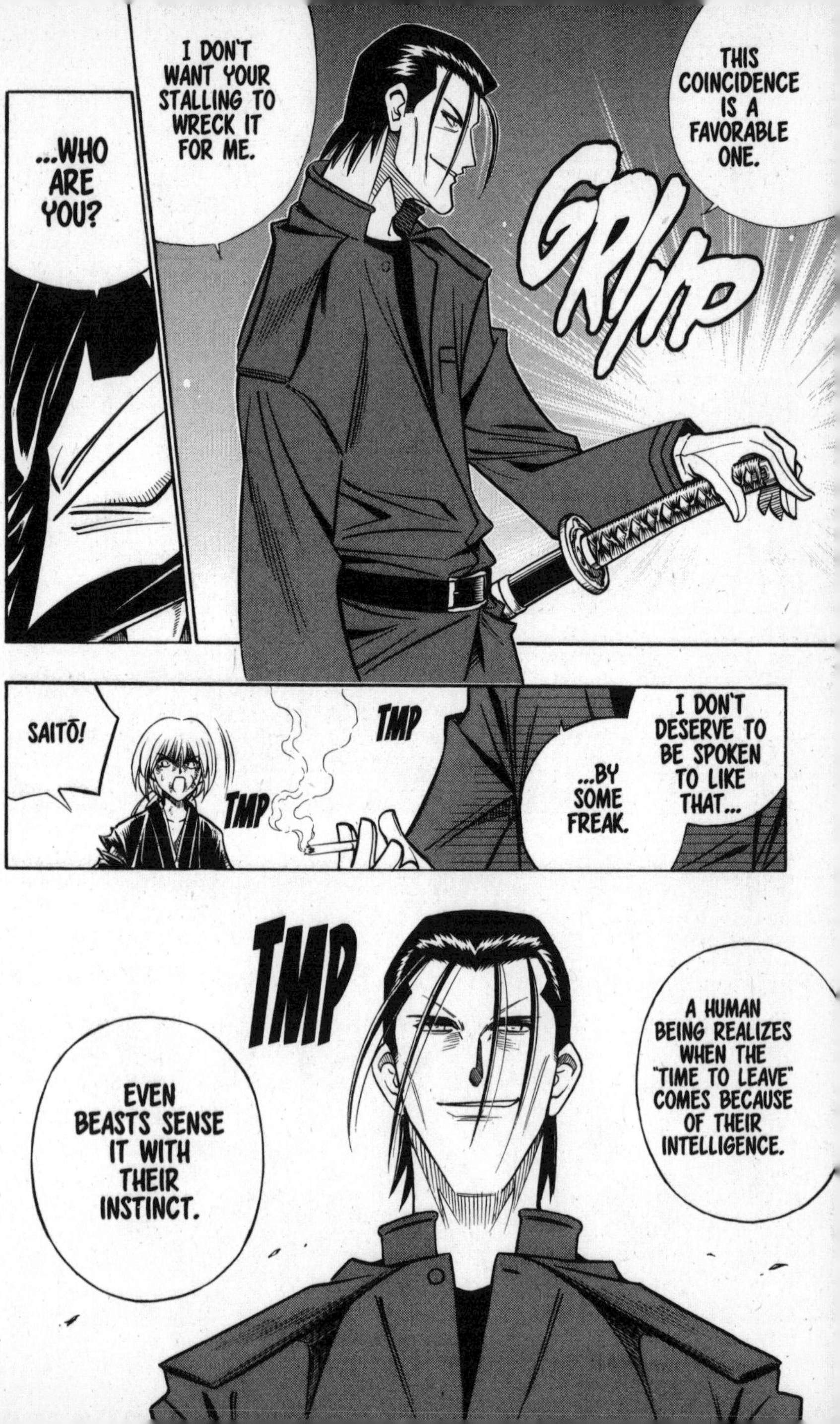
THIS COINCIDENCE IS A FAVORABLE ONE.
I DON'T WANT YOUR STALLING TO WRECK IT FOR ME.
GRIP
...WHO ARE YOU?
I DON'T DESERVE TO BE SPOKEN TO LIKE THAT...
...BY SOME FREAK.
TMP
TMP
SAITŌ!
A HUMAN BEING REALIZES WHEN THE "TIME TO LEAVE" COMES BECAUSE OF THEIR INTELLIGENCE.
TMP
EVEN BEASTS SENSE IT WITH THEIR INSTINCT.

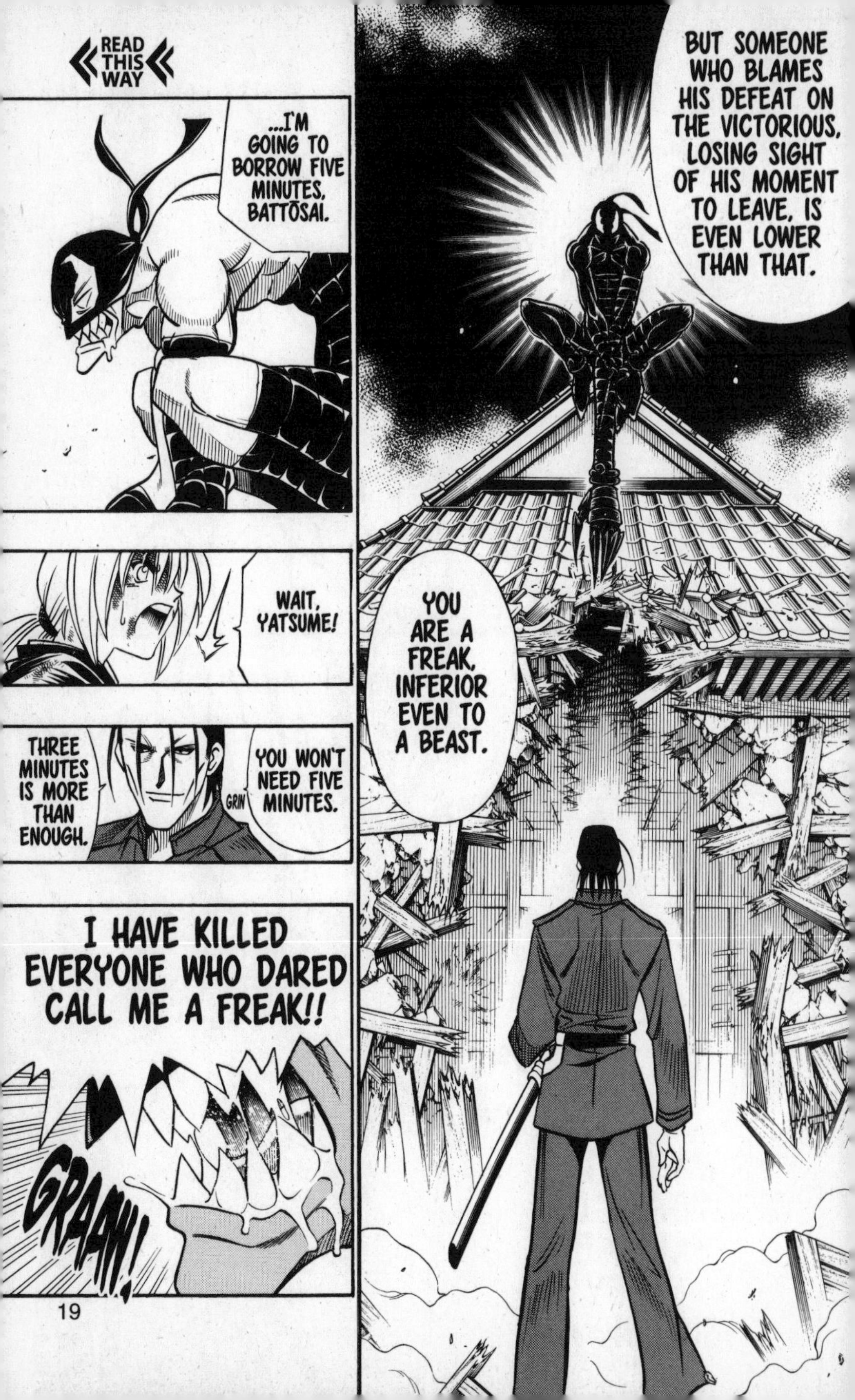
BUT SOMEONE WHO BLAMES HIS DEFEAT ON THE VICTORIOUS, LOSING SIGHT OF HIS MOMENT TO LEAVE, IS EVEN LOWER THAN THAT.
YOU ARE A FREAK, INFERIOR EVEN TO A BEAST.
READ THIS WAY
...I'M GOING TO BORROW FIVE MINUTES, BATTŌSAI.
WAIT, YATSUME!
YOU WON'T NEED FIVE MINUTES.
GRIN
THREE MINUTES IS MORE THAN ENOUGH.
I HAVE KILLED EVERYONE WHO DARED CALL ME A FREAK!!
GRAAH!!

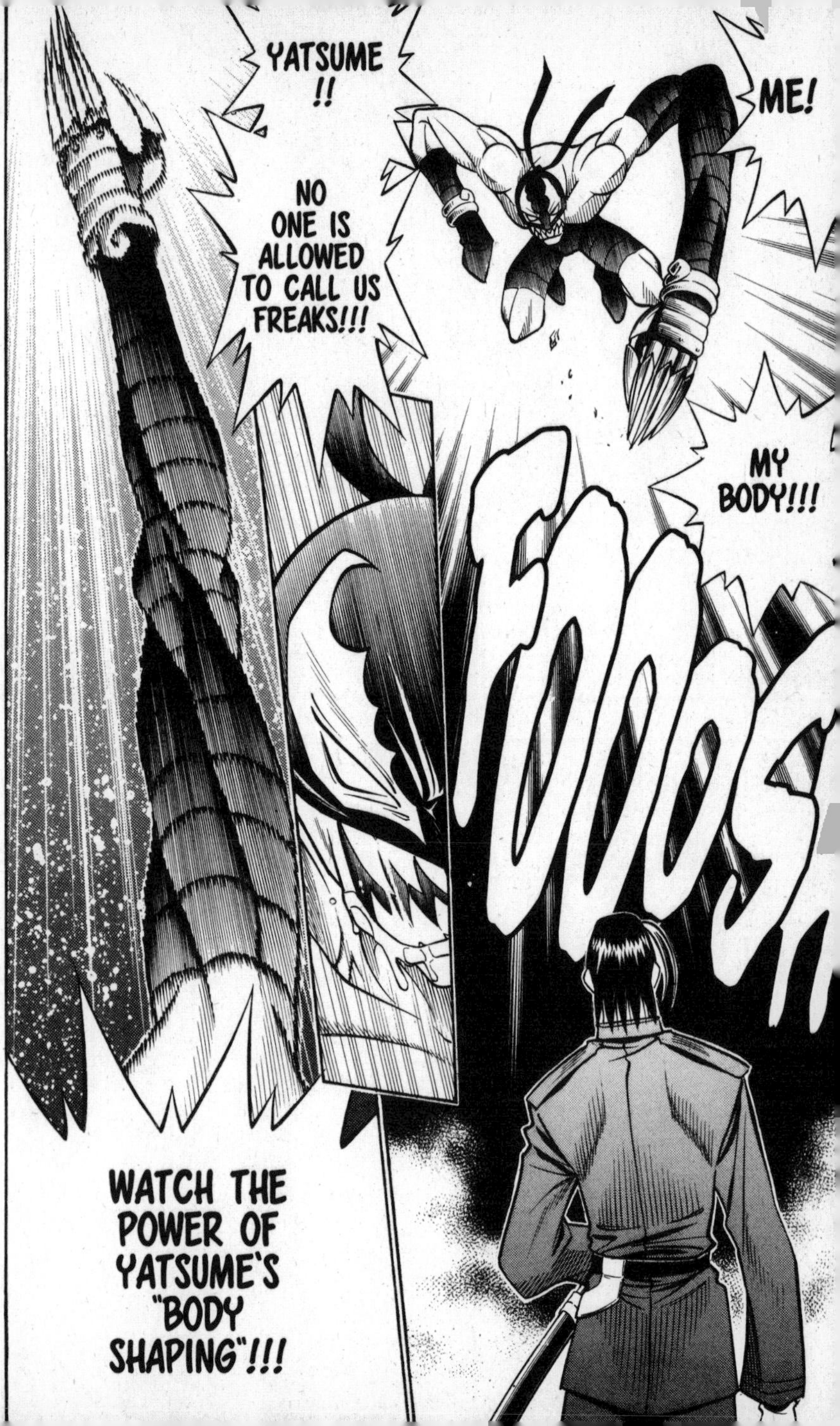
ME!
MY BODY!!!
YATSUME !!
NO ONE IS ALLOWED TO CALL US FREAKS!!!
WATCH THE POWER OF YATSUME'S "BODY SHAPING"!!!

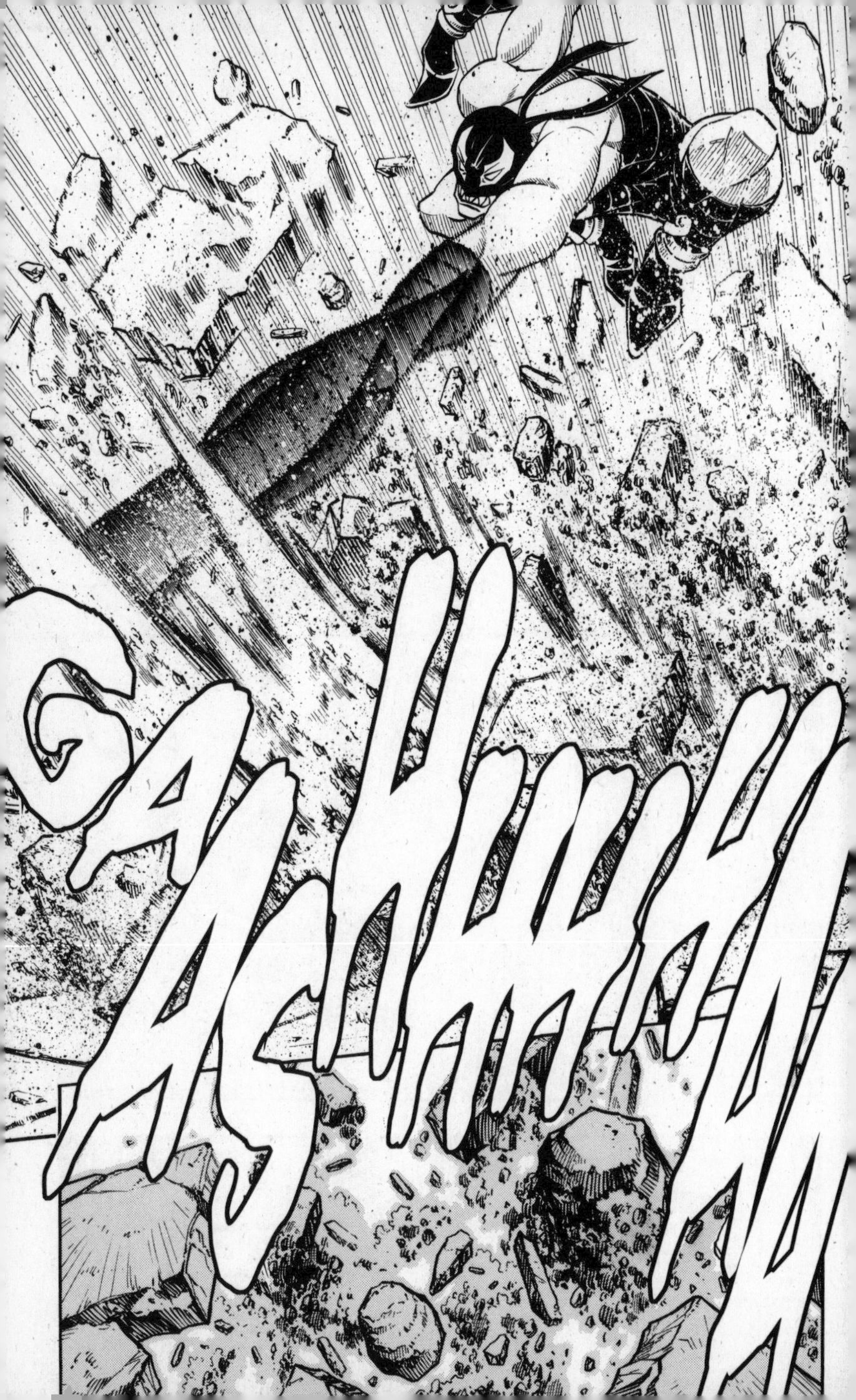

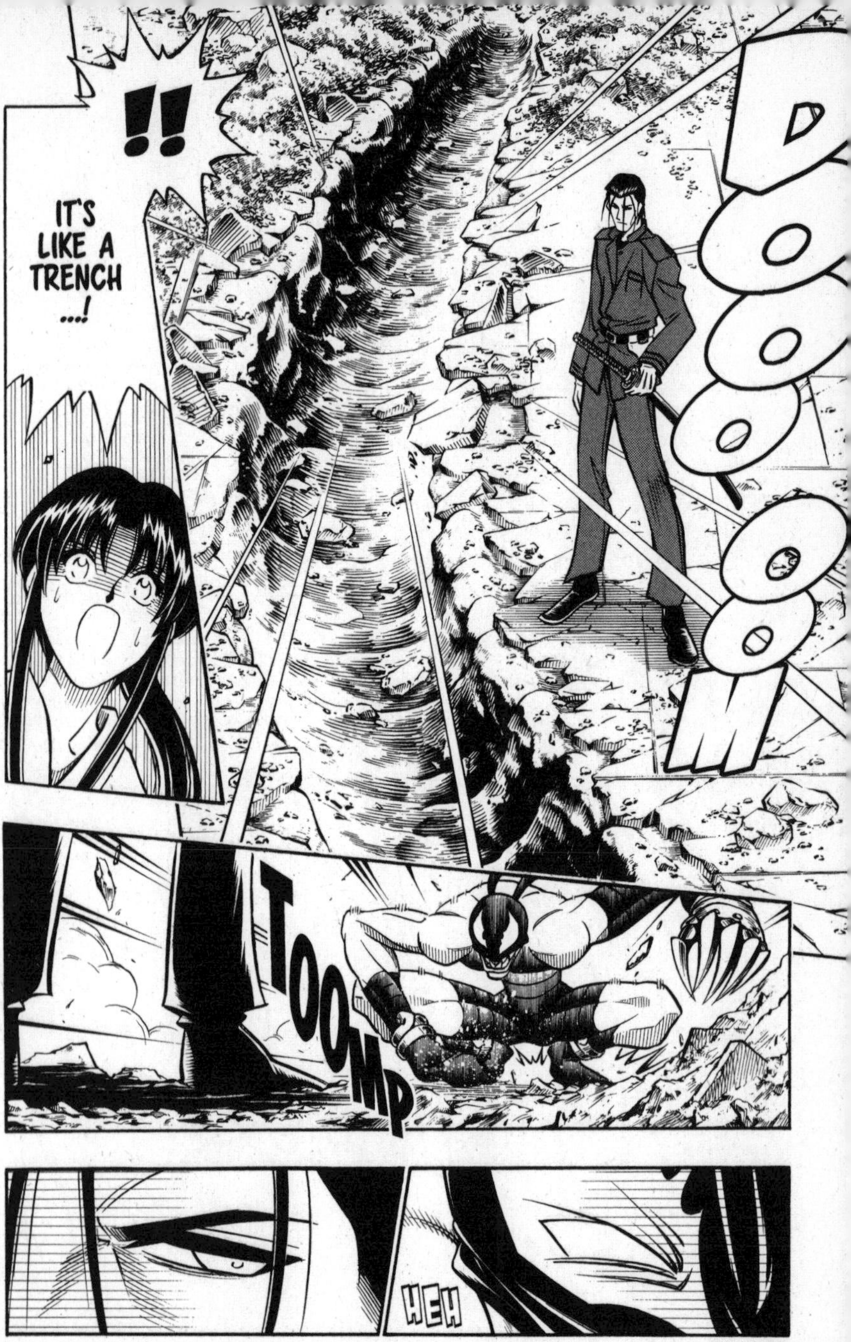
DOOOOOM
!!
IT'S LIKE A TRENCH ...!
TOOMP
HEH

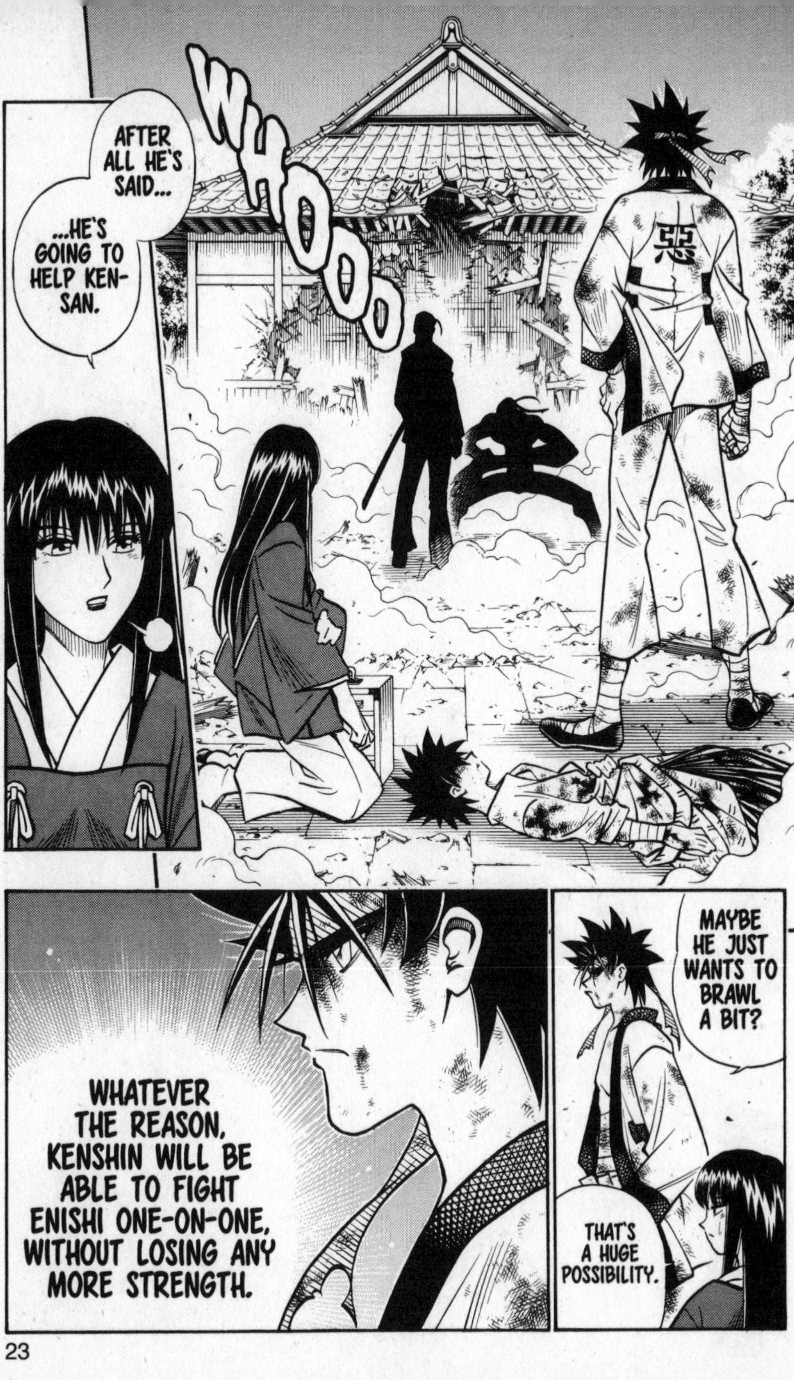
WHOOOO
悪
AFTER ALL HE'S SAID...
...HE'S GOING TO HELP KEN-SAN.
MAYBE HE JUST WANTS TO BRAWL A BIT?
THAT'S A HUGE POSSIBILITY.
WHATEVER THE REASON, KENSHIN WILL BE ABLE TO FIGHT ENISHI ONE-ON-ONE, WITHOUT LOSING ANY MORE STRENGTH.

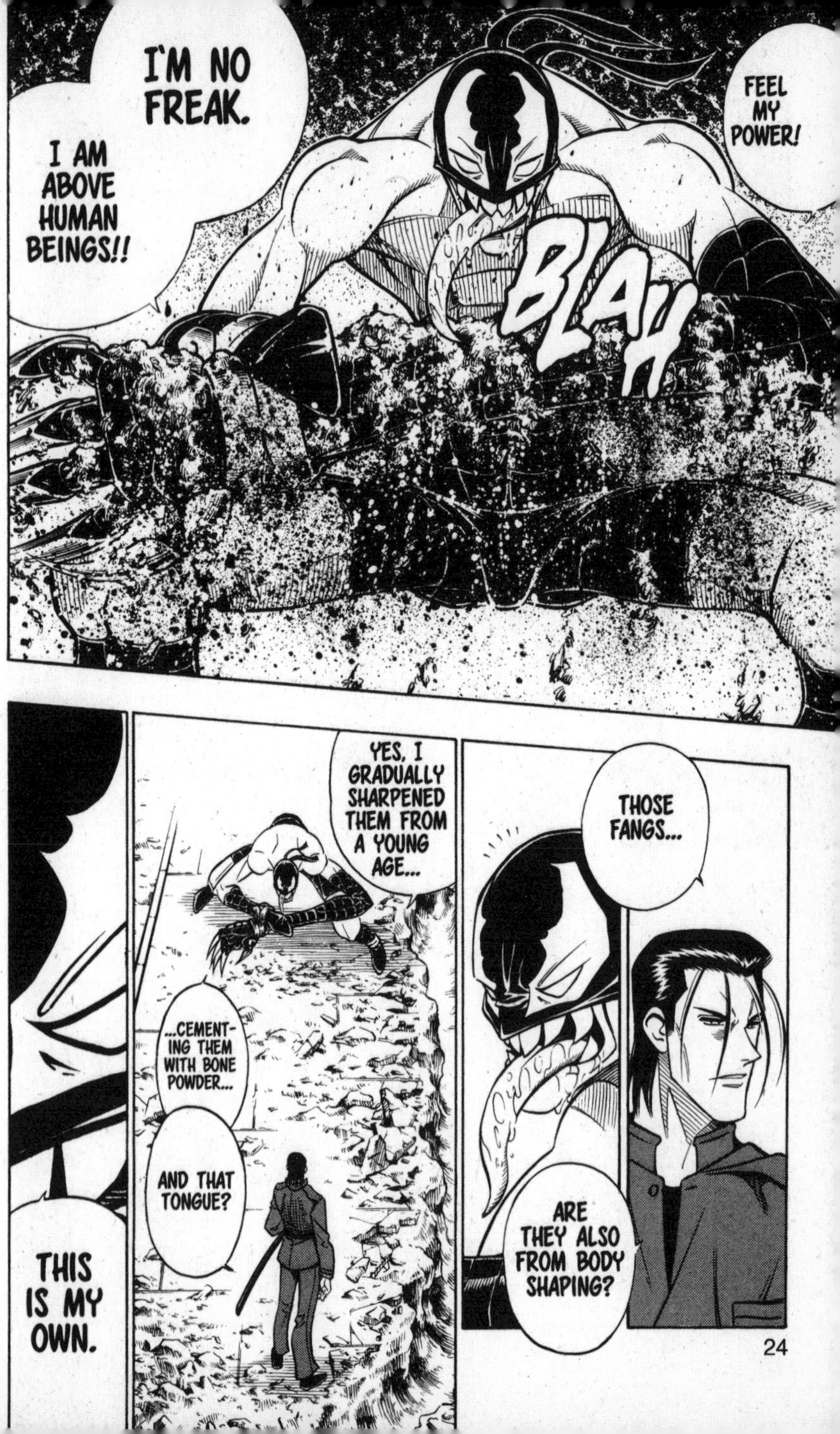
FEEL MY POWER!
BLAH
I'M NO FREAK.
I AM ABOVE HUMAN BEINGS!!
THOSE FANGS...
ARE THEY ALSO FROM BODY SHAPING?
YES, I GRADUALLY SHARPENED THEM FROM A YOUNG AGE...
...CEMENTING THEM WITH BONE POWDER...
AND THAT TONGUE?
THIS IS MY OWN.

READ THIS WAY

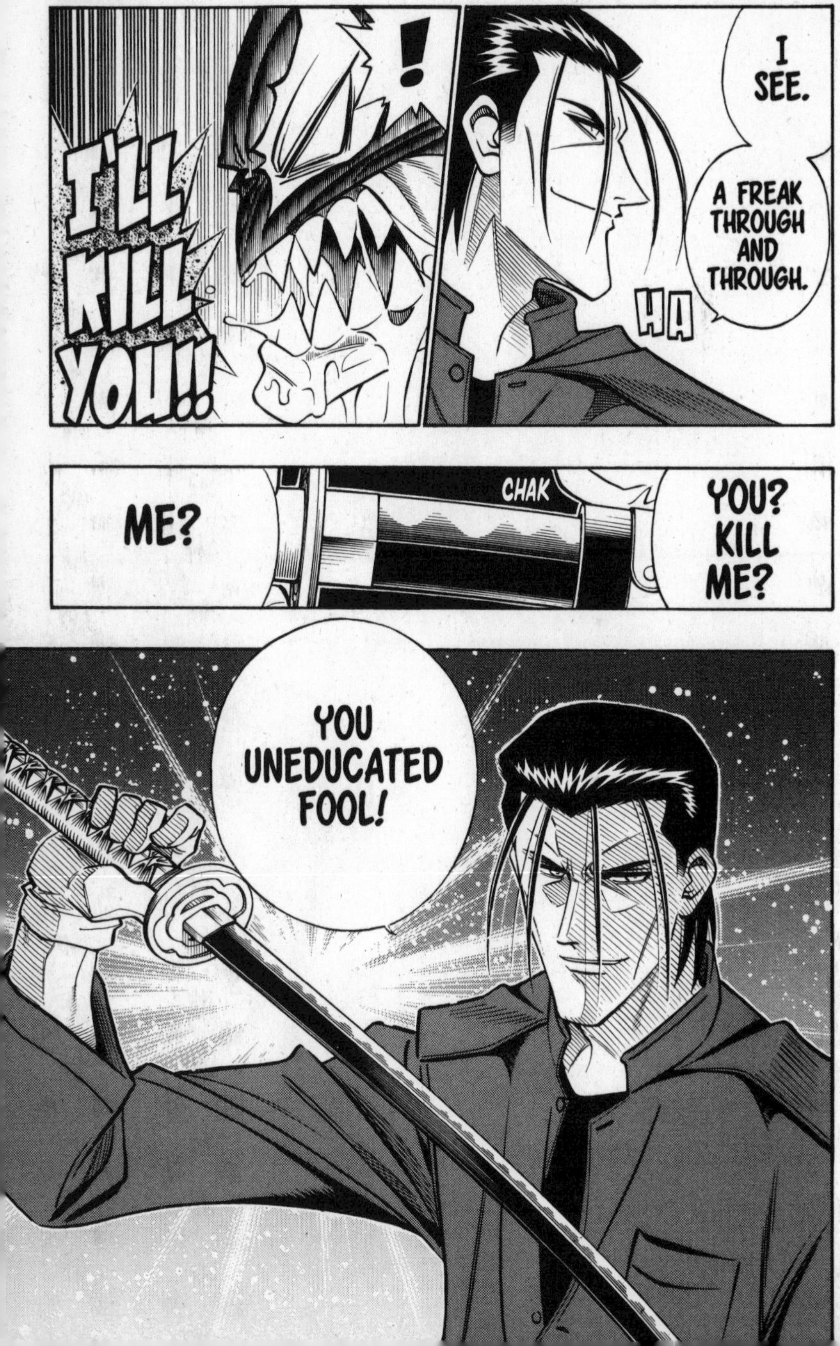
I SEE.
A FREAK THROUGH AND THROUGH.
HA
!
I'LL KILL YOU!!
YOU? KILL ME?
CHAK
ME?
YOU UNEDUCATED FOOL!

Rurouni Kenshin

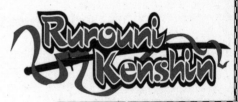

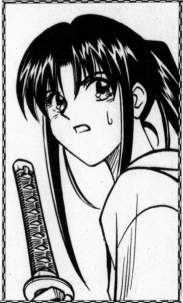

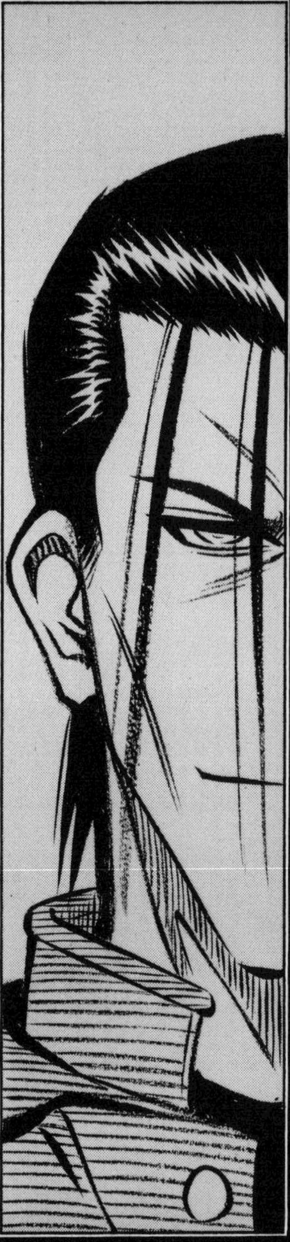

Act 198

I Can't See Him Losing

伸宏和月

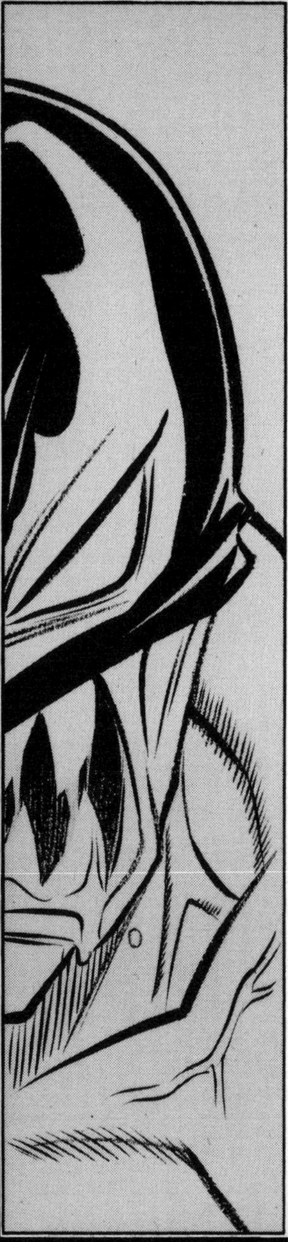

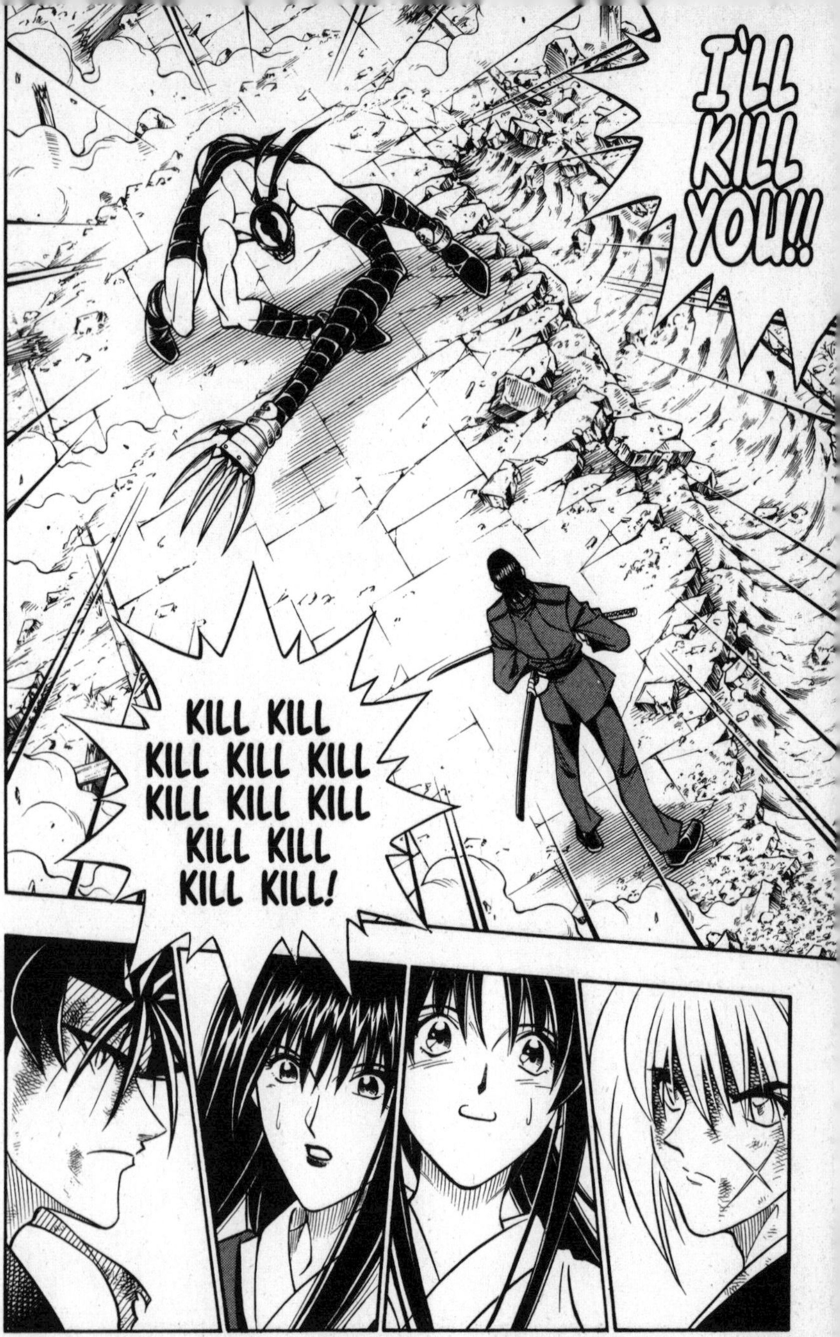
I'LL KILL YOU!!
KILL KILL KILL KILL KILL KILL KILL KILL KILL KILL KILL KILL!

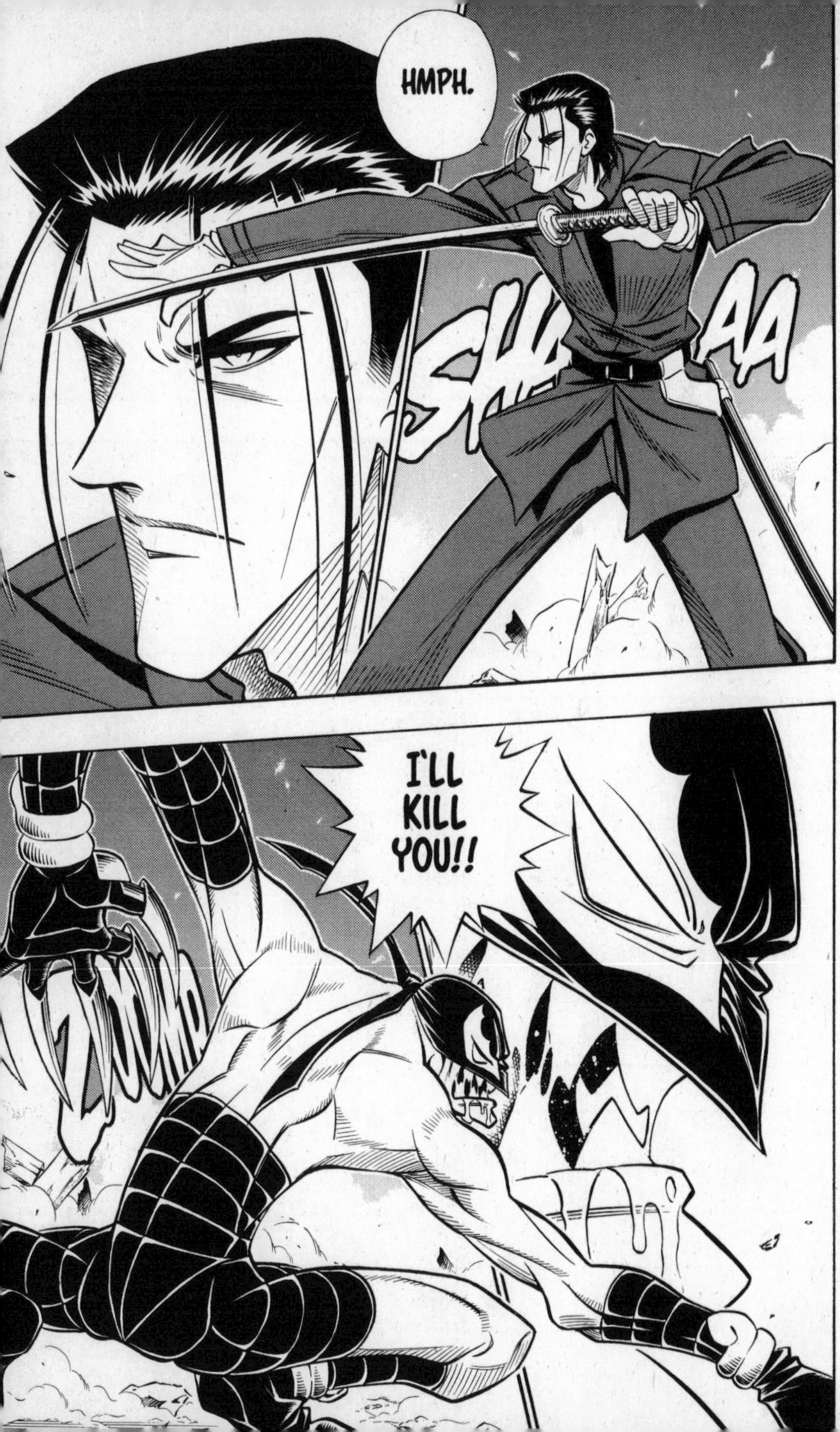
HMPH.
I'LL KILL YOU!!

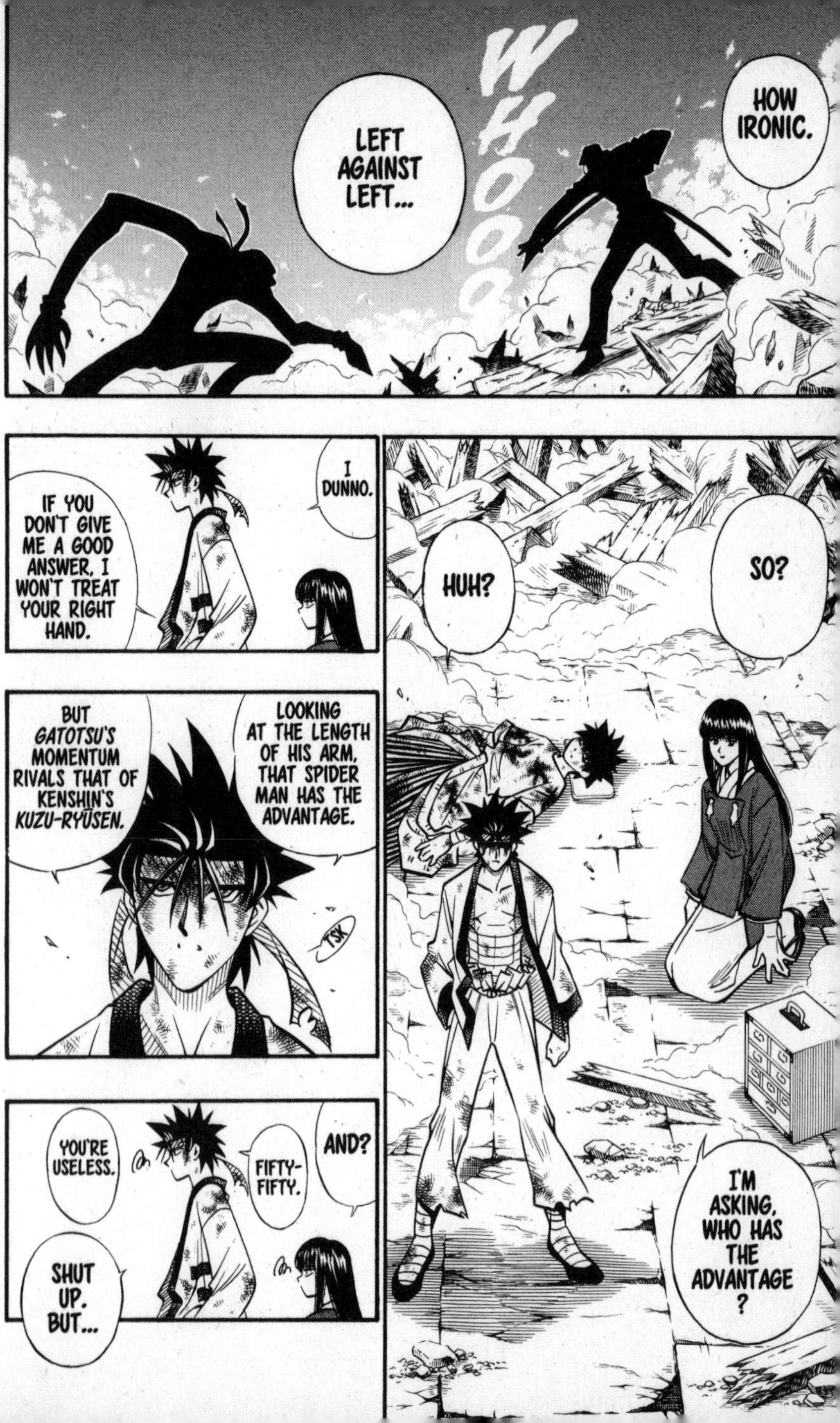
HOW IRONIC.
WHOOOO
LEFT AGAINST LEFT...
SO?
HUH?
I'M ASKING, WHO HAS THE ADVANTAGE?
I DUNNO.
IF YOU DON'T GIVE ME A GOOD ANSWER, I WON'T TREAT YOUR RIGHT HAND.
LOOKING AT THE LENGTH OF HIS ARM, THAT SPIDER MAN HAS THE ADVANTAGE.
BUT *GATOTSU'S* MOMENTUM RIVALS THAT OF KENSHIN'S *KUZU-RYŪSEN.*
TSK
AND?
FIFTY-FIFTY.
YOU'RE USELESS.
SHUT UP. BUT...

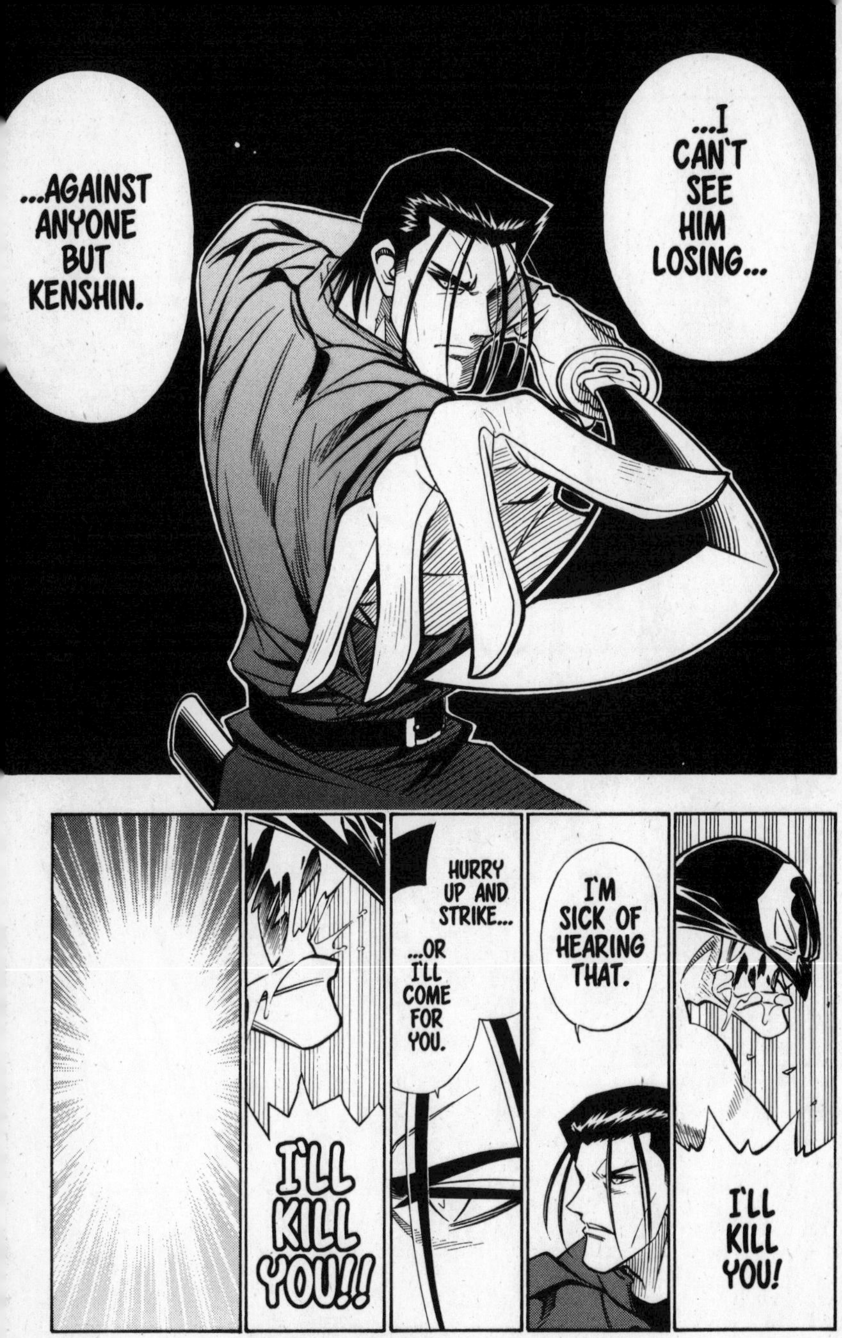
...I CAN'T SEE HIM LOSING...
...AGAINST ANYONE BUT KENSHIN.
I'LL KILL YOU!
I'M SICK OF HEARING THAT.
HURRY UP AND STRIKE...
...OR I'LL COME FOR YOU.
I'LL KILL YOU!!

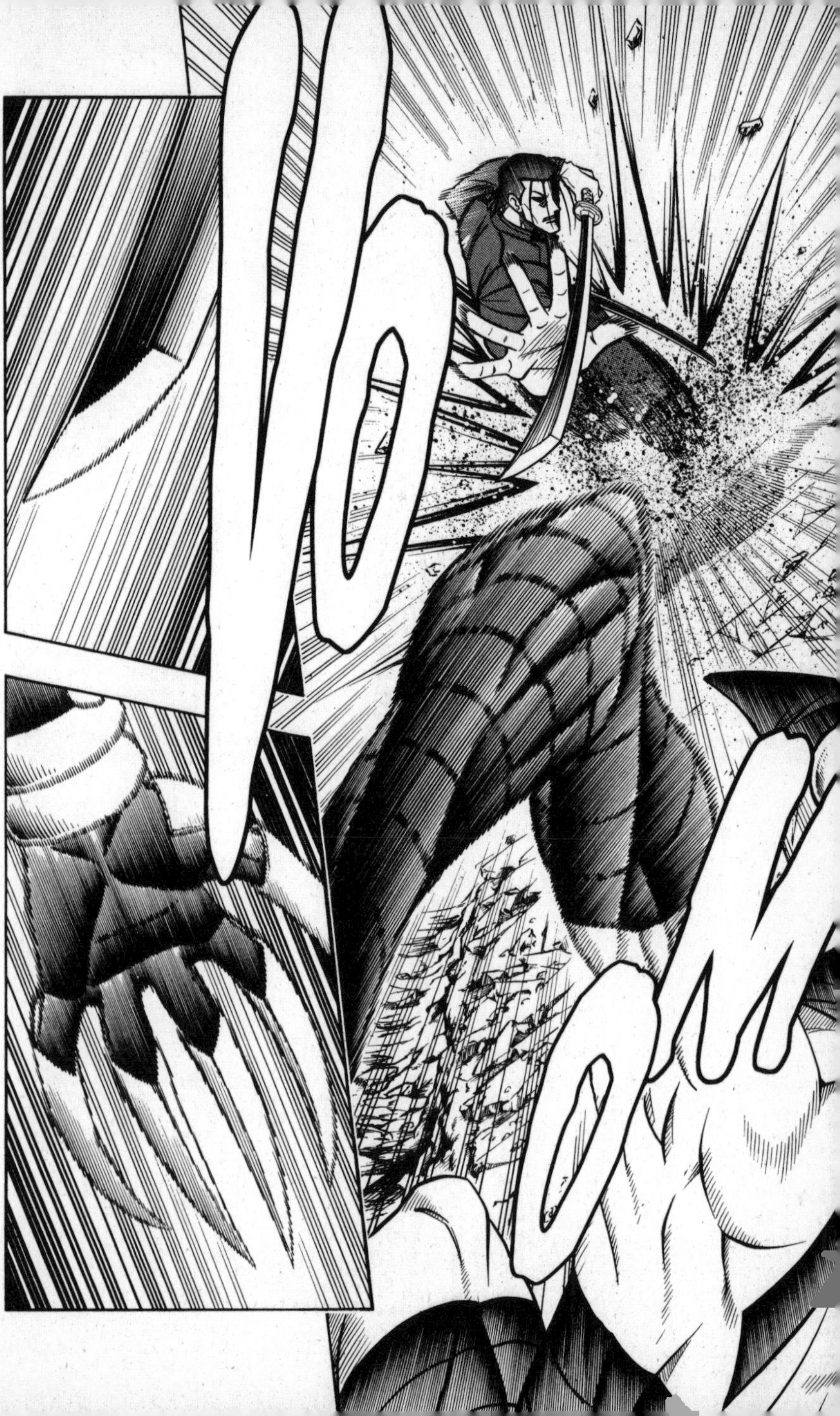

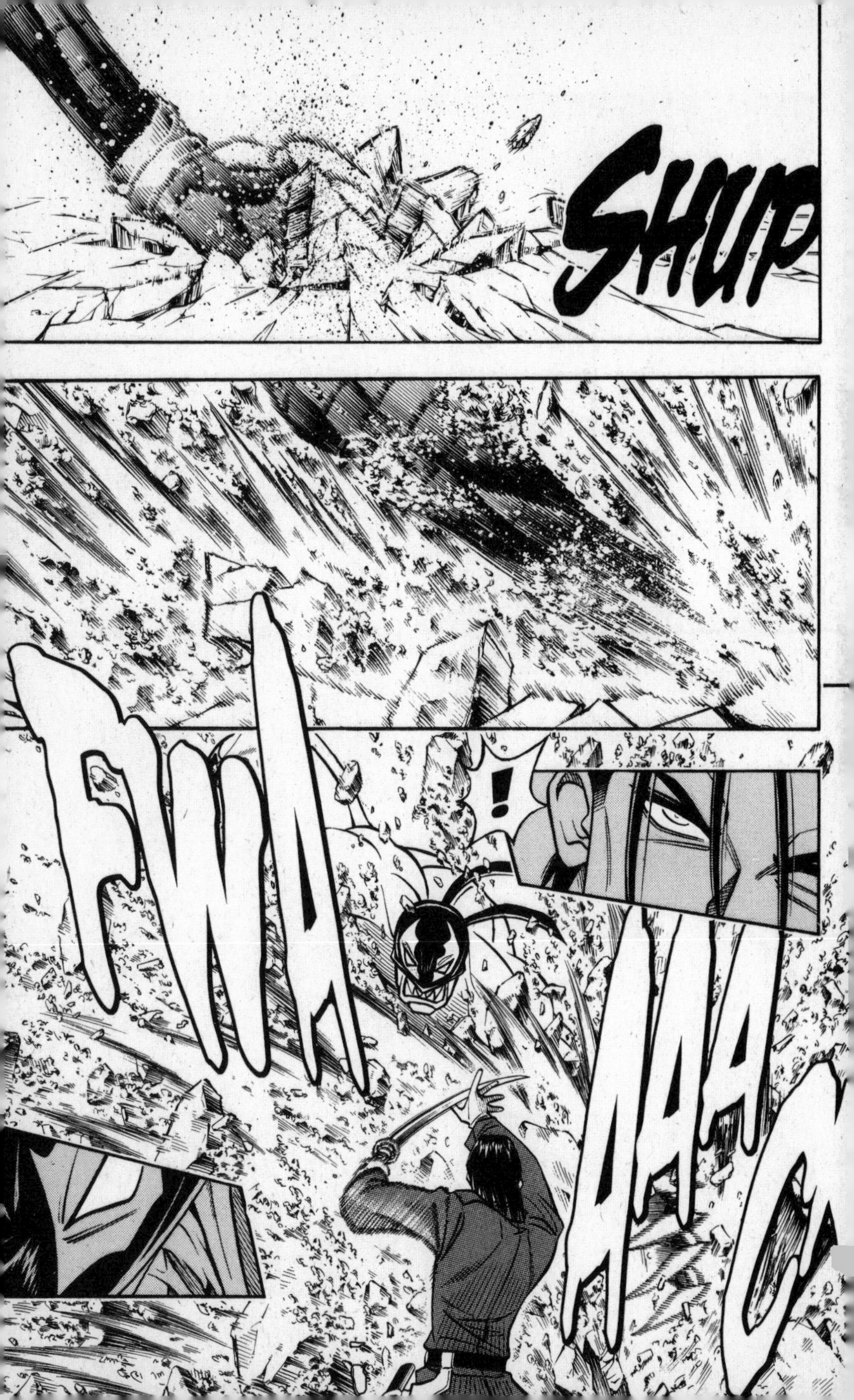
SHUP
!
FWAAAA

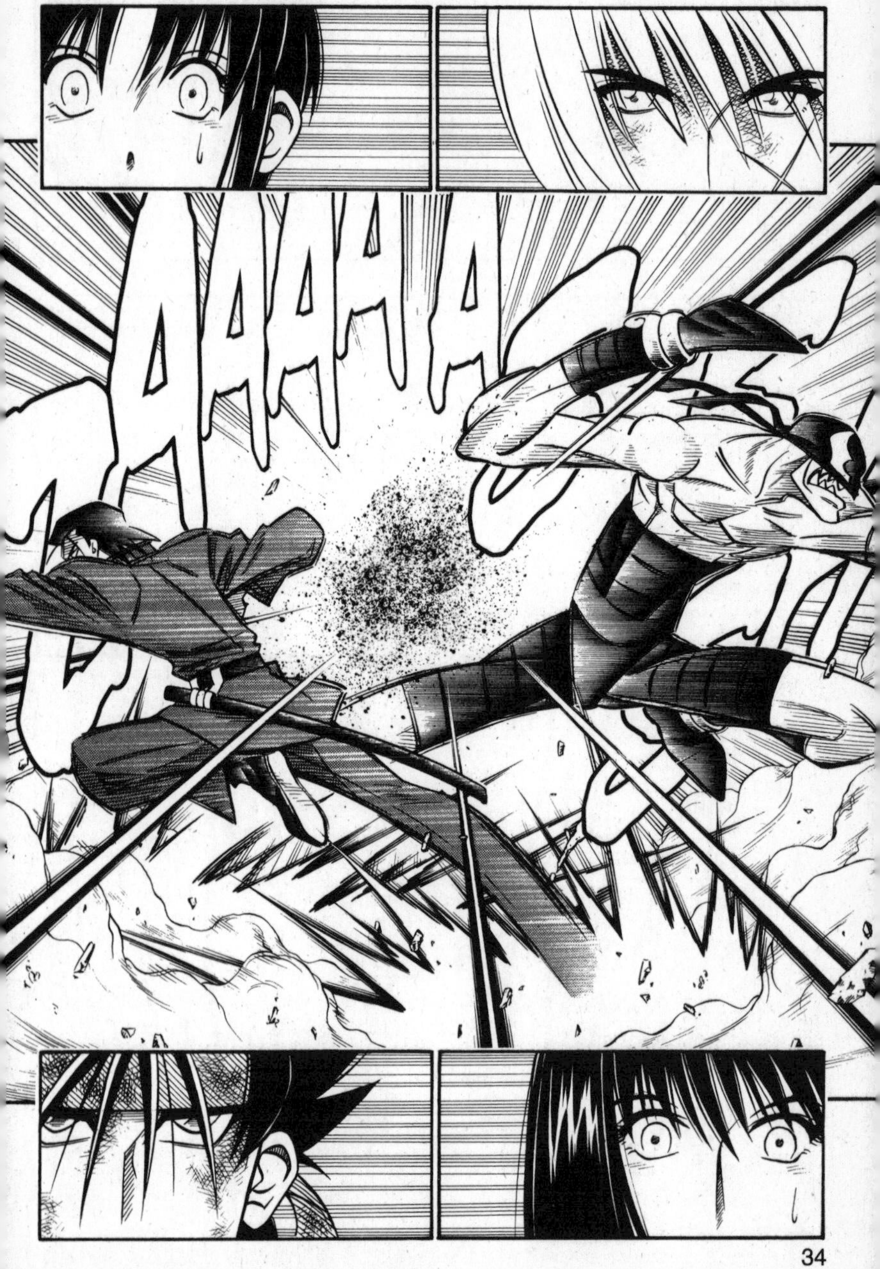
AAAAA

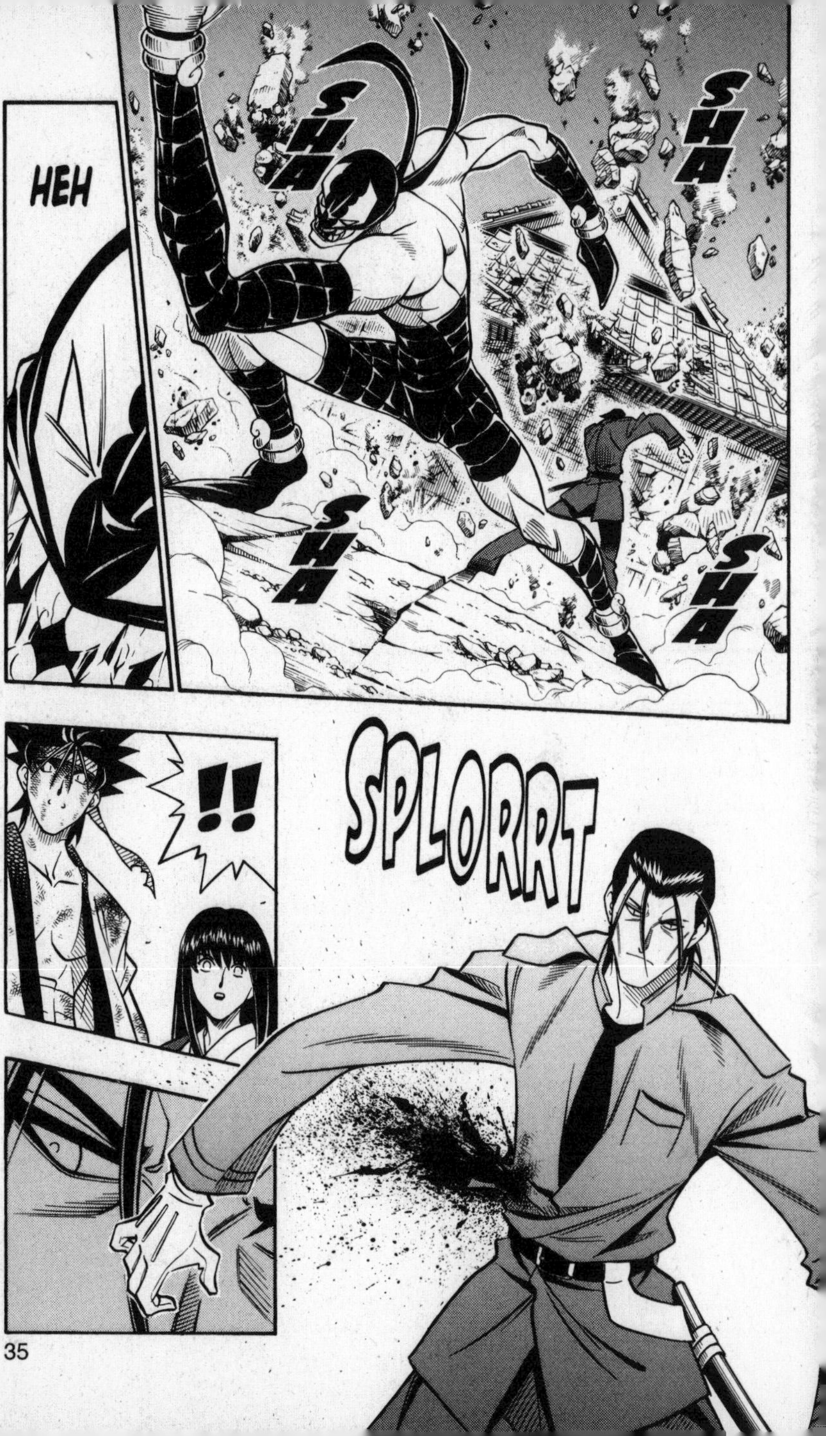

SHA
SHA
SHA
SHA
HEH
SPLORRT
!!

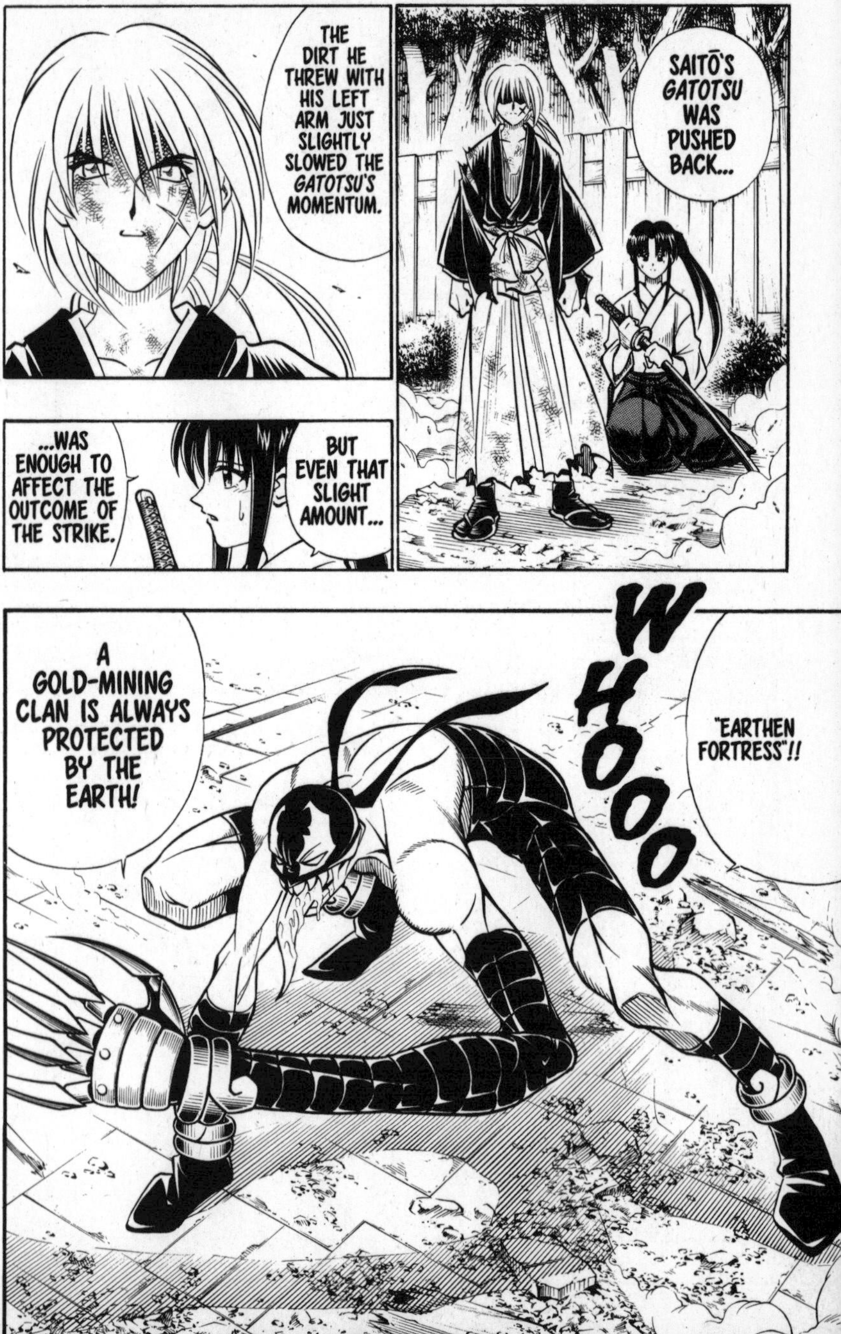

SAITŌ'S GATOTSU WAS PUSHED BACK...
THE DIRT HE THREW WITH HIS LEFT ARM JUST SLIGHTLY SLOWED THE *GATOTSU'S* MOMENTUM.
BUT EVEN THAT SLIGHT AMOUNT...
...WAS ENOUGH TO AFFECT THE OUTCOME OF THE STRIKE.
"EARTHEN FORTRESS"!!
WHOOO
A GOLD-MINING CLAN IS ALWAYS PROTECTED BY THE EARTH!

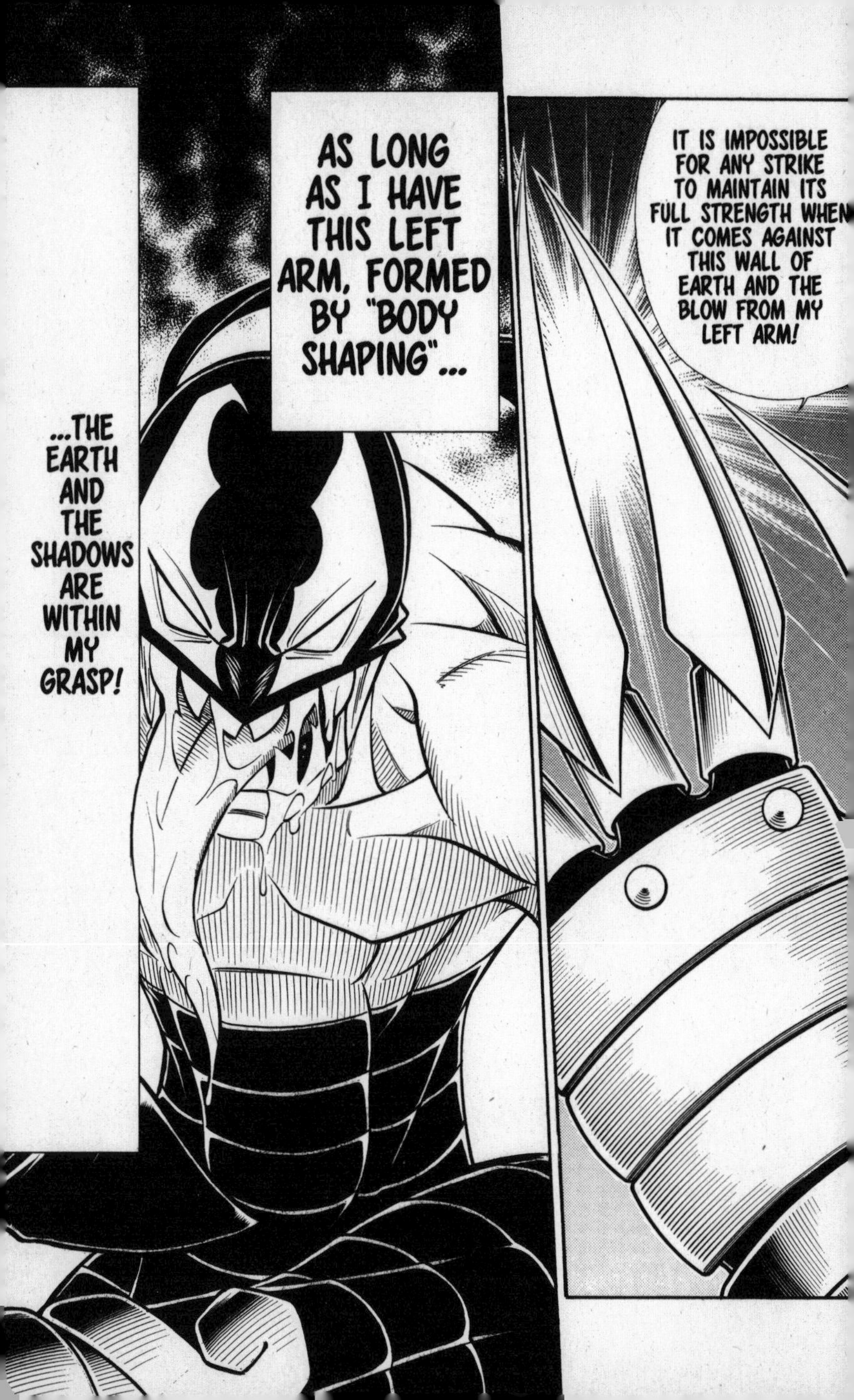
IT IS IMPOSSIBLE FOR ANY STRIKE TO MAINTAIN ITS FULL STRENGTH WHEN IT COMES AGAINST THIS WALL OF EARTH AND THE BLOW FROM MY LEFT ARM!
AS LONG AS I HAVE THIS LEFT ARM, FORMED BY "BODY SHAPING"...
...THE EARTH AND THE SHADOWS ARE WITHIN MY GRASP!

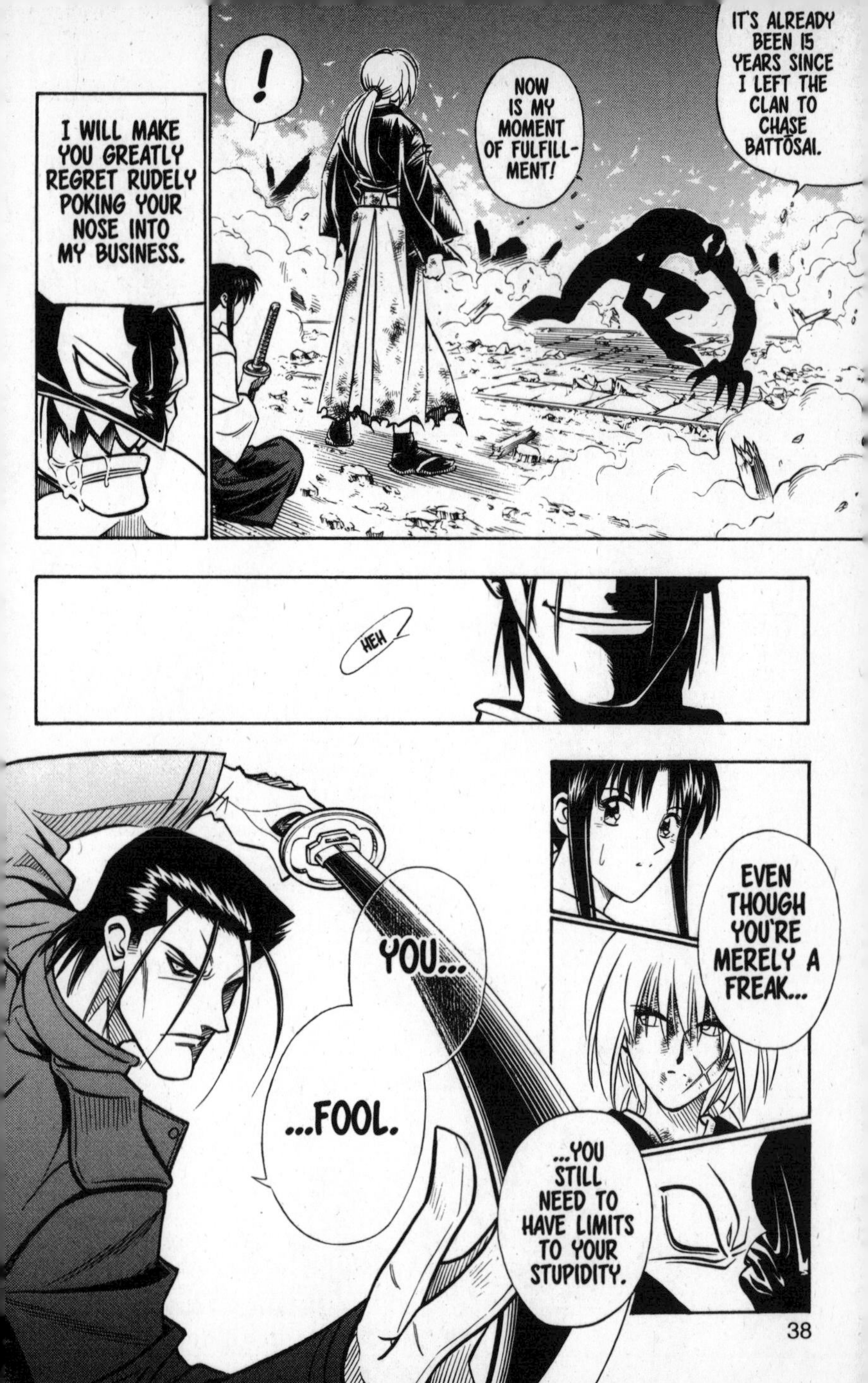

IT'S ALREADY BEEN 15 YEARS SINCE I LEFT THE CLAN TO CHASE BATTŌSAI.
NOW IS MY MOMENT OF FULFILL-MENT!
!
I WILL MAKE YOU GREATLY REGRET RUDELY POKING YOUR NOSE INTO MY BUSINESS.
HEH
EVEN THOUGH YOU'RE MERELY A FREAK...
...YOU STILL NEED TO HAVE LIMITS TO YOUR STUPIDITY.
YOU...
...FOOL.

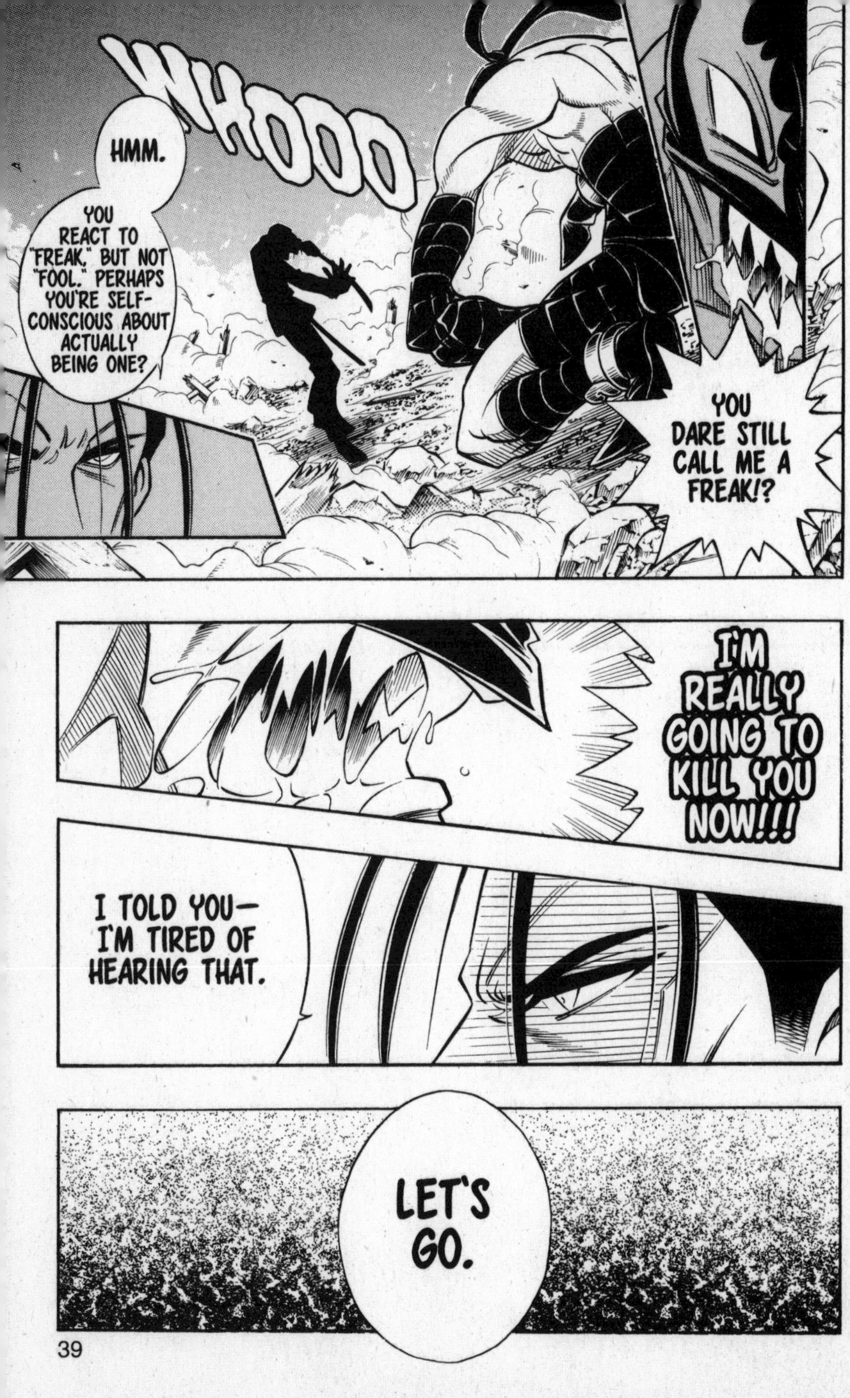
WHOOO
YOU DARE STILL CALL ME A FREAK!?
HMM.
YOU REACT TO "FREAK," BUT NOT "FOOL." PERHAPS YOU'RE SELF-CONSCIOUS ABOUT ACTUALLY BEING ONE?
I'M REALLY GOING TO KILL YOU NOW!!!
I TOLD YOU— I'M TIRED OF HEARING THAT.
LET'S GO.

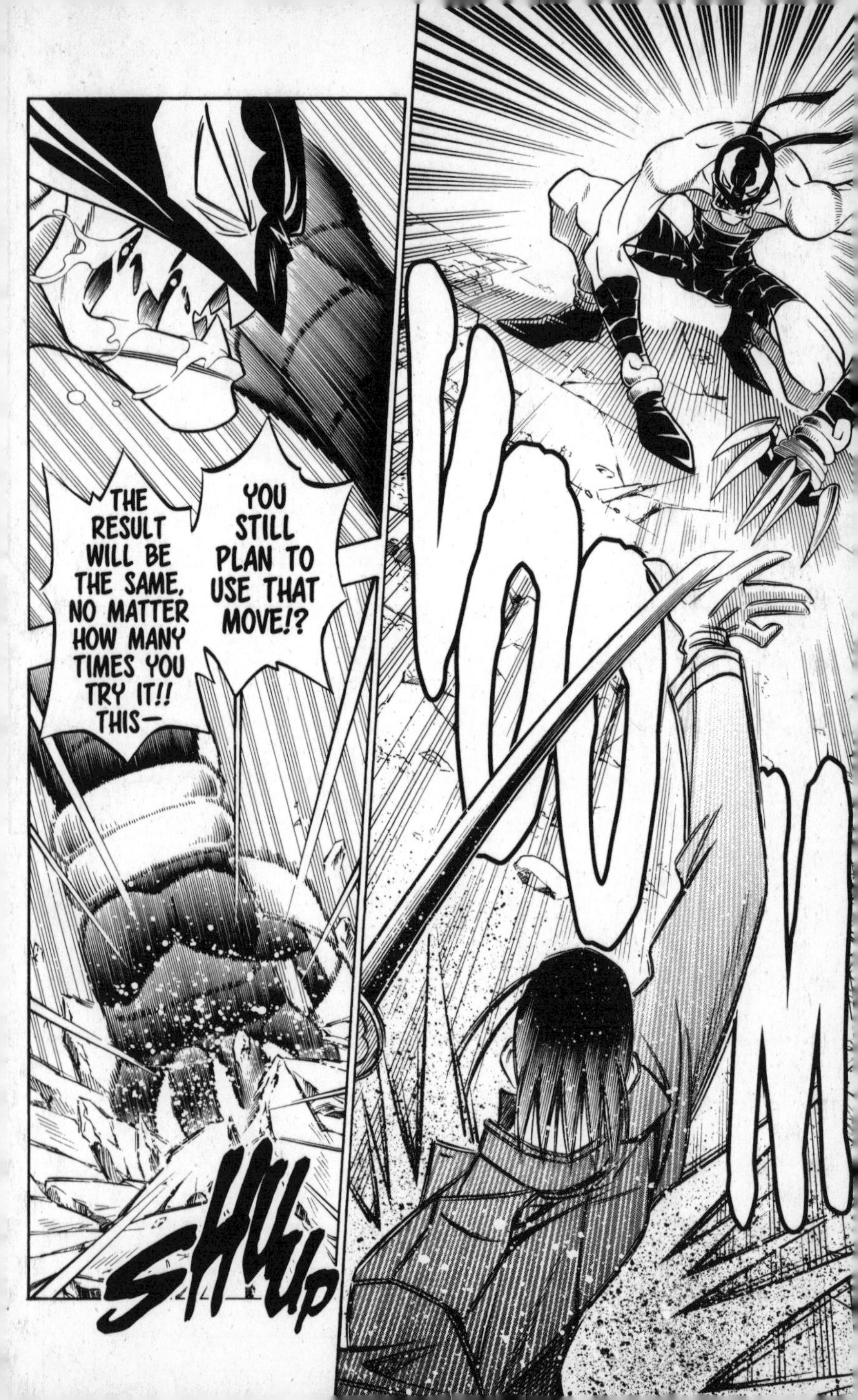
YOU STILL PLAN TO USE THAT MOVE!?
THE RESULT WILL BE THE SAME, NO MATTER HOW MANY TIMES YOU TRY IT!! THIS—

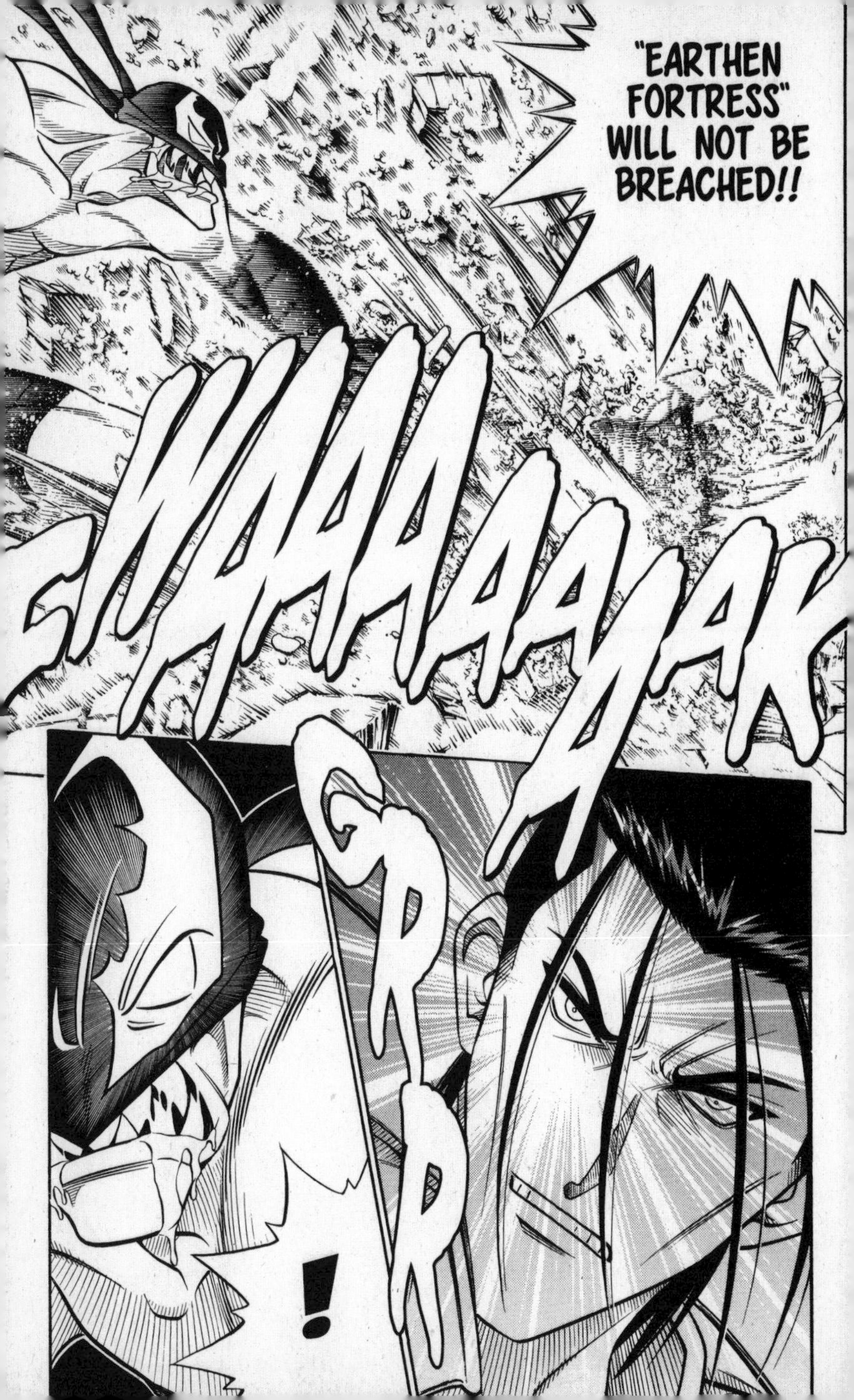
"EARTHEN FORTRESS" WILL NOT BE BREACHED!!
SHAAAAAK
GRRR
!

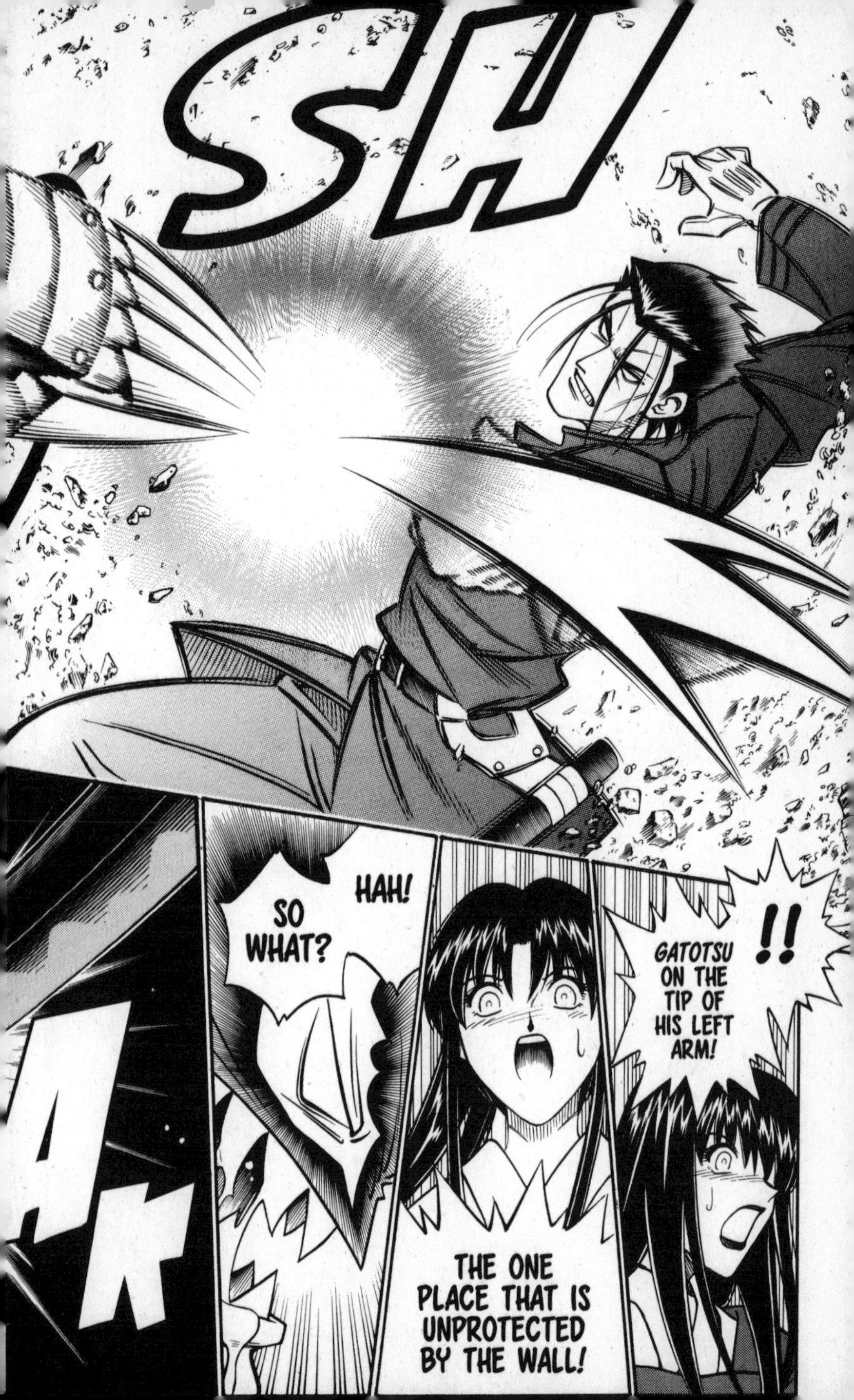
SH
!!
GATOTSU ON THE TIP OF HIS LEFT ARM!
THE ONE PLACE THAT IS UNPROTECTED BY THE WALL!
HAH!
SO WHAT?

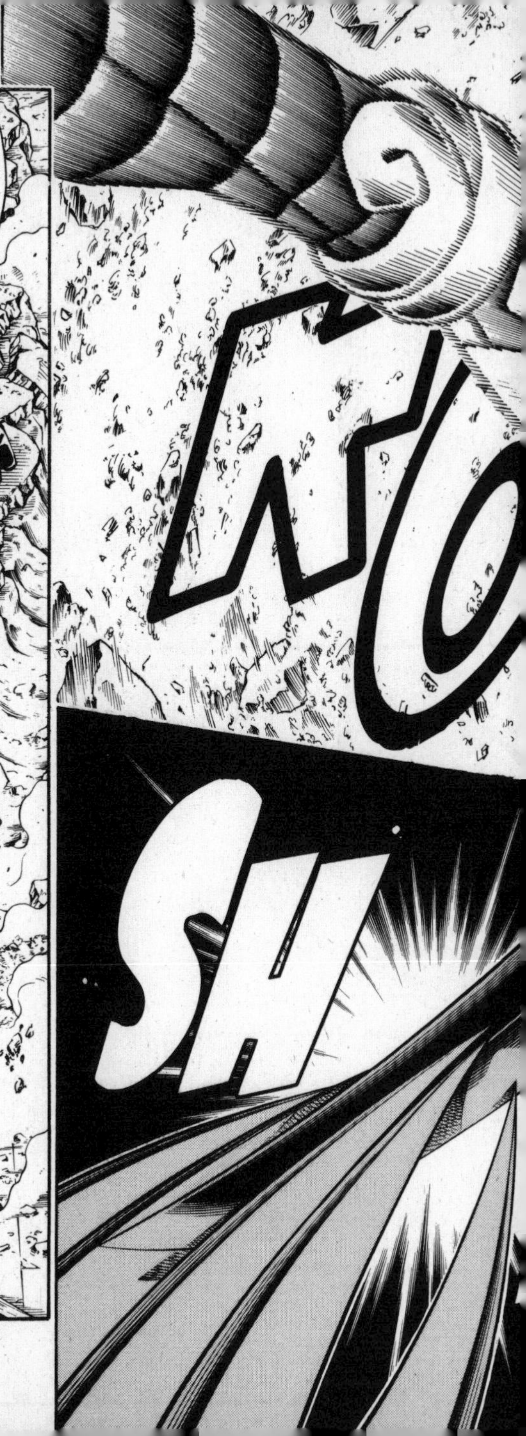
SH

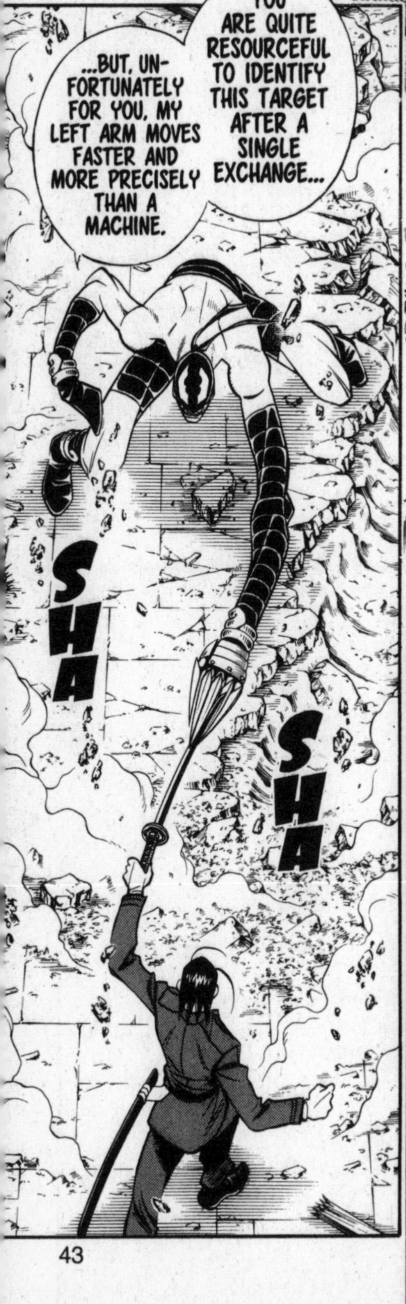
YOU ARE QUITE RESOURCEFUL TO IDENTIFY THIS TARGET AFTER A SINGLE EXCHANGE...
...BUT, UN-FORTUNATELY FOR YOU, MY LEFT ARM MOVES FASTER AND MORE PRECISELY THAN A MACHINE.
SHA
SHA

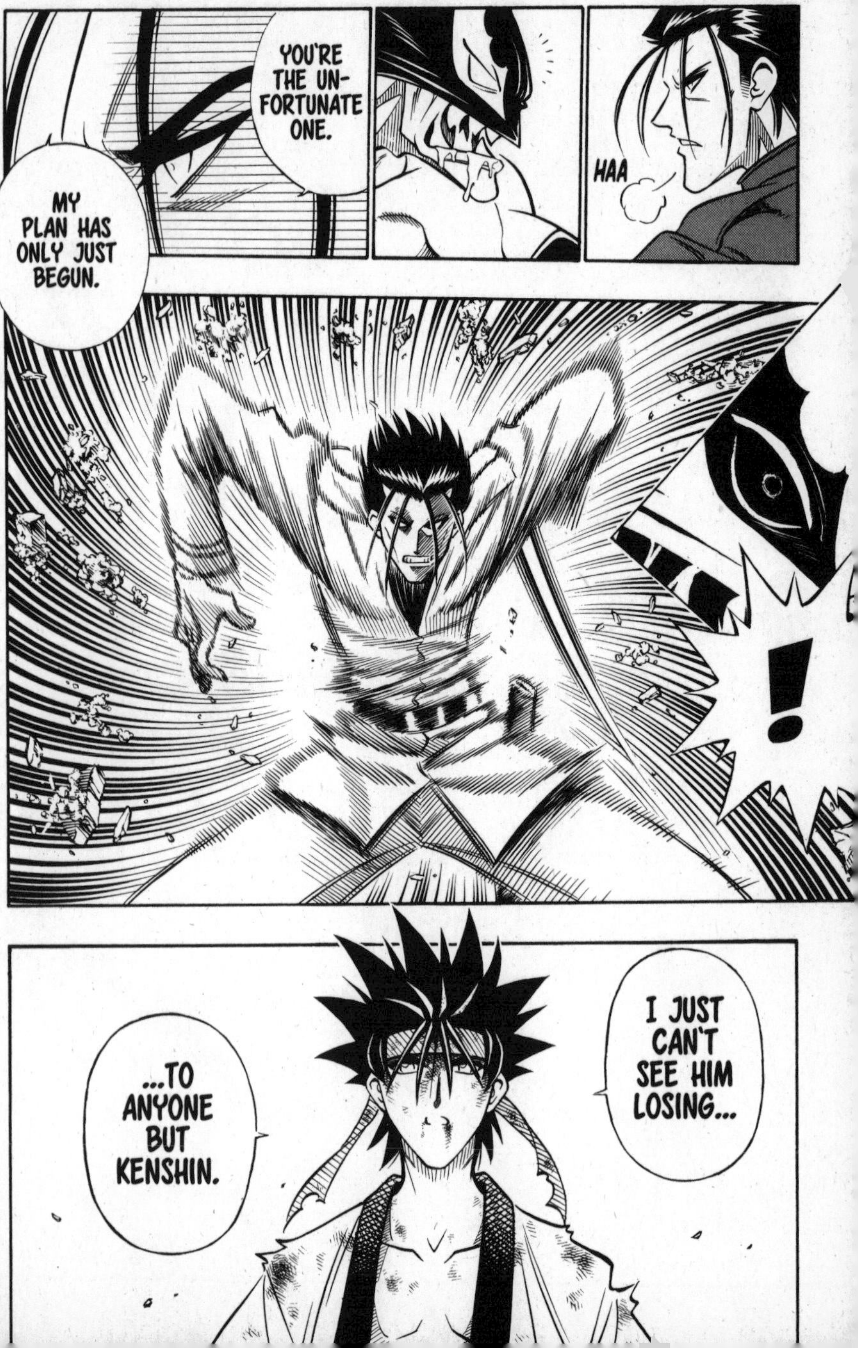
HAA
YOU'RE THE UN-FORTUNATE ONE.
MY PLAN HAS ONLY JUST BEGUN.
!
I JUST CAN'T SEE HIM LOSING...
...TO ANYONE BUT KENSHIN.

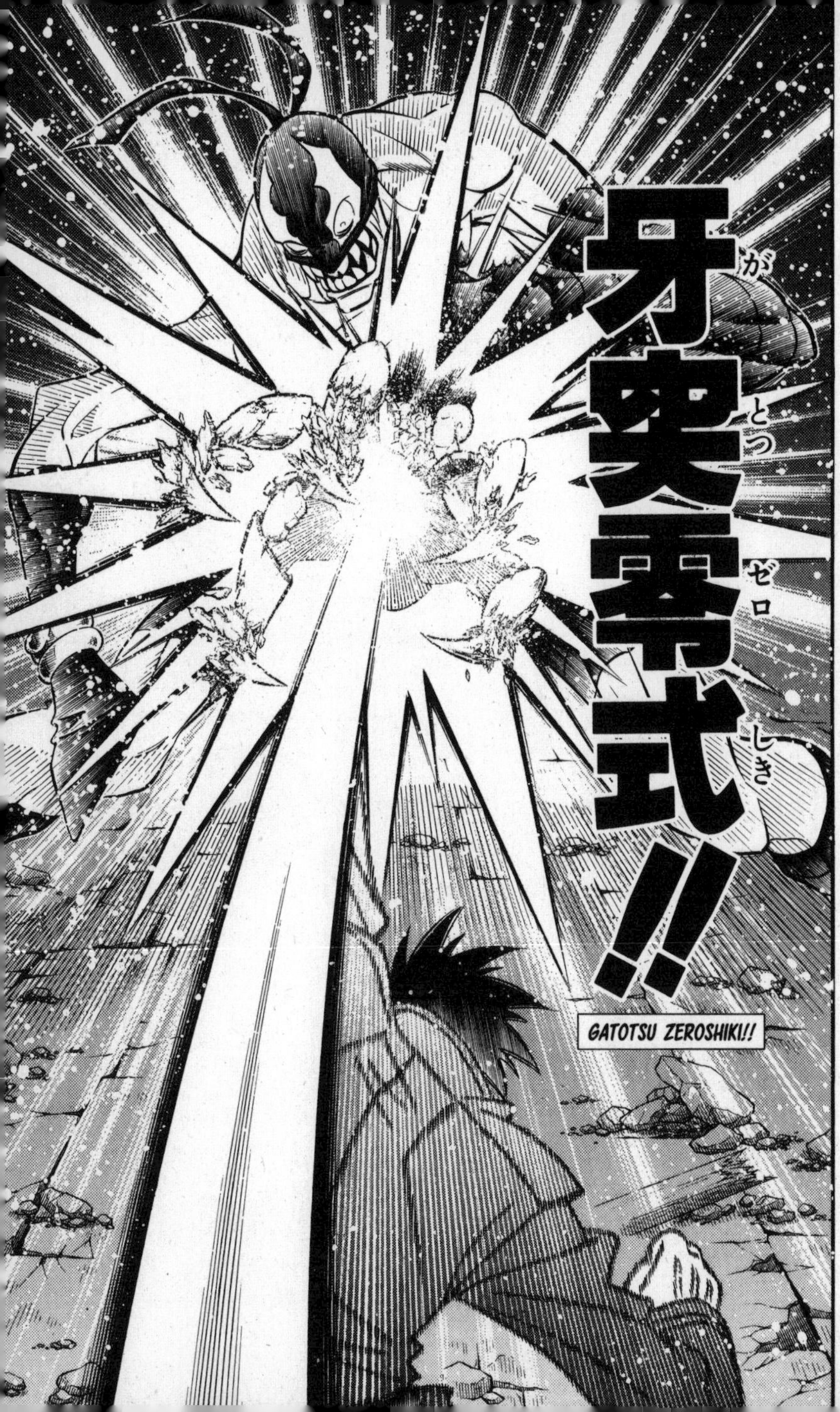
牙突零式!!
GATOTSU ZEROSHIKI!!

Rurouni Kenshin

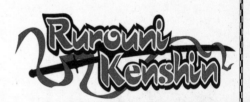

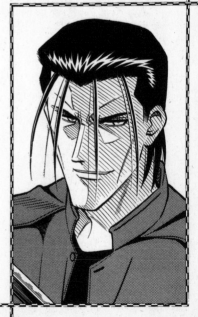

Act 199—Inadequate Strategy

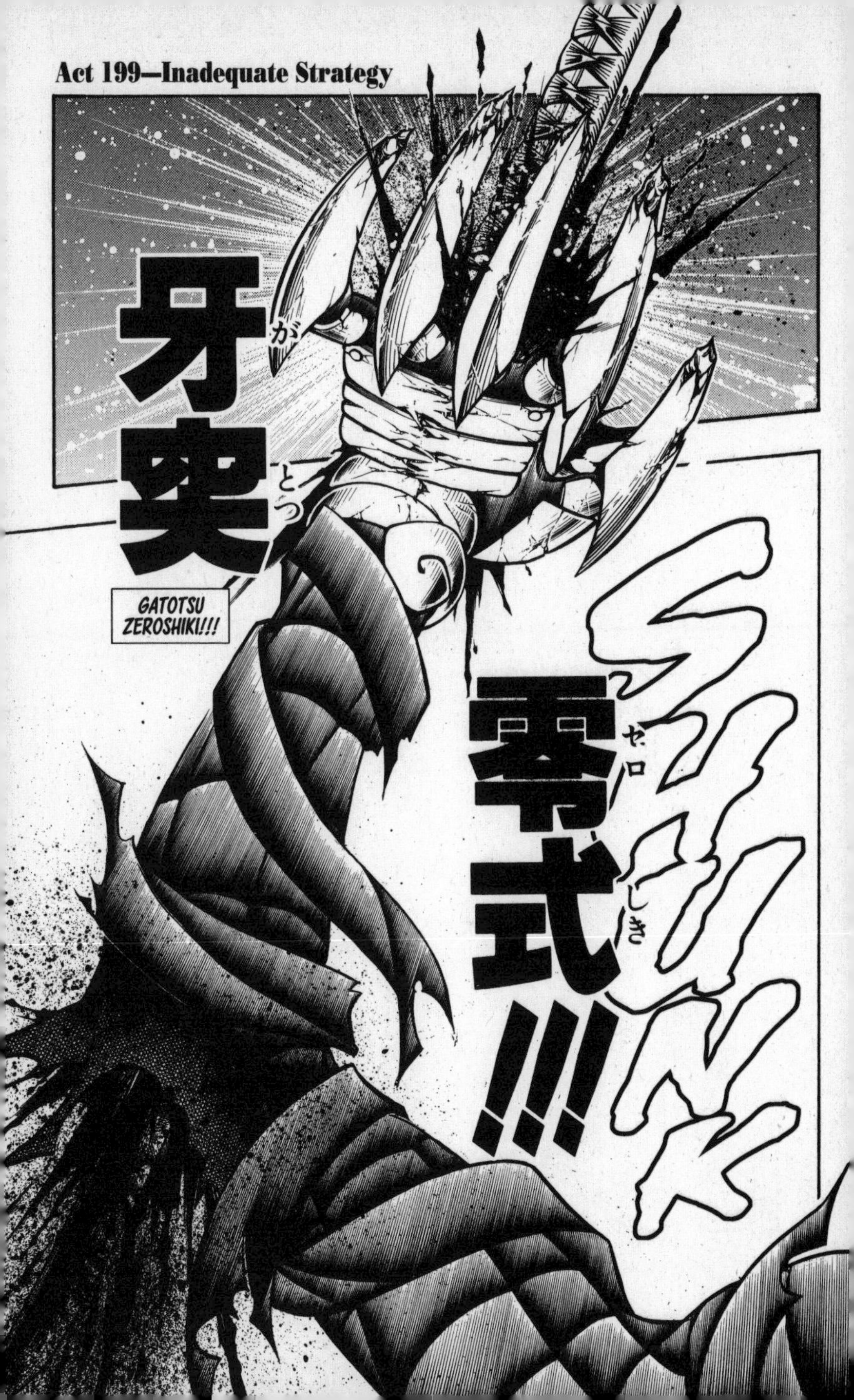

牙突零式!!!
GATOTSU ZEROSHIKI!!!

Inadequate Strategy

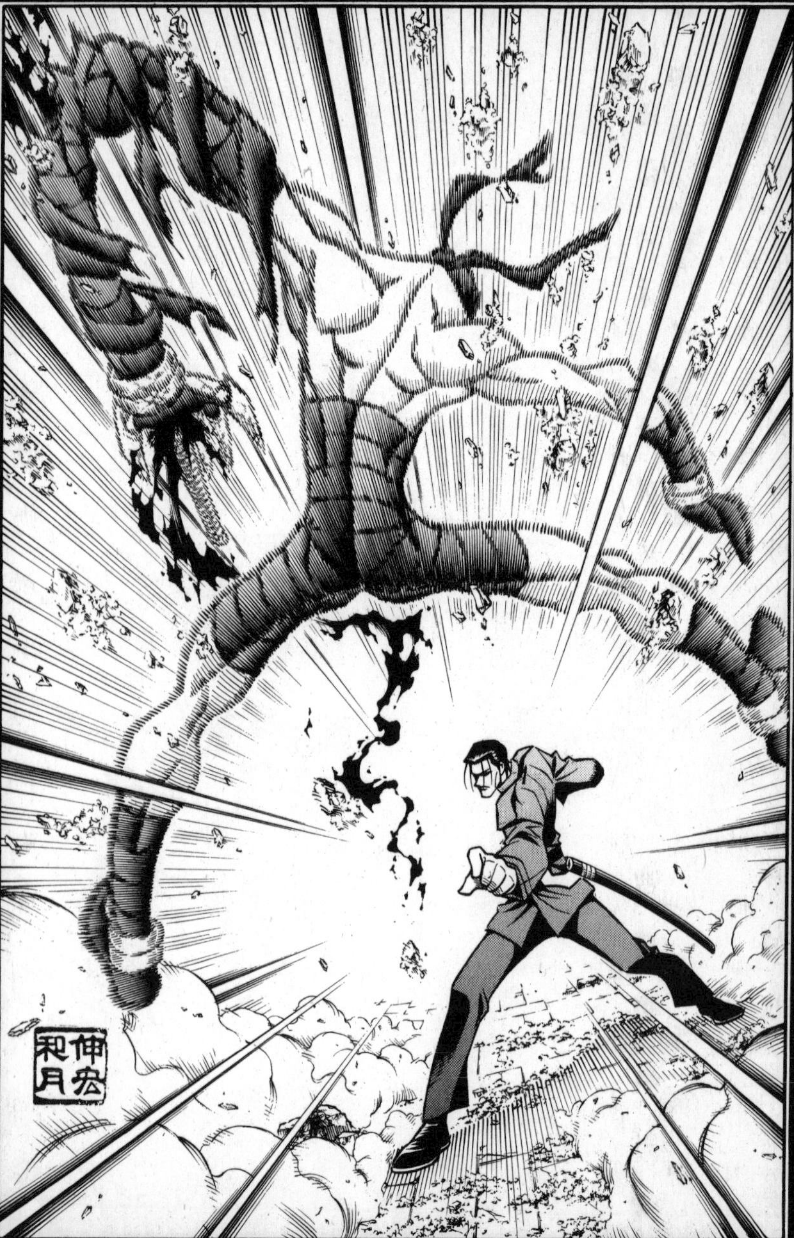
伸宏
和月

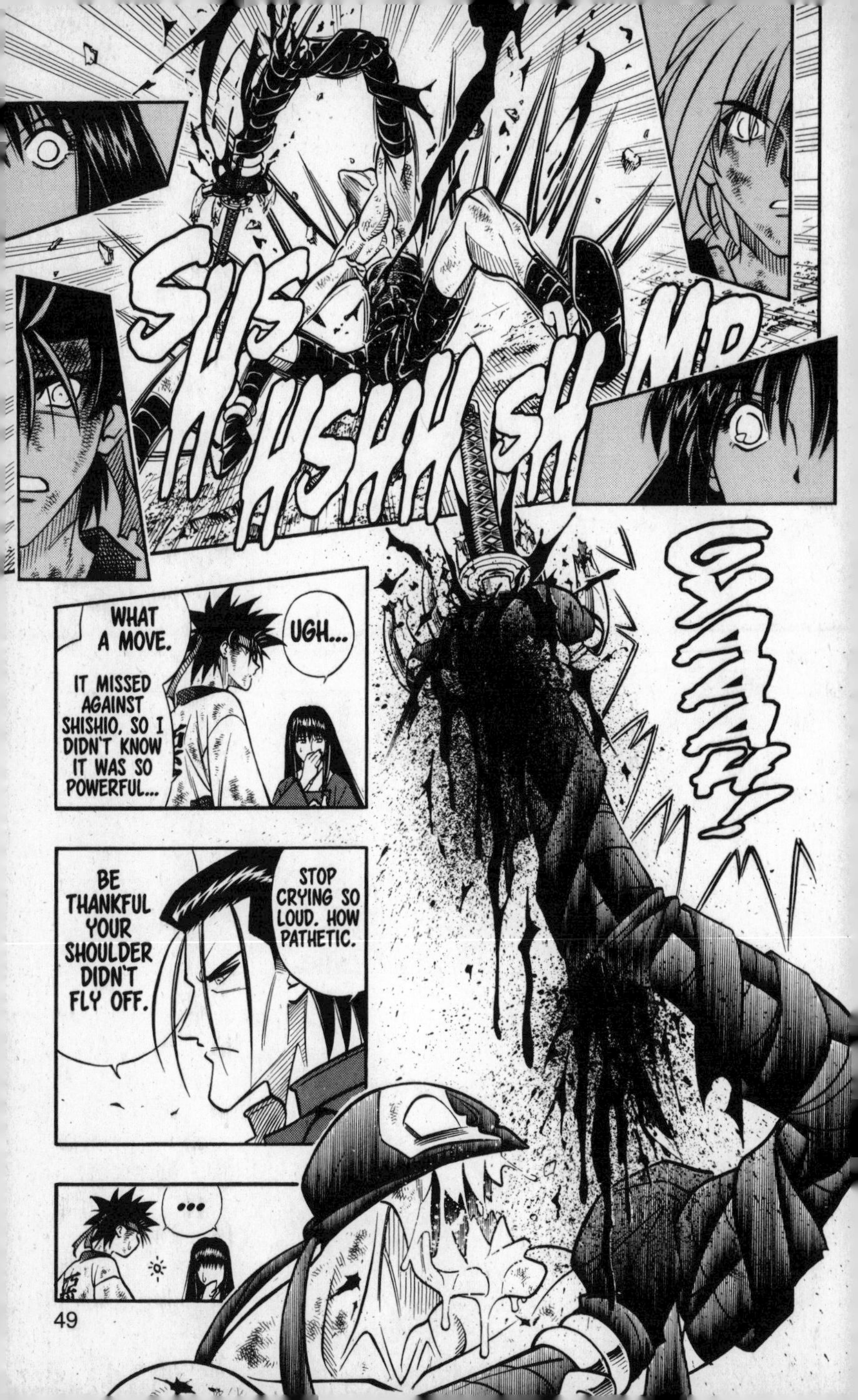
UGH...
WHAT A MOVE.
IT MISSED AGAINST SHISHIO, SO I DIDN'T KNOW IT WAS SO POWERFUL...
STOP CRYING SO LOUD. HOW PATHETIC.
BE THANKFUL YOUR SHOULDER DIDN'T FLY OFF.
...

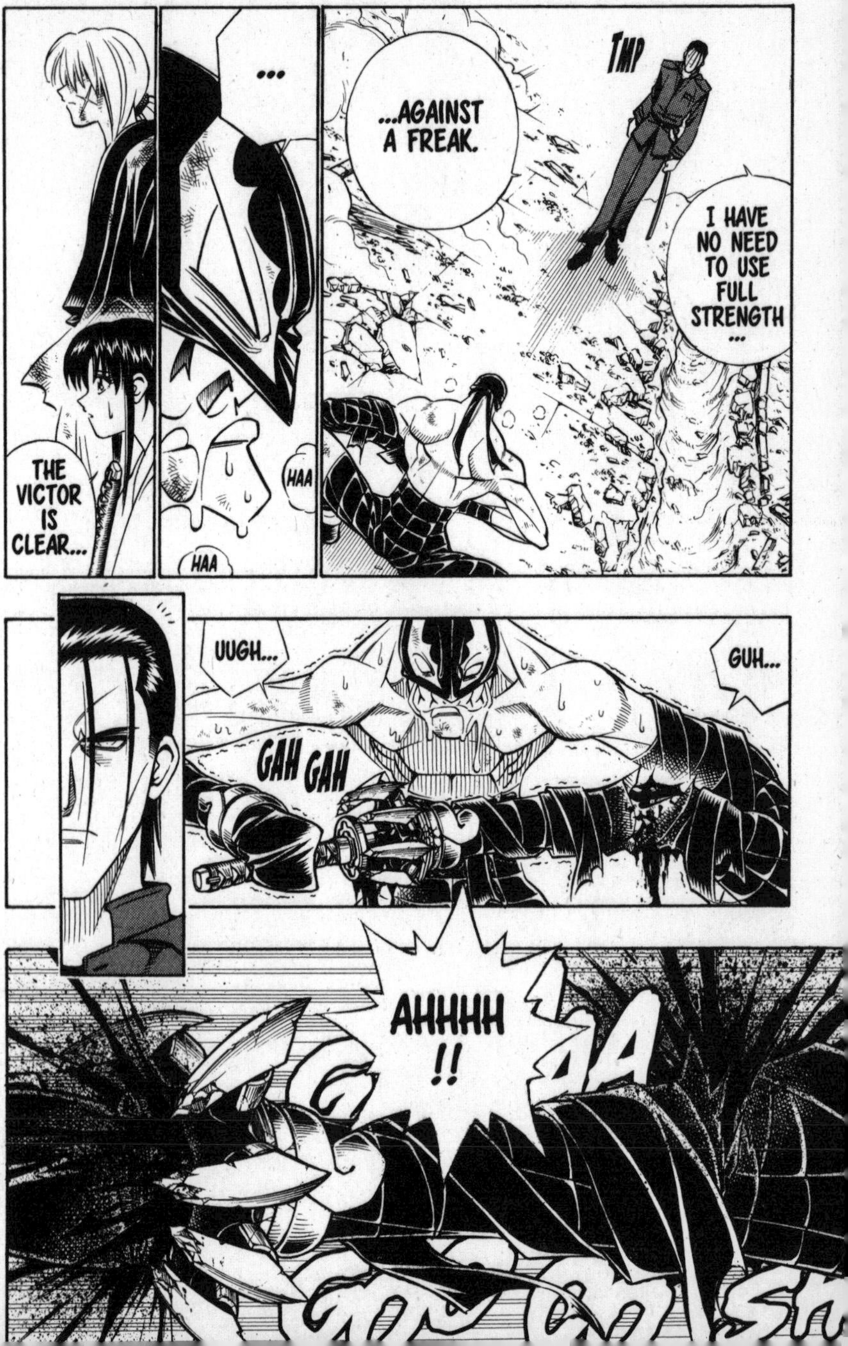
TMP
I HAVE NO NEED TO USE FULL STRENGTH...
...AGAINST A FREAK.
...
HAA
HAA
THE VICTOR IS CLEAR...
GUH...
UUGH...
GAH GAH
AHHHH !!

READ THIS WAY

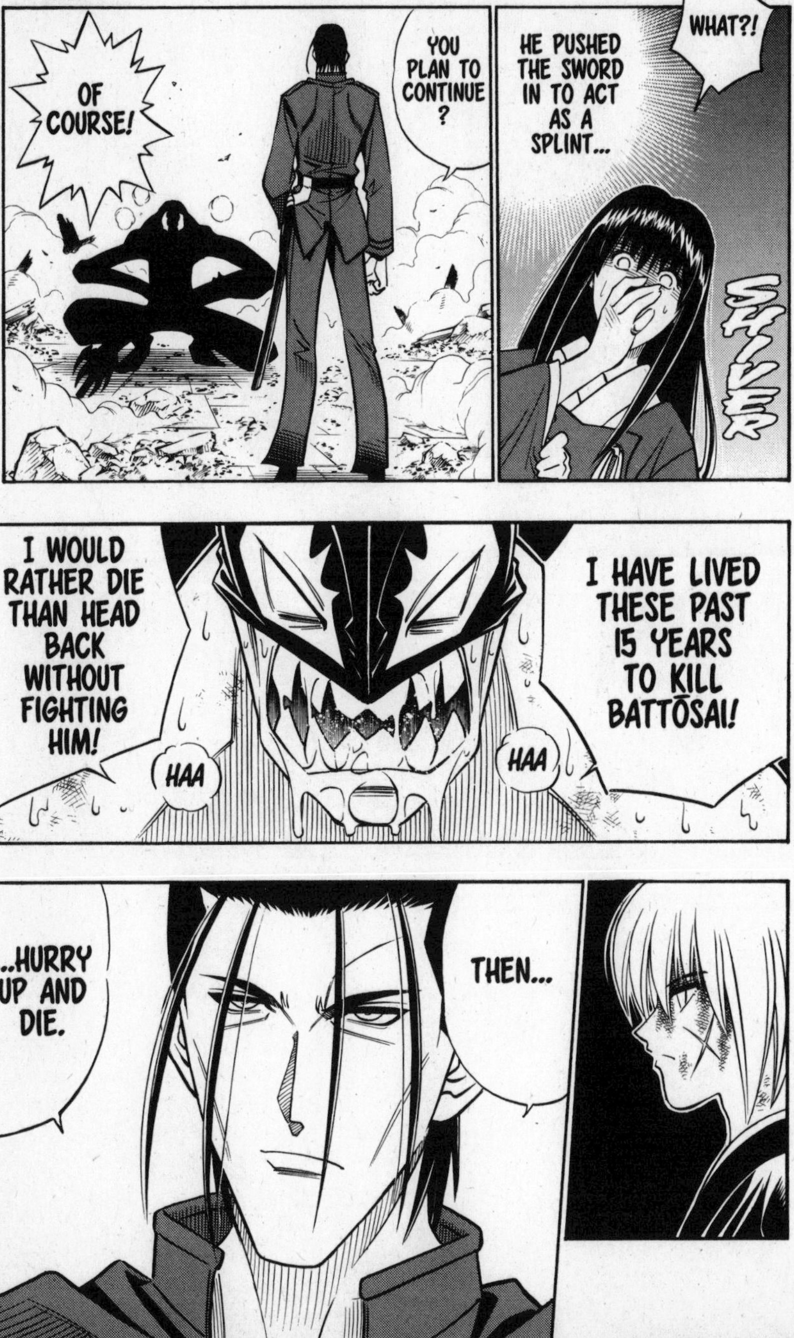

WHAT?!
HE PUSHED THE SWORD IN TO ACT AS A SPLINT...
SHIVER
YOU PLAN TO CONTINUE?
OF COURSE!
I HAVE LIVED THESE PAST 15 YEARS TO KILL BATTŌSAI!
HAA
HAA
I WOULD RATHER DIE THAN HEAD BACK WITHOUT FIGHTING HIM!
THEN...
...HURRY UP AND DIE.

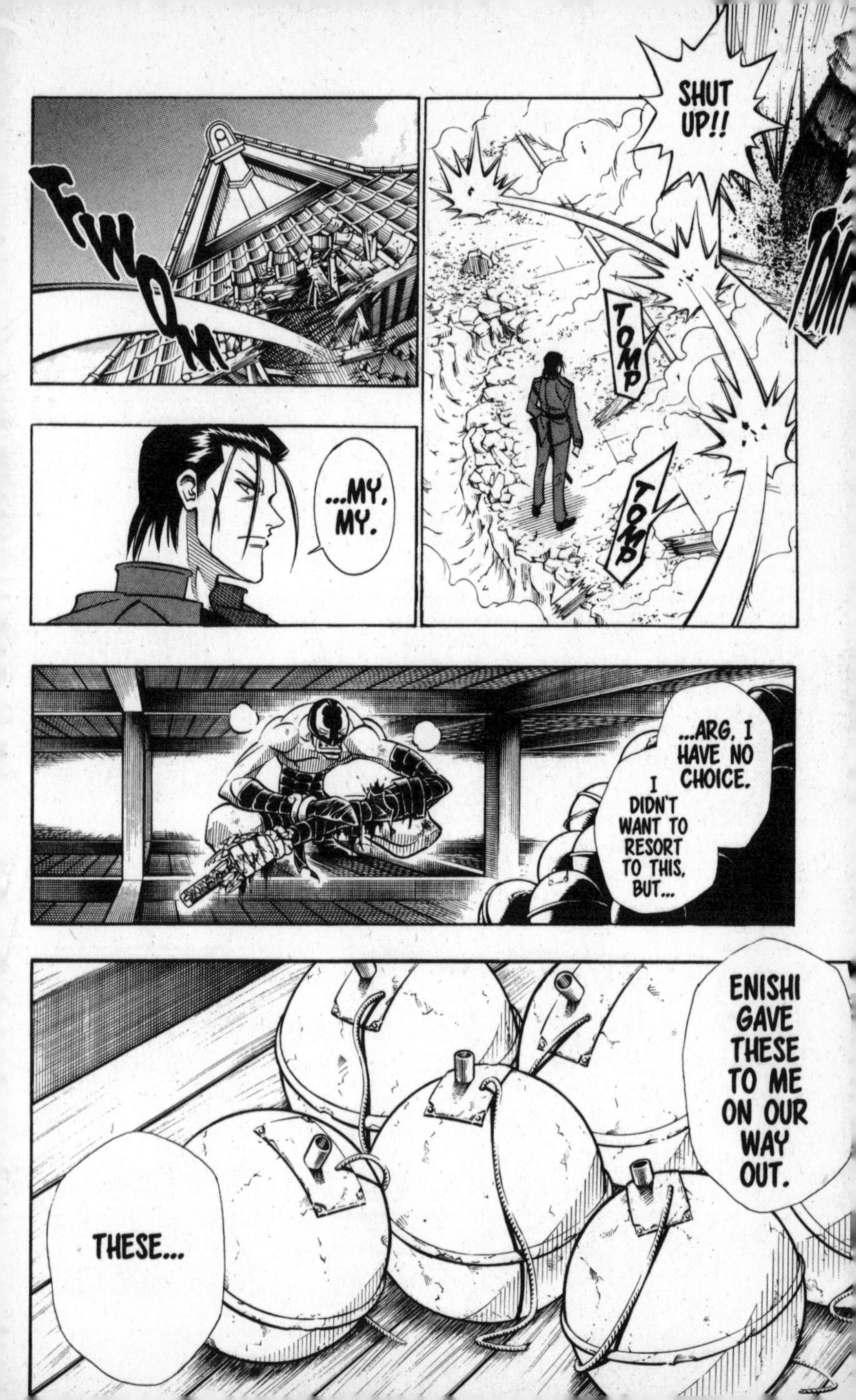
SHUT UP!!
TOMP
TOMP
TOMP
FWOOM
...MY, MY.
...ARG, I HAVE NO CHOICE.
I DIDN'T WANT TO RESORT TO THIS, BUT...
ENISHI GAVE THESE TO ME ON OUR WAY OUT.
THESE...

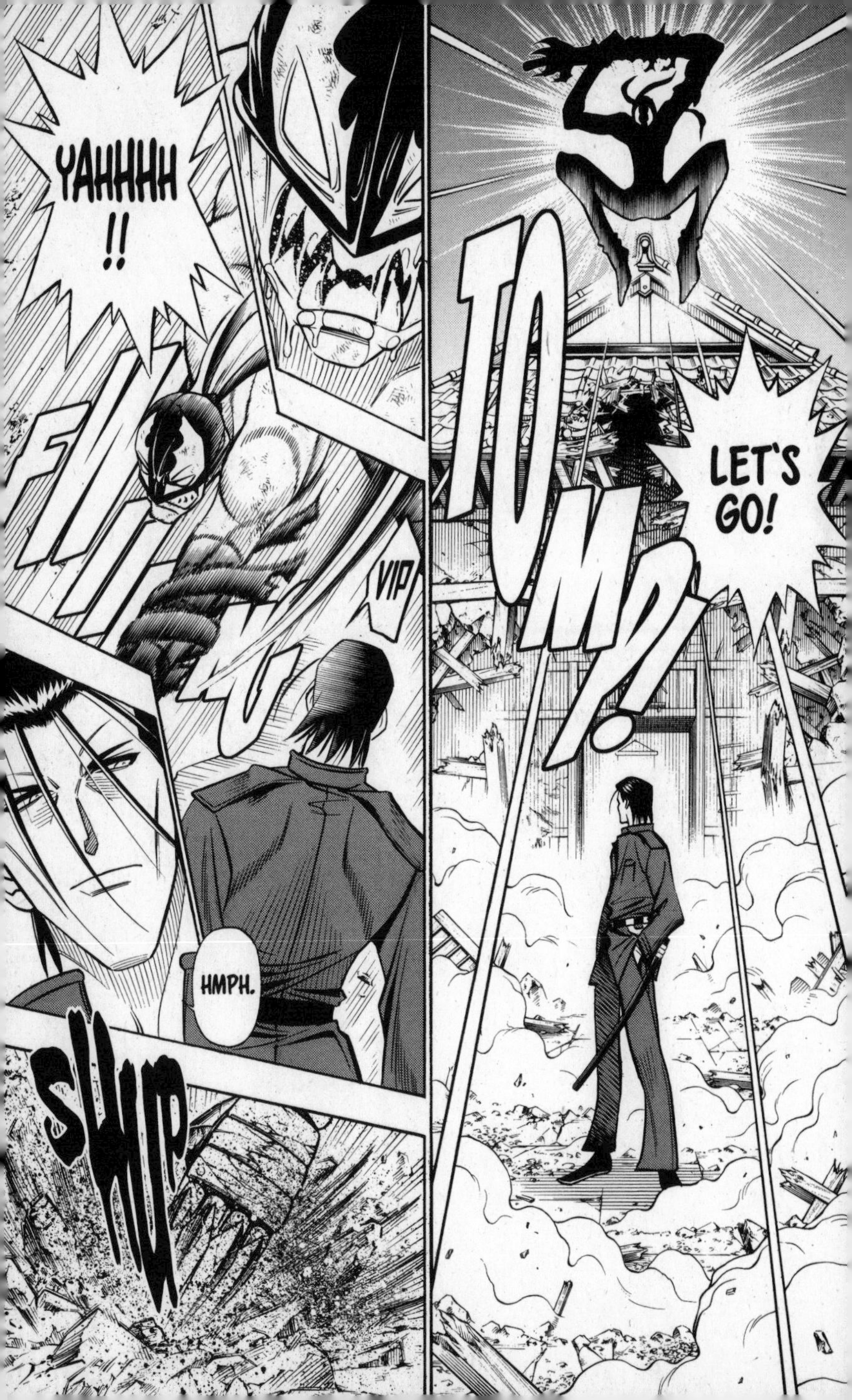
LET'S GO!
TOMP!
YAHHHH!!
VIP
HMPH.
SHUP

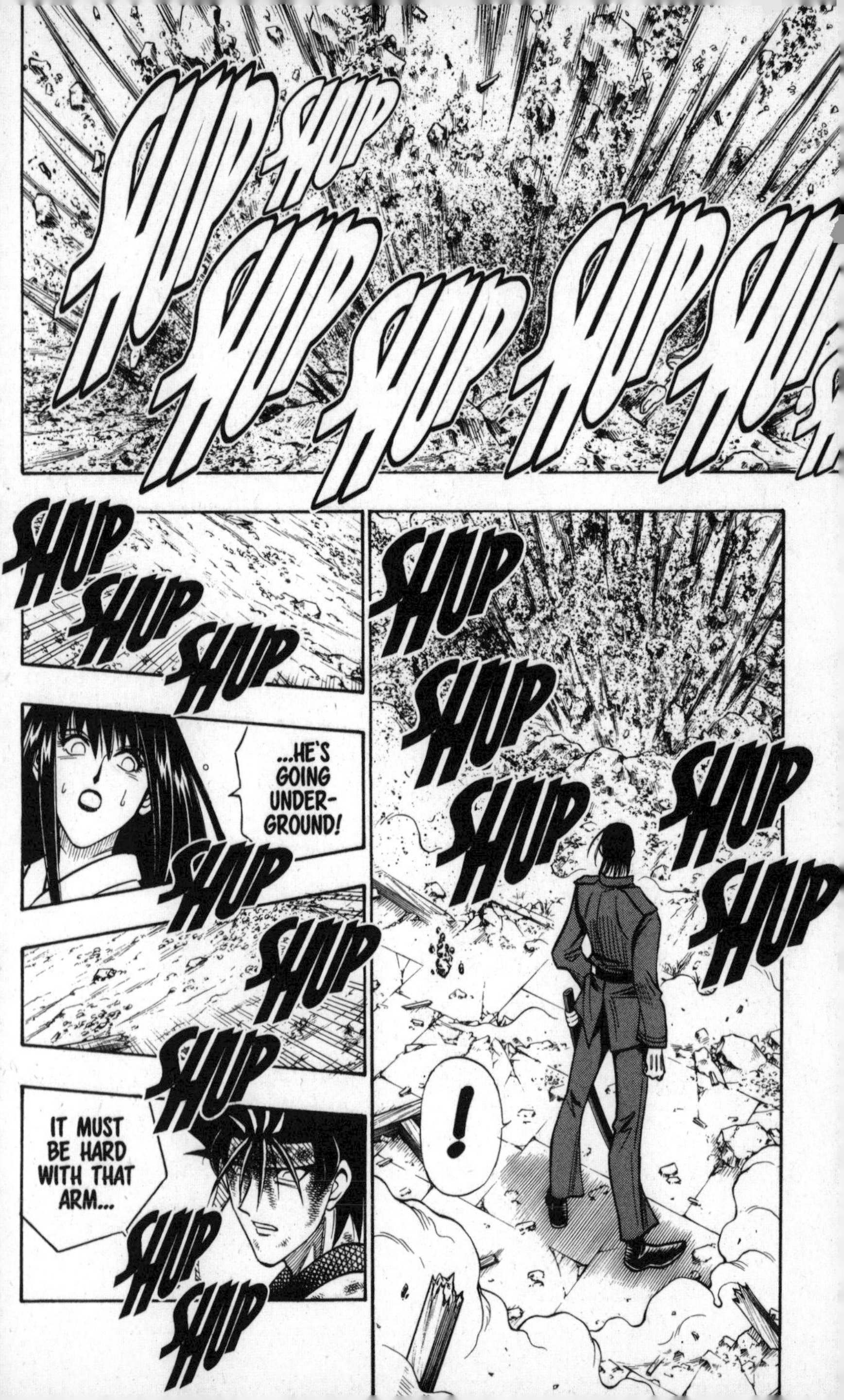
SHUP SHUP SHUP SHUP SHUP SHUP SHUP
SHUP SHUP SHUP SHUP SHUP
!
SHUP SHUP SHUP
...HE'S GOING UNDER-GROUND!
SHUP SHUP SHUP
IT MUST BE HARD WITH THAT ARM...
SHUP SHUP

READ THIS WAY

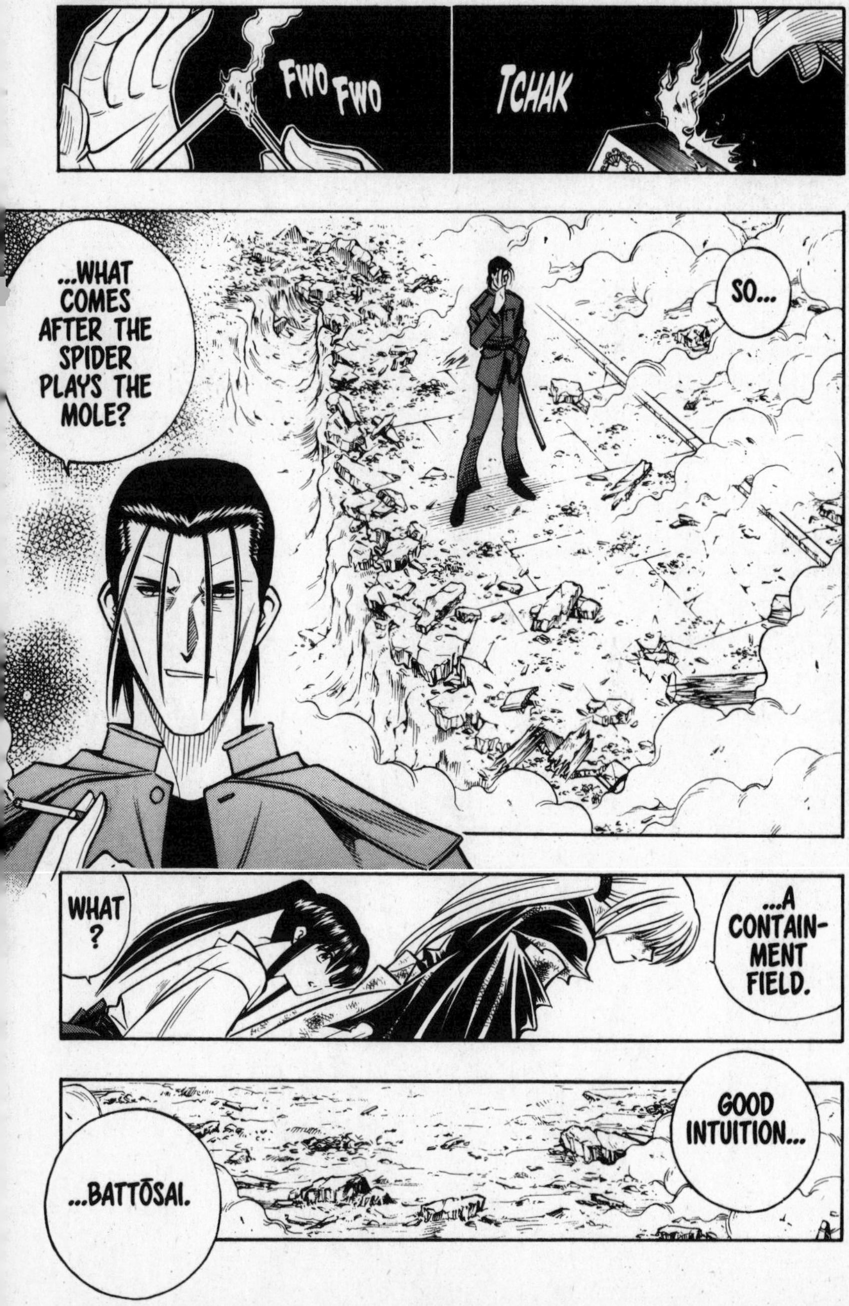
TCHAK
FWO FWO
SO...
...WHAT COMES AFTER THE SPIDER PLAYS THE MOLE?
...A CONTAIN-MENT FIELD.
WHAT?
GOOD INTUITION...
...BATTŌSAI.

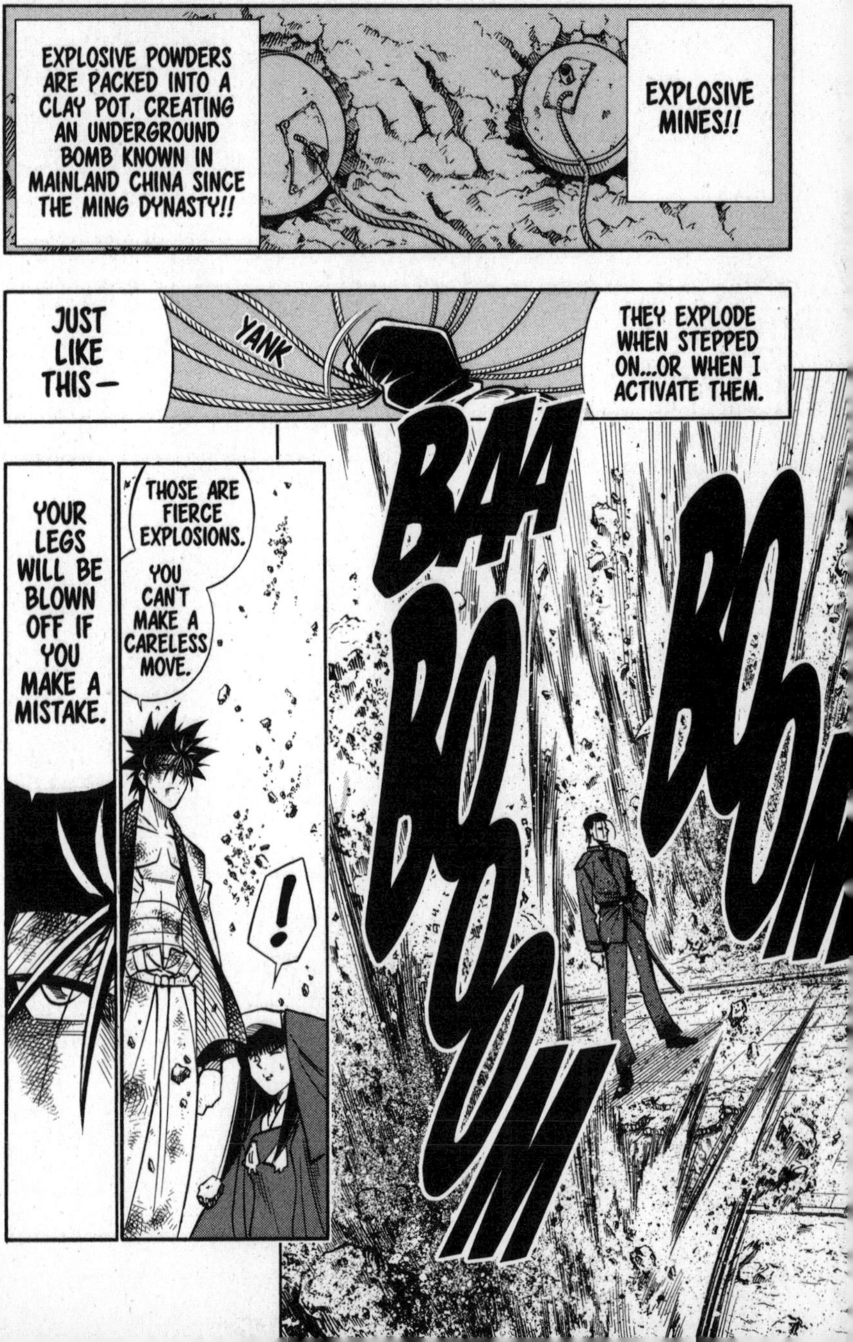
EXPLOSIVE MINES!!
EXPLOSIVE POWDERS ARE PACKED INTO A CLAY POT, CREATING AN UNDERGROUND BOMB KNOWN IN MAINLAND CHINA SINCE THE MING DYNASTY!!
THEY EXPLODE WHEN STEPPED ON...OR WHEN I ACTIVATE THEM.
YANK
JUST LIKE THIS—
THOSE ARE FIERCE EXPLOSIONS.
YOU CAN'T MAKE A CARELESS MOVE.
!
YOUR LEGS WILL BE BLOWN OFF IF YOU MAKE A MISTAKE.

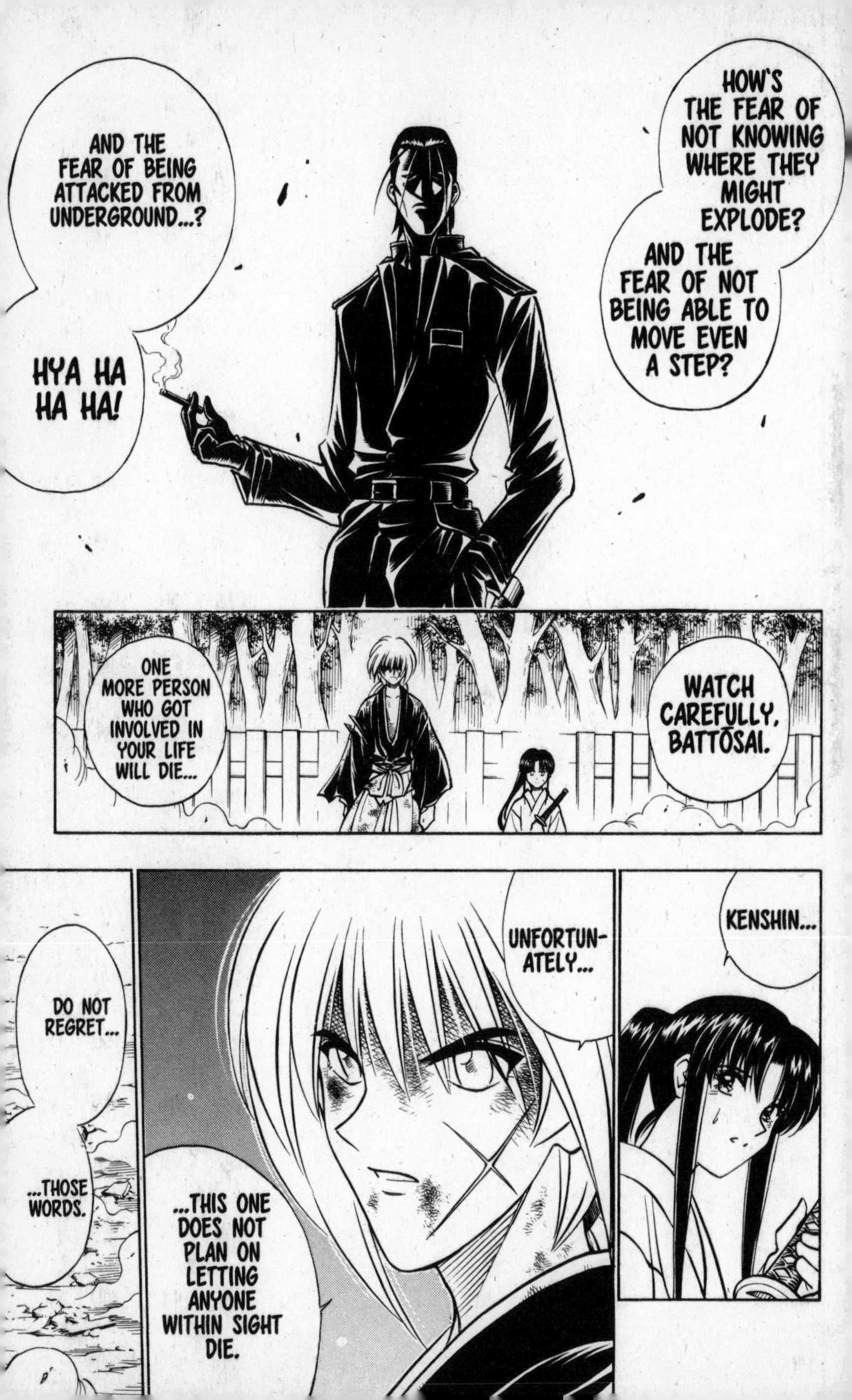
HOW'S THE FEAR OF NOT KNOWING WHERE THEY MIGHT EXPLODE?
AND THE FEAR OF NOT BEING ABLE TO MOVE EVEN A STEP?
AND THE FEAR OF BEING ATTACKED FROM UNDERGROUND...?
HYA HA HA HA!
WATCH CAREFULLY, BATTŌSAI.
ONE MORE PERSON WHO GOT INVOLVED IN YOUR LIFE WILL DIE...
KENSHIN...
UNFORTUN-ATELY...
...THIS ONE DOES NOT PLAN ON LETTING ANYONE WITHIN SIGHT DIE.
DO NOT REGRET...
...THOSE WORDS.

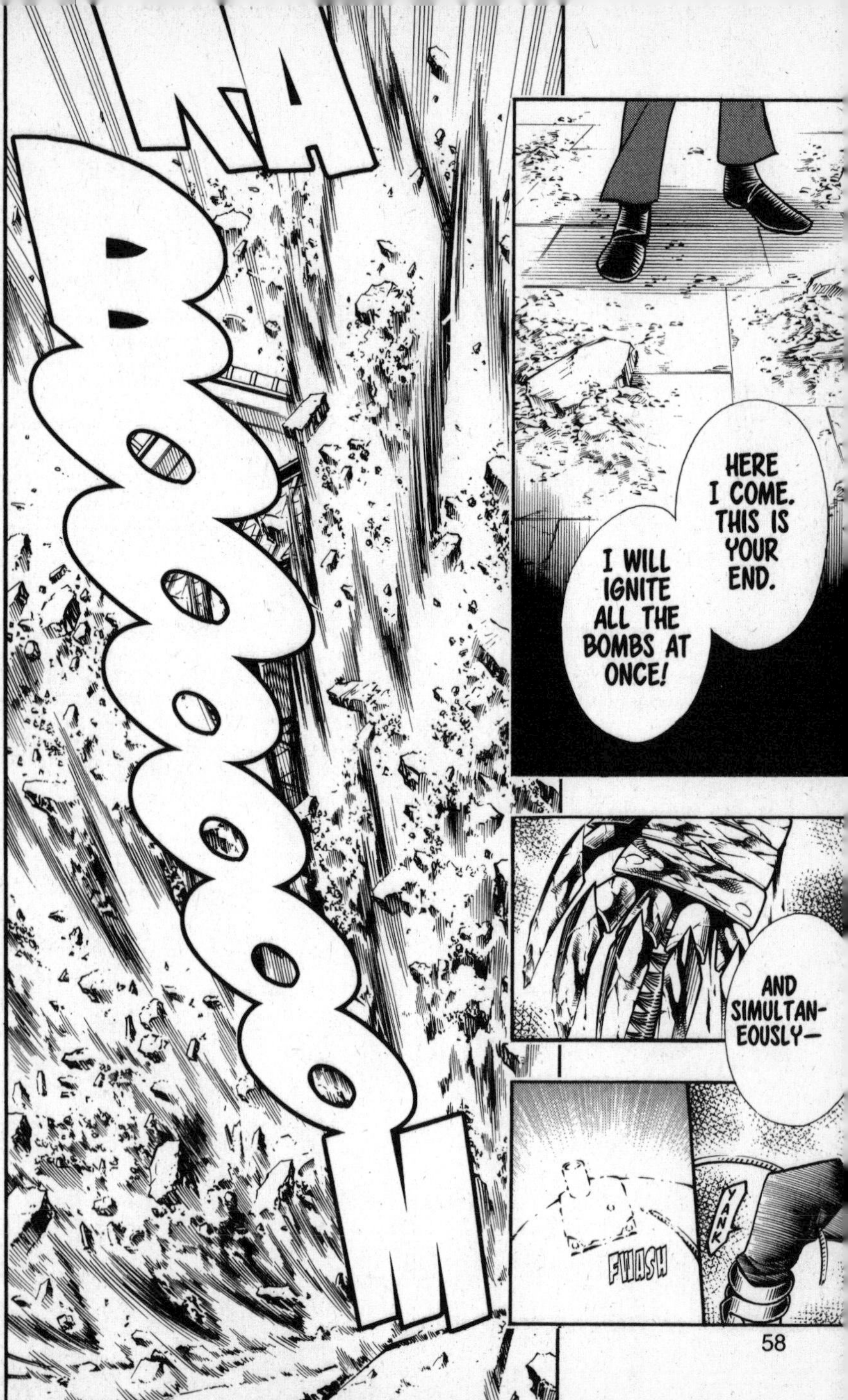
HERE I COME. THIS IS YOUR END.
I WILL IGNITE ALL THE BOMBS AT ONCE!
AND SIMULTANEOUSLY—
YANK
FWASH
KABOOOOOOM

READ THIS WAY

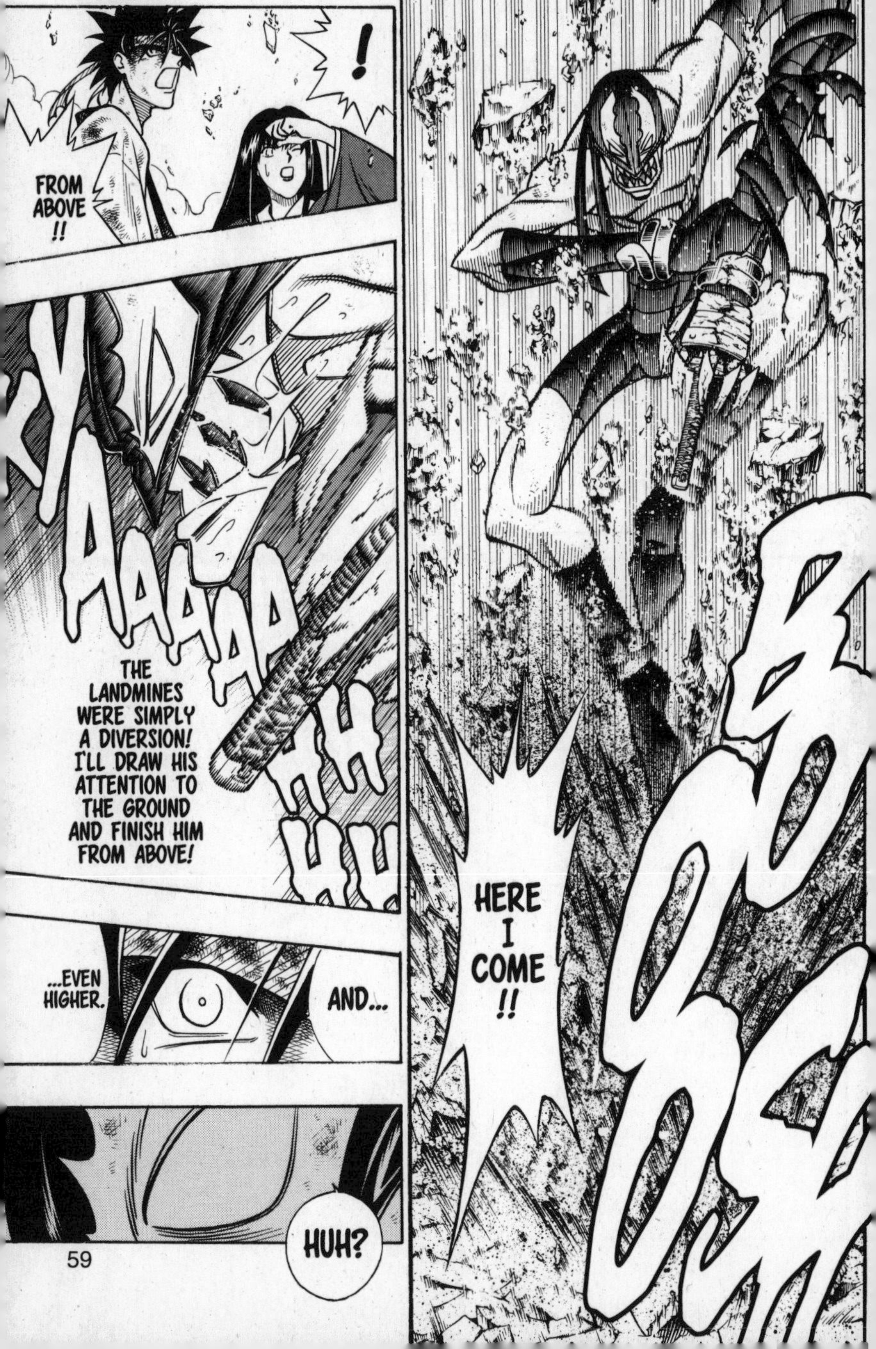
HERE I COME !!
!
FROM ABOVE !!
THE LANDMINES WERE SIMPLY A DIVERSION! I'LL DRAW HIS ATTENTION TO THE GROUND AND FINISH HIM FROM ABOVE!
AND...
...EVEN HIGHER.
HUH?

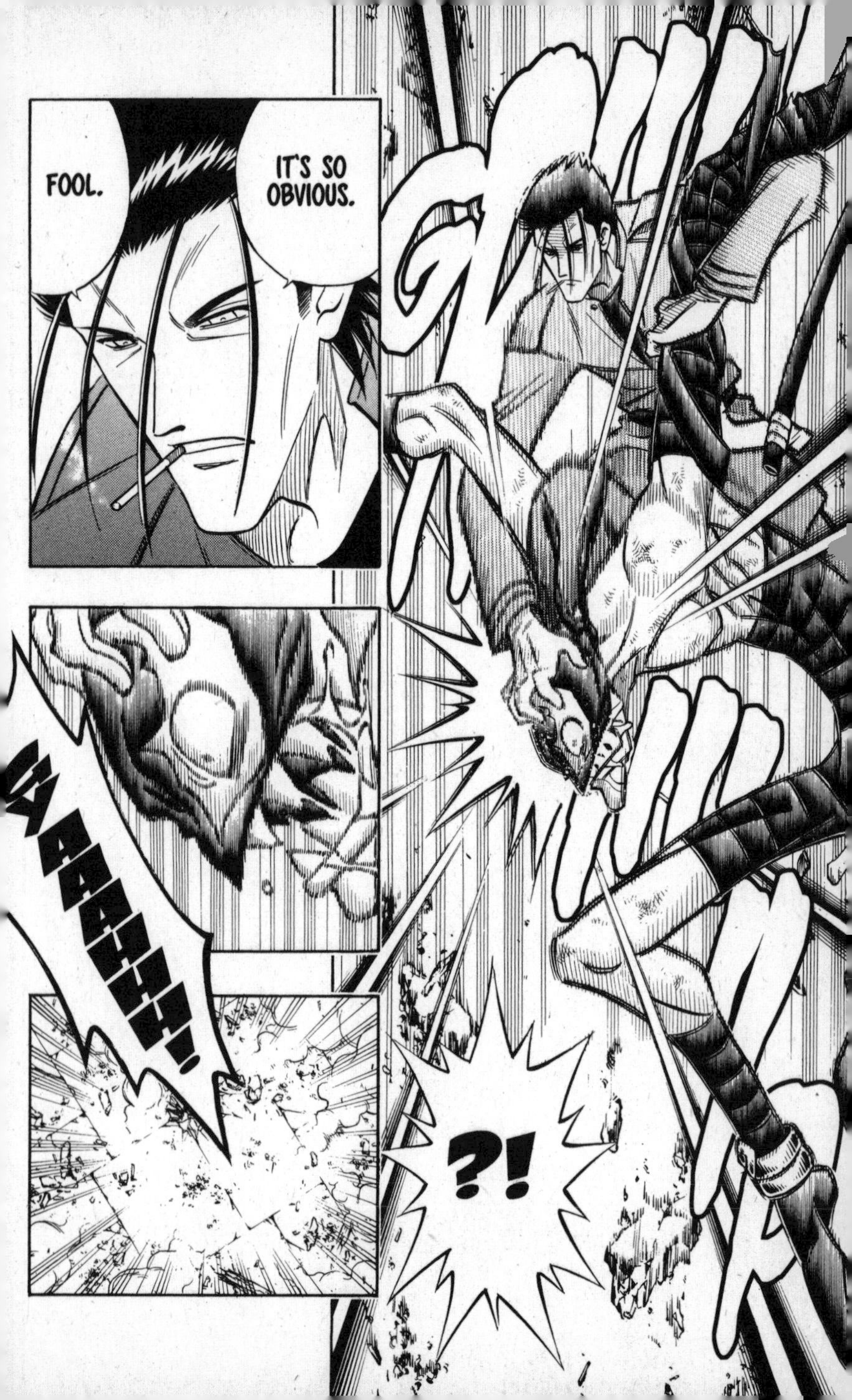
?!
IT'S SO OBVIOUS.
FOOL.
WAAAAHH!

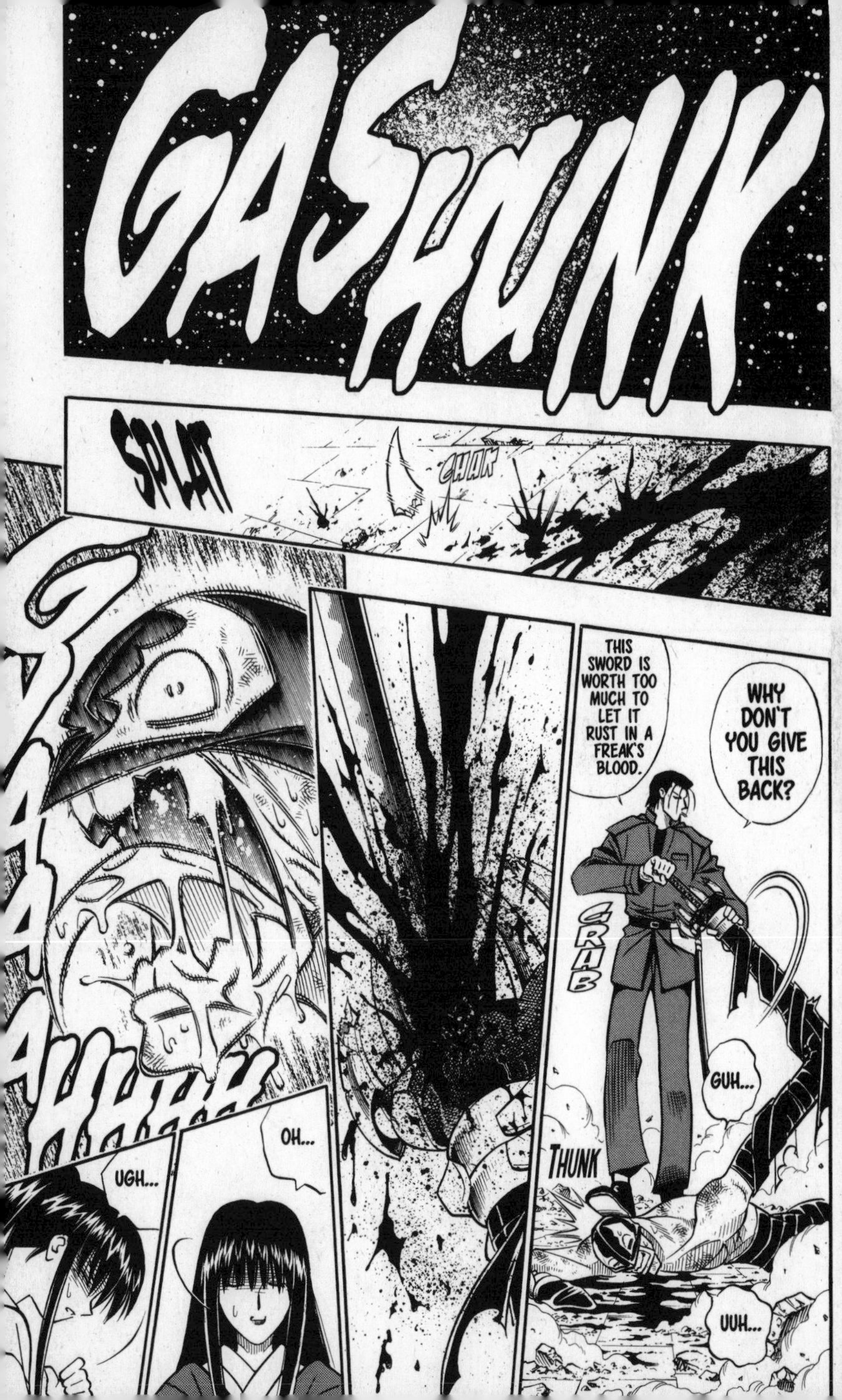
GASHUNK
SPLAT
CHAK
WHY DON'T YOU GIVE THIS BACK?
THIS SWORD IS WORTH TOO MUCH TO LET IT RUST IN A FREAK'S BLOOD.
GRAB
GUH...
THUNK
UUH...
OH...
UGH...

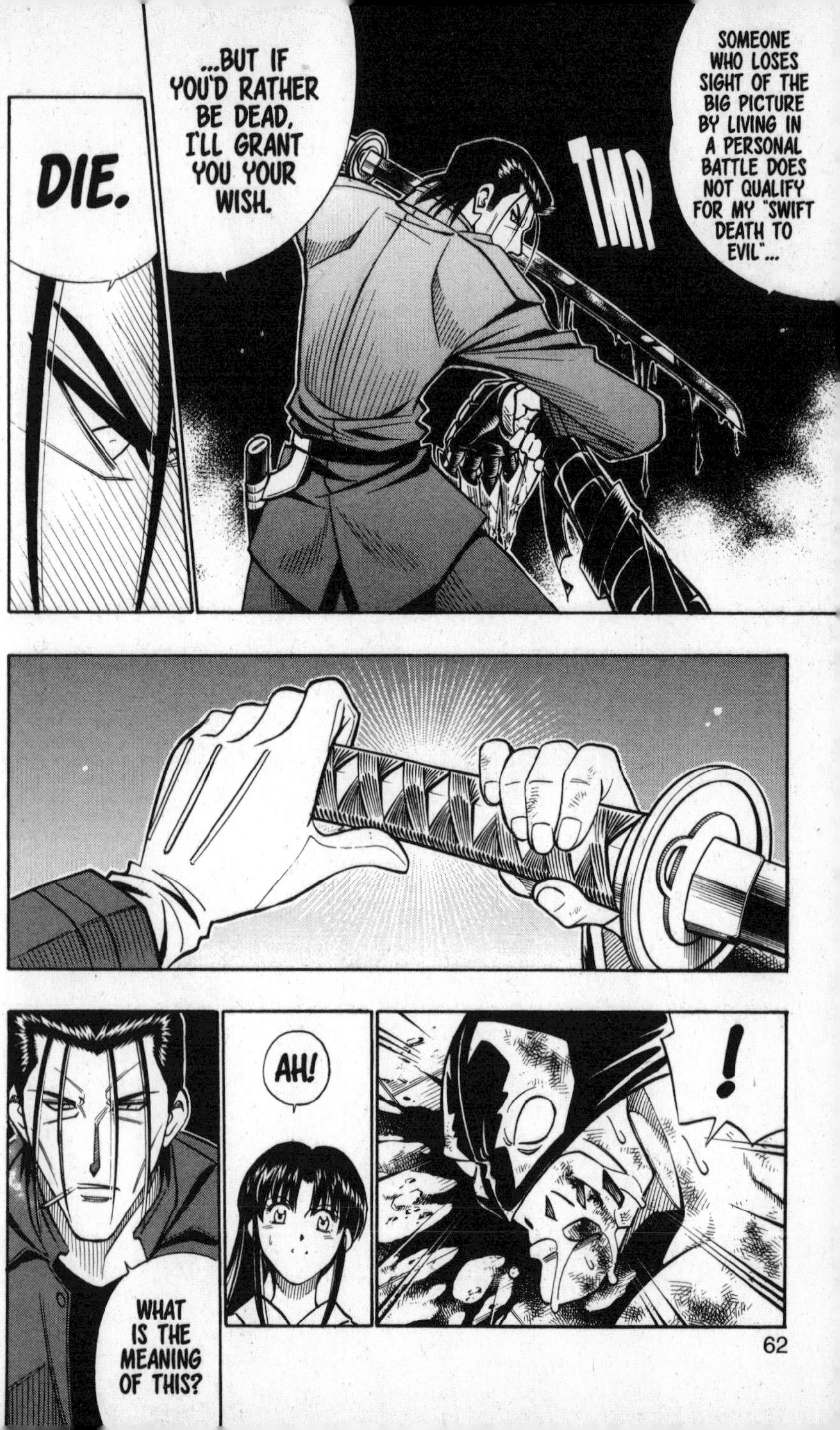
SOMEONE WHO LOSES SIGHT OF THE BIG PICTURE BY LIVING IN A PERSONAL BATTLE DOES NOT QUALIFY FOR MY "SWIFT DEATH TO EVIL"...
TMP
...BUT IF YOU'D RATHER BE DEAD, I'LL GRANT YOU YOUR WISH.
DIE.
!
AH!
WHAT IS THE MEANING OF THIS?

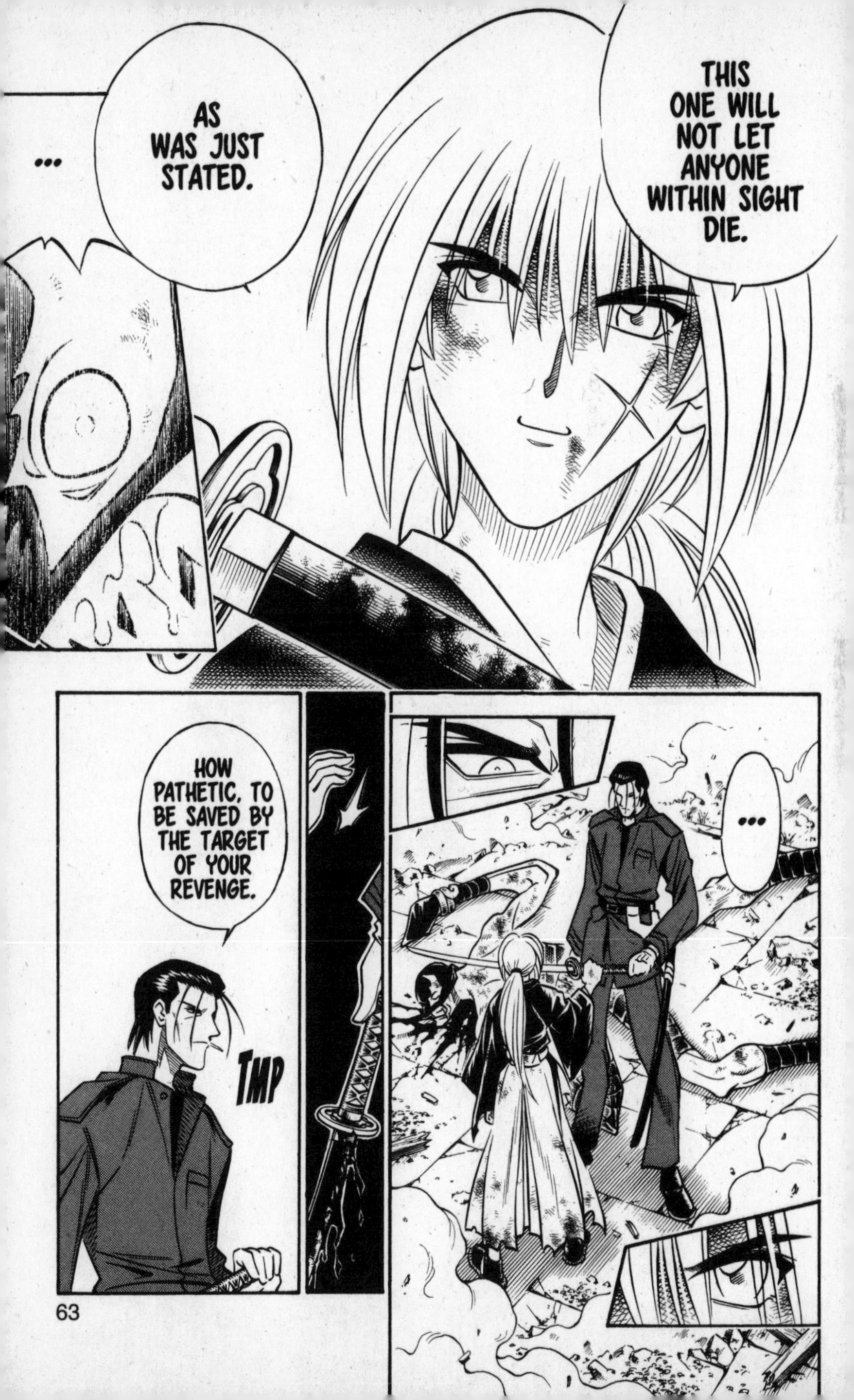
THIS ONE WILL NOT LET ANYONE WITHIN SIGHT DIE.
AS WAS JUST STATED.
...
...
HOW PATHETIC, TO BE SAVED BY THE TARGET OF YOUR REVENGE.
TMP

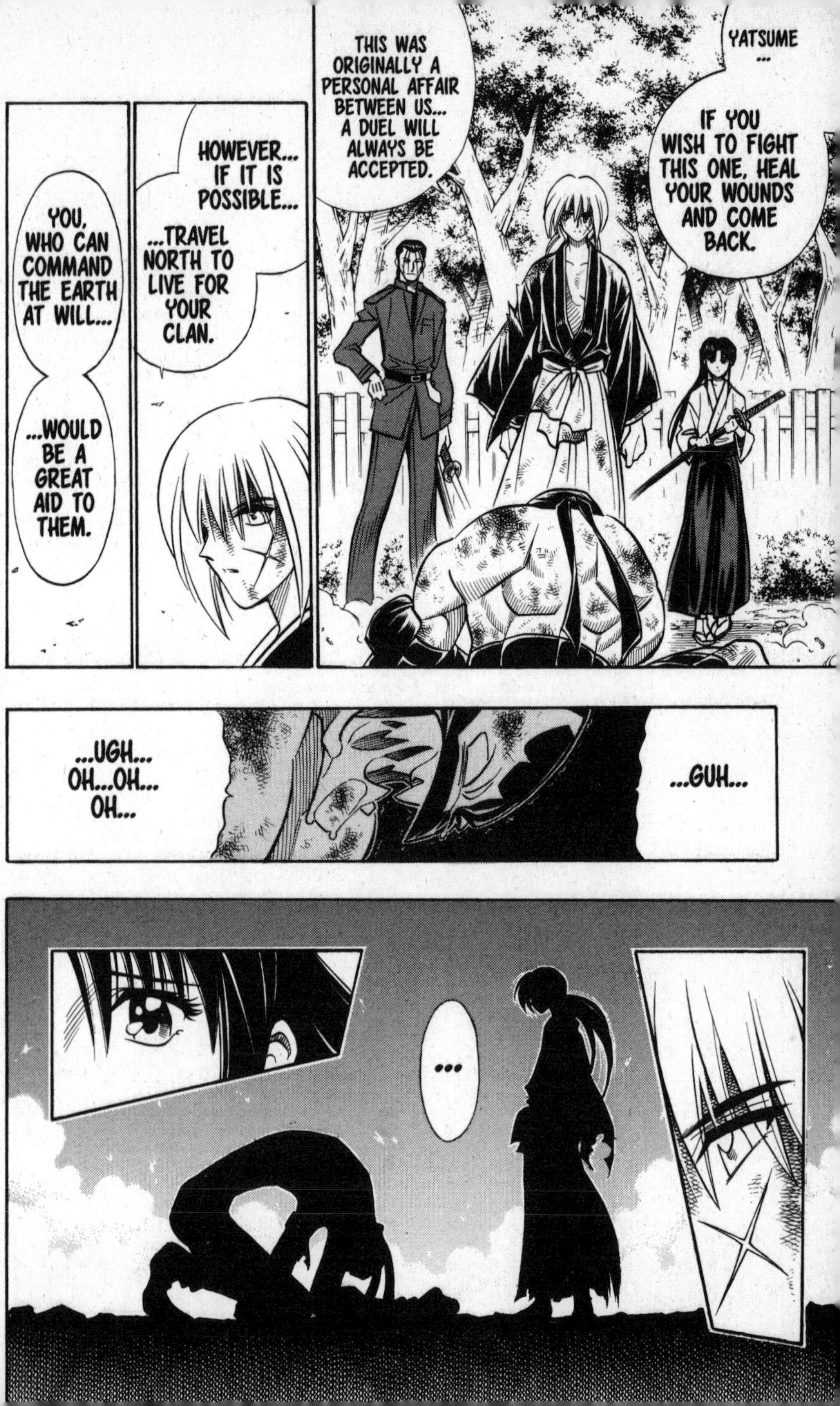
YATSUME ...
IF YOU WISH TO FIGHT THIS ONE, HEAL YOUR WOUNDS AND COME BACK.
THIS WAS ORIGINALLY A PERSONAL AFFAIR BETWEEN US... A DUEL WILL ALWAYS BE ACCEPTED.
HOWEVER... IF IT IS POSSIBLE...
...TRAVEL NORTH TO LIVE FOR YOUR CLAN.
YOU, WHO CAN COMMAND THE EARTH AT WILL...
...WOULD BE A GREAT AID TO THEM.
...GUH...
...UGH... OH...OH... OH...
...

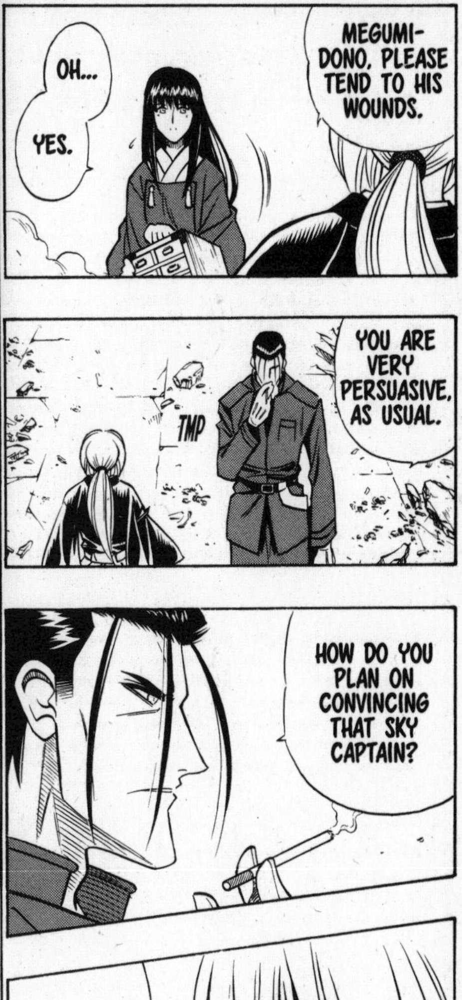
MEGUMI-DONO, PLEASE TEND TO HIS WOUNDS.
OH... YES.
YOU ARE VERY PERSUASIVE, AS USUAL.
TMP
HOW DO YOU PLAN ON CONVINCING THAT SKY CAPTAIN?
...

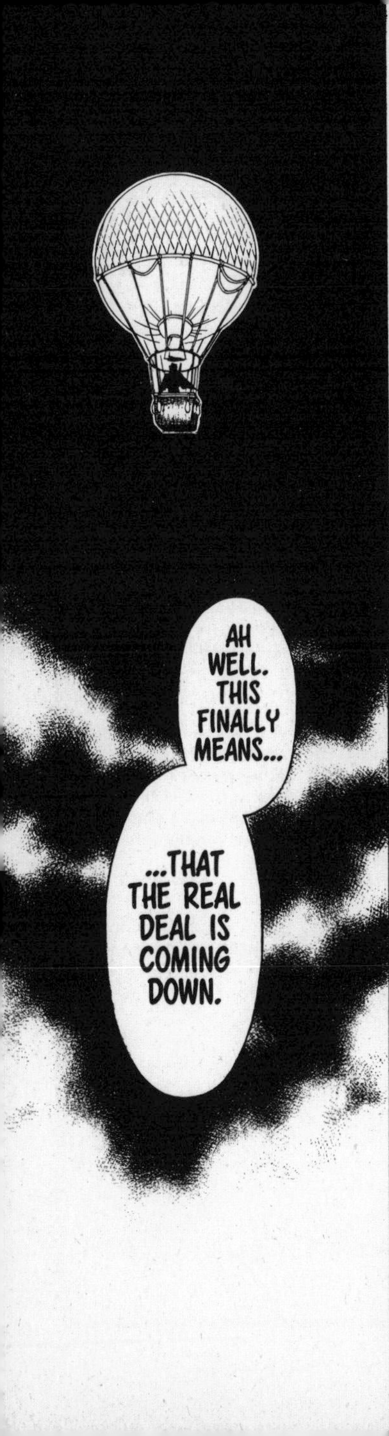
AH WELL. THIS FINALLY MEANS...
...THAT THE REAL DEAL IS COMING DOWN.

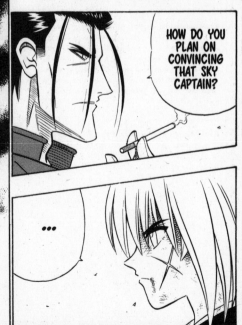

The Secret Life of Characters (46)
—Yatsume Mumyōi—

The model is quite old. It is *kumo otoko*, but not the American version. So, he has similar roots as Han'nya. I meant this to be a second attempt at the "freaks" theme, which did not go so well with Han'nya. Looking at the result, I honestly think I was utterly defeated. The biggest reason for the defeat is Saitō Hajime. Usui was the same way, but in front of this man, any character turns into a weakling... In that sense, Saitō is a death gate for characters. Mumyōi's body shaping is one of the ideas that I personally like, but it seems a little unfitting for a shonen manga. Either way, a topic like deformation of the body is a very sensitive issue, and I had to be very careful with how I dealt with it—but this may have detracted from the attention I needed to pay to the story as a whole. (Of course, Watsuki's lack of competence is a huge factor...) I have changed my thoughts a bit these days to "there should be more positive themes that ought to be in a shonen manga, rather than a negative theme like 'freaks.' I want to be dealing with more positive themes in the future." So there will be no more attempts at the "freaks" theme. But I will continue to challenge freaks in terms of design, since I do still like them.

The model in terms of design, as you can see, is all jumbled up. In the silhouette stage, the image was the bandana mask version of Wolverine from *X-Men* + Carnage from *Spider-man*. I was told by various people to do *Spider-man*, or to do Spawn and such, so I became agitated and said, "I'll throw in Venom also!" digging my own grave and self-destructing. I added the gold-mining clan bit after the fact, but he still ended up as a character that stands out from the time period.

I'm stupid. I'm a fool. I am a failure as a manga artist. I want to go up into the mountain and train myself from step one. Actually, once my work comes to a closure, I will seriously go train myself. I'll be hit by the waterfall and have an epiphany. (Seriously.)

Act 200
The Destined Duel

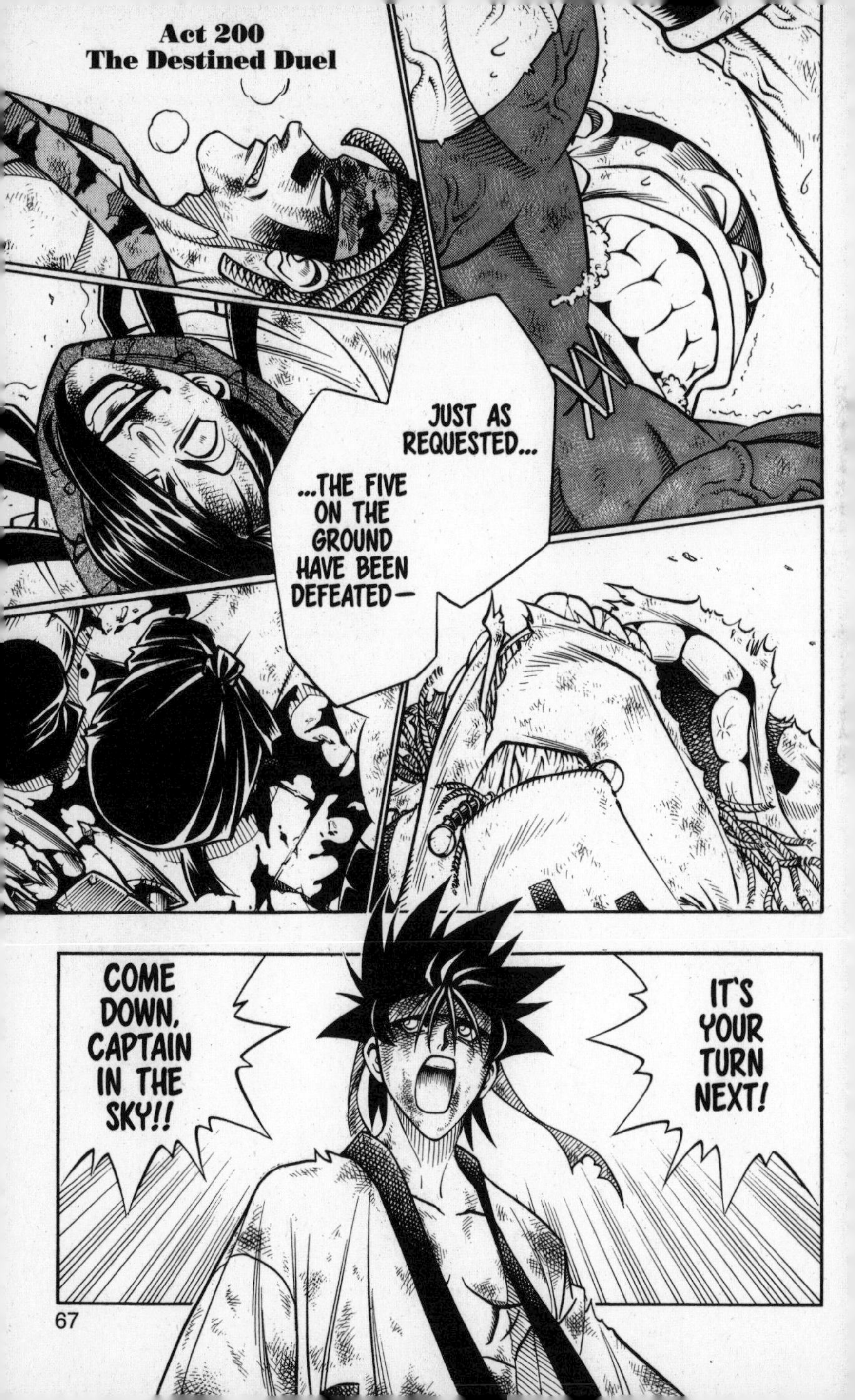
JUST AS REQUESTED...
...THE FIVE ON THE GROUND HAVE BEEN DEFEATED—
IT'S YOUR TURN NEXT!
COME DOWN, CAPTAIN IN THE SKY!!

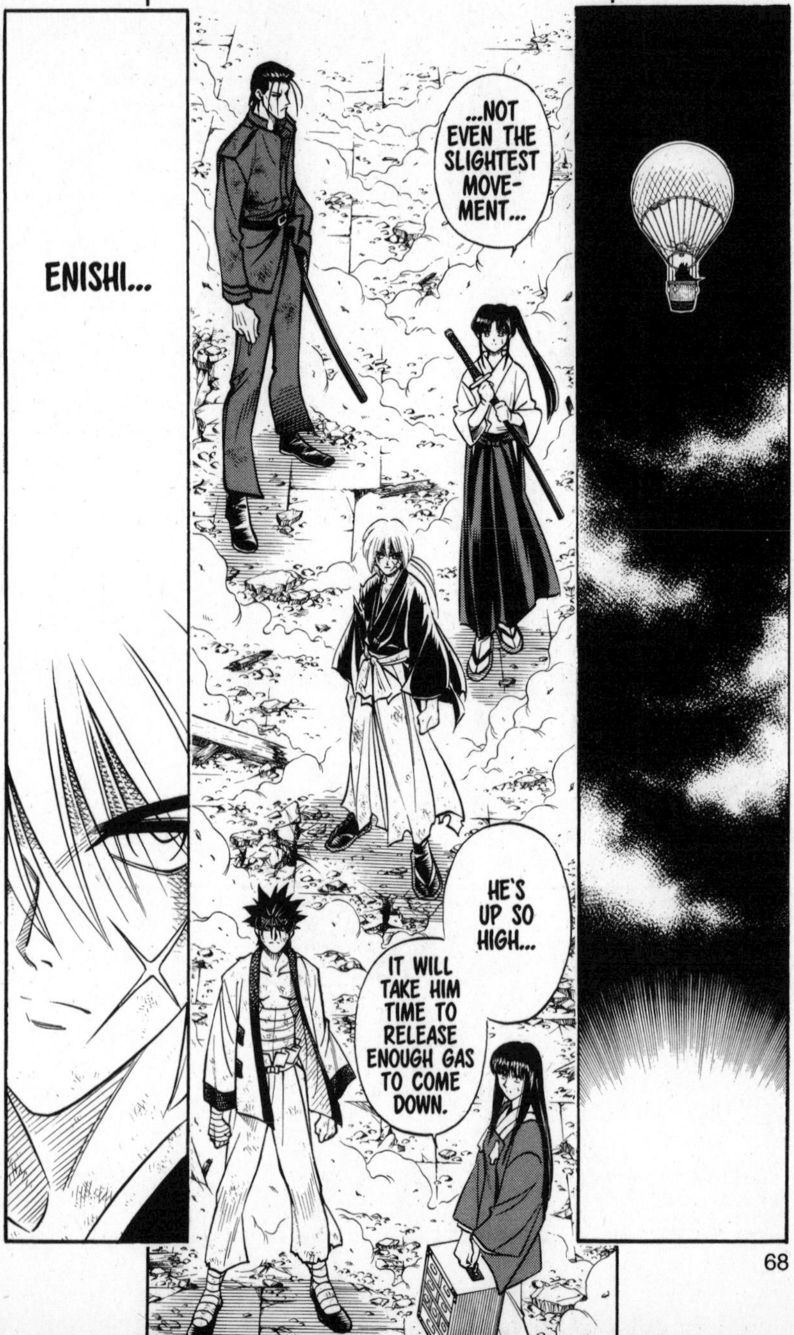
...NOT EVEN THE SLIGHTEST MOVE- MENT...
HE'S UP SO HIGH...
IT WILL TAKE HIM TIME TO RELEASE ENOUGH GAS TO COME DOWN.
ENISHI...

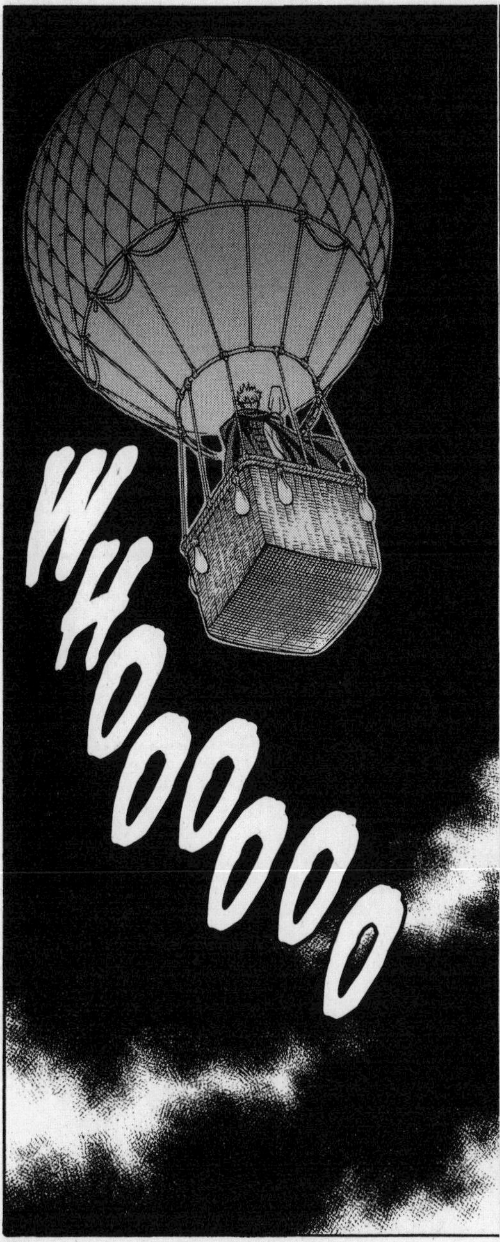
WHOOOOOO

Act 200

The Destined Duel

伸宏
和月

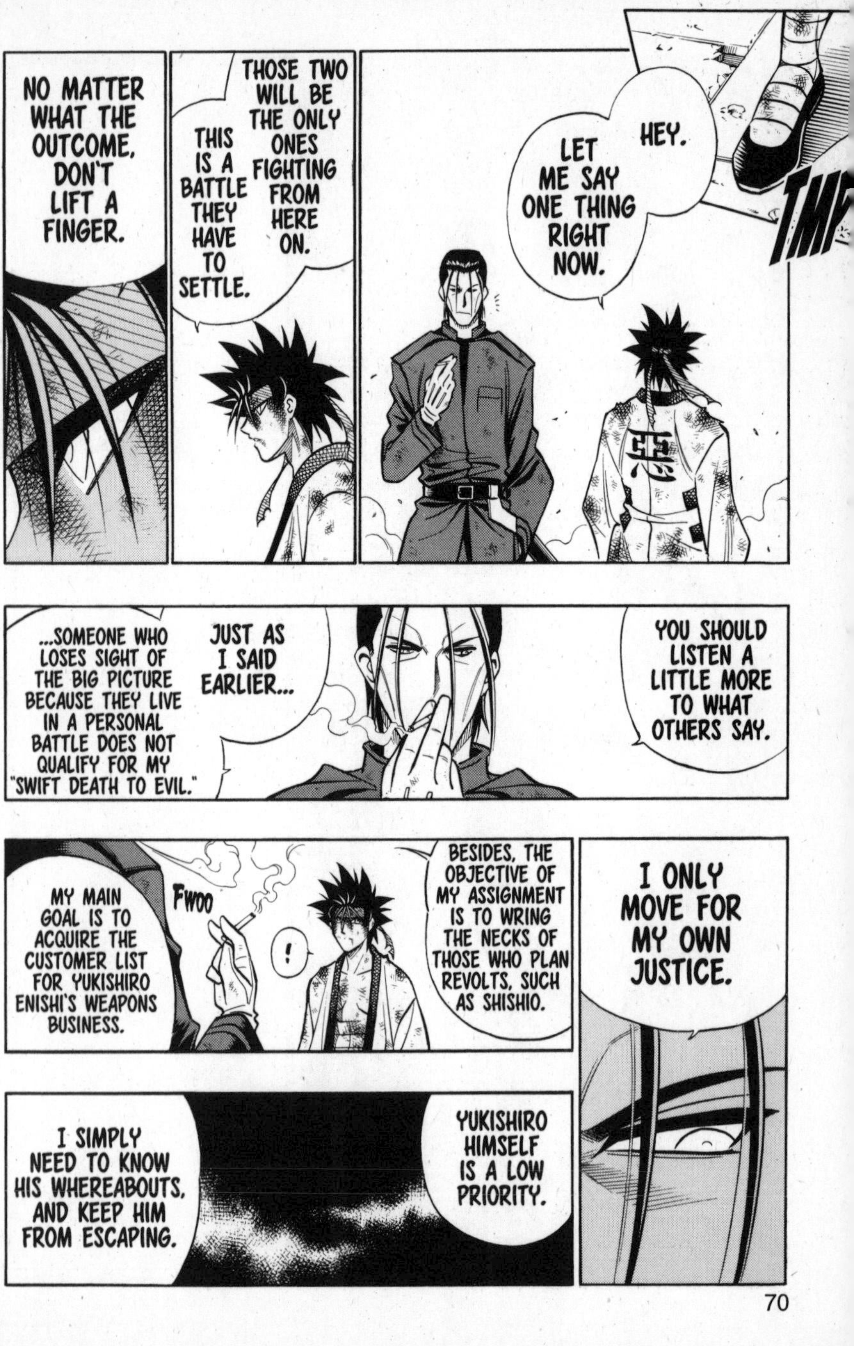
HEY.
LET ME SAY ONE THING RIGHT NOW.
THOSE TWO WILL BE THE ONLY ONES FIGHTING FROM HERE ON.
THIS IS A BATTLE THEY HAVE TO SETTLE.
NO MATTER WHAT THE OUTCOME, DON'T LIFT A FINGER.
YOU SHOULD LISTEN A LITTLE MORE TO WHAT OTHERS SAY.
JUST AS I SAID EARLIER...
...SOMEONE WHO LOSES SIGHT OF THE BIG PICTURE BECAUSE THEY LIVE IN A PERSONAL BATTLE DOES NOT QUALIFY FOR MY "SWIFT DEATH TO EVIL."
I ONLY MOVE FOR MY OWN JUSTICE.
BESIDES, THE OBJECTIVE OF MY ASSIGNMENT IS TO WRING THE NECKS OF THOSE WHO PLAN REVOLTS, SUCH AS SHISHIO.
!
Fwoo
MY MAIN GOAL IS TO ACQUIRE THE CUSTOMER LIST FOR YUKISHIRO ENISHI'S WEAPONS BUSINESS.
YUKISHIRO HIMSELF IS A LOW PRIORITY.
I SIMPLY NEED TO KNOW HIS WHEREABOUTS, AND KEEP HIM FROM ESCAPING.

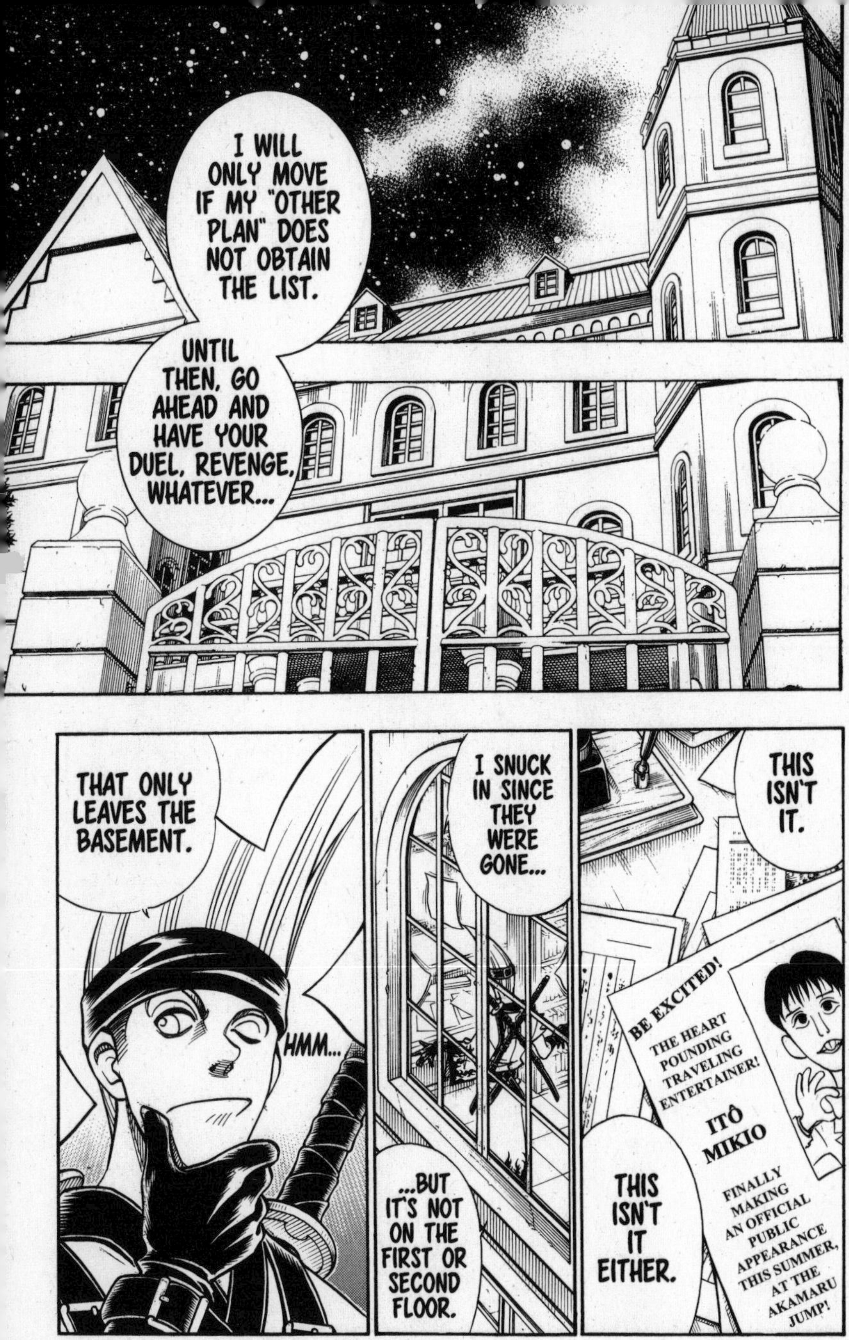

I WILL ONLY MOVE IF MY "OTHER PLAN" DOES NOT OBTAIN THE LIST.
UNTIL THEN, GO AHEAD AND HAVE YOUR DUEL, REVENGE, WHATEVER...
THIS ISN'T IT.
BE EXCITED!
THE HEART POUNDING TRAVELING ENTERTAINER!
ITÔ MIKIO
FINALLY MAKING AN OFFICIAL PUBLIC APPEARANCE THIS SUMMER, AT THE AKAMARU JUMP!
THIS ISN'T IT EITHER.
I SNUCK IN SINCE THEY WERE GONE...
...BUT IT'S NOT ON THE FIRST OR SECOND FLOOR.
THAT ONLY LEAVES THE BASEMENT.
HMM...

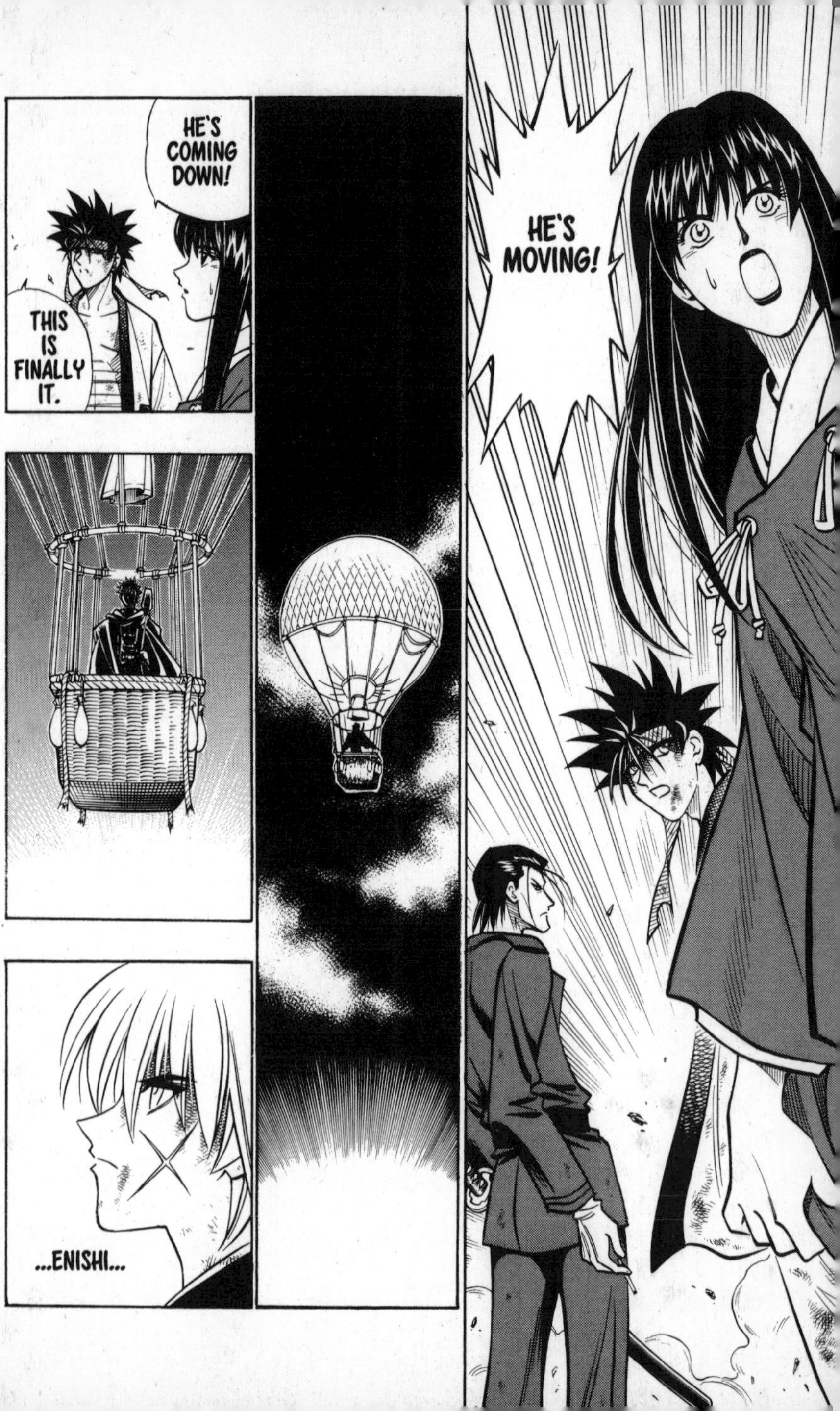
HE'S MOVING!
HE'S COMING DOWN!
THIS IS FINALLY IT.
...ENISHI...

READ THIS WAY

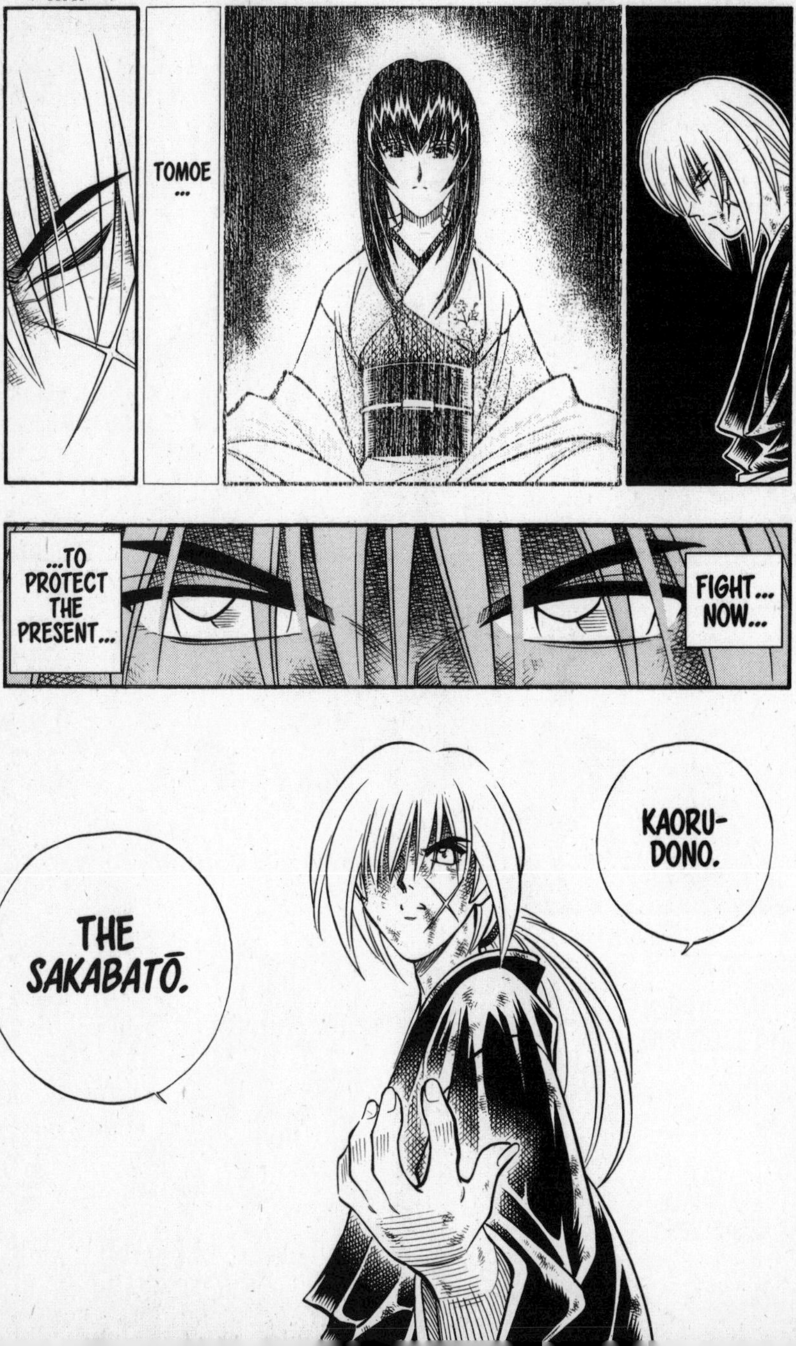
TOMOE ...
FIGHT... NOW...
...TO PROTECT THE PRESENT...
KAORU-DONO.
THE SAKABATŌ.

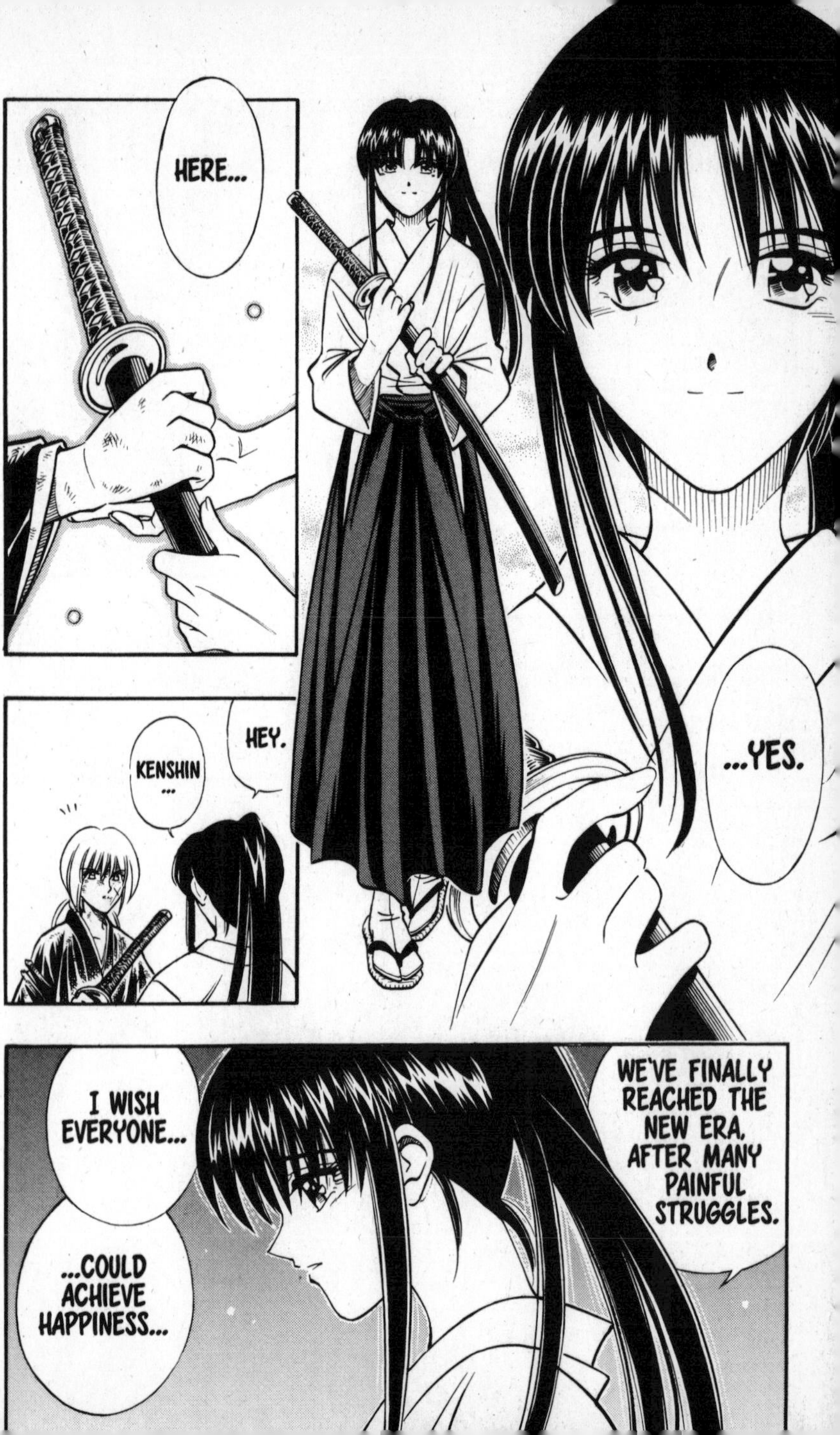
...YES.
HERE...
HEY.
KENSHIN ...
WE'VE FINALLY REACHED THE NEW ERA, AFTER MANY PAINFUL STRUGGLES.
I WISH EVERYONE...
...COULD ACHIEVE HAPPINESS...

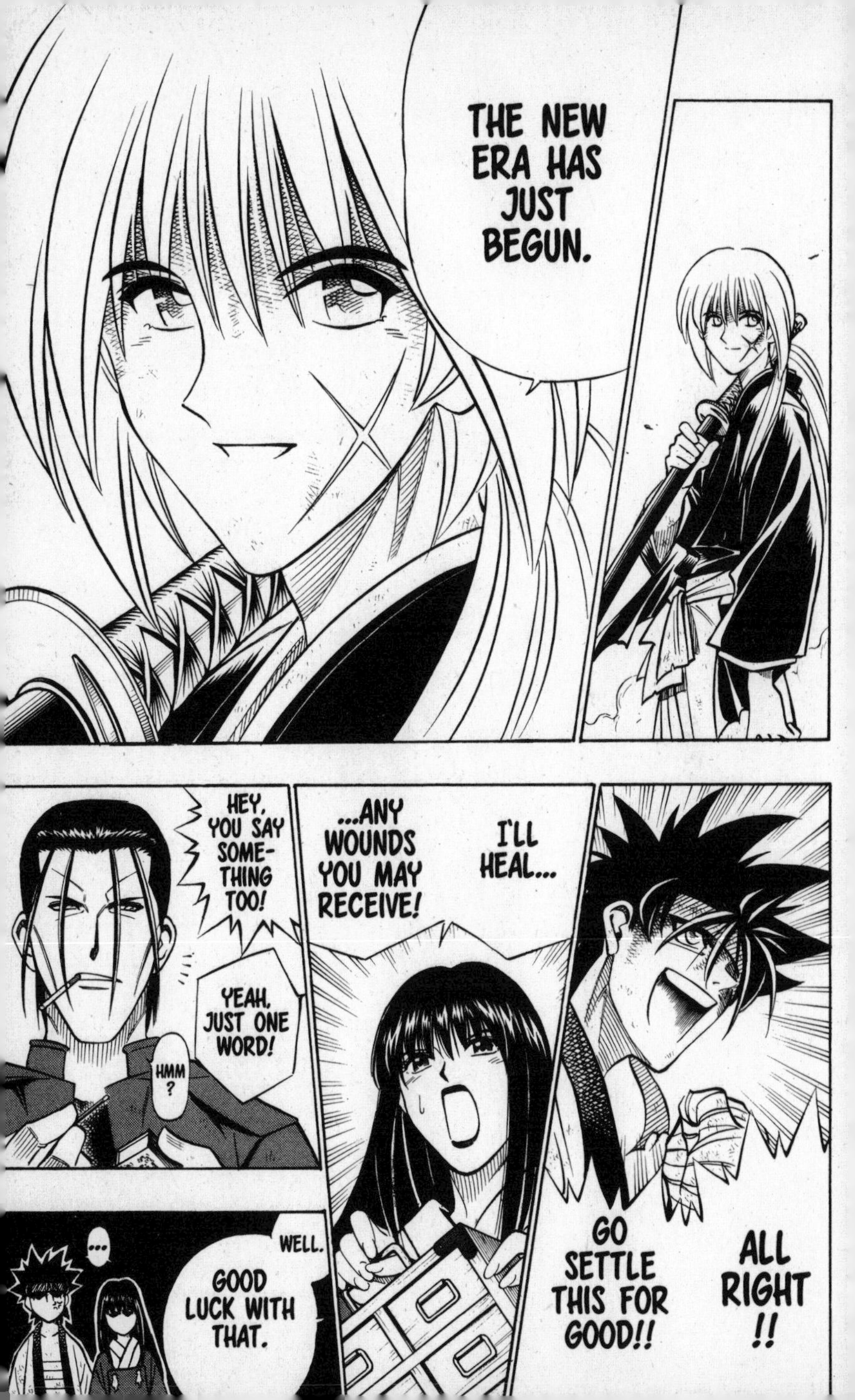
THE NEW ERA HAS JUST BEGUN.
ALL RIGHT!!
GO SETTLE THIS FOR GOOD!!
I'LL HEAL...
...ANY WOUNDS YOU MAY RECEIVE!
HEY, YOU SAY SOME-THING TOO!
YEAH, JUST ONE WORD!
HMM?
WELL.
...
GOOD LUCK WITH THAT.

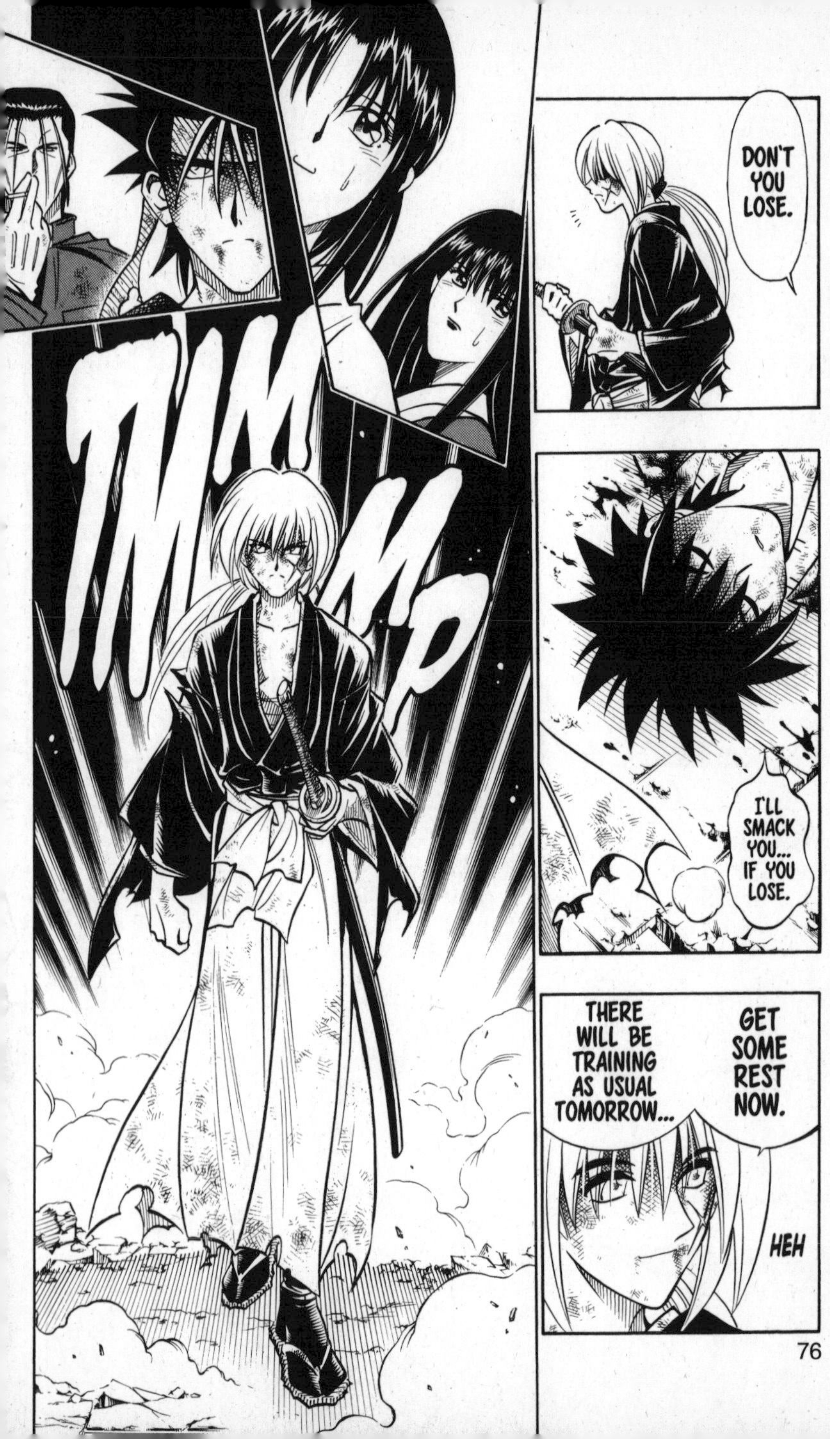
DON'T YOU LOSE.
I'LL SMACK YOU... IF YOU LOSE.
GET SOME REST NOW.
THERE WILL BE TRAINING AS USUAL TOMORROW...
HEH

READ THIS WAY

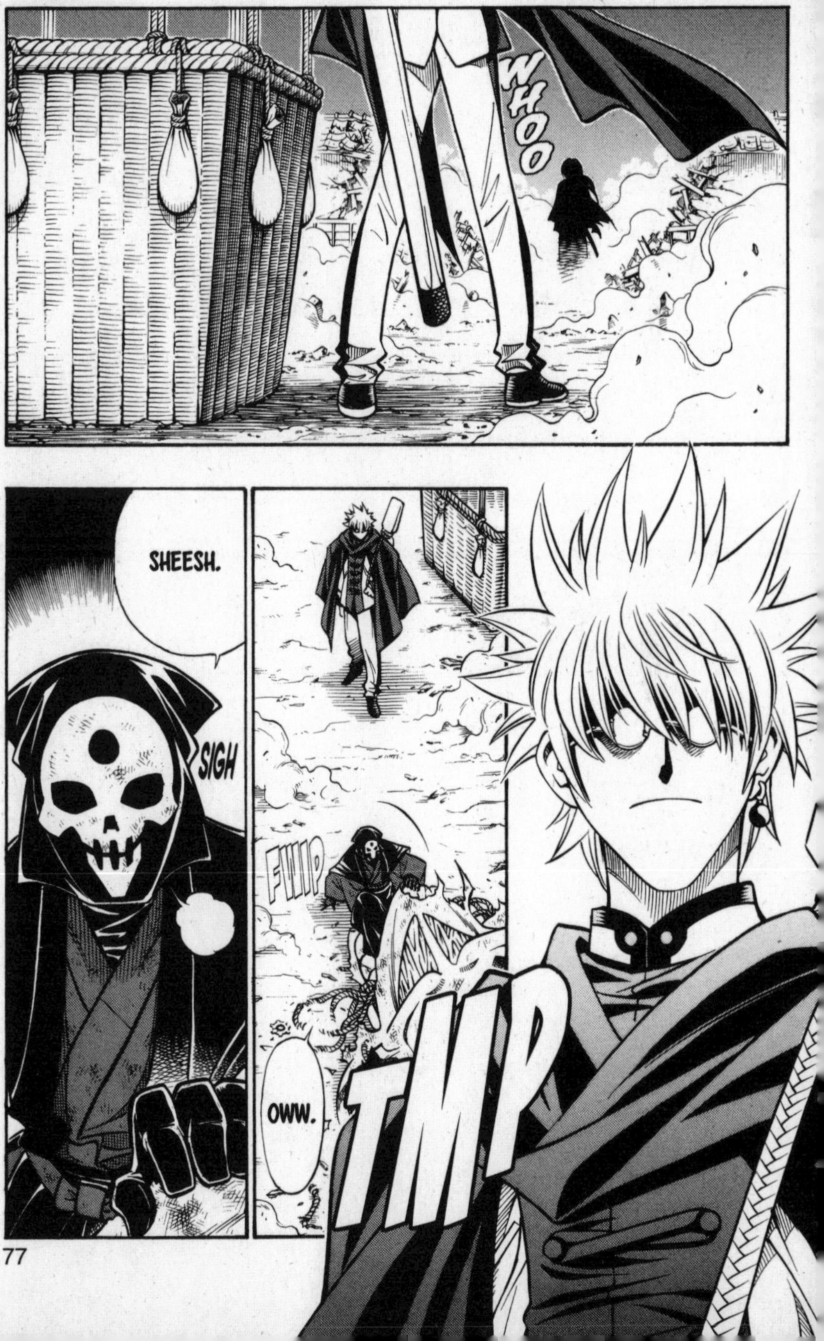
WHOO
TMP
FWIP
OWW.
SHEESH.
SIGH

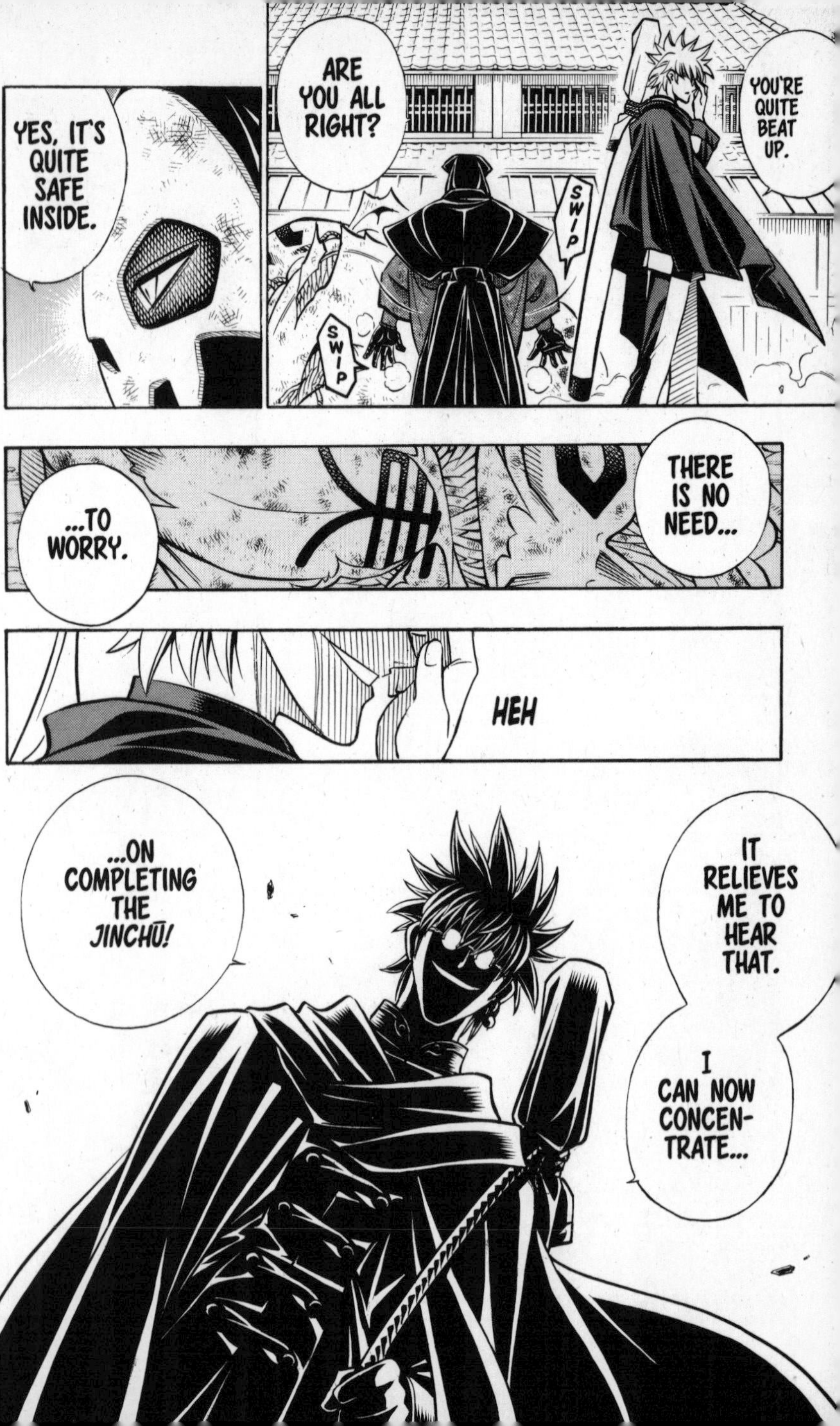
YOU'RE QUITE BEAT UP.
SWIP
ARE YOU ALL RIGHT?
SWIP
YES, IT'S QUITE SAFE INSIDE.
THERE IS NO NEED...
...TO WORRY.
HEH
IT RELIEVES ME TO HEAR THAT.
I CAN NOW CONCENTRATE...
...ON COMPLETING THE JINCHŪ!

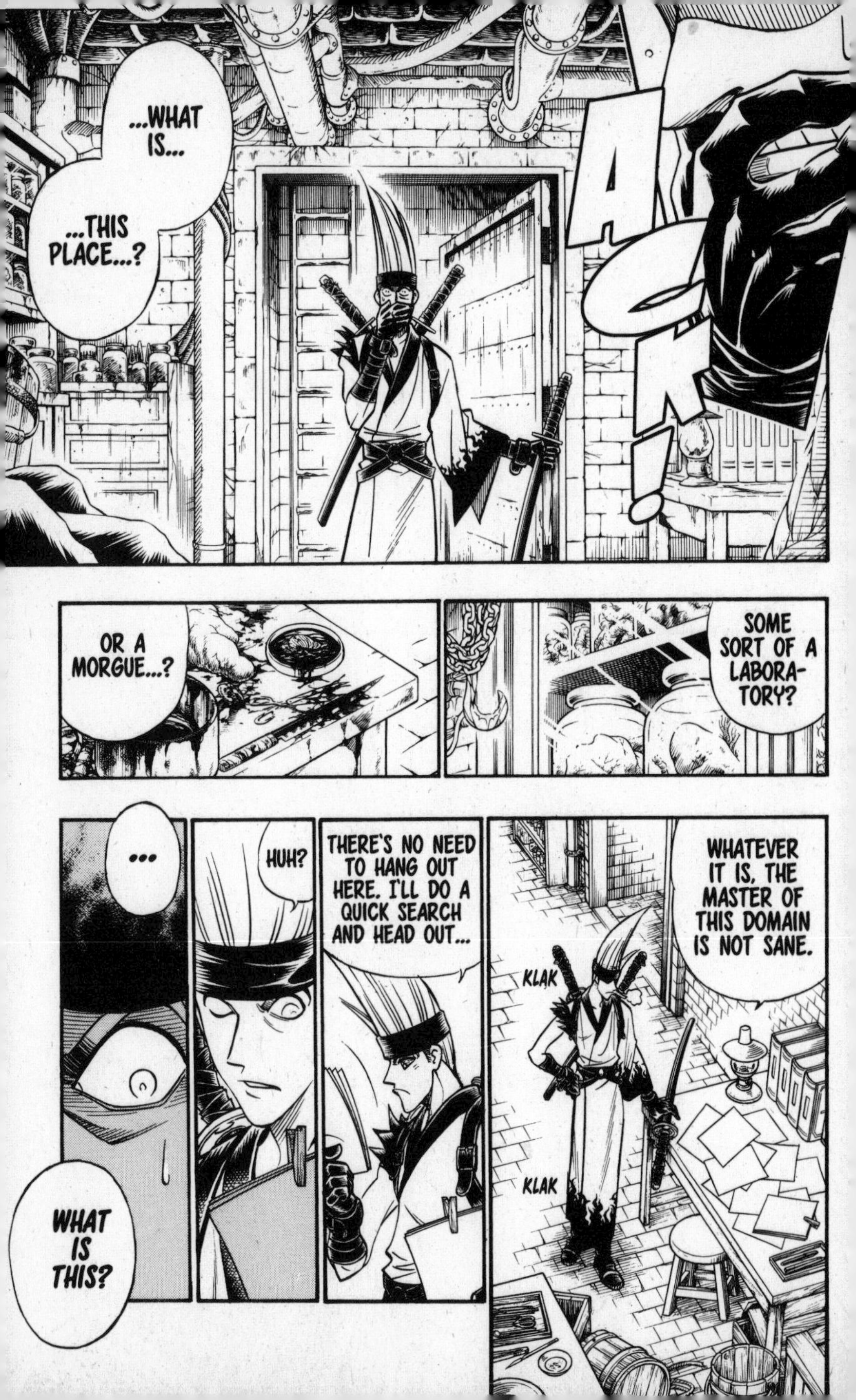
...WHAT IS...
...THIS PLACE...?
SOME SORT OF A LABORA-TORY?
OR A MORGUE...?
WHATEVER IT IS, THE MASTER OF THIS DOMAIN IS NOT SANE.
KLAK
KLAK
THERE'S NO NEED TO HANG OUT HERE. I'LL DO A QUICK SEARCH AND HEAD OUT...
HUH?
...
WHAT IS THIS?

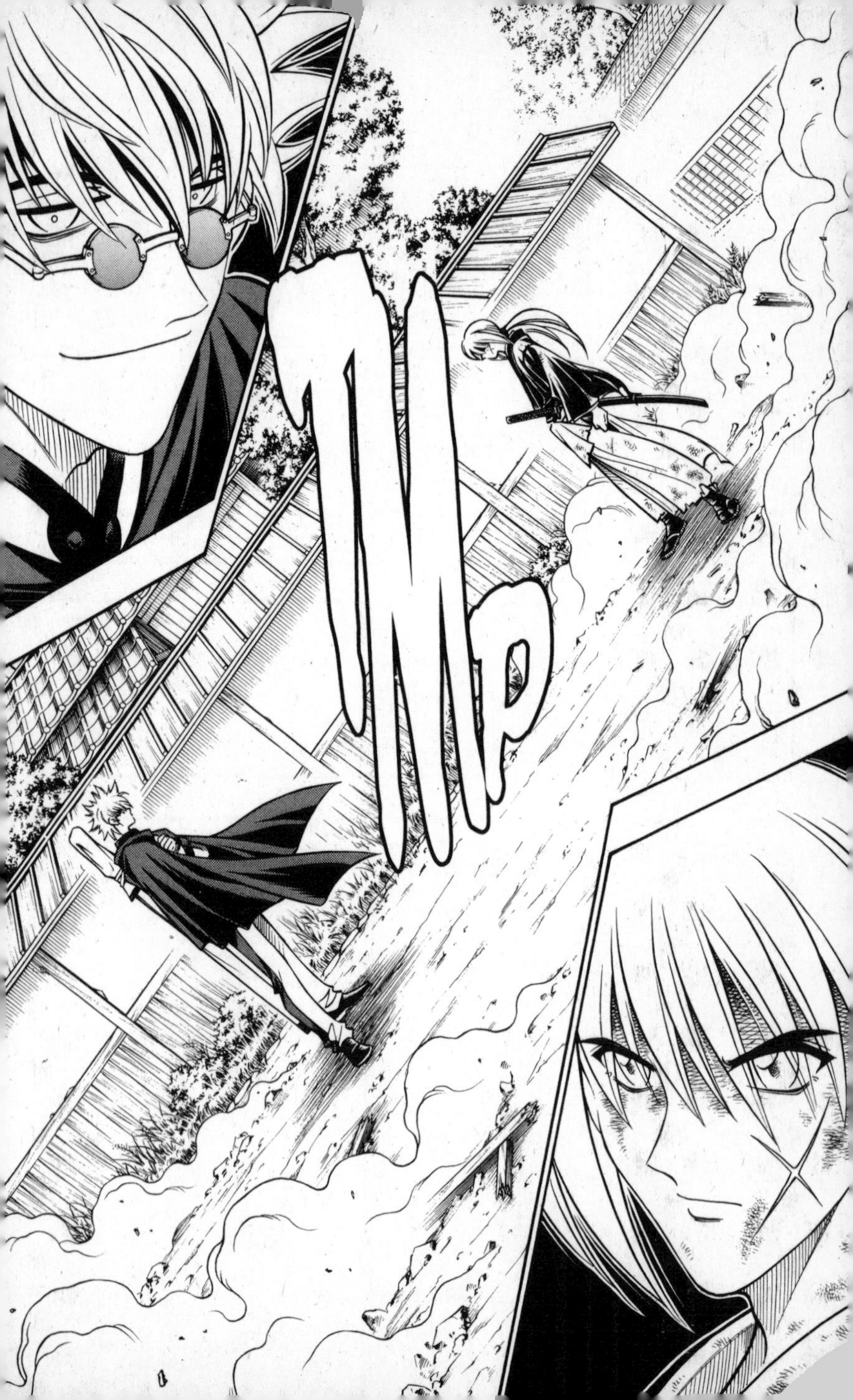
TMP

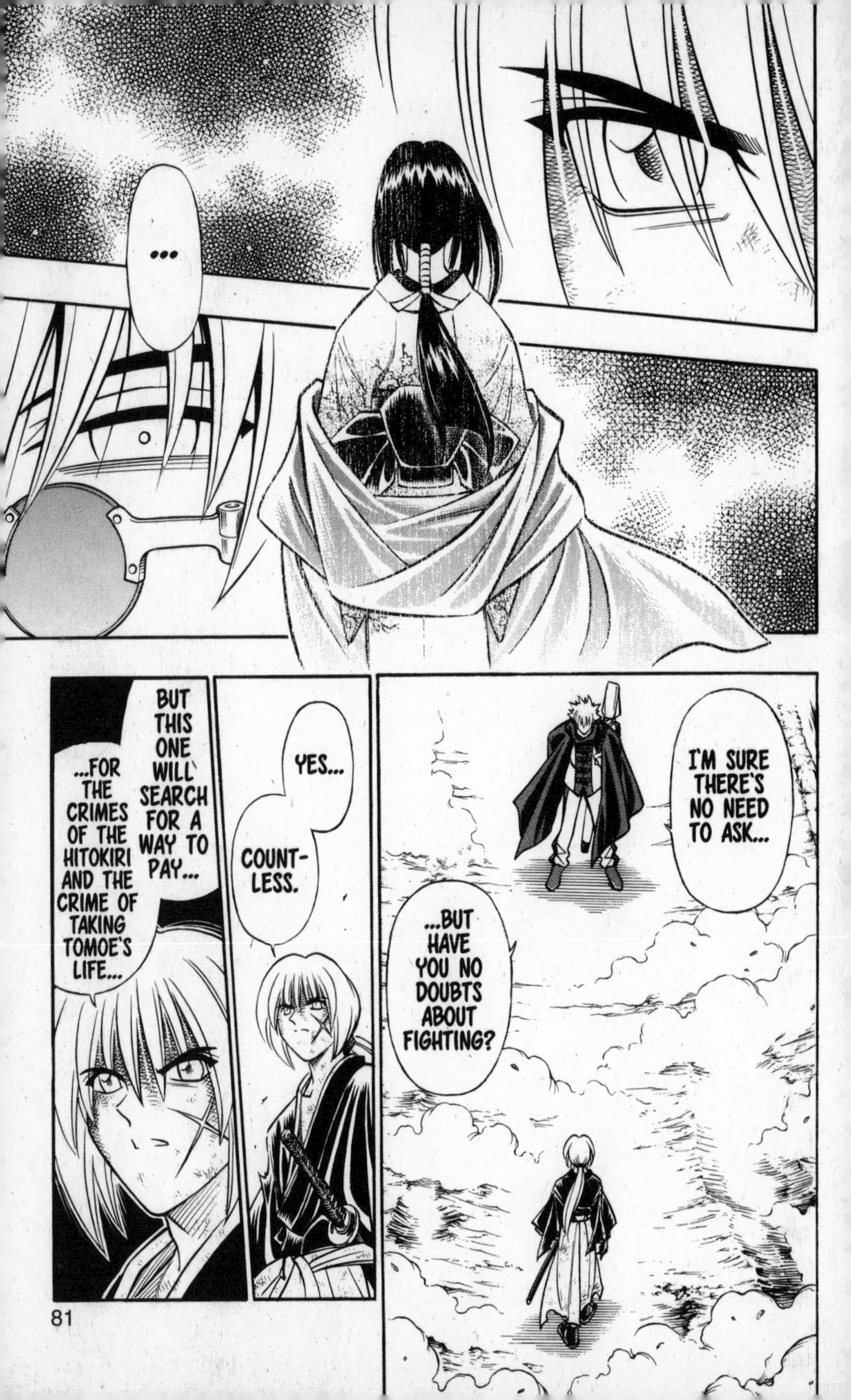
...
I'M SURE THERE'S NO NEED TO ASK...
...BUT HAVE YOU NO DOUBTS ABOUT FIGHTING?
YES...
COUNT-LESS.
BUT THIS ONE WILL SEARCH FOR A WAY TO PAY...
...FOR THE CRIMES OF THE HITOKIRI AND THE CRIME OF TAKING TOMOE'S LIFE...

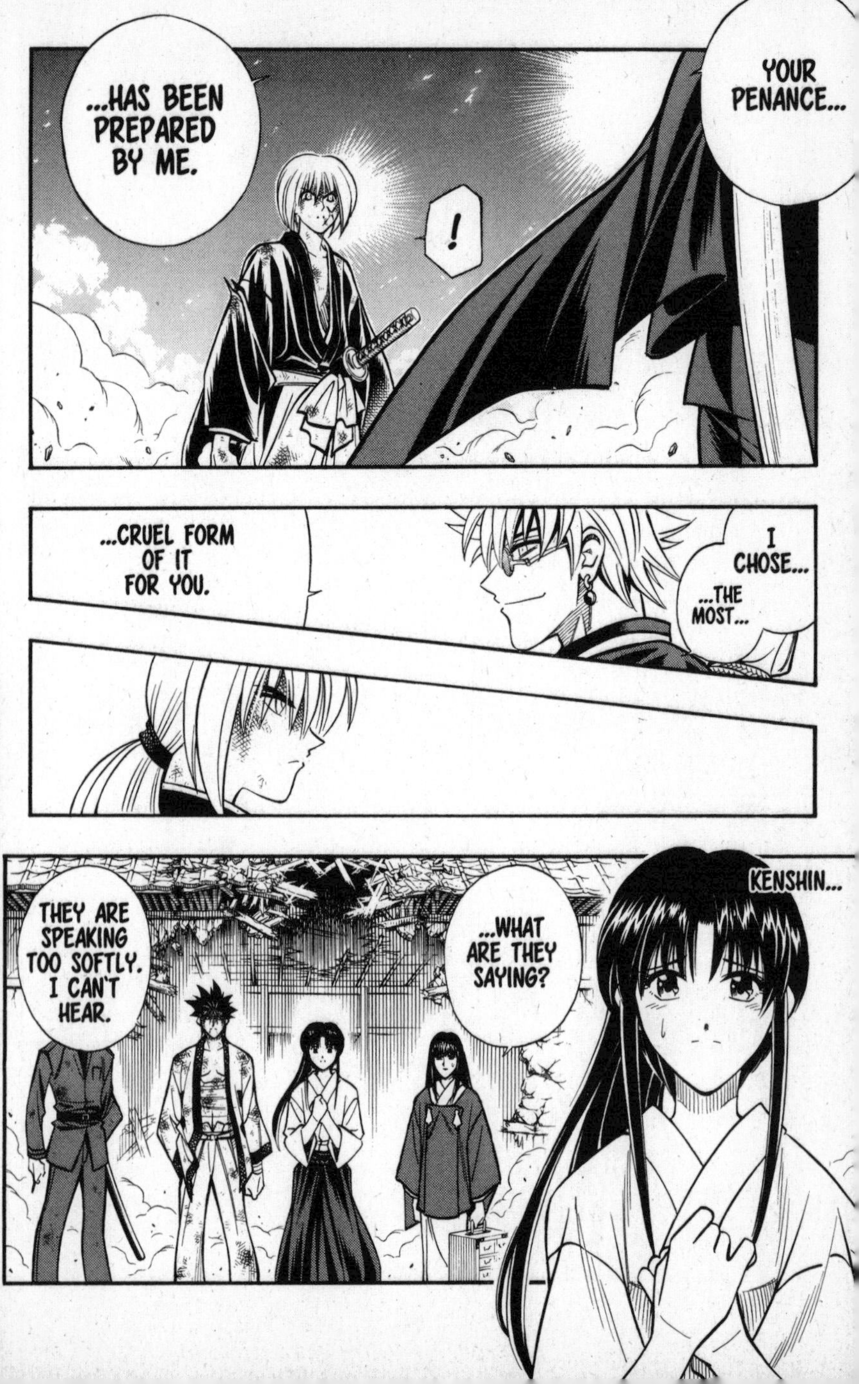
YOUR PENANCE...
!
...HAS BEEN PREPARED BY ME.
I CHOSE...
...THE MOST...
...CRUEL FORM OF IT FOR YOU.
KENSHIN...
...WHAT ARE THEY SAYING?
THEY ARE SPEAKING TOO SOFTLY. I CAN'T HEAR.

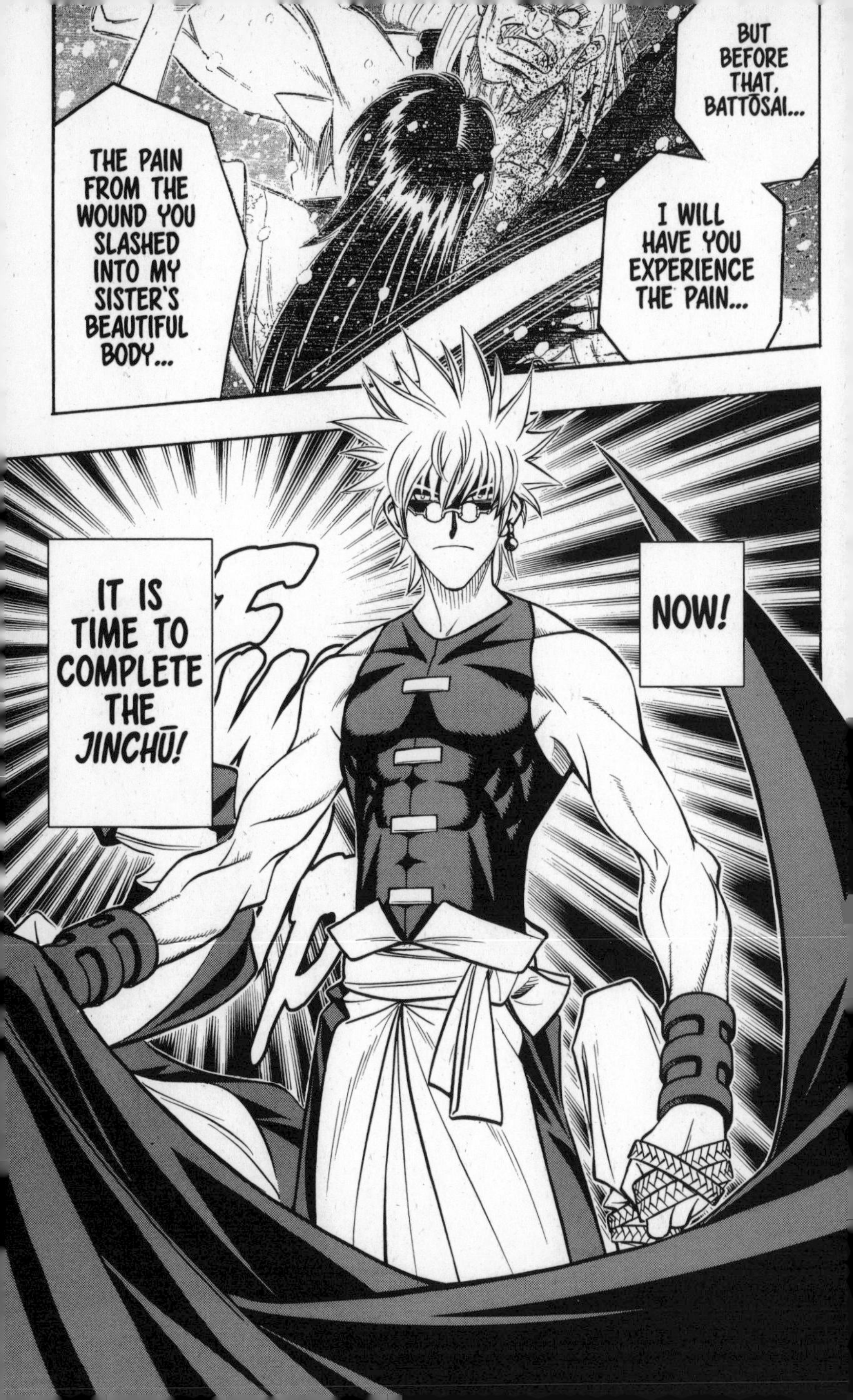
BUT BEFORE THAT, BATTŌSAI...
I WILL HAVE YOU EXPERIENCE THE PAIN...
THE PAIN FROM THE WOUND YOU SLASHED INTO MY SISTER'S BEAUTIFUL BODY...
NOW!
IT IS TIME TO COMPLETE THE *JINCHŪ*!

Rurouni Kenshin

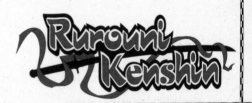

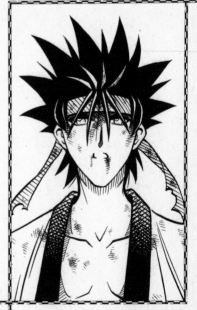

Act 201—Another Strength

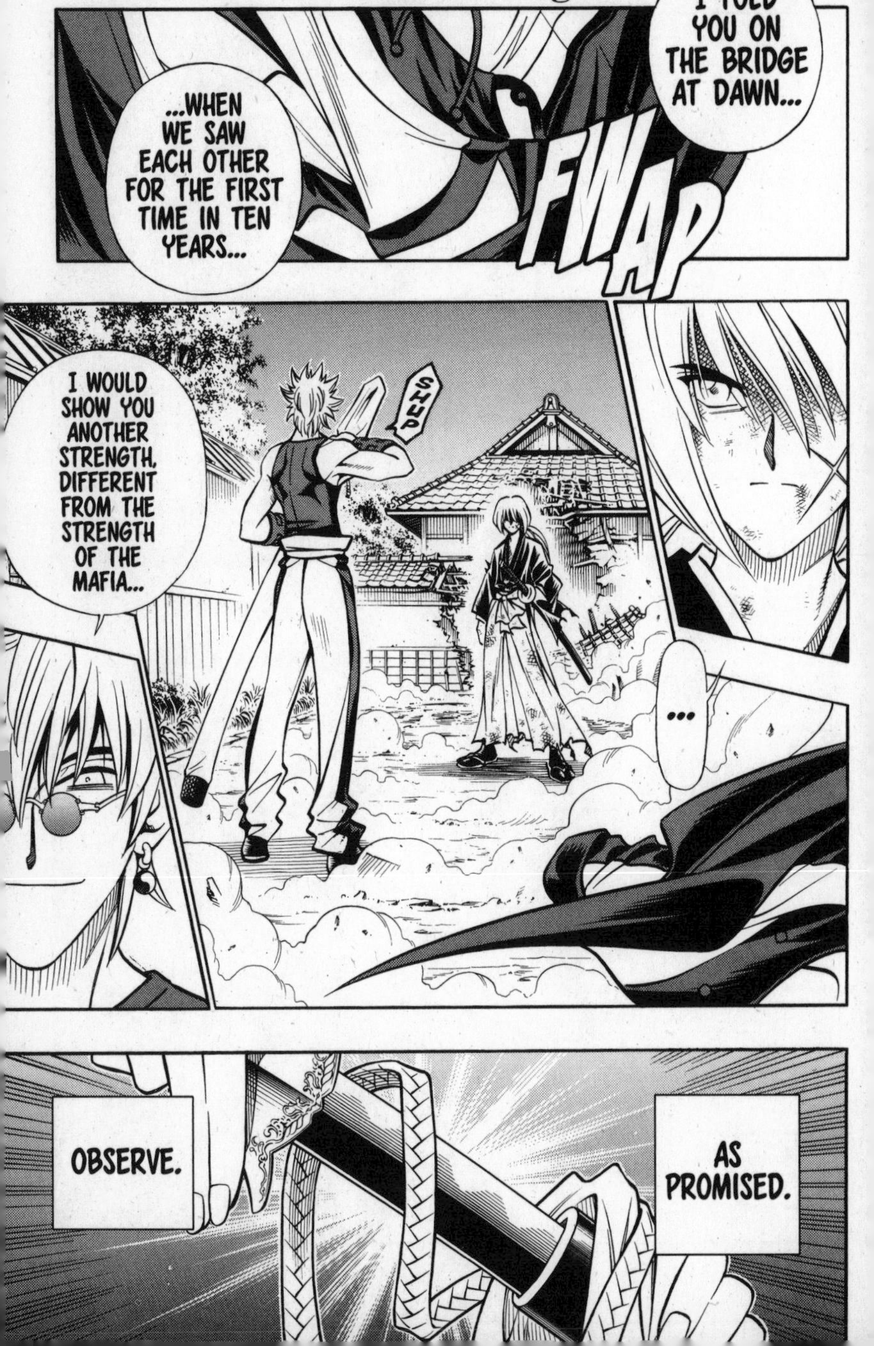
I TOLD YOU ON THE BRIDGE AT DAWN...
...WHEN WE SAW EACH OTHER FOR THE FIRST TIME IN TEN YEARS...
FWAP
...
SHUP
I WOULD SHOW YOU ANOTHER STRENGTH, DIFFERENT FROM THE STRENGTH OF THE MAFIA...
AS PROMISED.
OBSERVE.

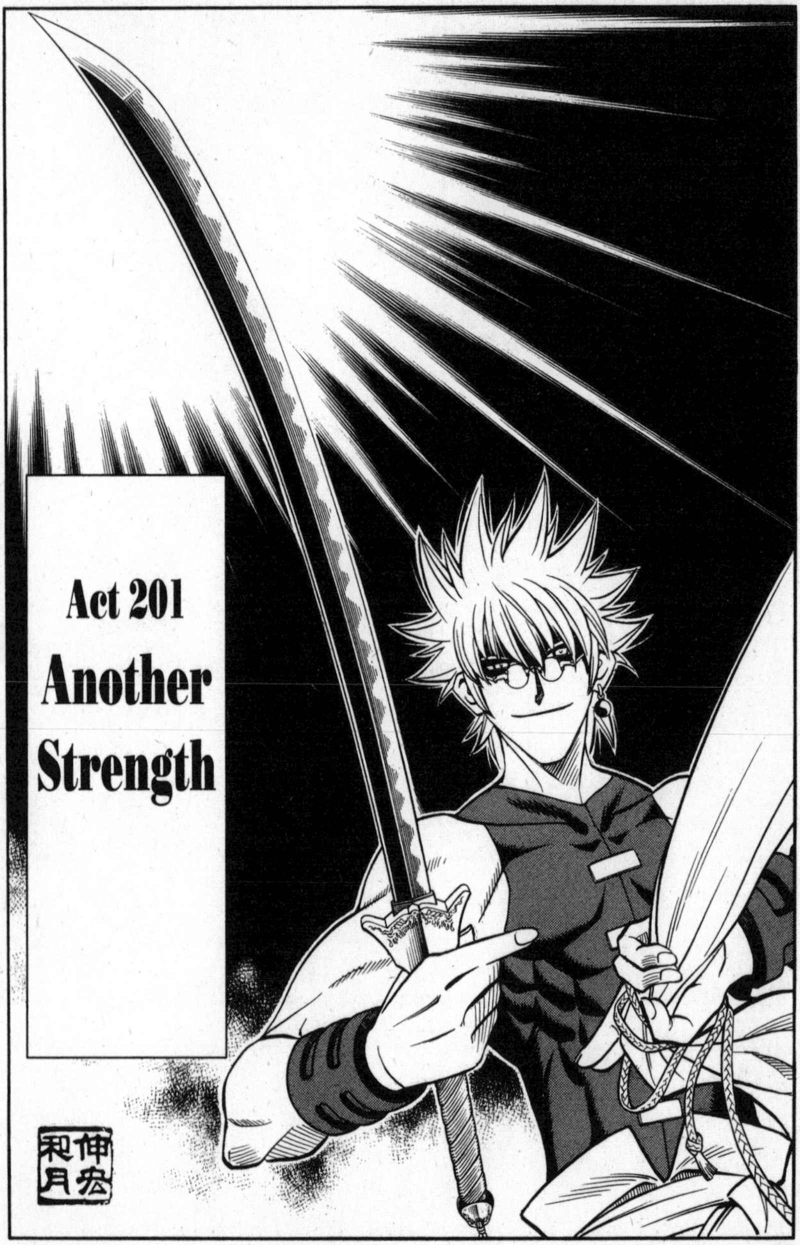
Act 201
Another Strength

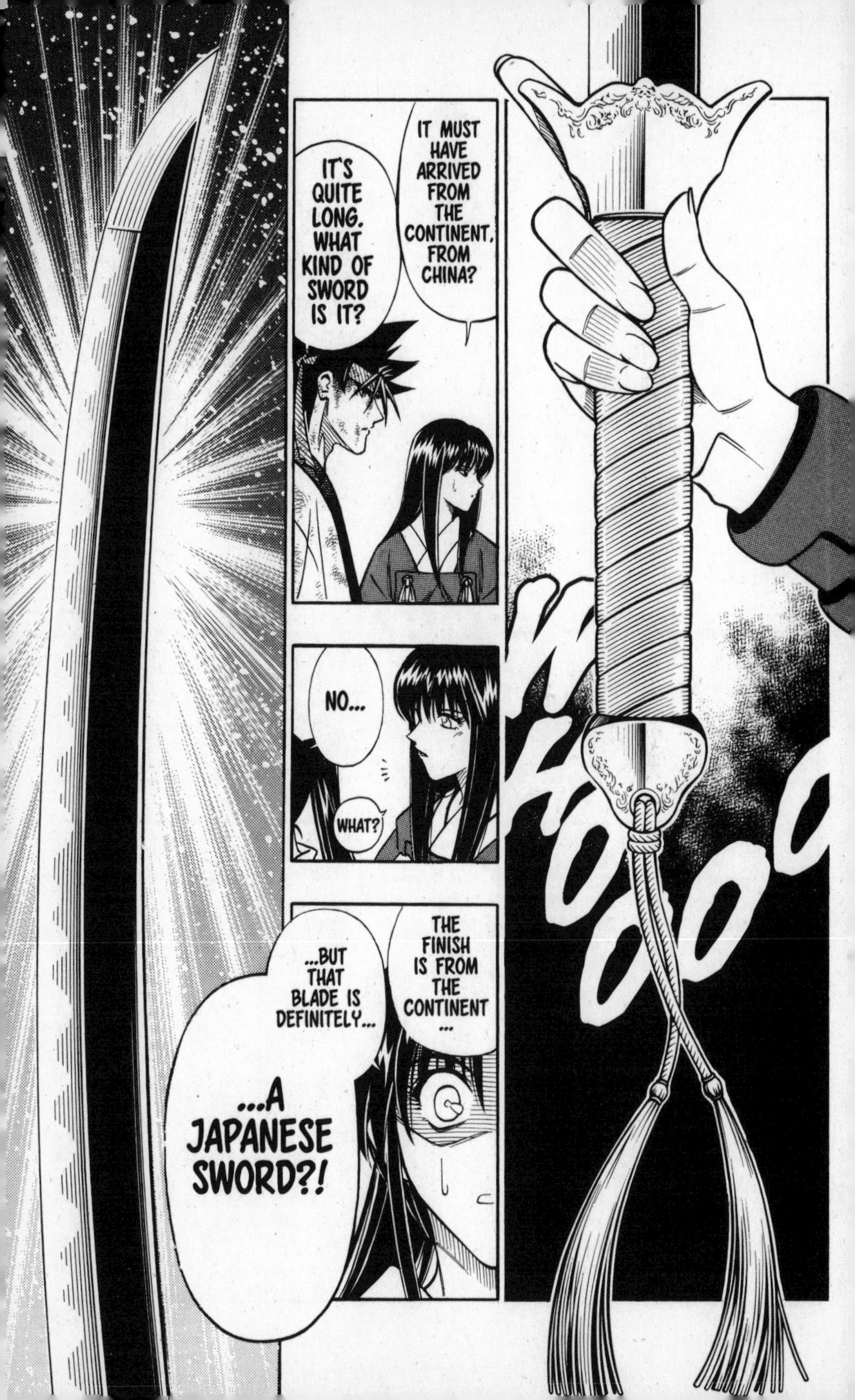
IT MUST HAVE ARRIVED FROM THE CONTINENT, FROM CHINA?
IT'S QUITE LONG. WHAT KIND OF SWORD IS IT?
NO...
WHAT?
THE FINISH IS FROM THE CONTINENT...
...BUT THAT BLADE IS DEFINITELY...
...A JAPANESE SWORD?!

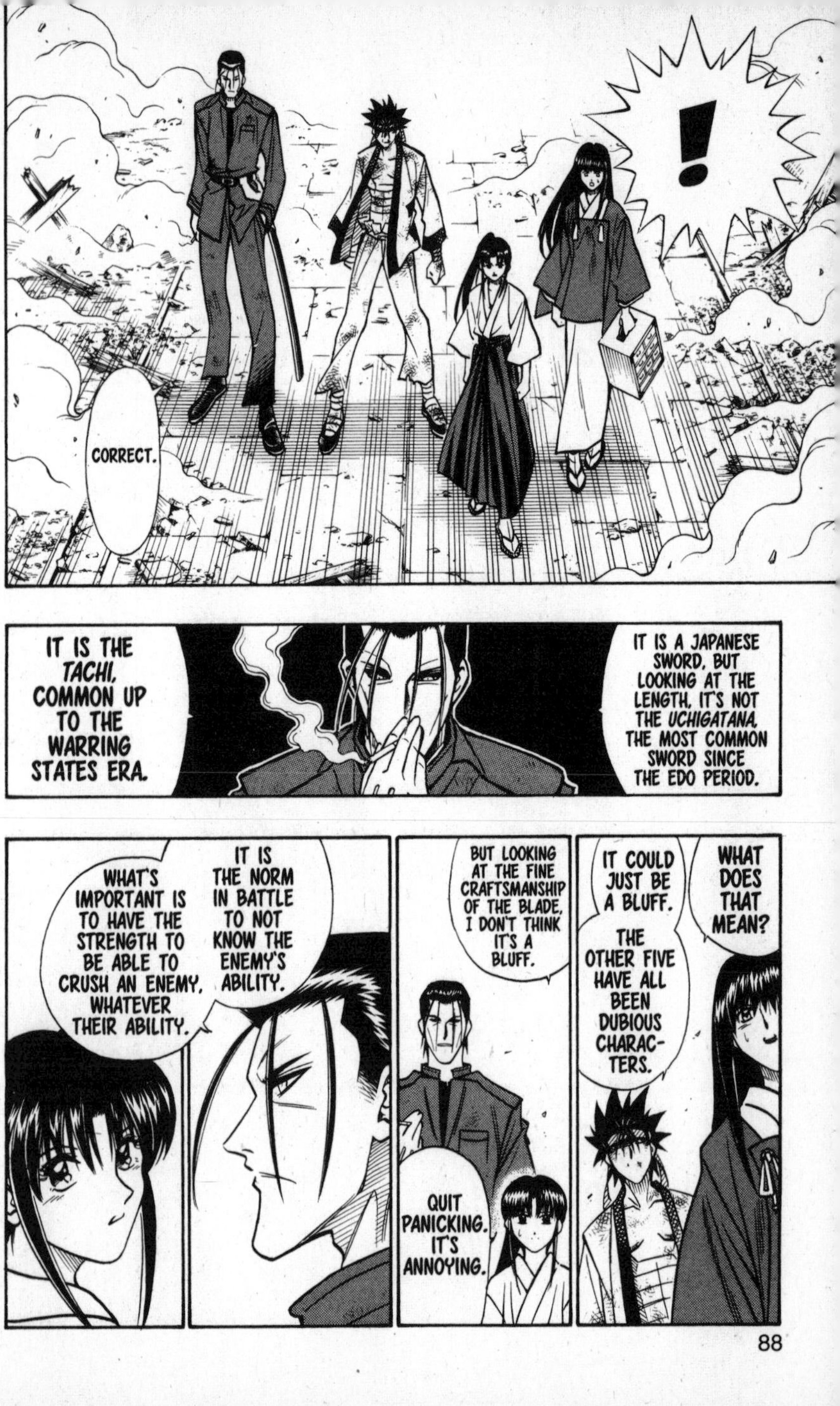
!
CORRECT.
IT IS A JAPANESE SWORD, BUT LOOKING AT THE LENGTH, IT'S NOT THE *UCHIGATANA*, THE MOST COMMON SWORD SINCE THE EDO PERIOD.
IT IS THE *TACHI*, COMMON UP TO THE WARRING STATES ERA.
WHAT DOES THAT MEAN?
IT COULD JUST BE A BLUFF.
THE OTHER FIVE HAVE ALL BEEN DUBIOUS CHARAC-TERS.
BUT LOOKING AT THE FINE CRAFTSMANSHIP OF THE BLADE, I DON'T THINK IT'S A BLUFF.
QUIT PANICKING. IT'S ANNOYING.
IT IS THE NORM IN BATTLE TO NOT KNOW THE ENEMY'S ABILITY.
WHAT'S IMPORTANT IS TO HAVE THE STRENGTH TO BE ABLE TO CRUSH AN ENEMY, WHATEVER THEIR ABILITY.

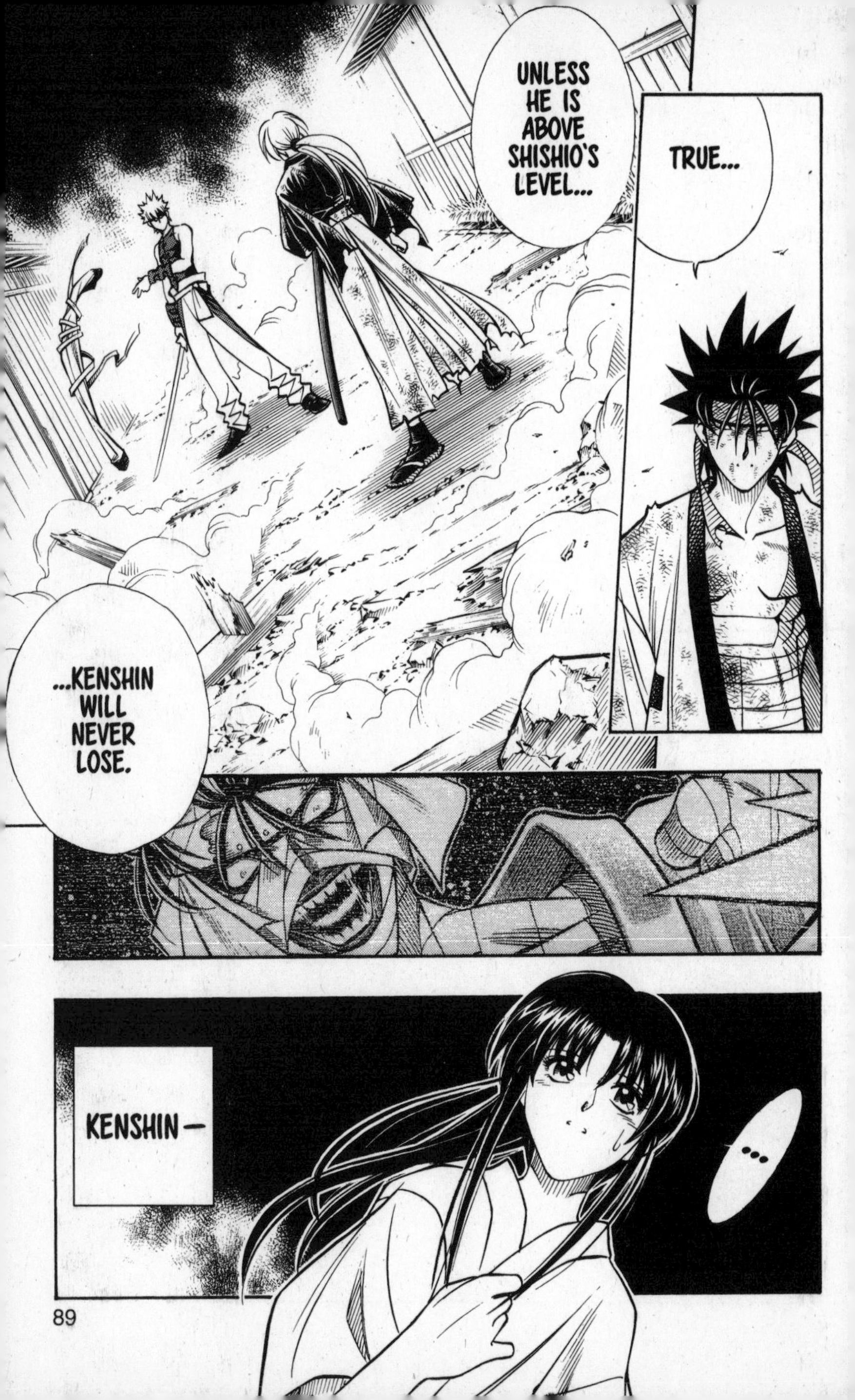

TRUE...
UNLESS HE IS ABOVE SHISHIO'S LEVEL...
...KENSHIN WILL NEVER LOSE.
...
KENSHIN—

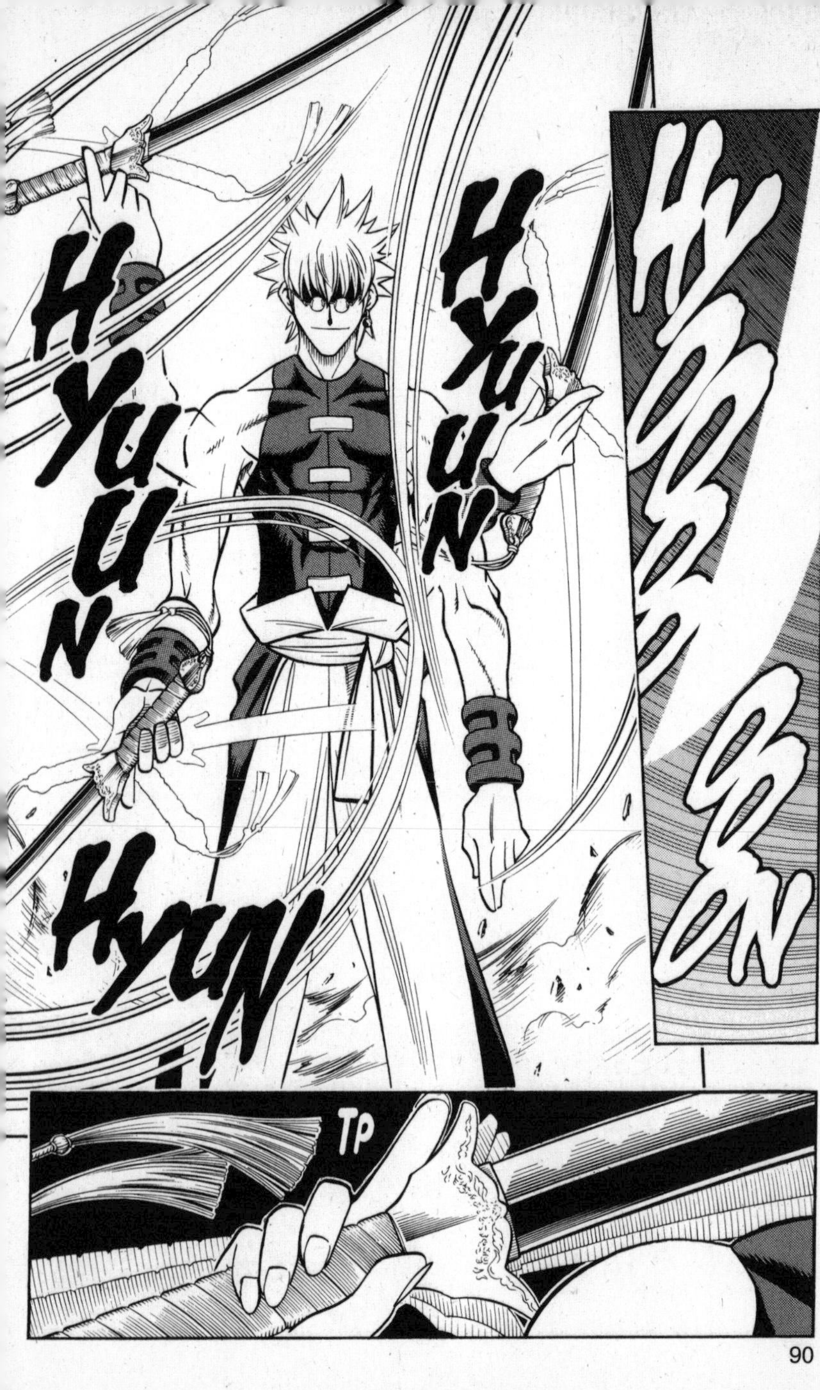
HYOOSH
OOON
HYUUN
HYUUN
HYUN
TP

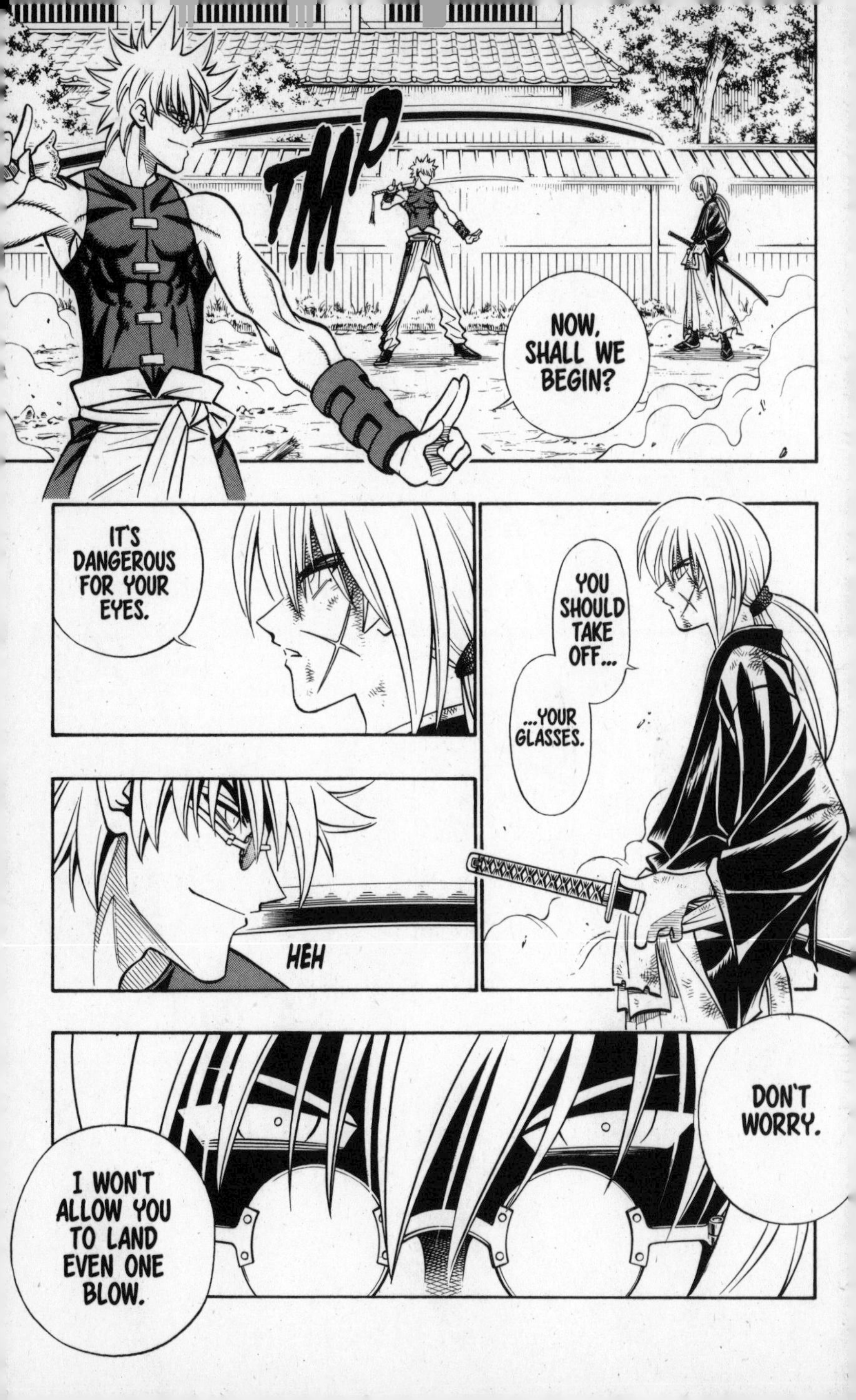
TMP
NOW, SHALL WE BEGIN?
YOU SHOULD TAKE OFF...
...YOUR GLASSES.
IT'S DANGEROUS FOR YOUR EYES.
HEH
DON'T WORRY.
I WON'T ALLOW YOU TO LAND EVEN ONE BLOW.

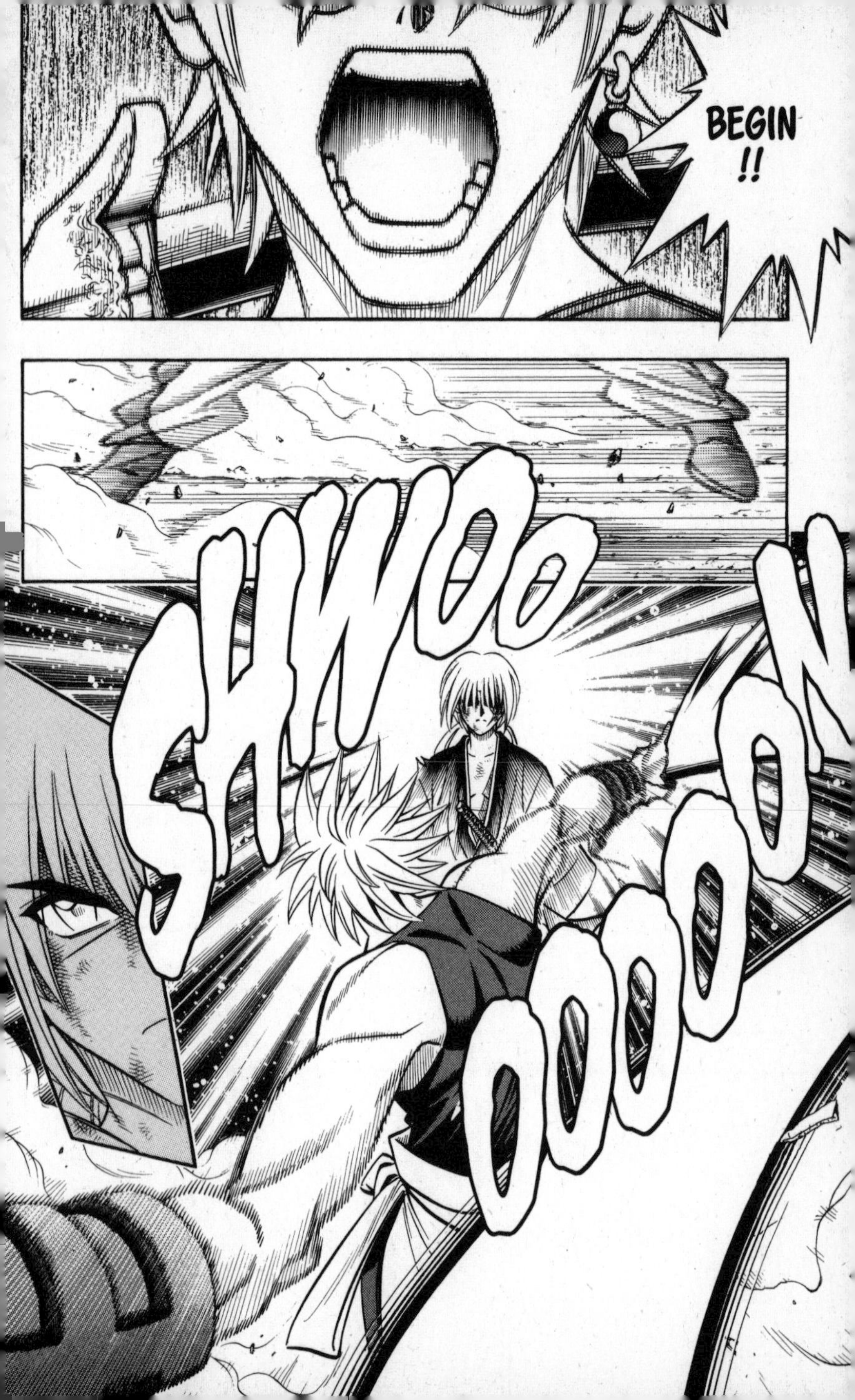
BEGIN !!
SHWOOOOOOOOON

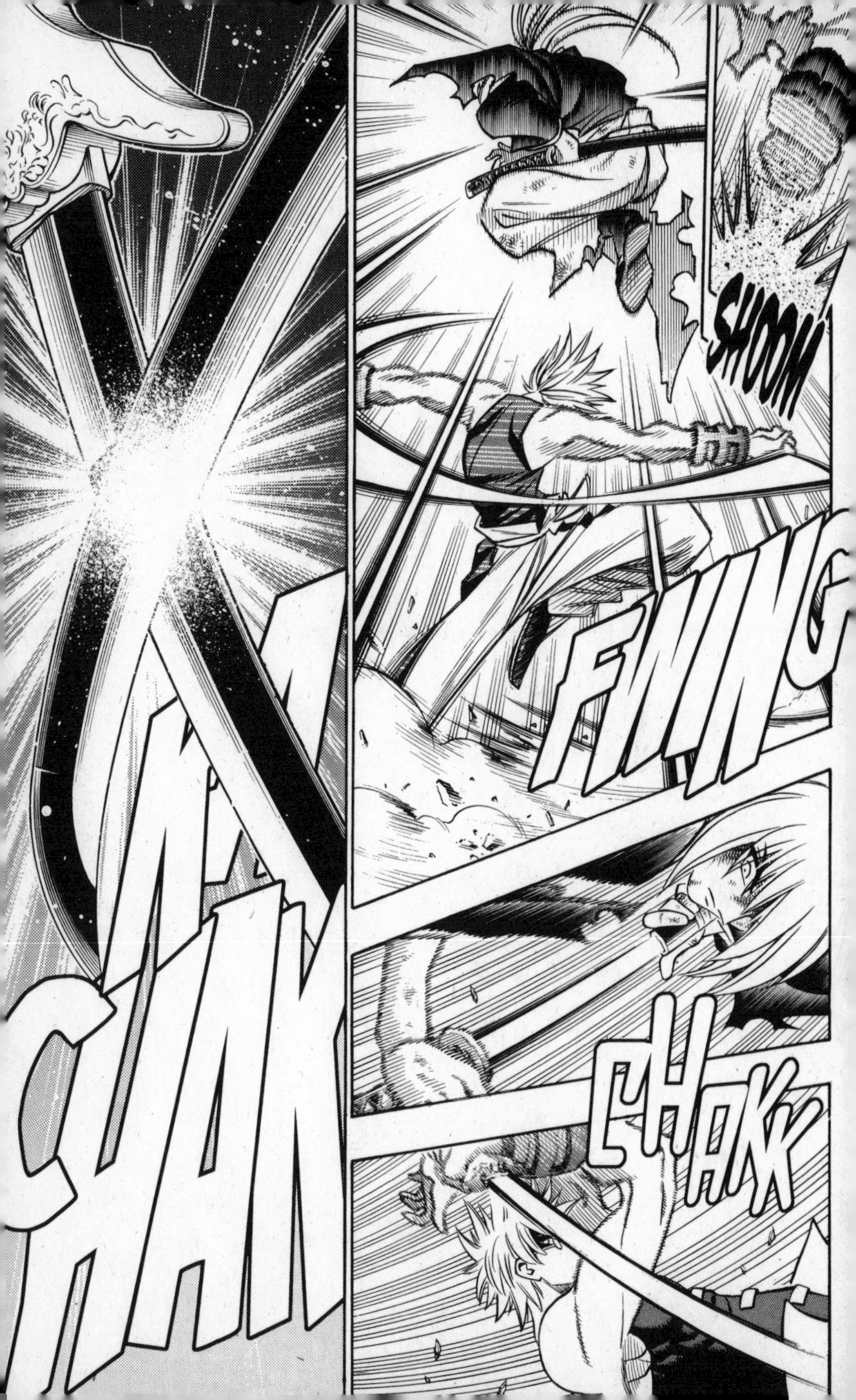
SHOOM
FWING
CHAK
CHAN

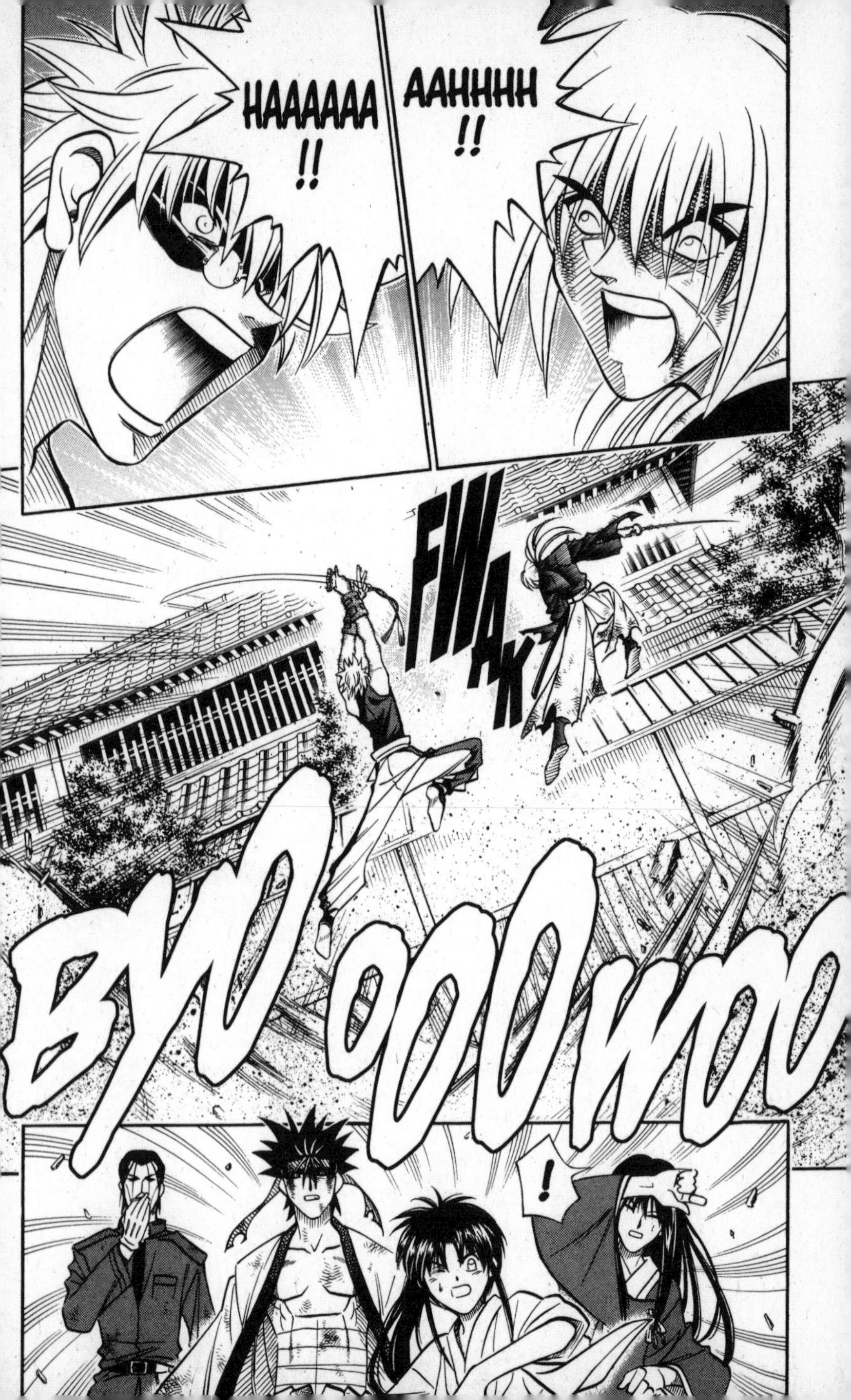
AAHHHH !!
HAAAAAA !!
FWAK
BWOOOWOO
!

READ THIS WAY

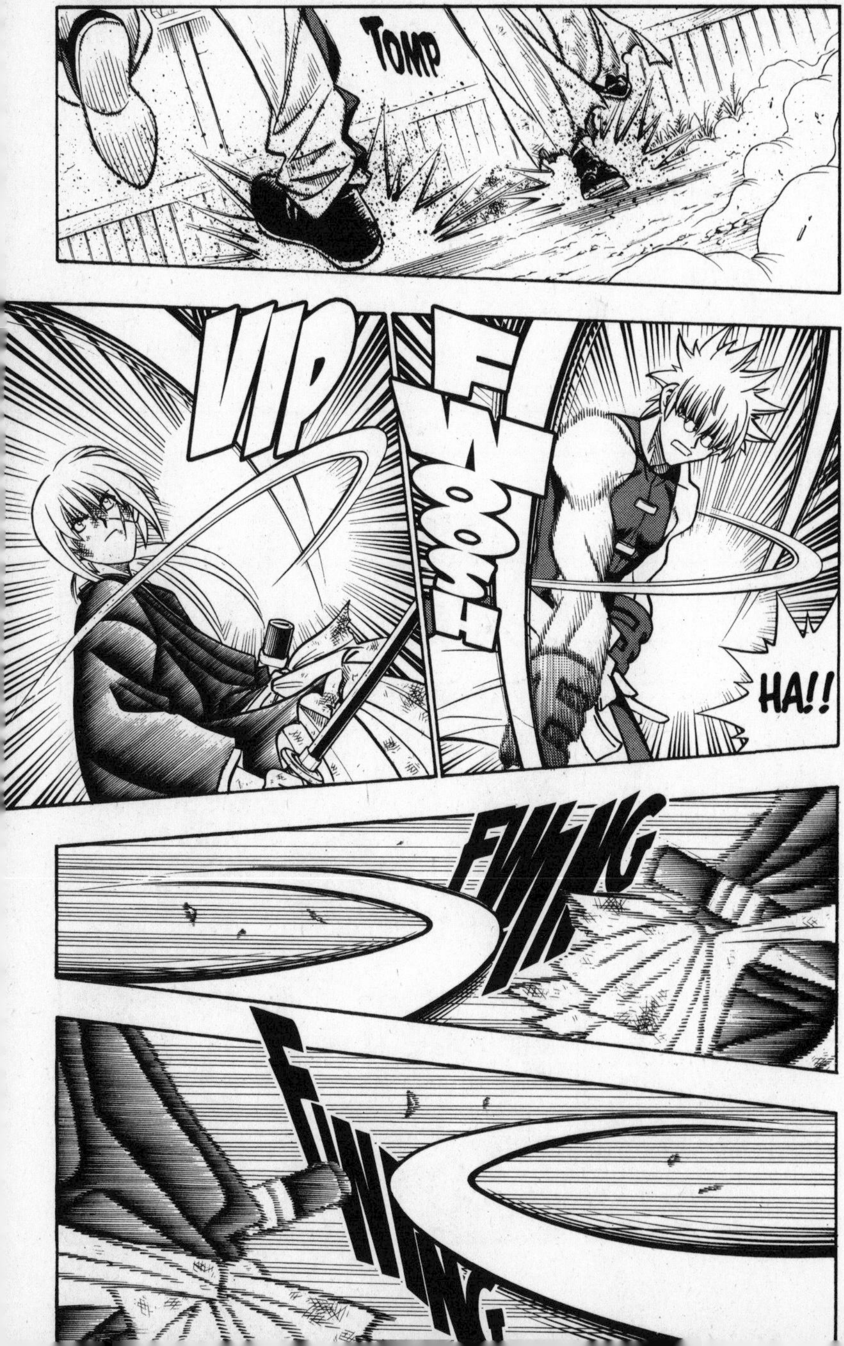
TOMP
FWOOSH!!
HA!!
VIP
FWING
FWING

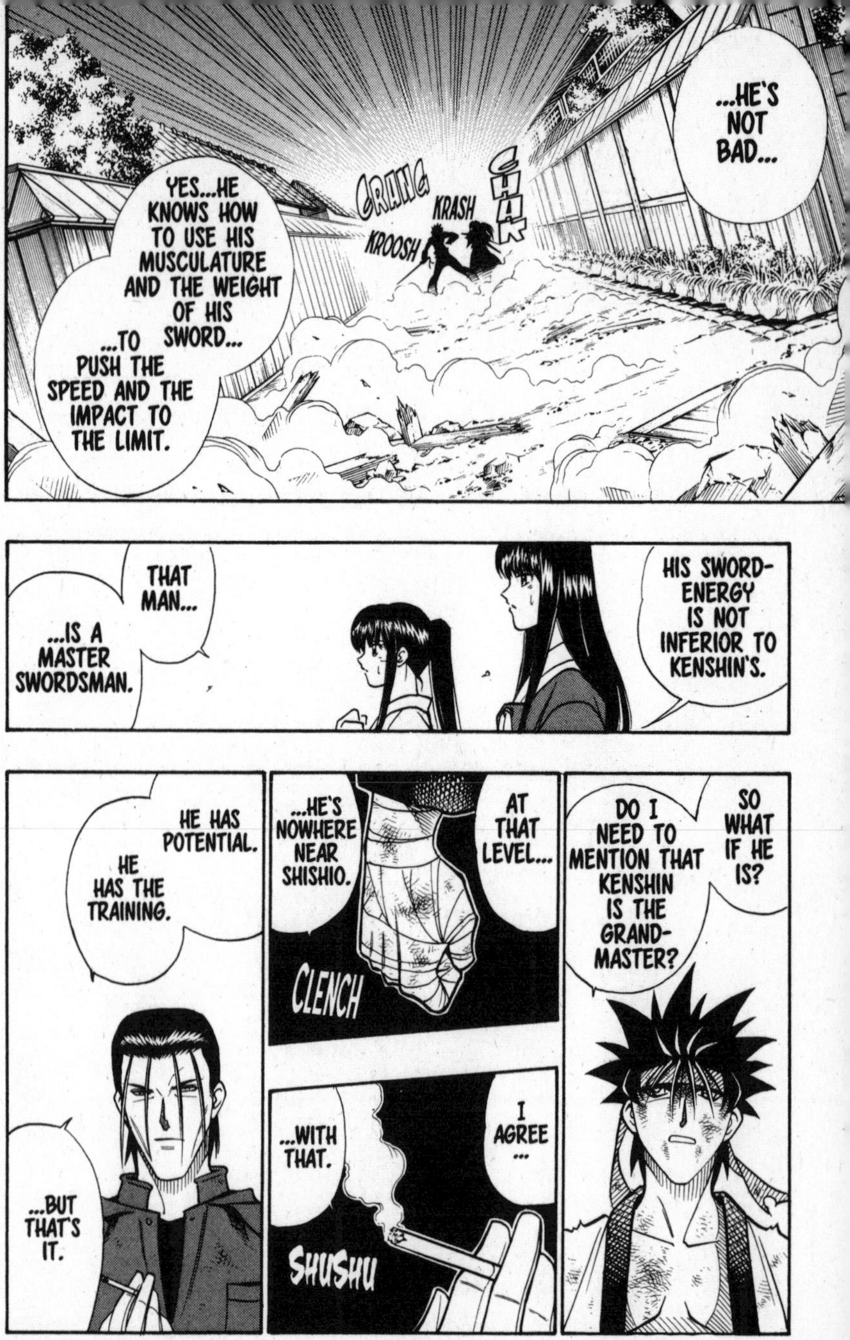
...HE'S NOT BAD...
CHAK
KRASH
CRANG
KROOSH
YES...HE KNOWS HOW TO USE HIS MUSCULATURE AND THE WEIGHT OF HIS SWORD...
...TO PUSH THE SPEED AND THE IMPACT TO THE LIMIT.
HIS SWORD-ENERGY IS NOT INFERIOR TO KENSHIN'S.
THAT MAN...
...IS A MASTER SWORDSMAN.
SO WHAT IF HE IS?
DO I NEED TO MENTION THAT KENSHIN IS THE GRAND-MASTER?
AT THAT LEVEL...
...HE'S NOWHERE NEAR SHISHIO.
CLENCH
I AGREE ...
...WITH THAT.
SHUSHU
HE HAS POTENTIAL.
HE HAS THE TRAINING.
...BUT THAT'S IT.

READ THIS WAY

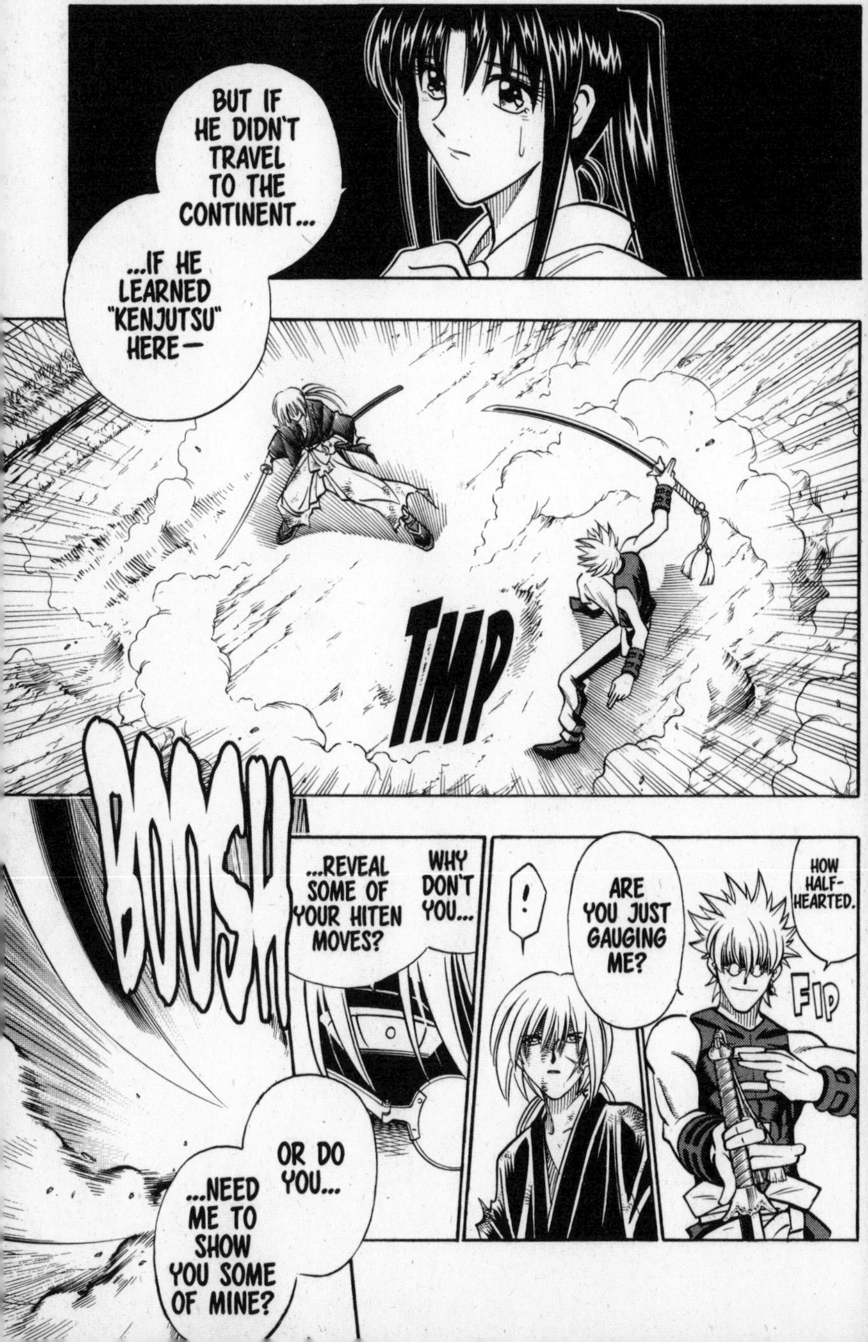
BUT IF HE DIDN'T TRAVEL TO THE CONTINENT...
...IF HE LEARNED "KENJUTSU" HERE—
TMP
BOOSH
HOW HALF-HEARTED.
FIP
ARE YOU JUST GAUGING ME?
!
WHY DON'T YOU...
...REVEAL SOME OF YOUR HITEN MOVES?
OR DO YOU...
...NEED ME TO SHOW YOU SOME OF MINE?

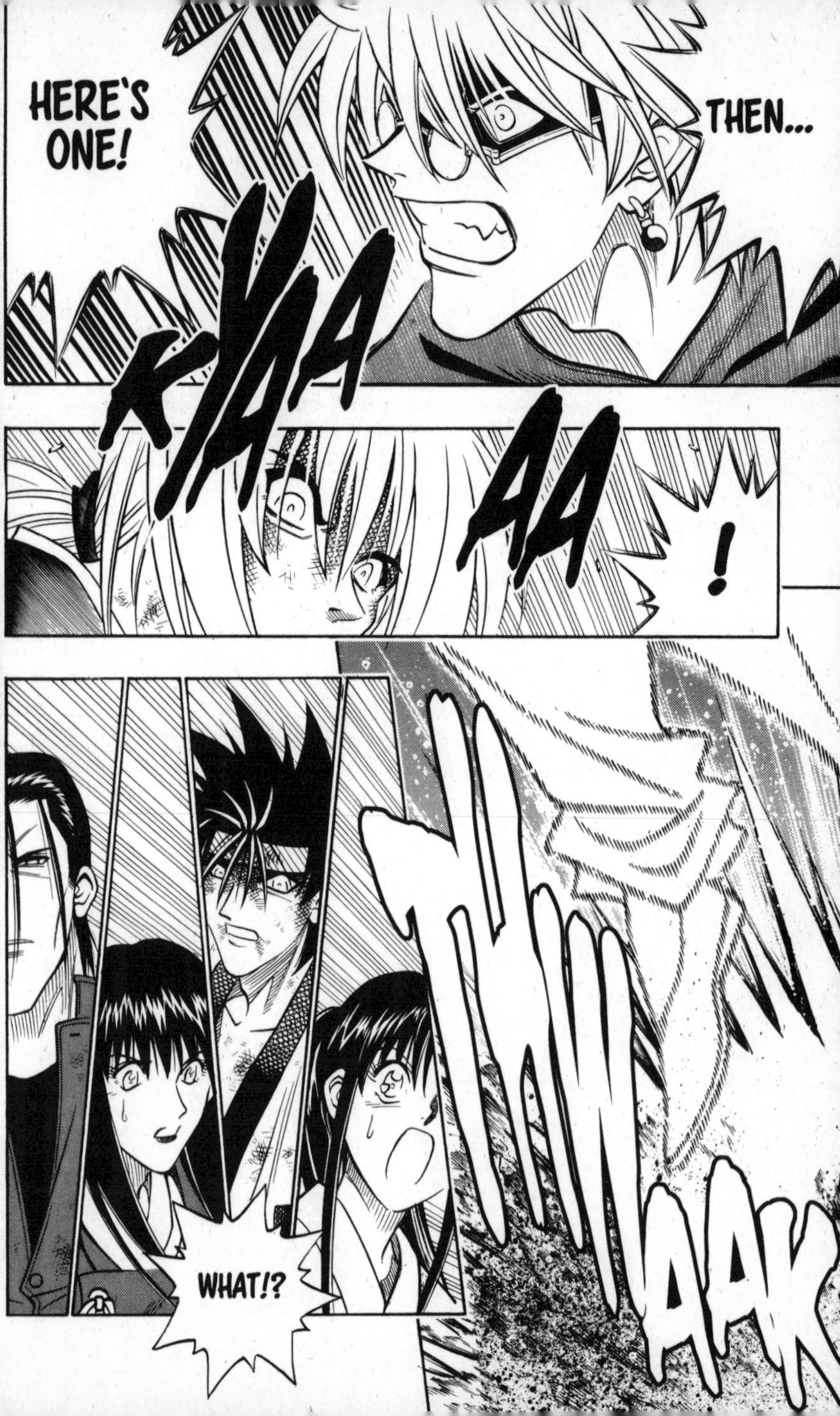
THEN...
HERE'S ONE!
KYAA AA!
THWAAK
WHAT!?

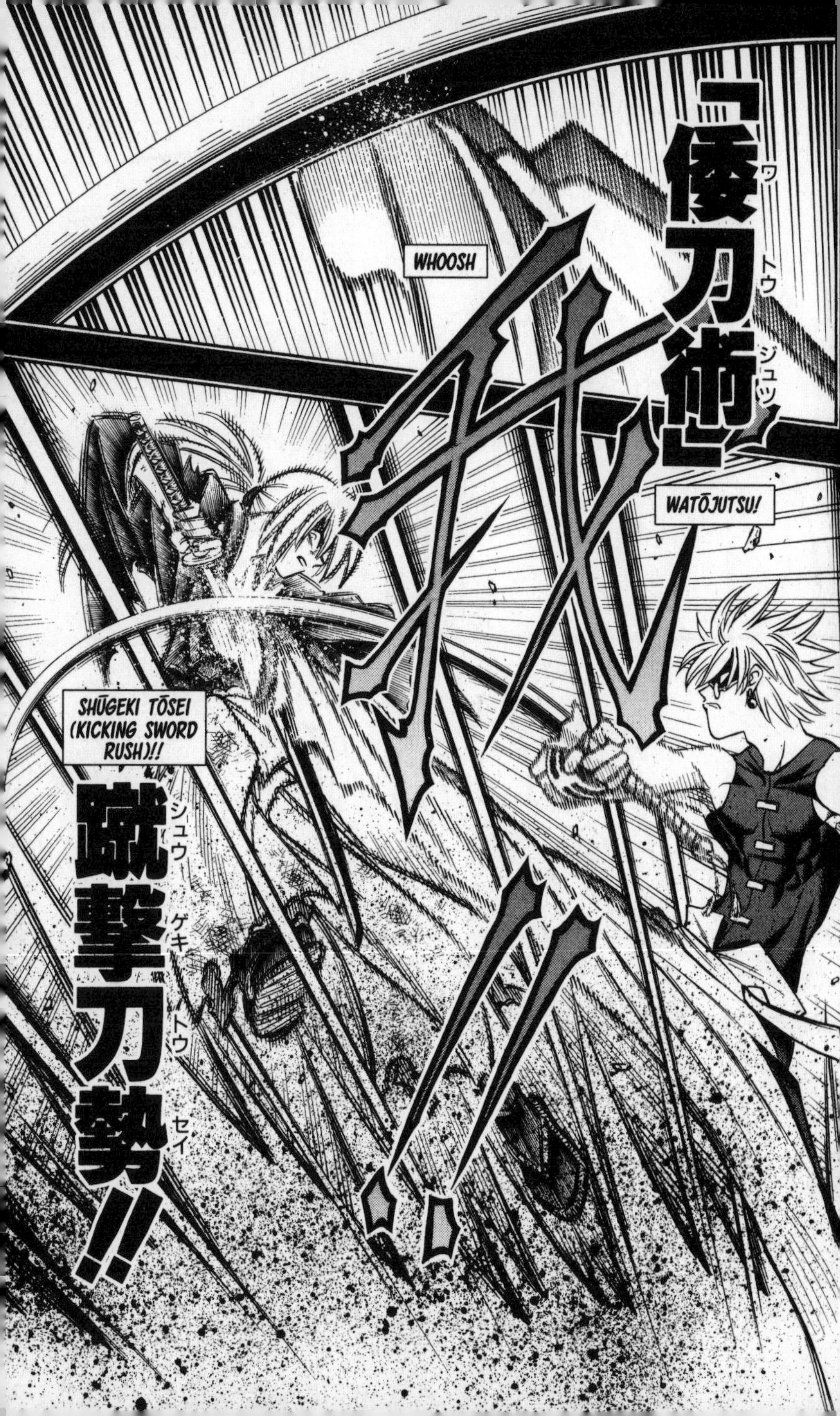
「倭刀術」
WATŌJUTSU!
WHOOSH
蹴撃刀勢!!
SHŪGEKI TŌSEI (KICKING SWORD RUSH)!!

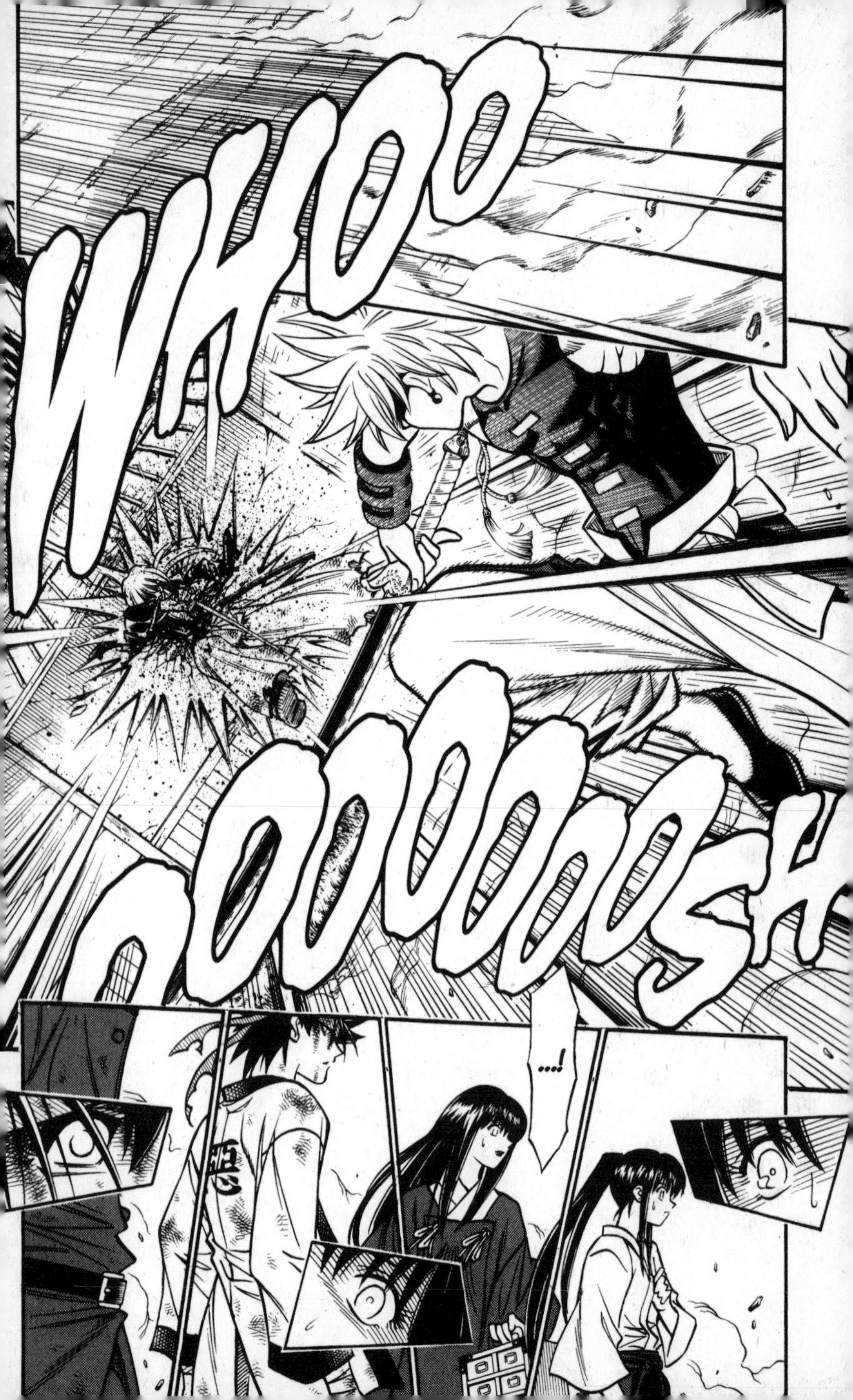
WHOO
OOOOOOOSH
...!

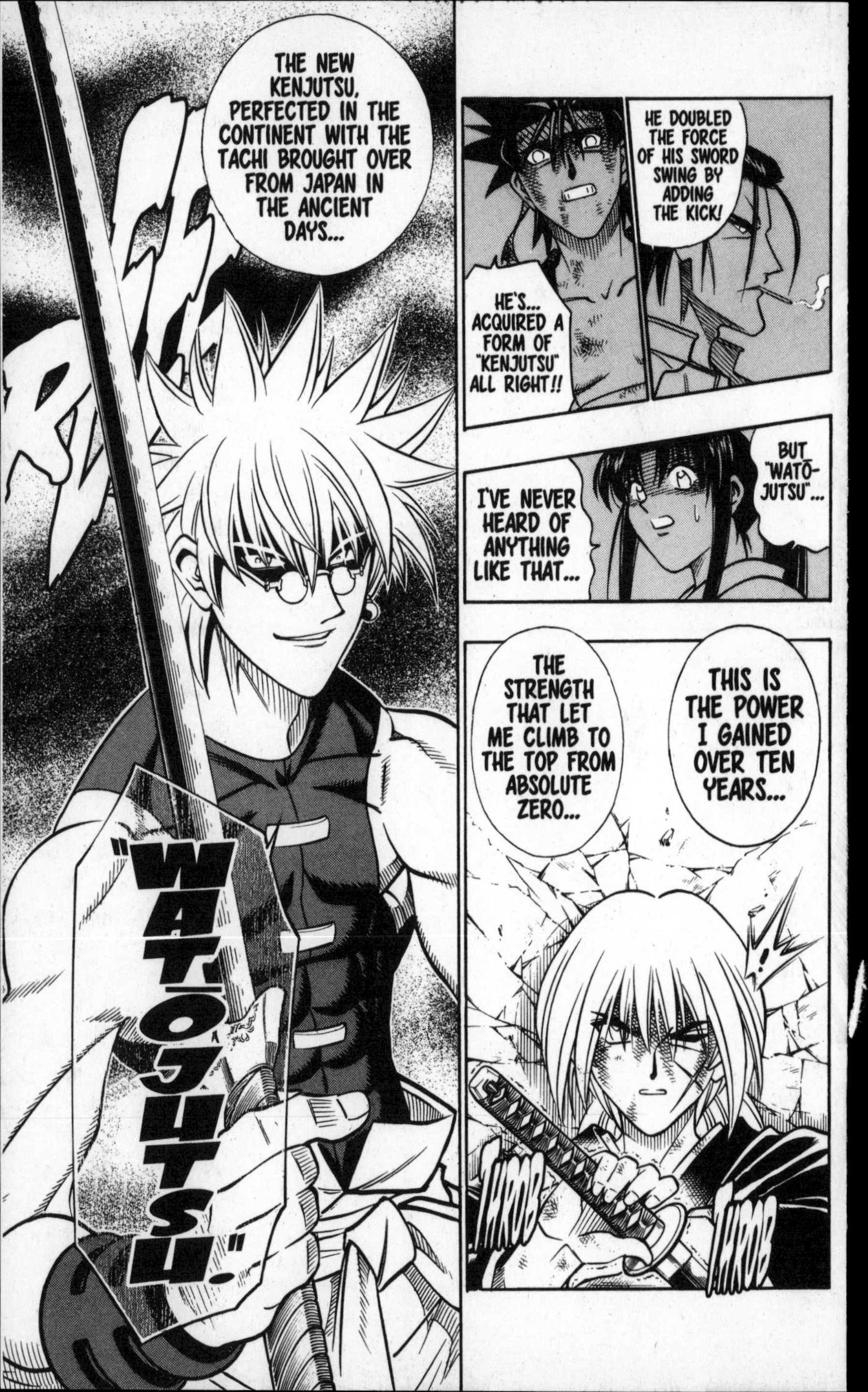
HE DOUBLED THE FORCE OF HIS SWORD SWING BY ADDING THE KICK!
HE'S... ACQUIRED A FORM OF "KENJUTSU" ALL RIGHT!!
BUT "WATŌ-JUTSU"...
I'VE NEVER HEARD OF ANYTHING LIKE THAT...
THIS IS THE POWER I GAINED OVER TEN YEARS...
THE STRENGTH THAT LET ME CLIMB TO THE TOP FROM ABSOLUTE ZERO...
THROB
THROB
THE NEW KENJUTSU, PERFECTED IN THE CONTINENT WITH THE TACHI BROUGHT OVER FROM JAPAN IN THE ANCIENT DAYS...
"WATŌJUTSU."

Rurouni Kenshin

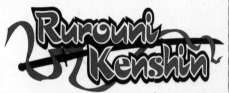

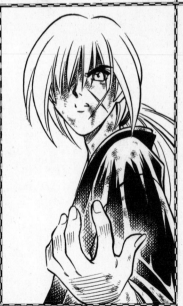

Act 202—Tales of the Past

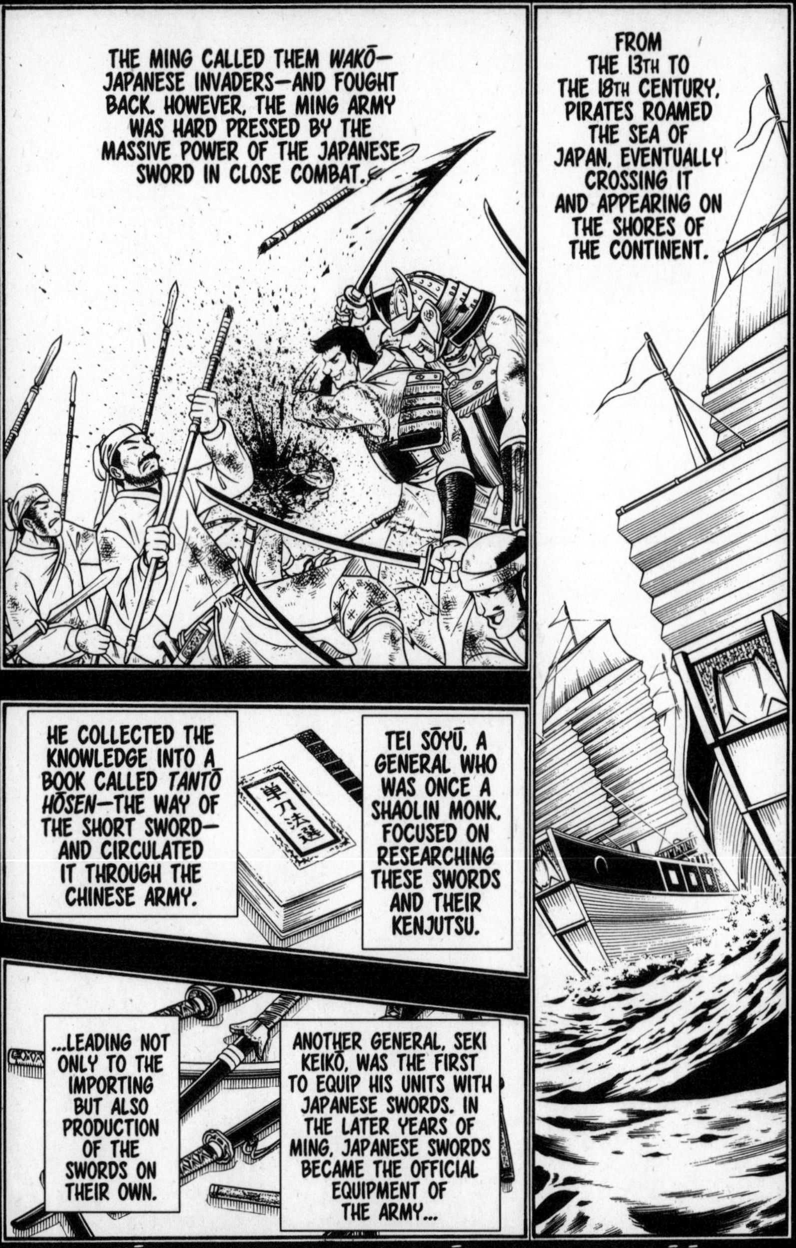
FROM THE 13TH TO THE 18TH CENTURY, PIRATES ROAMED THE SEA OF JAPAN, EVENTUALLY CROSSING IT AND APPEARING ON THE SHORES OF THE CONTINENT.
THE MING CALLED THEM *WAKŌ*—JAPANESE INVADERS—AND FOUGHT BACK. HOWEVER, THE MING ARMY WAS HARD PRESSED BY THE MASSIVE POWER OF THE JAPANESE SWORD IN CLOSE COMBAT.
TEI SŌYŪ, A GENERAL WHO WAS ONCE A SHAOLIN MONK, FOCUSED ON RESEARCHING THESE SWORDS AND THEIR KENJUTSU.
単刀法選
HE COLLECTED THE KNOWLEDGE INTO A BOOK CALLED *TANTŌ HŌSEN*—THE WAY OF THE SHORT SWORD—AND CIRCULATED IT THROUGH THE CHINESE ARMY.
ANOTHER GENERAL, SEKI KEIKŌ, WAS THE FIRST TO EQUIP HIS UNITS WITH JAPANESE SWORDS. IN THE LATER YEARS OF MING, JAPANESE SWORDS BECAME THE OFFICIAL EQUIPMENT OF THE ARMY...
...LEADING NOT ONLY TO THE IMPORTING BUT ALSO PRODUCTION OF THE SWORDS ON THEIR OWN.

RESOURCES: *CHŪGOKU BUJUTSUSHI DAIKAN* BY SASAO KYŌJI, PUBLISHED BY FUKUSHŌDŌ.

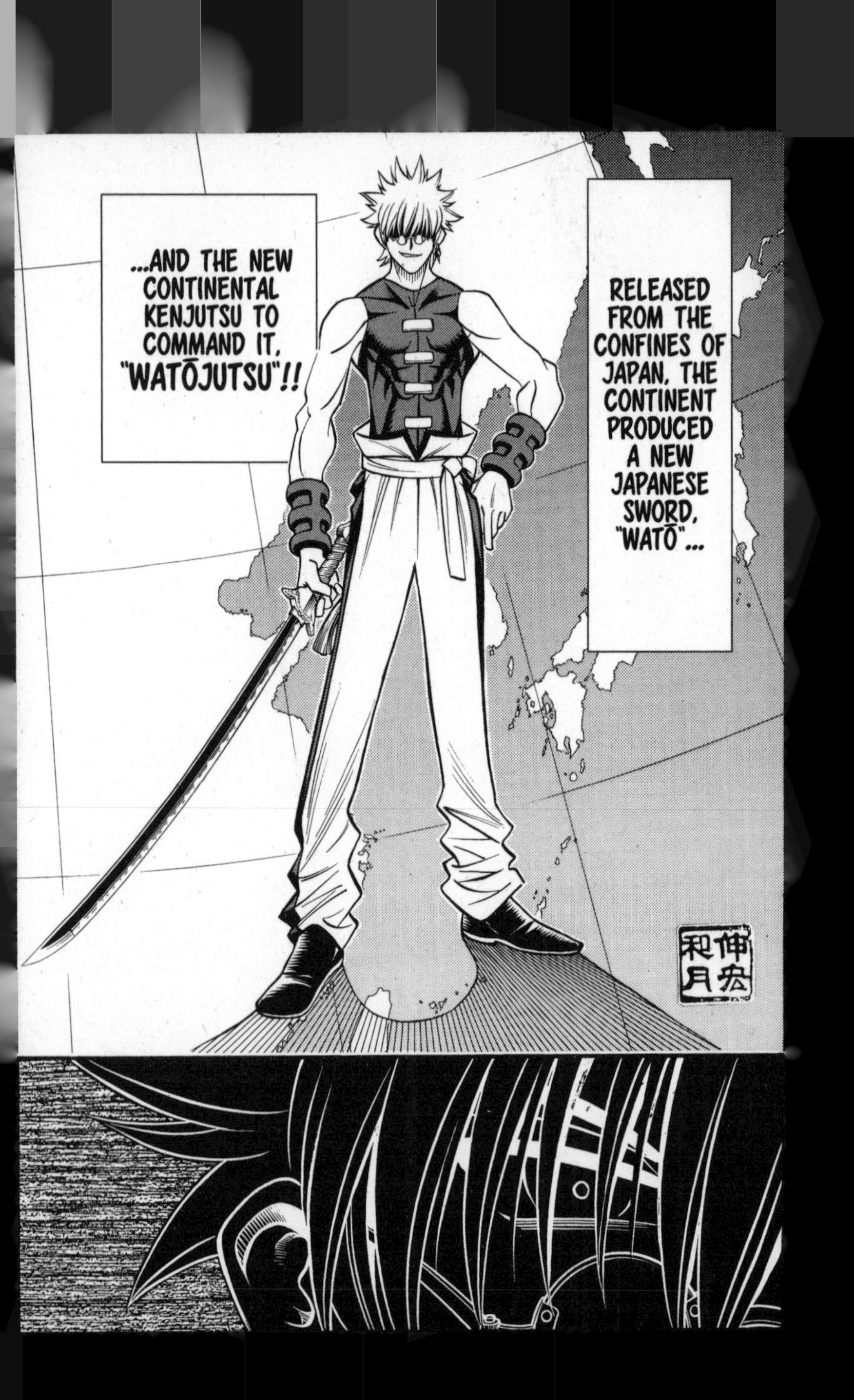
RELEASED FROM THE CONFINES OF JAPAN, THE CONTINENT PRODUCED A NEW JAPANESE SWORD, "WATŌ"...
...AND THE NEW CONTINENTAL KENJUTSU TO COMMAND IT, "WATŌJUTSU"!!
伸宏
和月

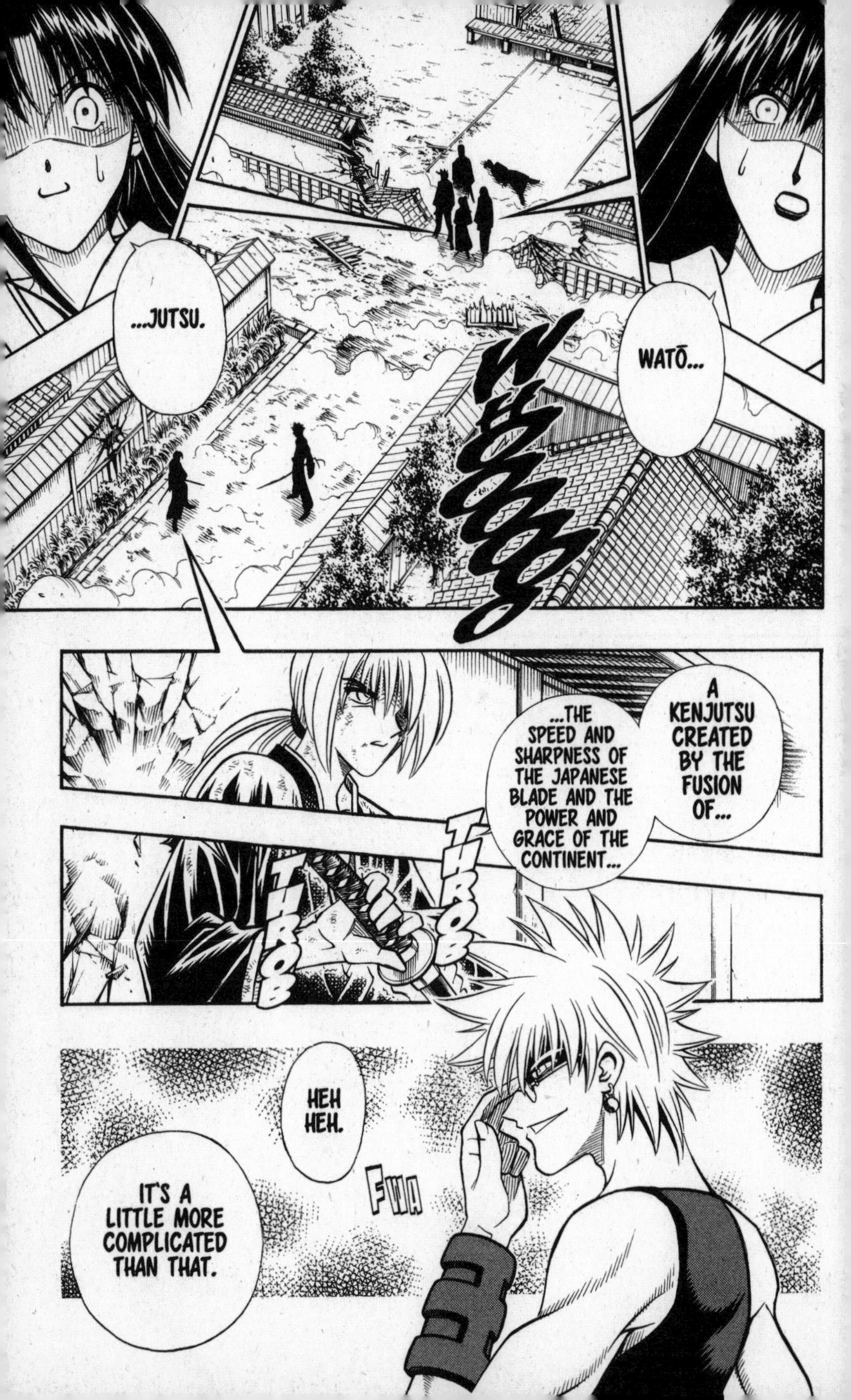
WATŌ...
...JUTSU.
A KENJUTSU CREATED BY THE FUSION OF...
...THE SPEED AND SHARPNESS OF THE JAPANESE BLADE AND THE POWER AND GRACE OF THE CONTINENT...
THROB
THROB
HEH HEH.
FWA
IT'S A LITTLE MORE COMPLICATED THAN THAT.

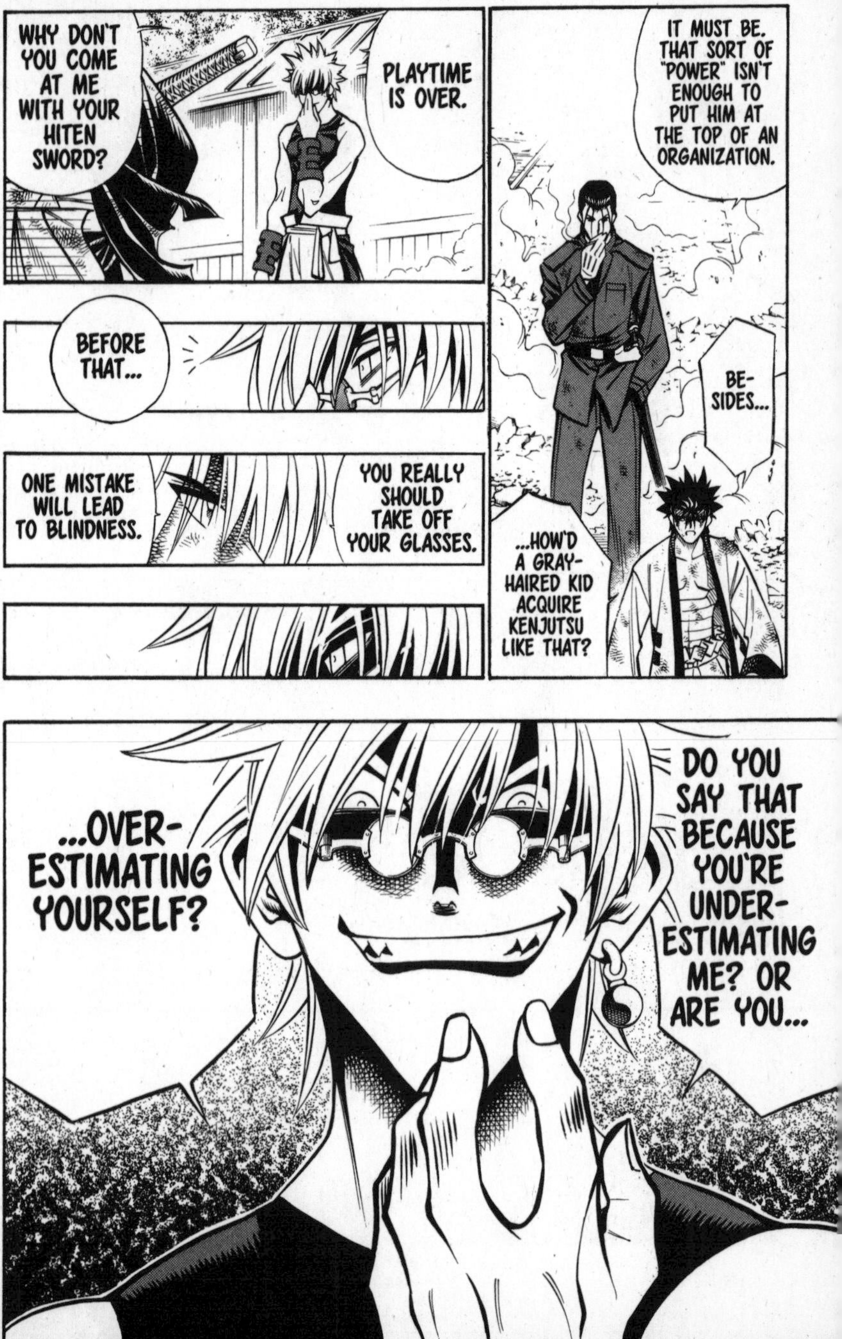
IT MUST BE. THAT SORT OF "POWER" ISN'T ENOUGH TO PUT HIM AT THE TOP OF AN ORGANIZATION.
BE-SIDES...
...HOW'D A GRAY-HAIRED KID ACQUIRE KENJUTSU LIKE THAT?
PLAYTIME IS OVER.
WHY DON'T YOU COME AT ME WITH YOUR HITEN SWORD?
BEFORE THAT...
YOU REALLY SHOULD TAKE OFF YOUR GLASSES.
ONE MISTAKE WILL LEAD TO BLINDNESS.
DO YOU SAY THAT BECAUSE YOU'RE UNDER-ESTIMATING ME? OR ARE YOU...
...OVER-ESTIMATING YOURSELF?

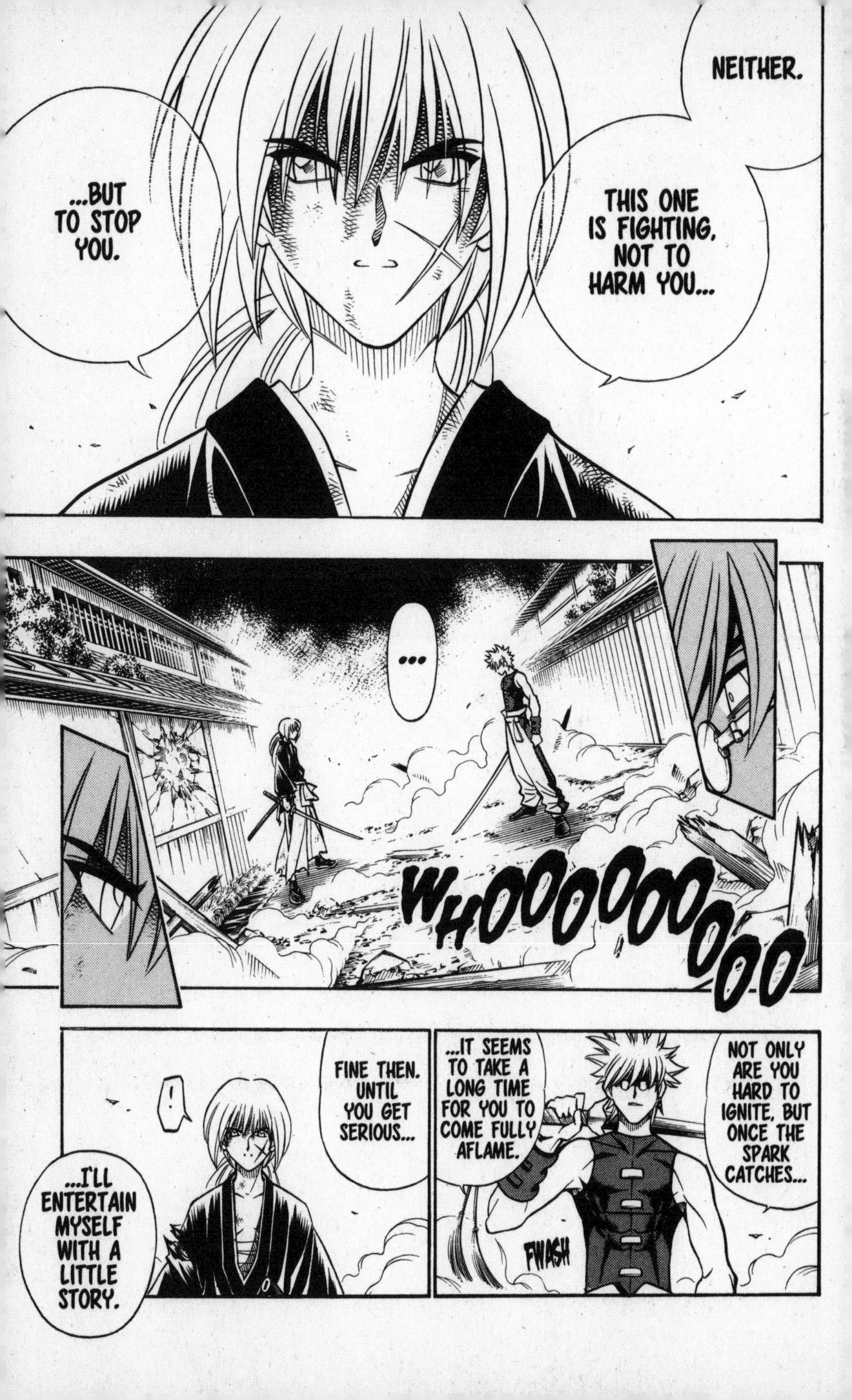
NEITHER.
THIS ONE IS FIGHTING, NOT TO HARM YOU...
...BUT TO STOP YOU.
...
WHOOOOOOOOOO
NOT ONLY ARE YOU HARD TO IGNITE, BUT ONCE THE SPARK CATCHES...
...IT SEEMS TO TAKE A LONG TIME FOR YOU TO COME FULLY AFLAME.
FWASH
FINE THEN. UNTIL YOU GET SERIOUS...
!
...I'LL ENTERTAIN MYSELF WITH A LITTLE STORY.

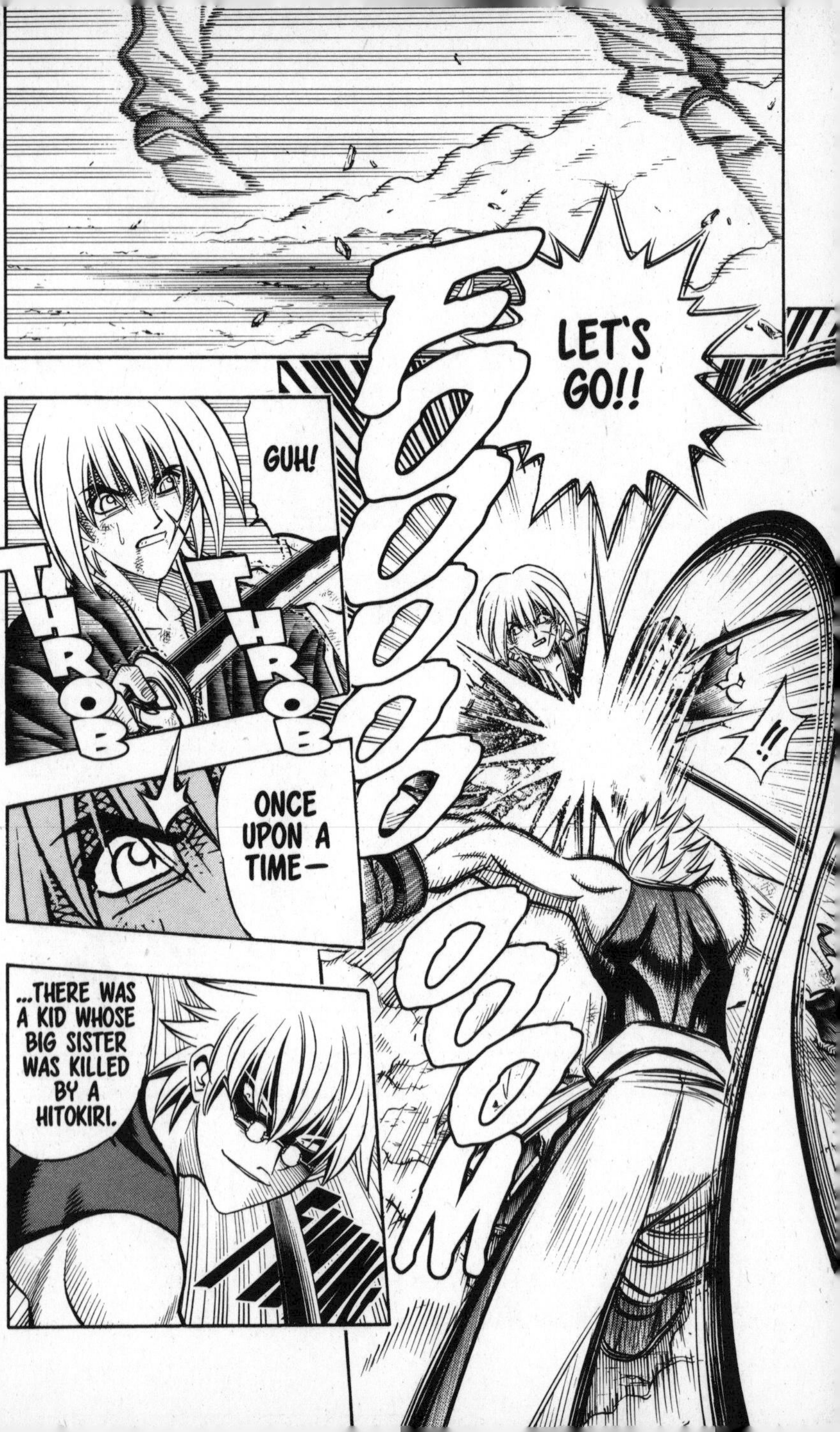
LET'S GO!!
FOOOOOOOOM
!!
GUH!
THROB THROB
ONCE UPON A TIME—
...THERE WAS A KID WHOSE BIG SISTER WAS KILLED BY A HITOKIRI.

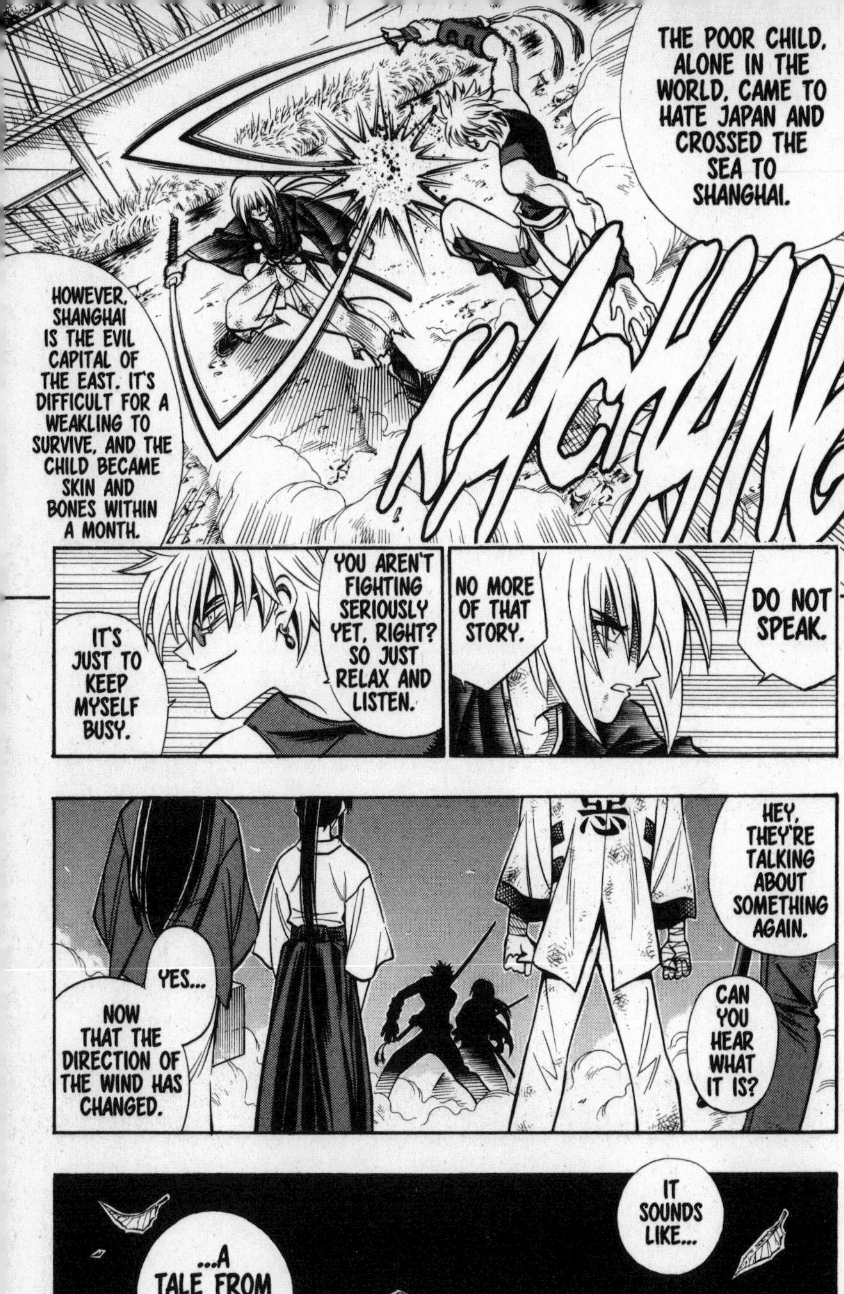
THE POOR CHILD, ALONE IN THE WORLD, CAME TO HATE JAPAN AND CROSSED THE SEA TO SHANGHAI.
KACHANG
HOWEVER, SHANGHAI IS THE EVIL CAPITAL OF THE EAST. IT'S DIFFICULT FOR A WEAKLING TO SURVIVE, AND THE CHILD BECAME SKIN AND BONES WITHIN A MONTH.
DO NOT SPEAK.
NO MORE OF THAT STORY.
YOU AREN'T FIGHTING SERIOUSLY YET, RIGHT? SO JUST RELAX AND LISTEN.
IT'S JUST TO KEEP MYSELF BUSY.
HEY, THEY'RE TALKING ABOUT SOMETHING AGAIN.
CAN YOU HEAR WHAT IT IS?
YES... NOW THAT THE DIRECTION OF THE WIND HAS CHANGED.
IT SOUNDS LIKE...
...A TALE FROM THE PAST.

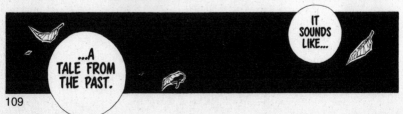

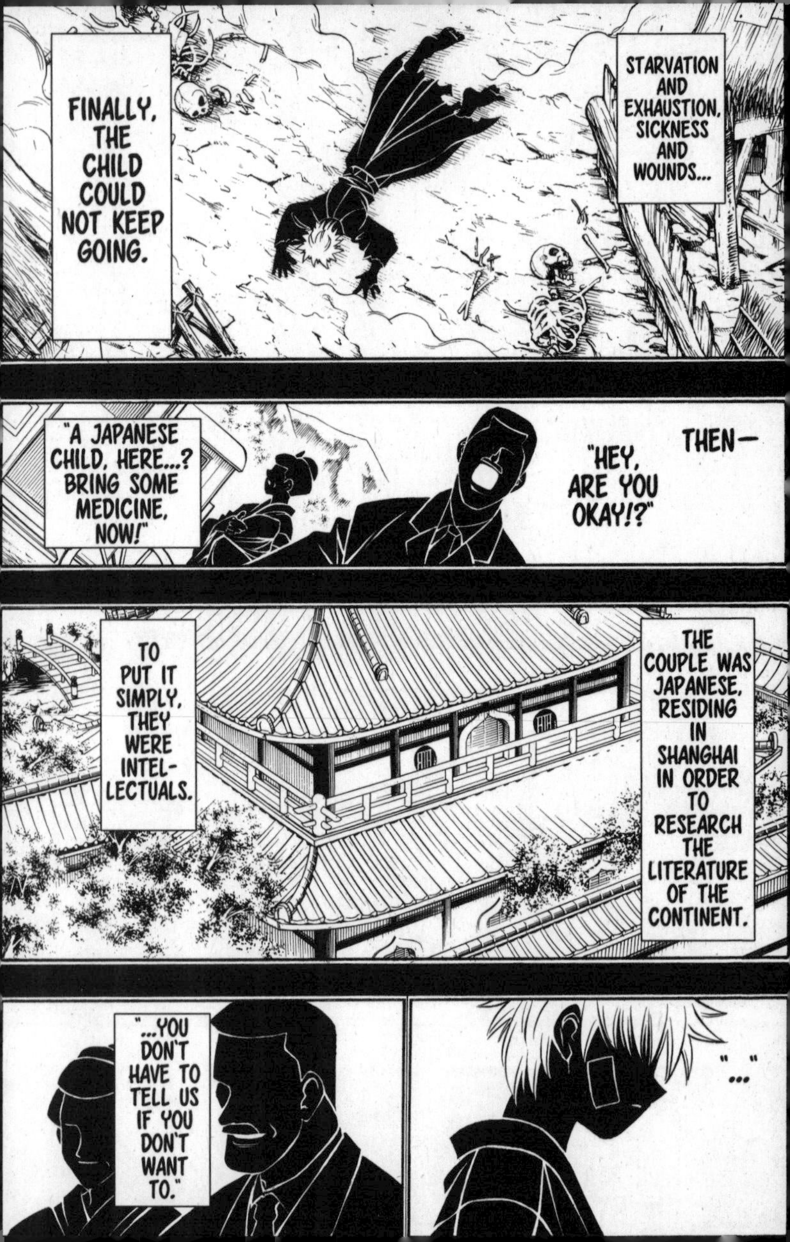
STARVATION AND EXHAUSTION, SICKNESS AND WOUNDS...
FINALLY, THE CHILD COULD NOT KEEP GOING.
THEN—
"HEY, ARE YOU OKAY!?"
"A JAPANESE CHILD, HERE...? BRING SOME MEDICINE, NOW!"
THE COUPLE WAS JAPANESE, RESIDING IN SHANGHAI IN ORDER TO RESEARCH THE LITERATURE OF THE CONTINENT.
TO PUT IT SIMPLY, THEY WERE INTEL-LECTUALS.
"..."
"...YOU DON'T HAVE TO TELL US IF YOU DON'T WANT TO."

READ THIS WAY

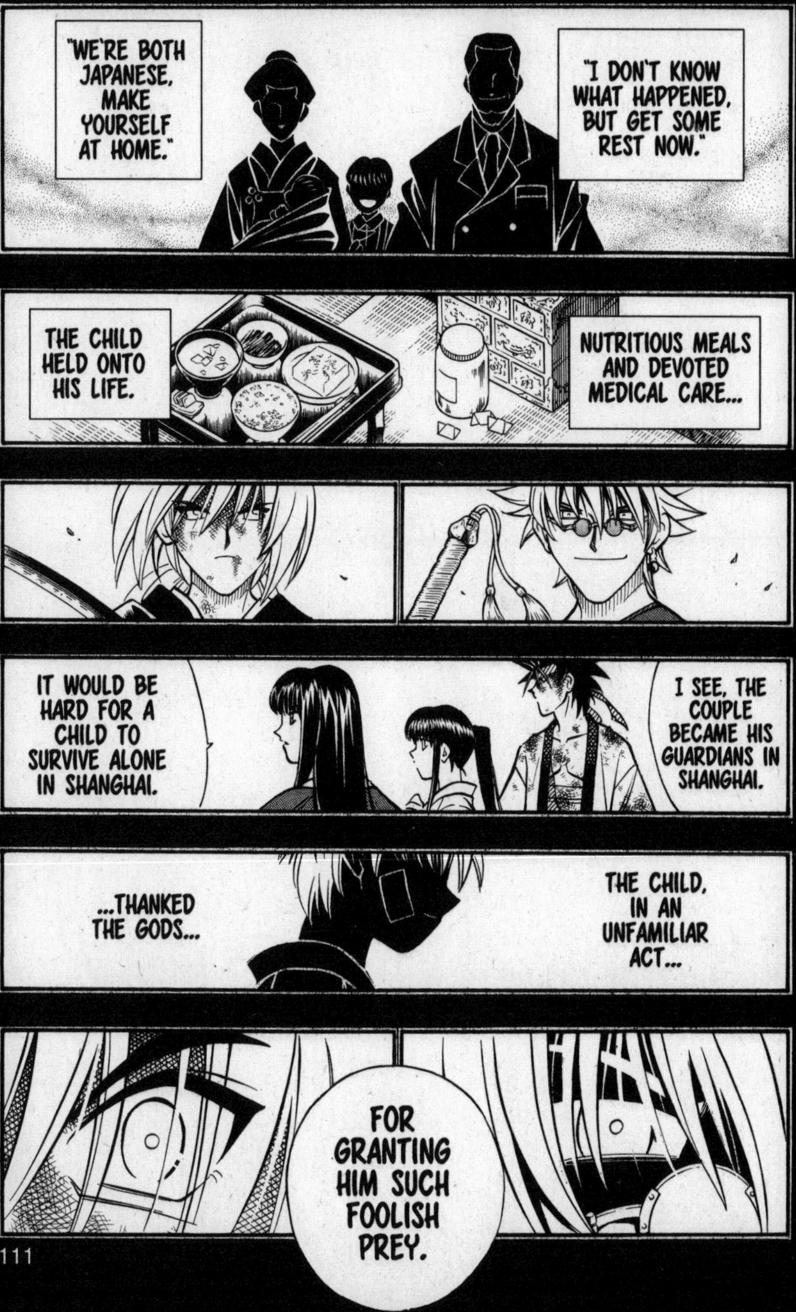
"I DON'T KNOW WHAT HAPPENED, BUT GET SOME REST NOW."
"WE'RE BOTH JAPANESE, MAKE YOURSELF AT HOME."
NUTRITIOUS MEALS AND DEVOTED MEDICAL CARE...
THE CHILD HELD ONTO HIS LIFE.
I SEE, THE COUPLE BECAME HIS GUARDIANS IN SHANGHAI.
IT WOULD BE HARD FOR A CHILD TO SURVIVE ALONE IN SHANGHAI.
THE CHILD, IN AN UNFAMILIAR ACT...
...THANKED THE GODS...
FOR GRANTING HIM SUCH FOOLISH PREY.

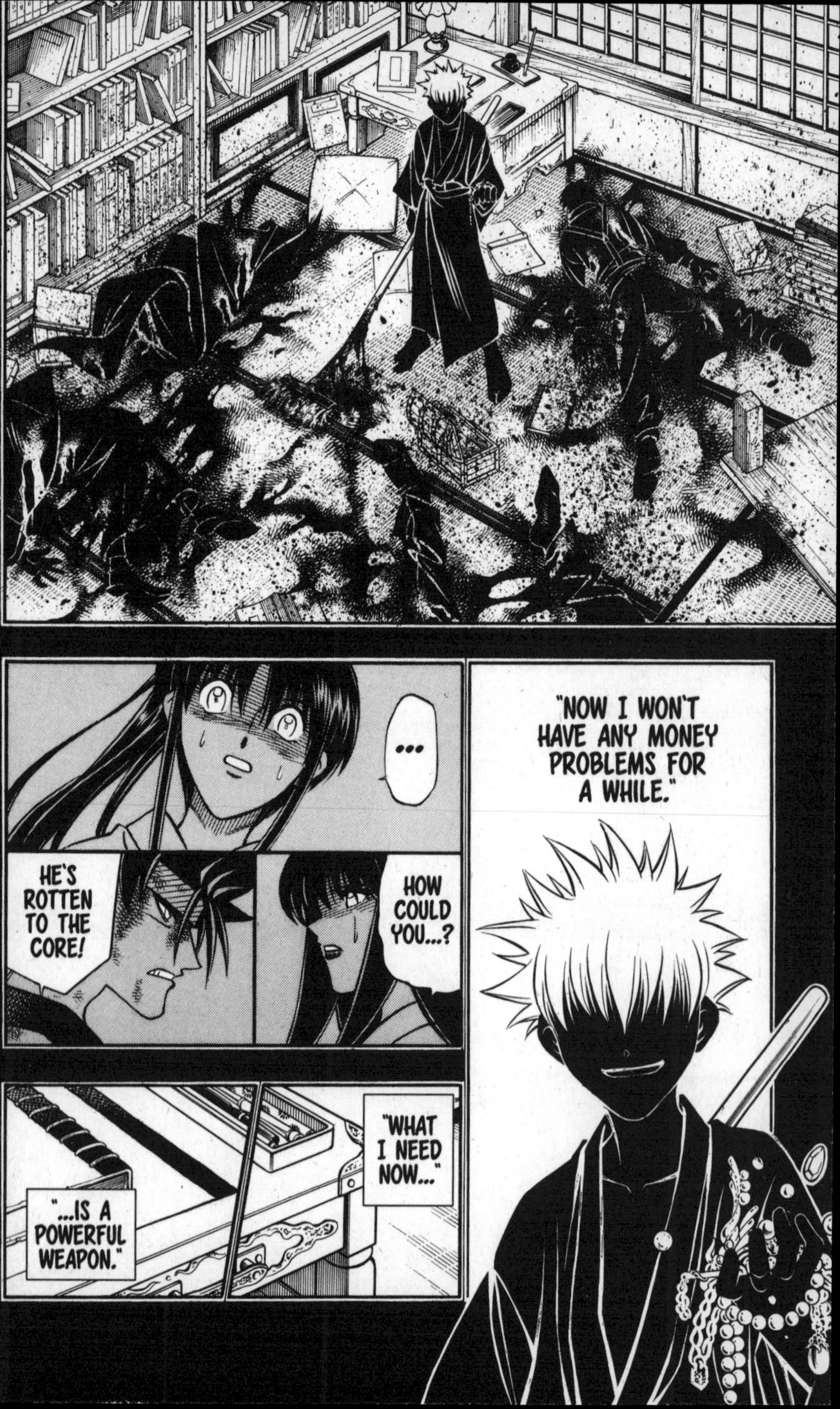
"NOW I WON'T HAVE ANY MONEY PROBLEMS FOR A WHILE."
...
HOW COULD YOU...?
HE'S ROTTEN TO THE CORE!
"WHAT I NEED NOW..."
"...IS A POWERFUL WEAPON."

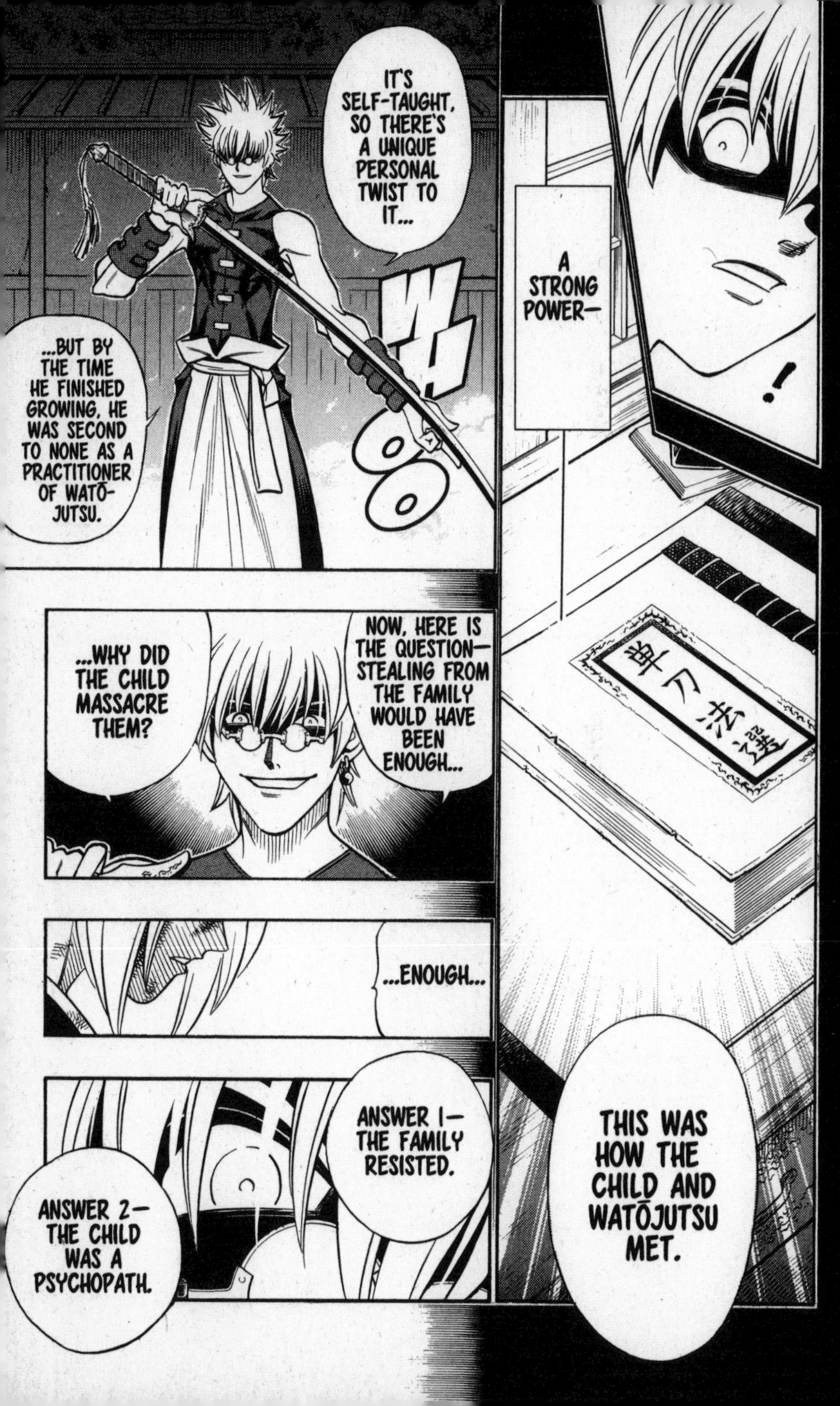
A STRONG POWER—
!
THIS WAS HOW THE CHILD AND WATŌJUTSU MET.
IT'S SELF-TAUGHT, SO THERE'S A UNIQUE PERSONAL TWIST TO IT...
...BUT BY THE TIME HE FINISHED GROWING, HE WAS SECOND TO NONE AS A PRACTITIONER OF WATŌ-JUTSU.
NOW, HERE IS THE QUESTION—STEALING FROM THE FAMILY WOULD HAVE BEEN ENOUGH...
...WHY DID THE CHILD MASSACRE THEM?
...ENOUGH...
ANSWER 1—THE FAMILY RESISTED.
ANSWER 2—THE CHILD WAS A PSYCHOPATH.

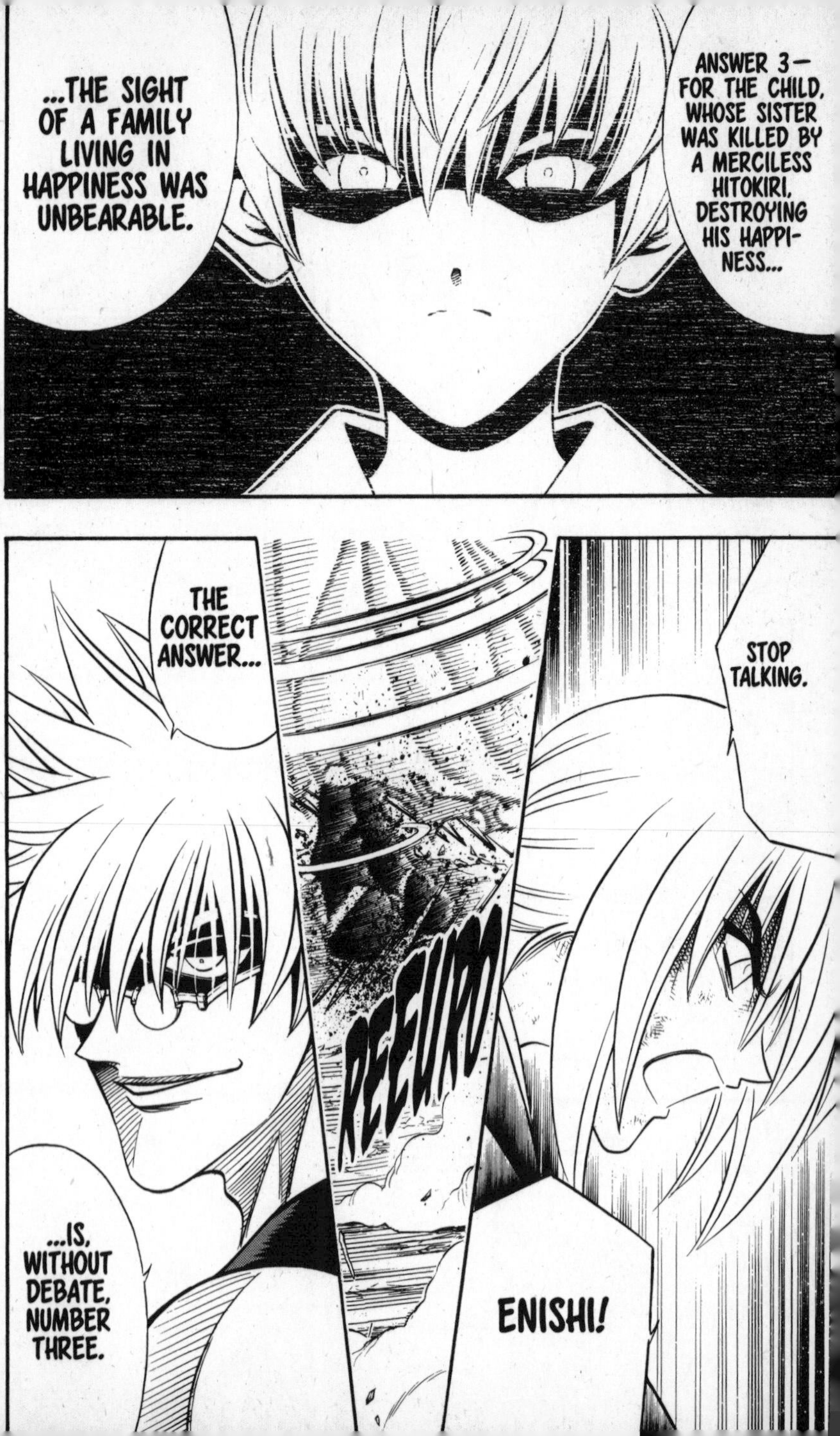
ANSWER 3— FOR THE CHILD, WHOSE SISTER WAS KILLED BY A MERCILESS HITOKIRI, DESTROYING HIS HAPPI- NESS...
...THE SIGHT OF A FAMILY LIVING IN HAPPINESS WAS UNBEARABLE.
STOP TALKING.
ENISHI!
THE CORRECT ANSWER...
...IS, WITHOUT DEBATE, NUMBER THREE.

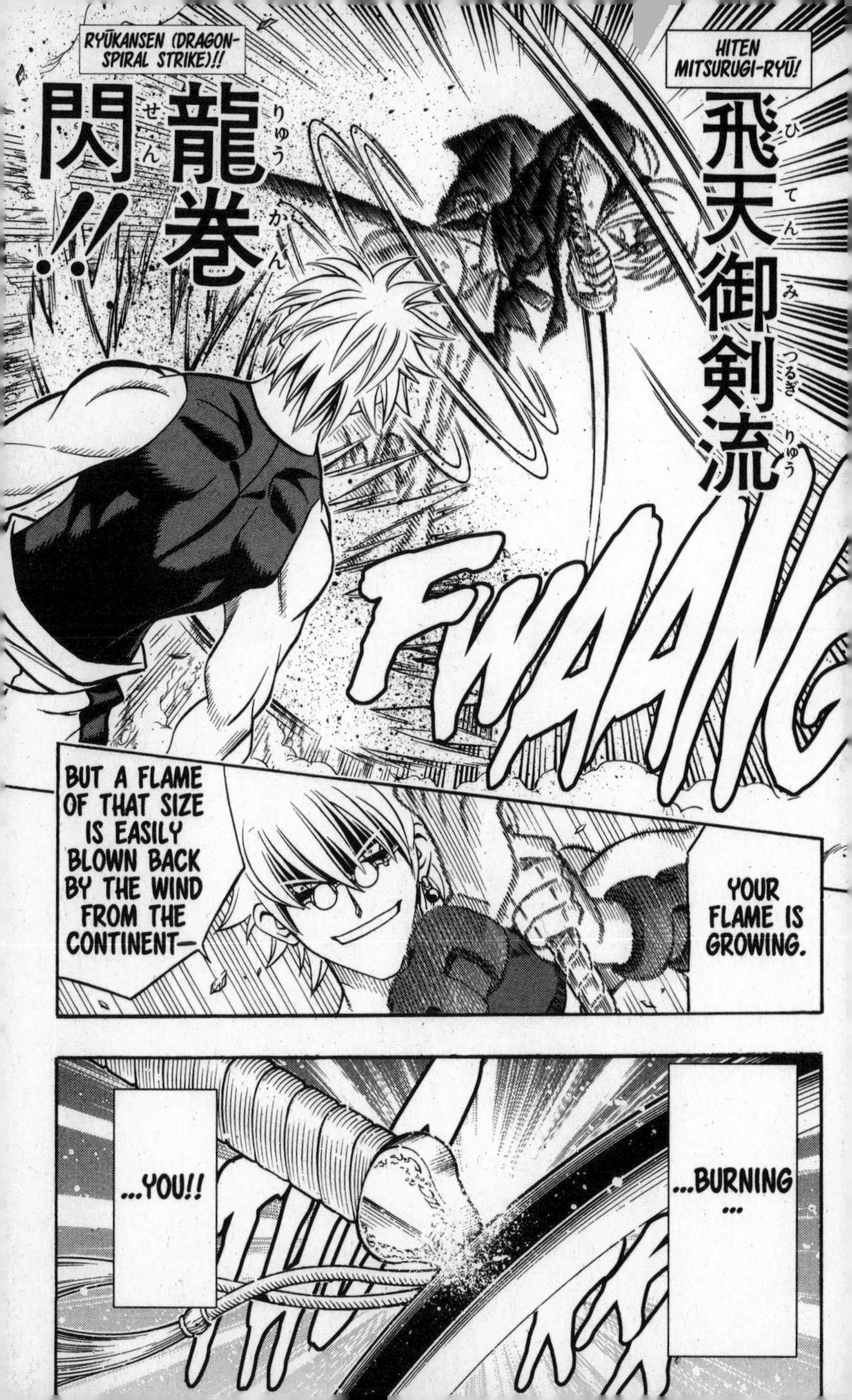
HITEN MITSURUGI-RYŪ!
飛天御剣流
RYŪKANSEN (DRAGON-SPIRAL STRIKE)!!
龍巻閃!!
FWANG
YOUR FLAME IS GROWING.
BUT A FLAME OF THAT SIZE IS EASILY BLOWN BACK BY THE WIND FROM THE CONTINENT—
...BURNING...
...YOU!!

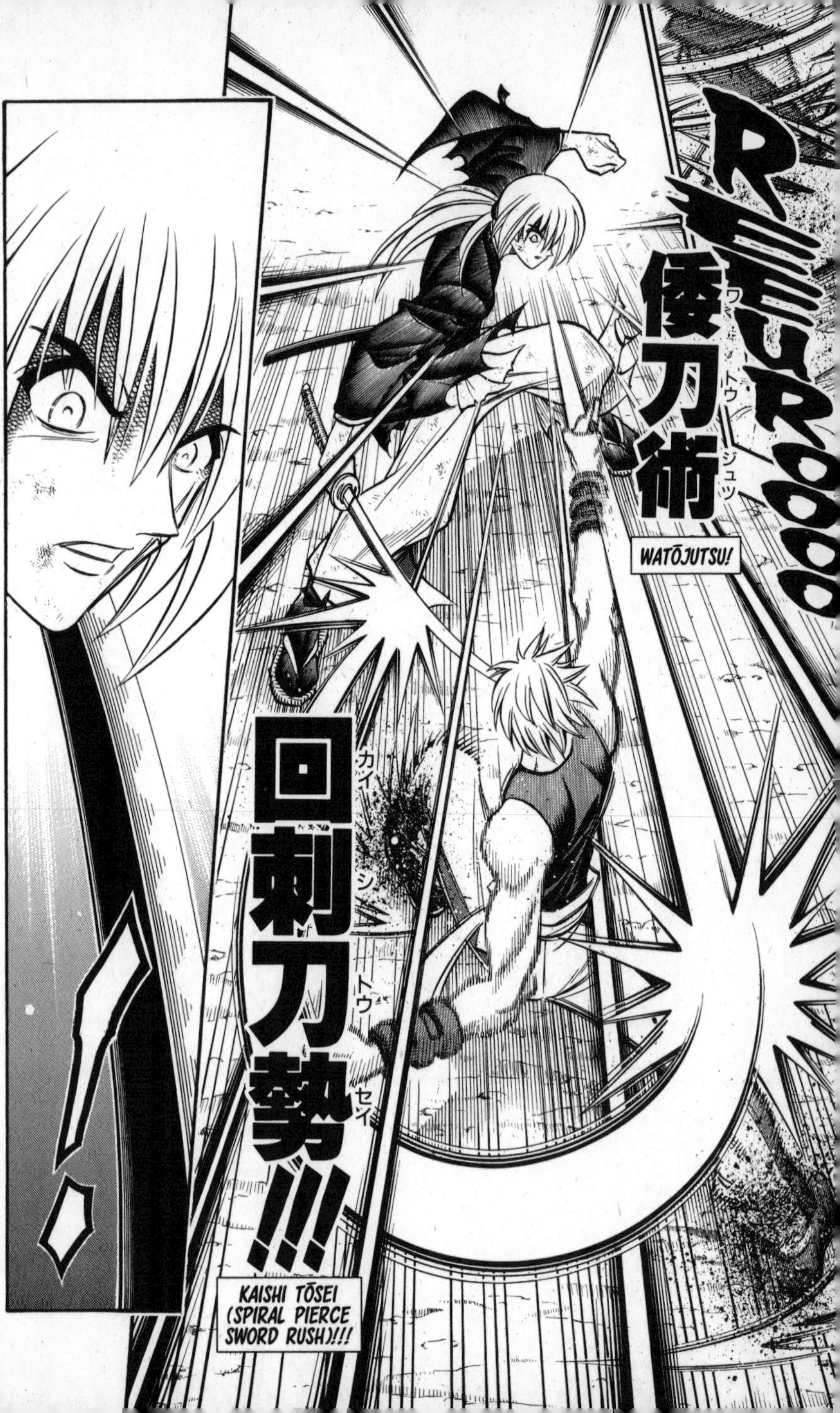
REEUROOOO
倭刀術
WATŌJUTSU!
回刺刀勢!!!
KAISHI TŌSEI (SPIRAL PIERCE SWORD RUSH)!!!

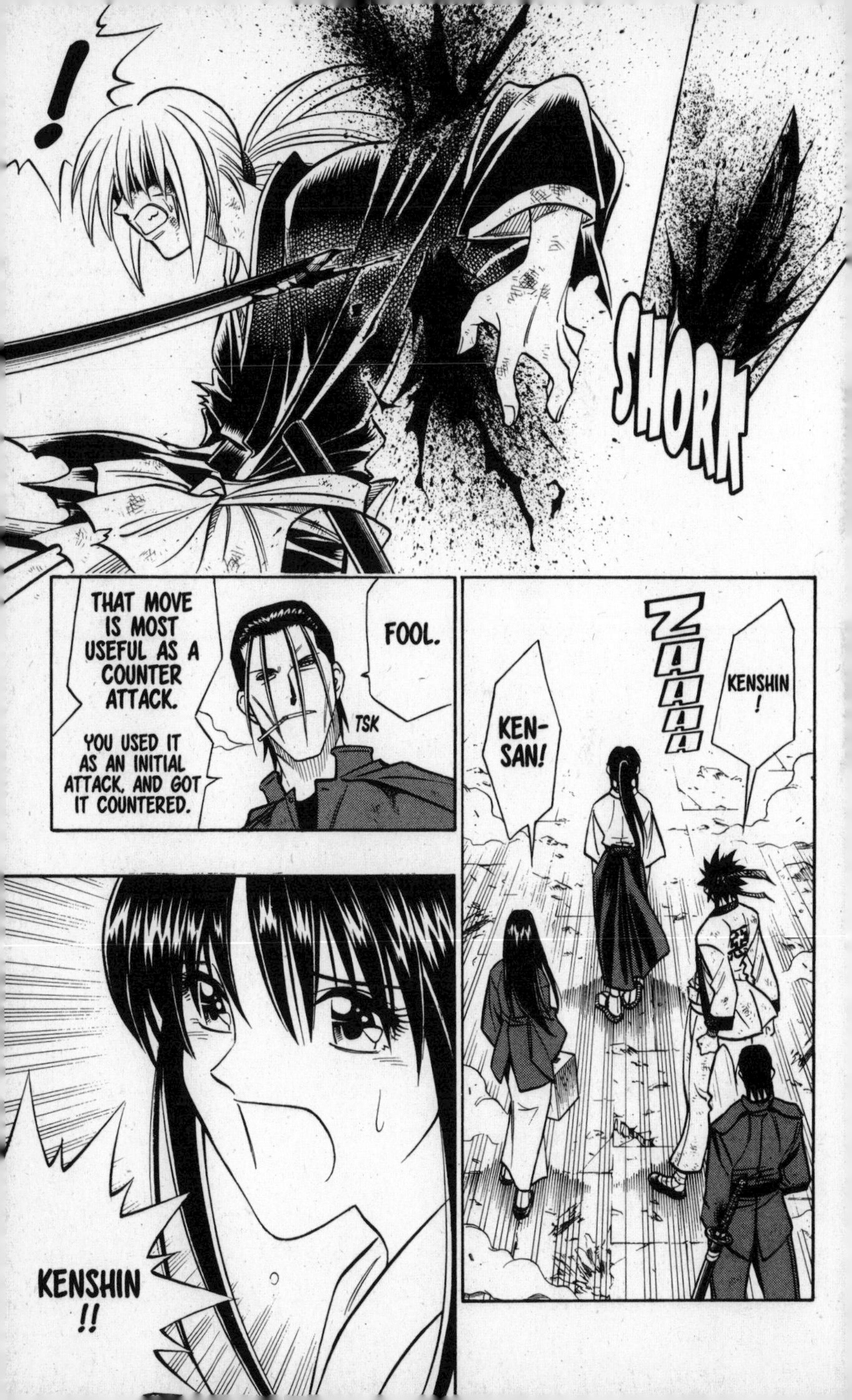
SHORK
!
KENSHIN!
ZAAAAA
KEN-SAN!
FOOL.
TSK
THAT MOVE IS MOST USEFUL AS A COUNTER ATTACK.
YOU USED IT AS AN INITIAL ATTACK, AND GOT IT COUNTERED.
KENSHIN!!

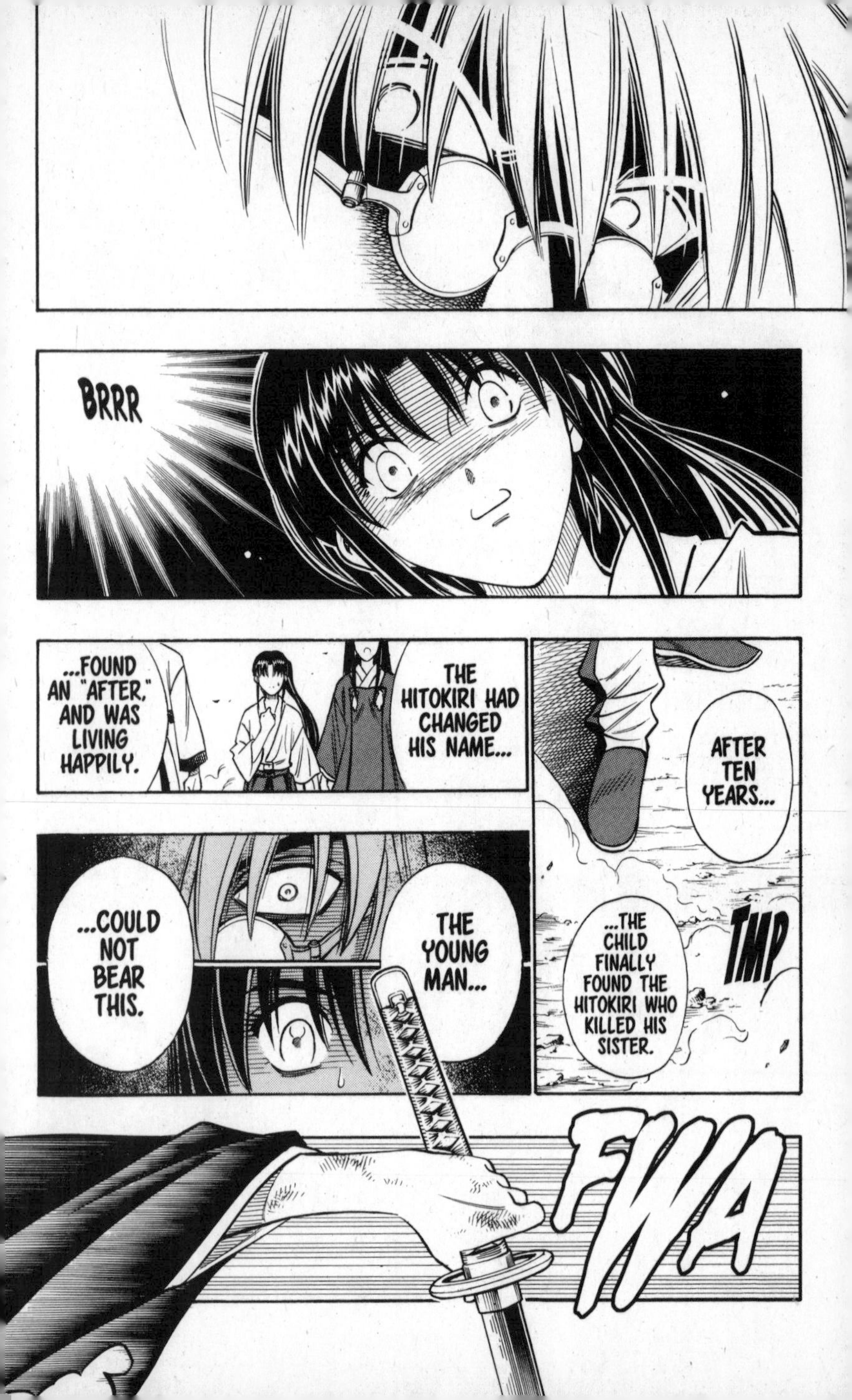
BRRR
AFTER TEN YEARS...
TMP
...THE CHILD FINALLY FOUND THE HITOKIRI WHO KILLED HIS SISTER.
THE HITOKIRI HAD CHANGED HIS NAME...
...FOUND AN "AFTER," AND WAS LIVING HAPPILY.
THE YOUNG MAN...
...COULD NOT BEAR THIS.
FWA

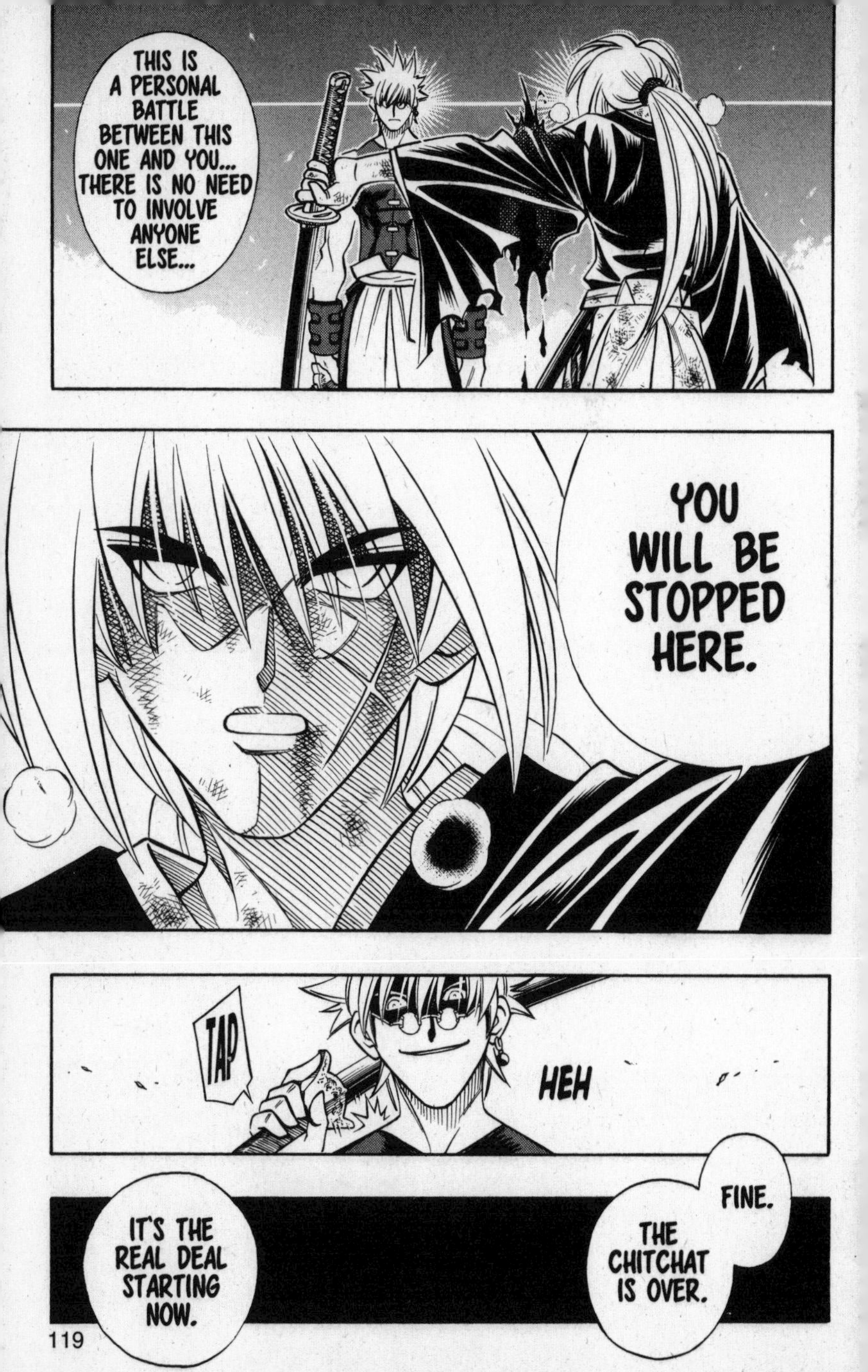
THIS IS A PERSONAL BATTLE BETWEEN THIS ONE AND YOU... THERE IS NO NEED TO INVOLVE ANYONE ELSE...
YOU WILL BE STOPPED HERE.
HEH
TAP
FINE.
THE CHITCHAT IS OVER.
IT'S THE REAL DEAL STARTING NOW.

Rurouni Kenshin

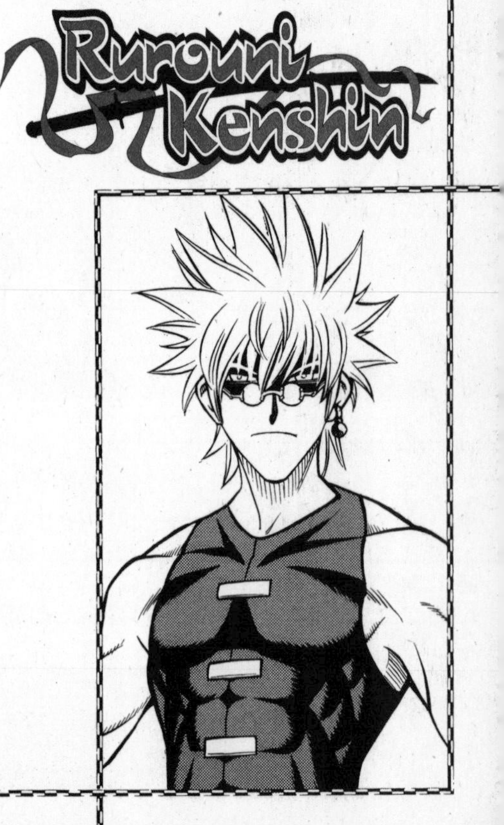

Act 203
A Pure and Simple End to a 15-Year Duel

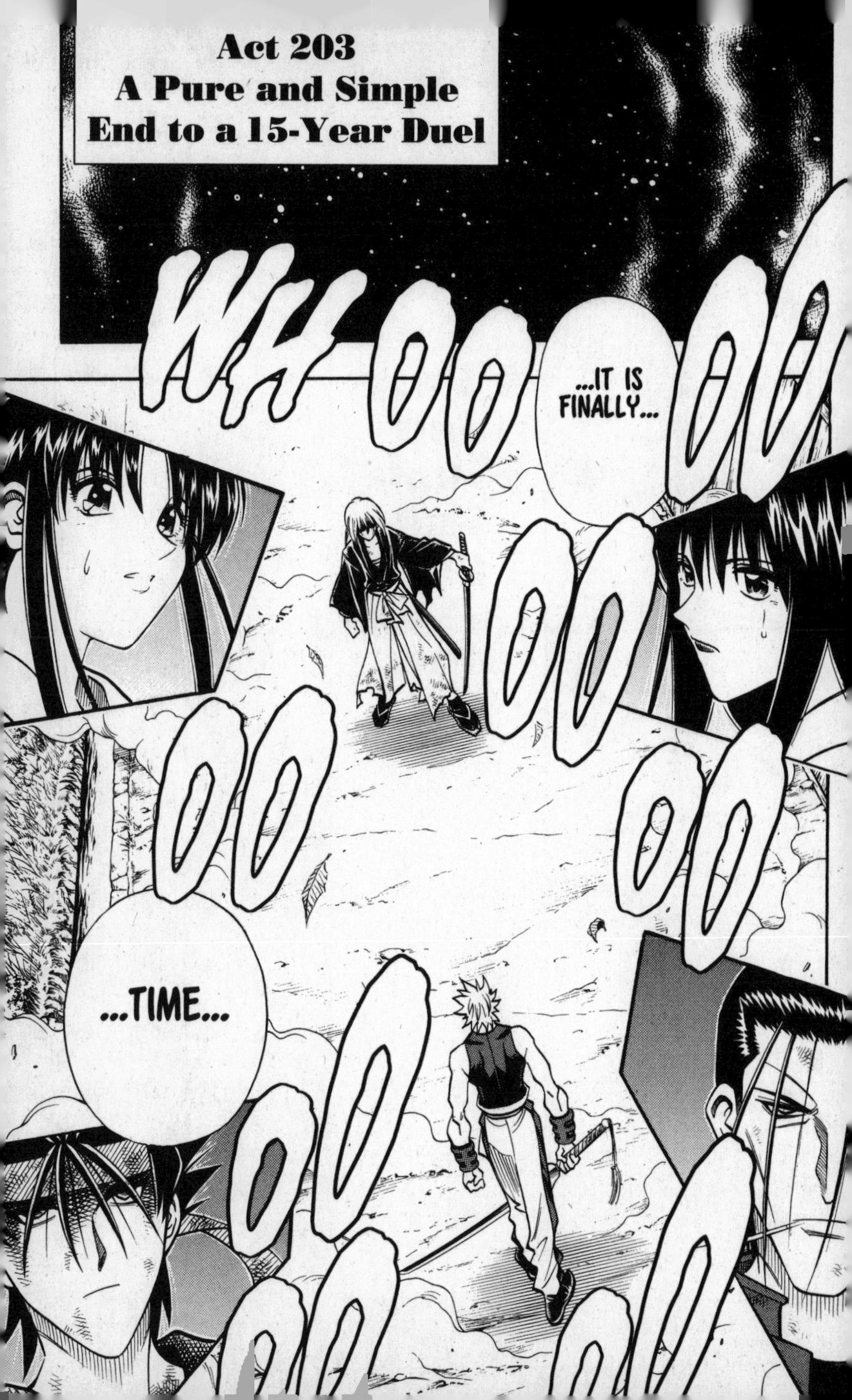

WHOOOOOOOOOOOOOOOOOO
...IT IS FINALLY...
...TIME...

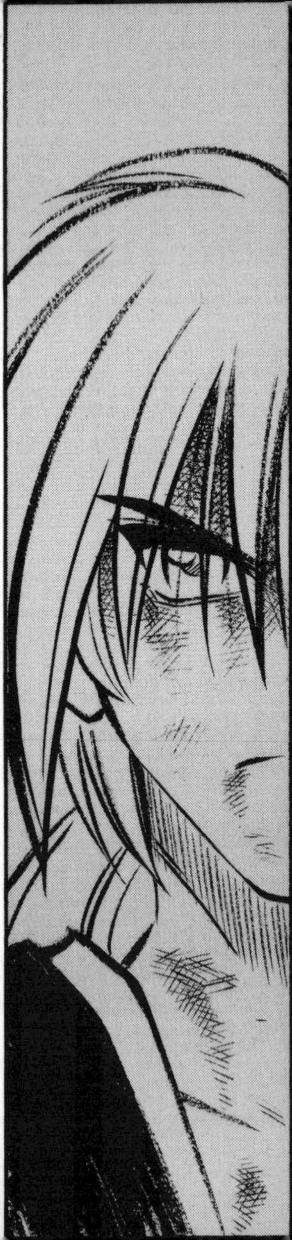

Act 203

A Pure and Simple End to a 15-Year Duel

伸宏和月

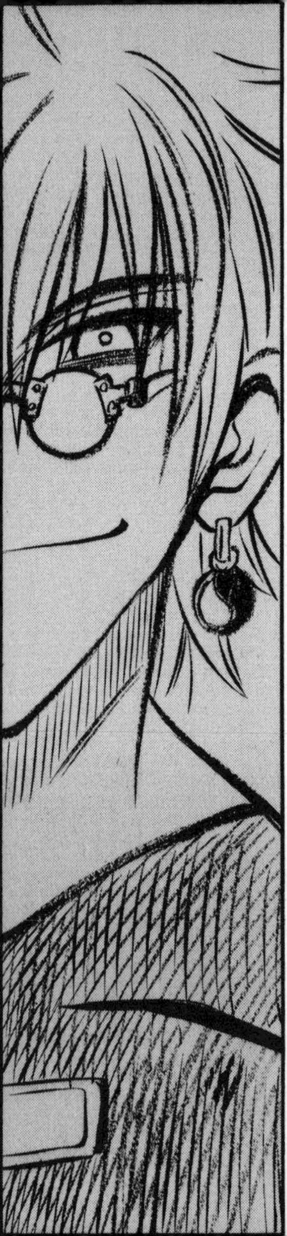

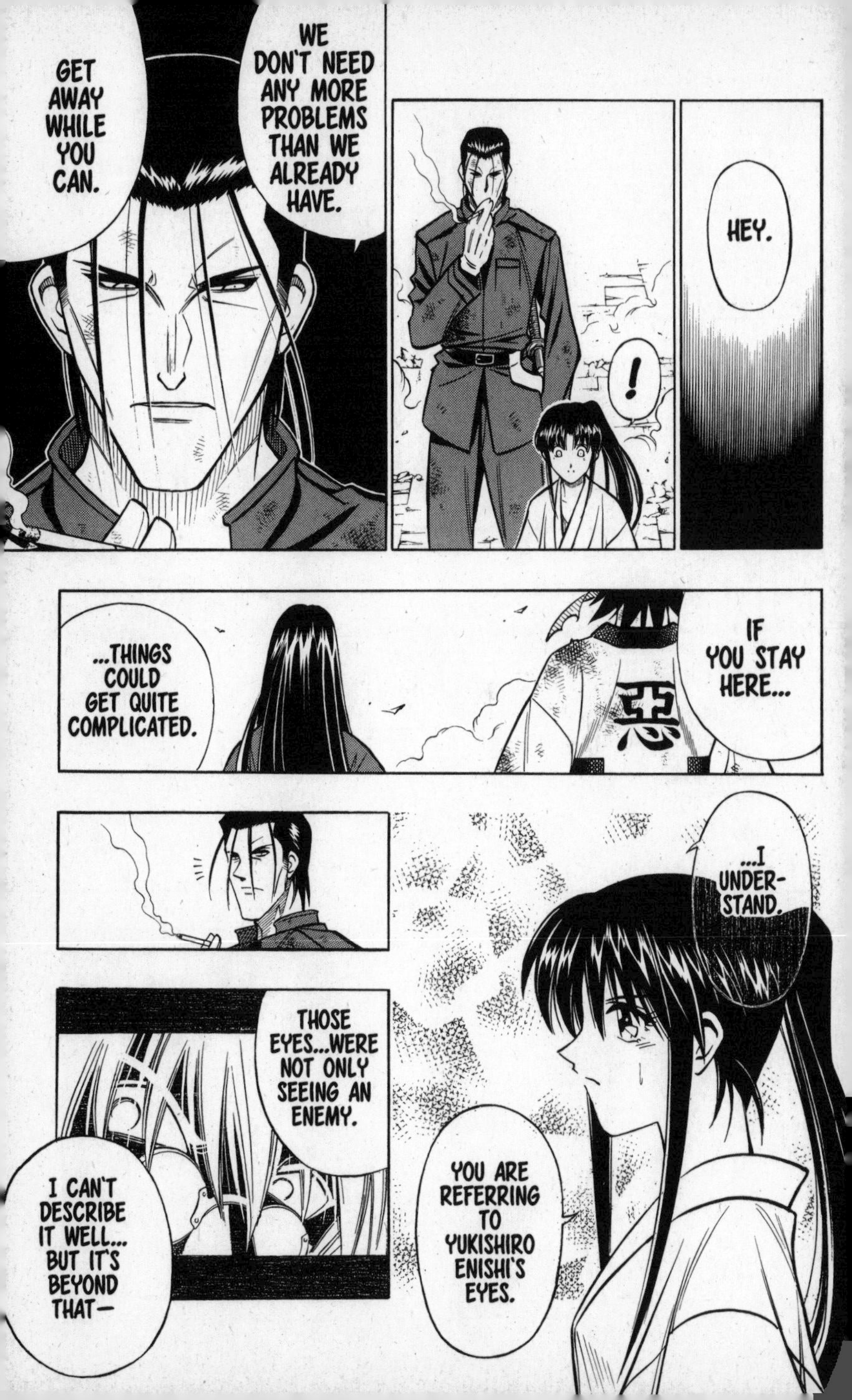
HEY.
!
WE DON'T NEED ANY MORE PROBLEMS THAN WE ALREADY HAVE.
GET AWAY WHILE YOU CAN.
IF YOU STAY HERE...
...THINGS COULD GET QUITE COMPLICATED.
...I UNDER-STAND.
YOU ARE REFERRING TO YUKISHIRO ENISHI'S EYES.
THOSE EYES...WERE NOT ONLY SEEING AN ENEMY.
I CAN'T DESCRIBE IT WELL... BUT IT'S BEYOND THAT—

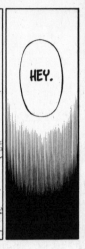

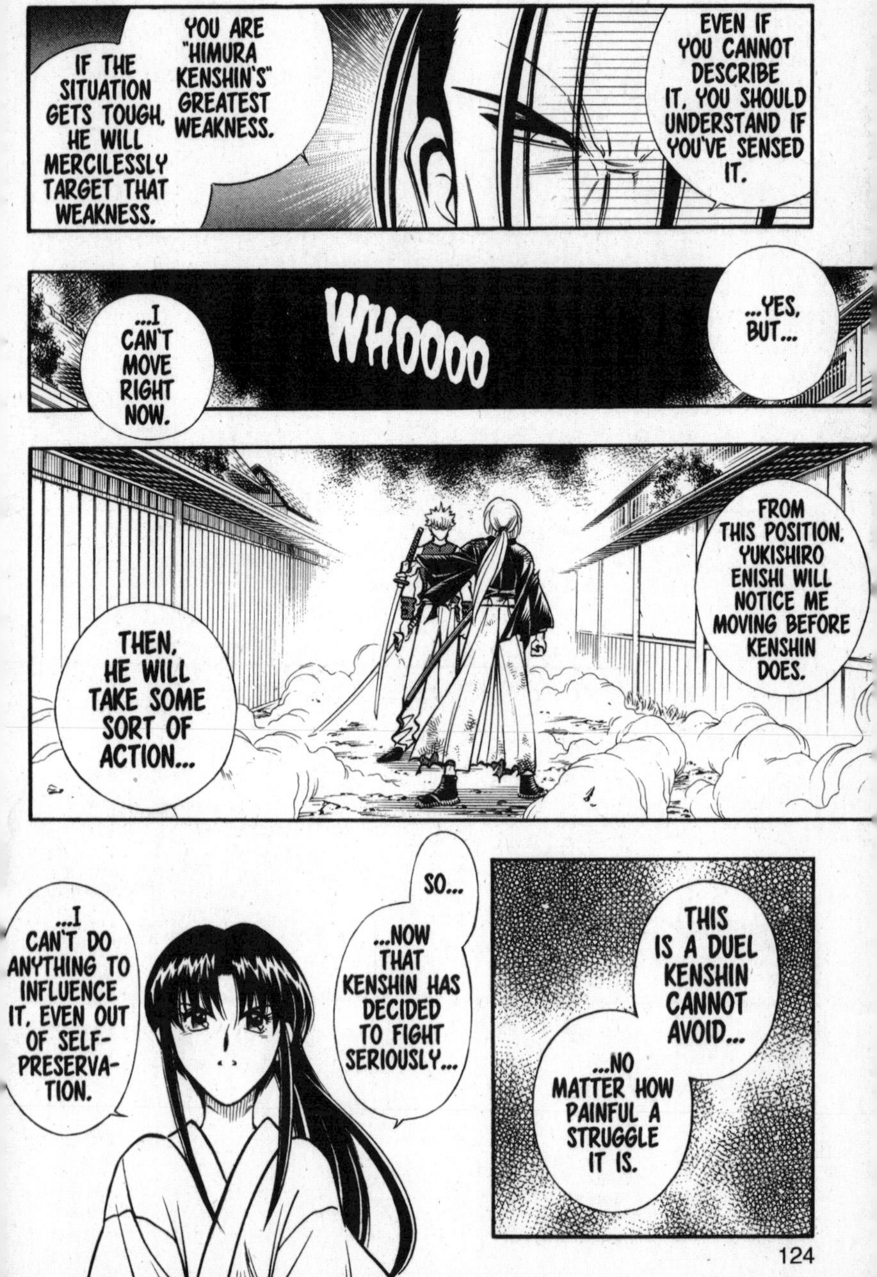
EVEN IF YOU CANNOT DESCRIBE IT, YOU SHOULD UNDERSTAND IF YOU'VE SENSED IT.
YOU ARE "HIMURA KENSHIN'S" GREATEST WEAKNESS.
IF THE SITUATION GETS TOUGH, HE WILL MERCILESSLY TARGET THAT WEAKNESS.
...YES, BUT...
WHOOOO
...I CAN'T MOVE RIGHT NOW.
FROM THIS POSITION, YUKISHIRO ENISHI WILL NOTICE ME MOVING BEFORE KENSHIN DOES.
THEN, HE WILL TAKE SOME SORT OF ACTION...
THIS IS A DUEL KENSHIN CANNOT AVOID...
...NO MATTER HOW PAINFUL A STRUGGLE IT IS.
SO...
...NOW THAT KENSHIN HAS DECIDED TO FIGHT SERIOUSLY...
...I CAN'T DO ANYTHING TO INFLUENCE IT, EVEN OUT OF SELF-PRESERVATION.

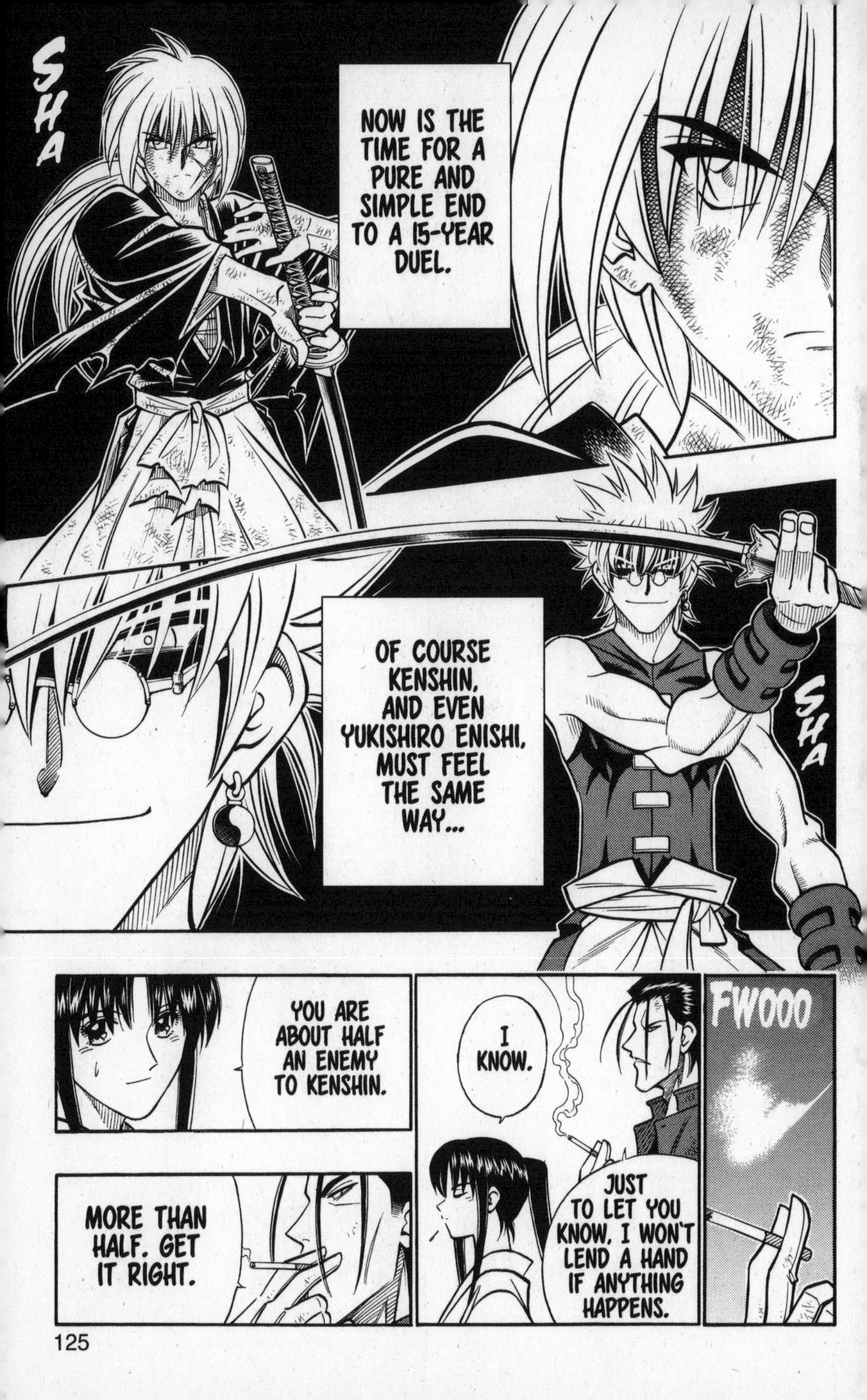
NOW IS THE TIME FOR A PURE AND SIMPLE END TO A 15-YEAR DUEL.
SHA
OF COURSE KENSHIN, AND EVEN YUKISHIRO ENISHI, MUST FEEL THE SAME WAY...
SHA
FWOOO
I KNOW.
JUST TO LET YOU KNOW, I WON'T LEND A HAND IF ANYTHING HAPPENS.
YOU ARE ABOUT HALF AN ENEMY TO KENSHIN.
MORE THAN HALF. GET IT RIGHT.

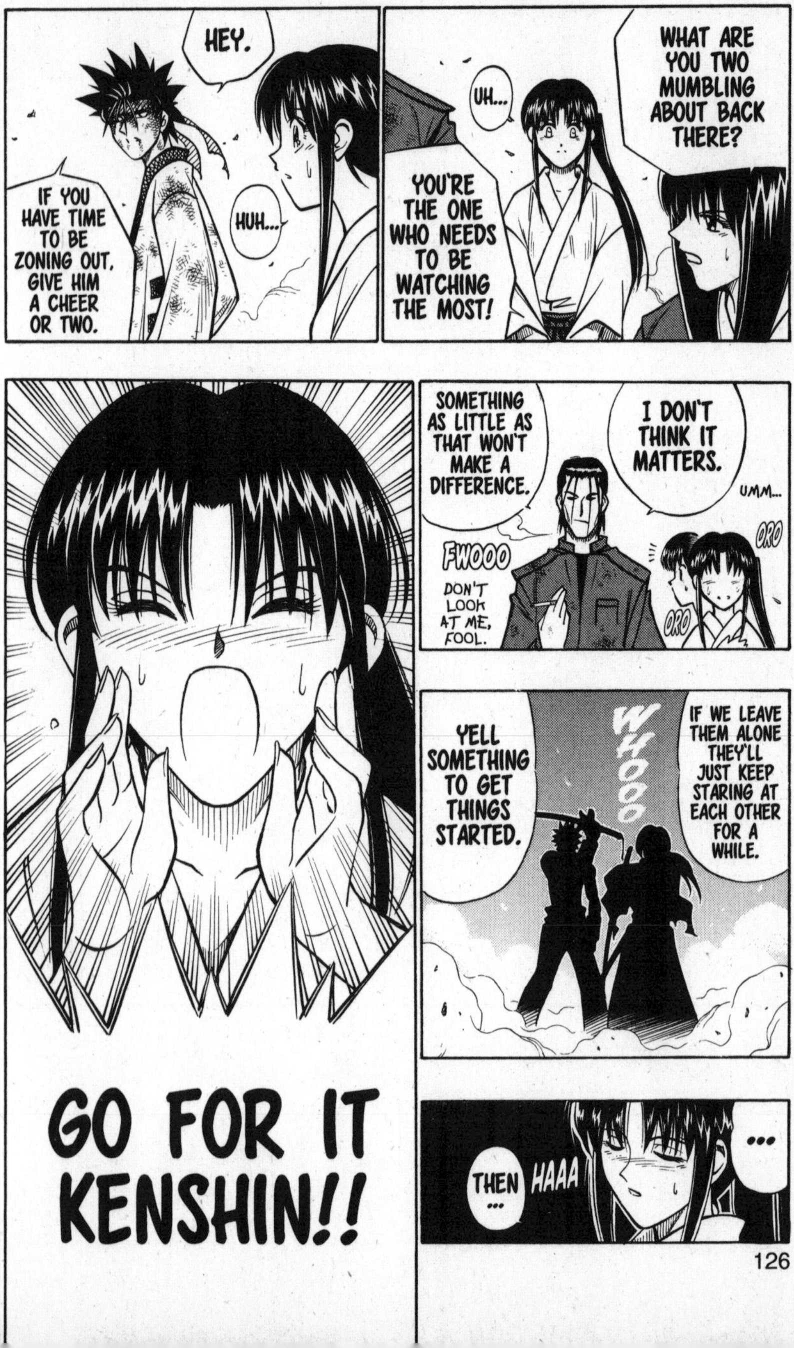
WHAT ARE YOU TWO MUMBLING ABOUT BACK THERE?
UH...
YOU'RE THE ONE WHO NEEDS TO BE WATCHING THE MOST!
HEY.
HUH...
IF YOU HAVE TIME TO BE ZONING OUT, GIVE HIM A CHEER OR TWO.
I DON'T THINK IT MATTERS.
UMM...
ORO
SOMETHING AS LITTLE AS THAT WON'T MAKE A DIFFERENCE.
FWOOO
DON'T LOOK AT ME, FOOL.
ORO
IF WE LEAVE THEM ALONE THEY'LL JUST KEEP STARING AT EACH OTHER FOR A WHILE.
WHOOO
YELL SOMETHING TO GET THINGS STARTED.
...
HAAA
THEN ...
GO FOR IT KENSHIN!!

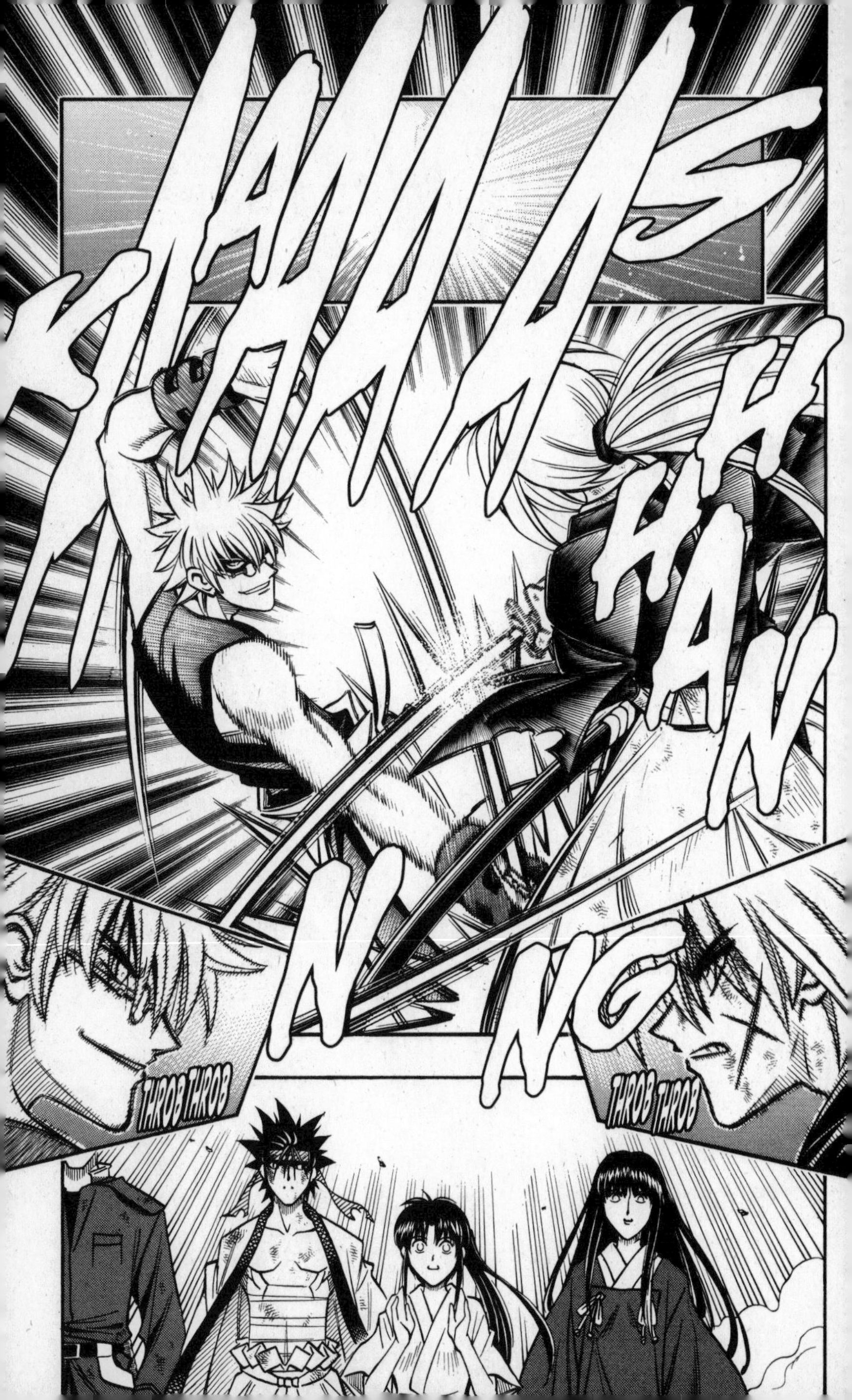
THROB THROB
THROB THROB

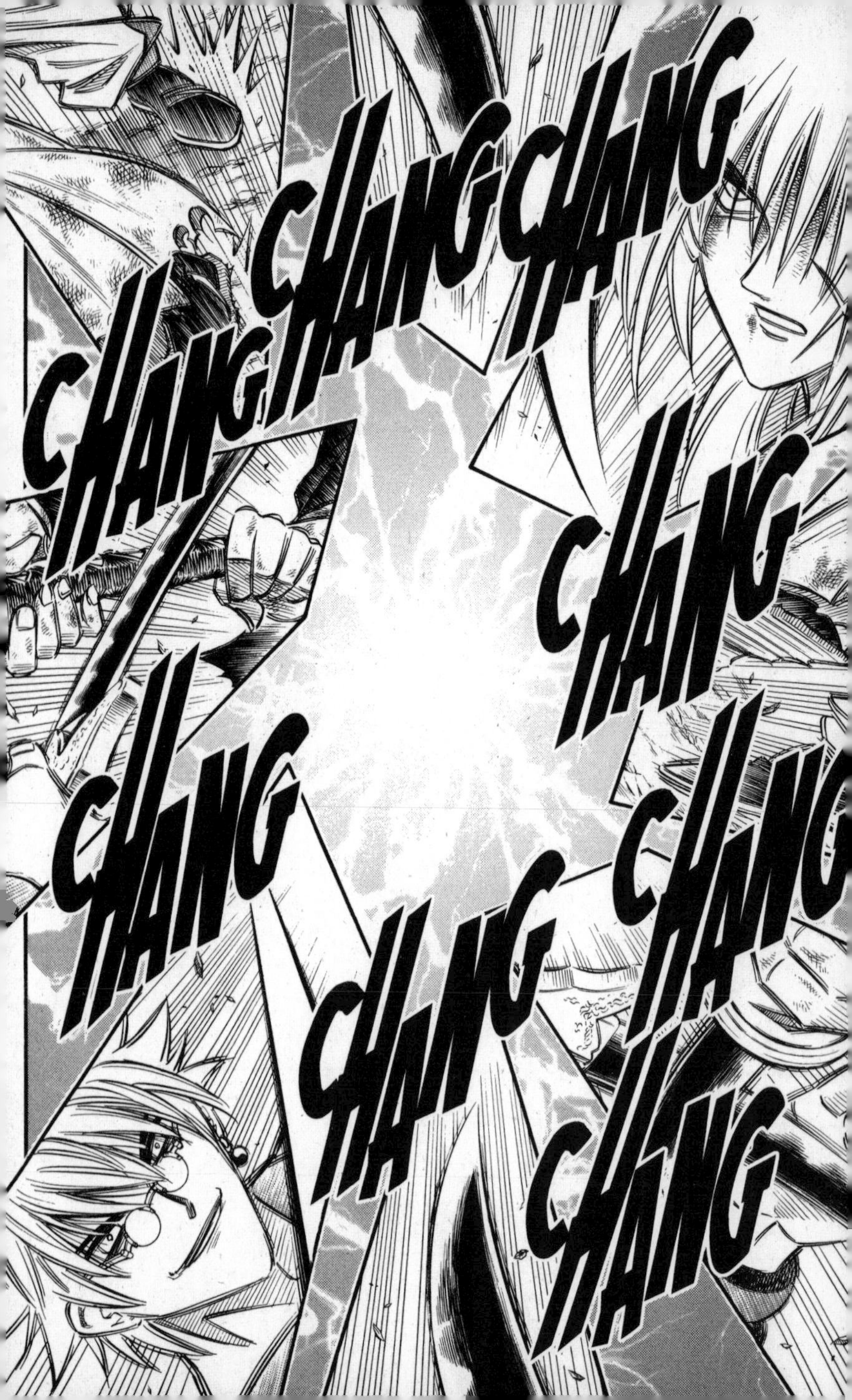
CHANG CHANG CHANG
CHANG
CHANG
CHANG
CHANG
CHANG
CHANG

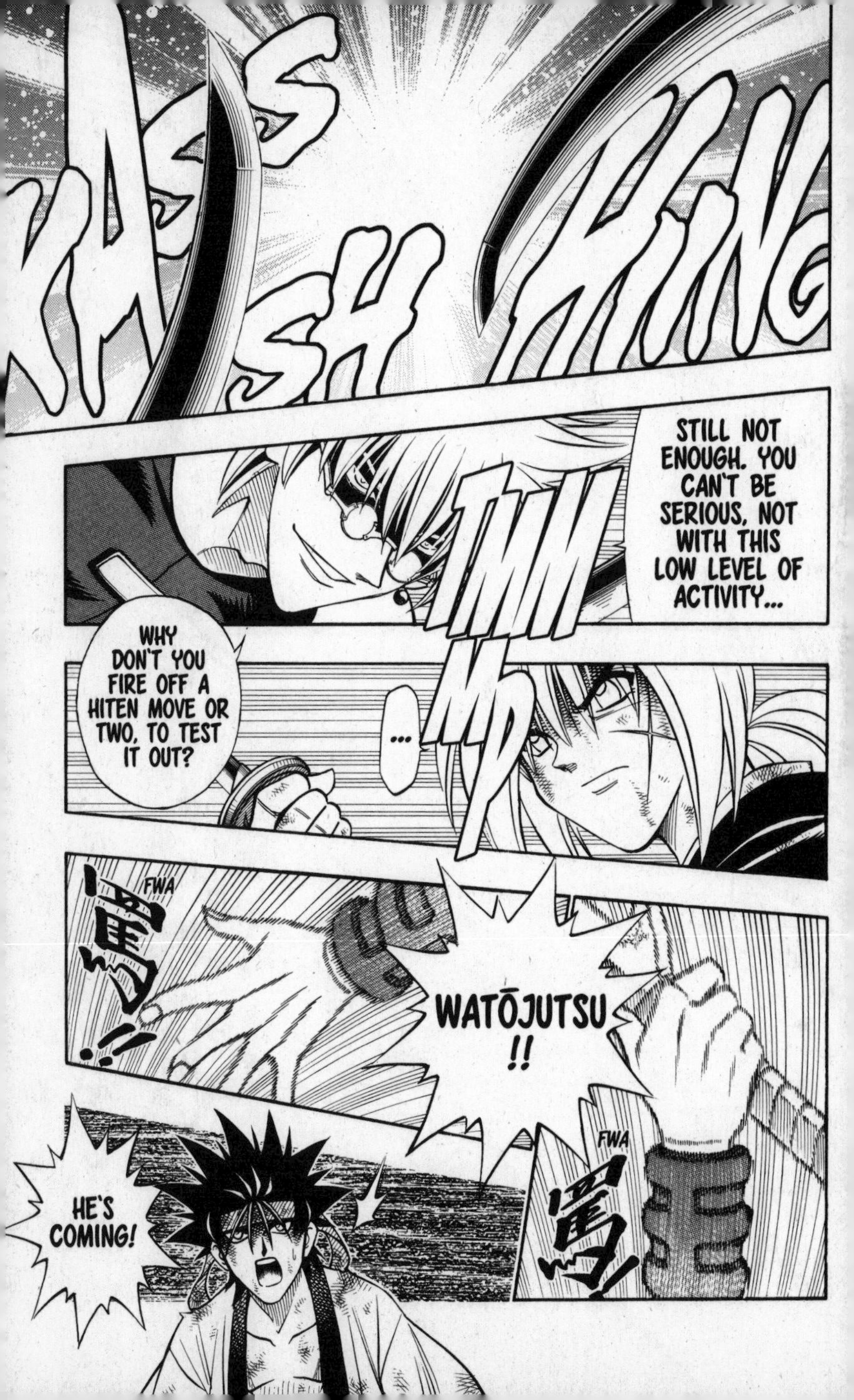
KASHHING
STILL NOT ENOUGH. YOU CAN'T BE SERIOUS, NOT WITH THIS LOW LEVEL OF ACTIVITY...
THMMP
WHY DON'T YOU FIRE OFF A HITEN MOVE OR TWO, TO TEST IT OUT?
...
FWA
WATŌJUTSU!!
FWA
HE'S COMING!

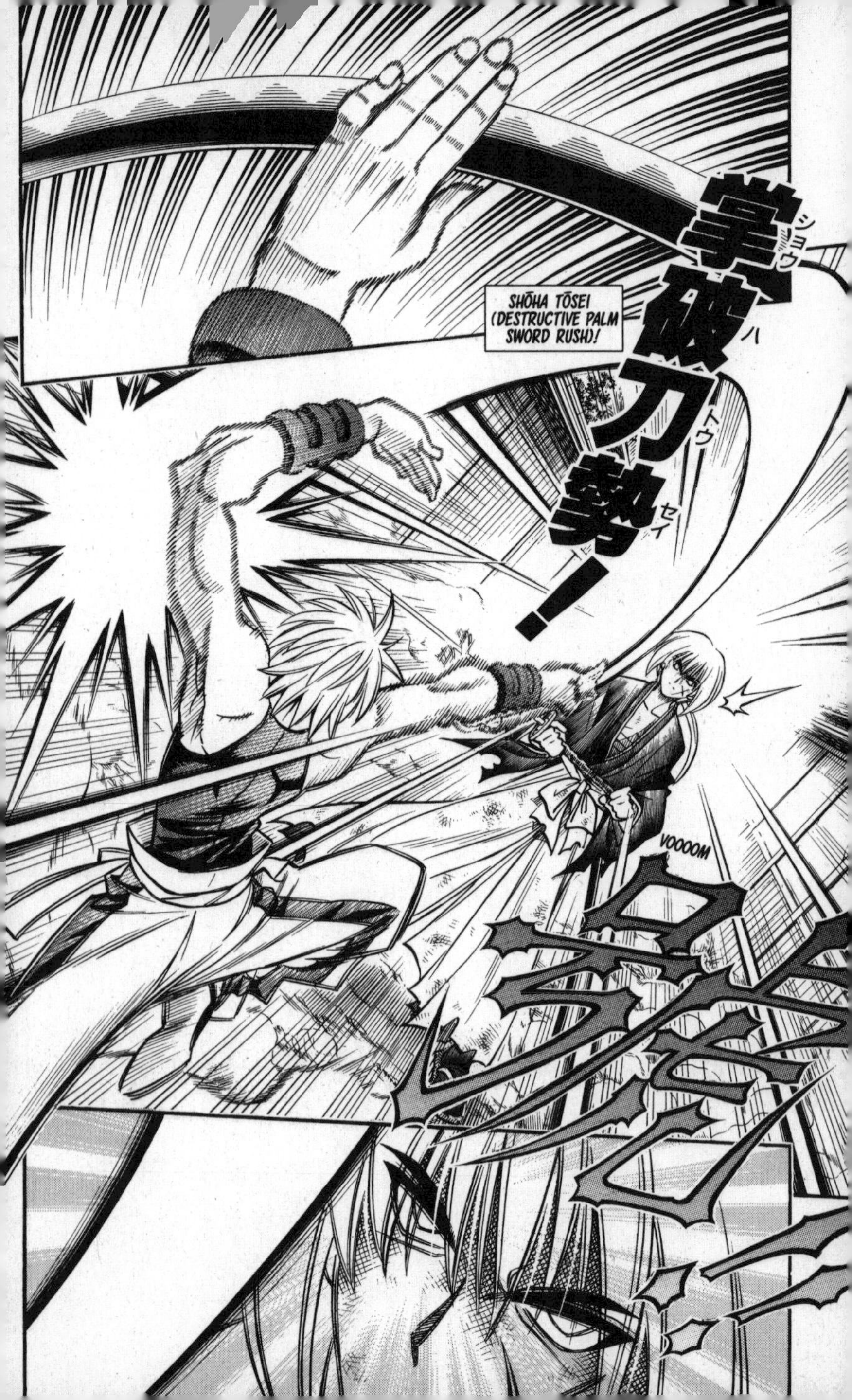
掌破刀勢!
SHŌHA TŌSEI (DESTRUCTIVE PALM SWORD RUSH)!
VOOOOM

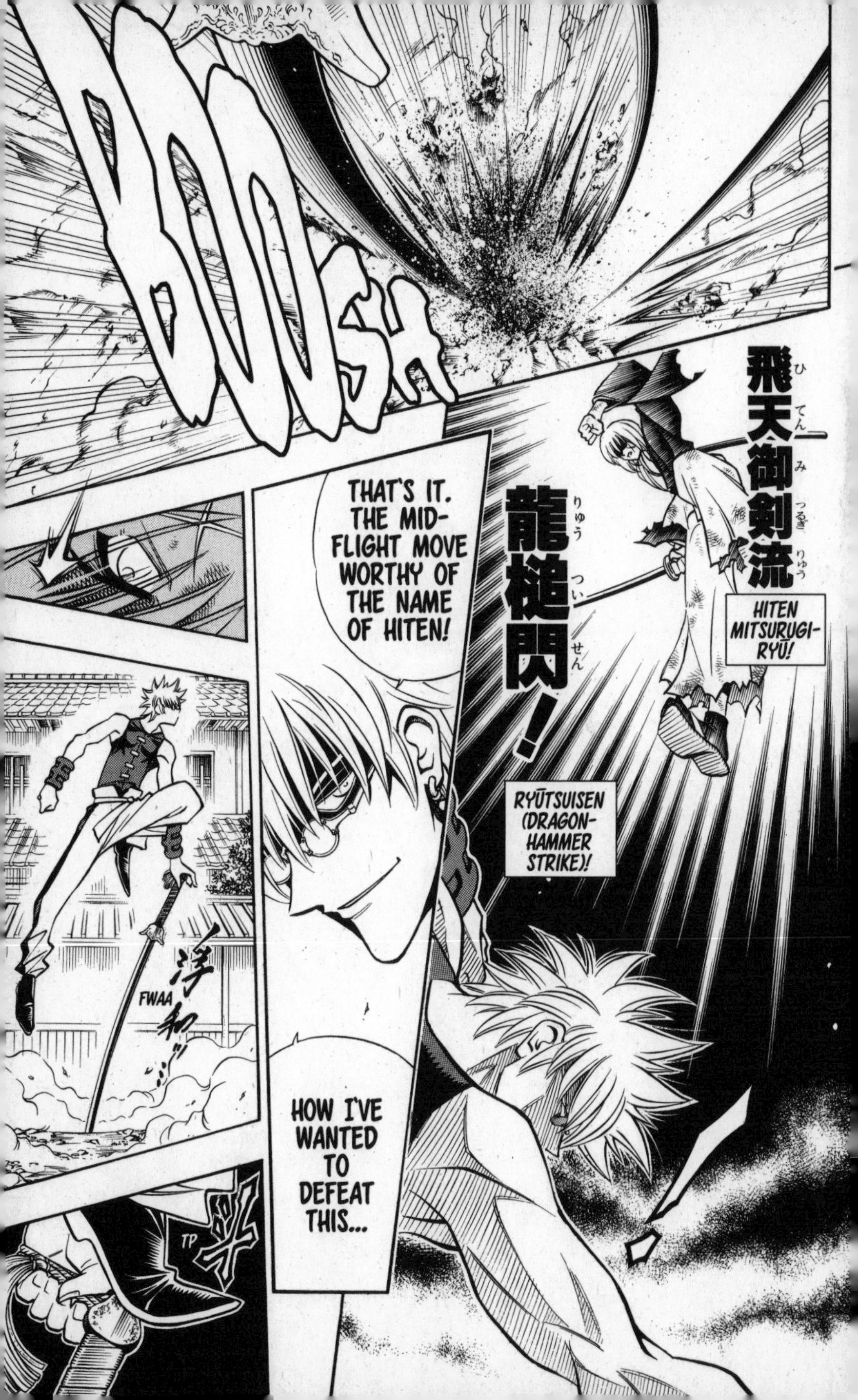
BOOSH
飛天御剣流
HITEN MITSURUGI-RYŪ!
龍槌閃!
RYŪTSUISEN (DRAGON-HAMMER STRIKE)!
THAT'S IT. THE MID-FLIGHT MOVE WORTHY OF THE NAME OF HITEN!
FWAA
HOW I'VE WANTED TO DEFEAT THIS...
TP

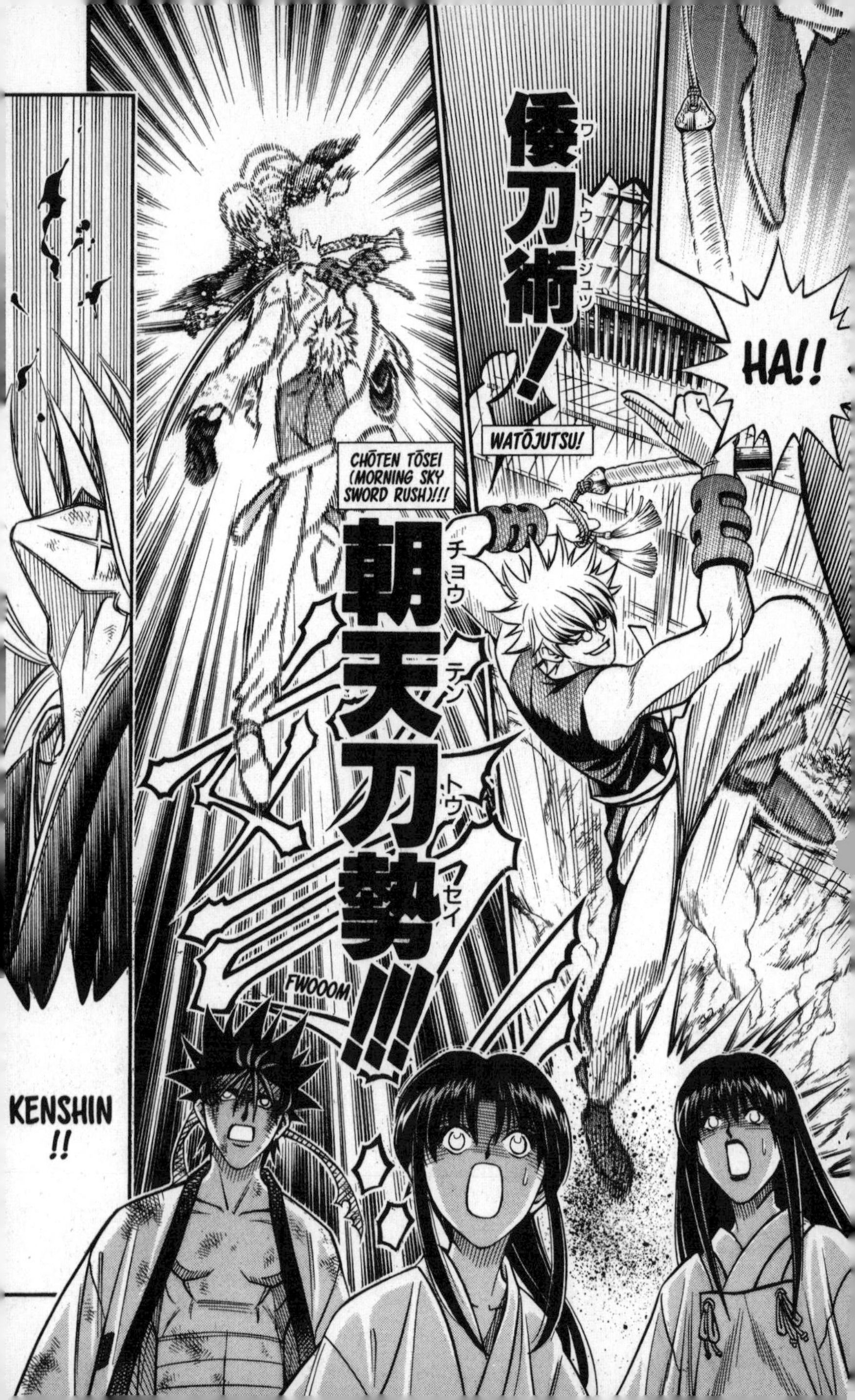
HA!!
倭刀術!
WATŌJUTSU!
CHŌTEN TŌSEI (MORNING SKY SWORD RUSH)!!!
朝天刀勢!!!
FWOOOM
KENSHIN !!

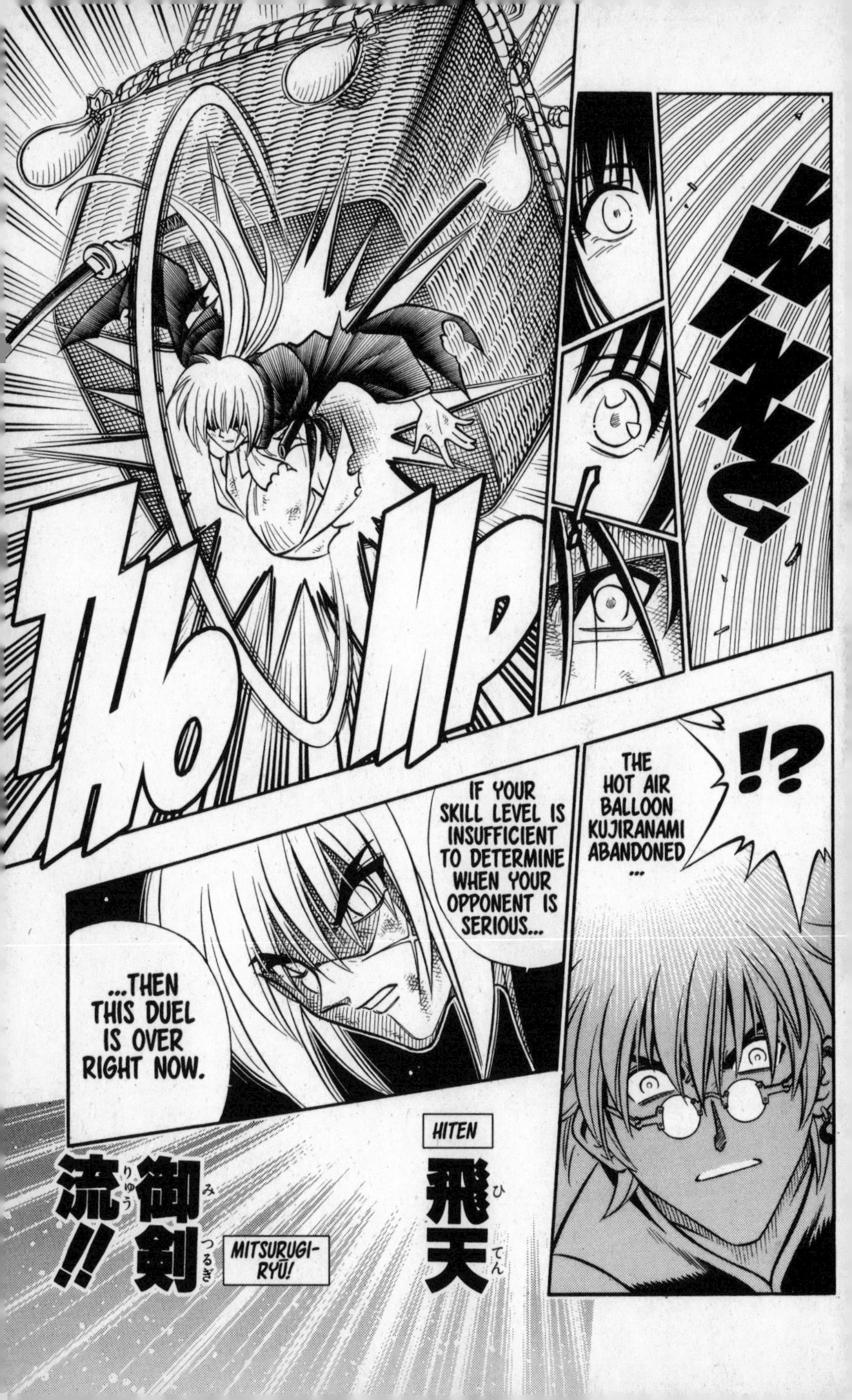
THOMP
!?
THE HOT AIR BALLOON KUJIRANAMI ABANDONED...
IF YOUR SKILL LEVEL IS INSUFFICIENT TO DETERMINE WHEN YOUR OPPONENT IS SERIOUS...
...THEN THIS DUEL IS OVER RIGHT NOW.
HITEN
飛天
MITSURUGI-RYŪ!
御剣流!!

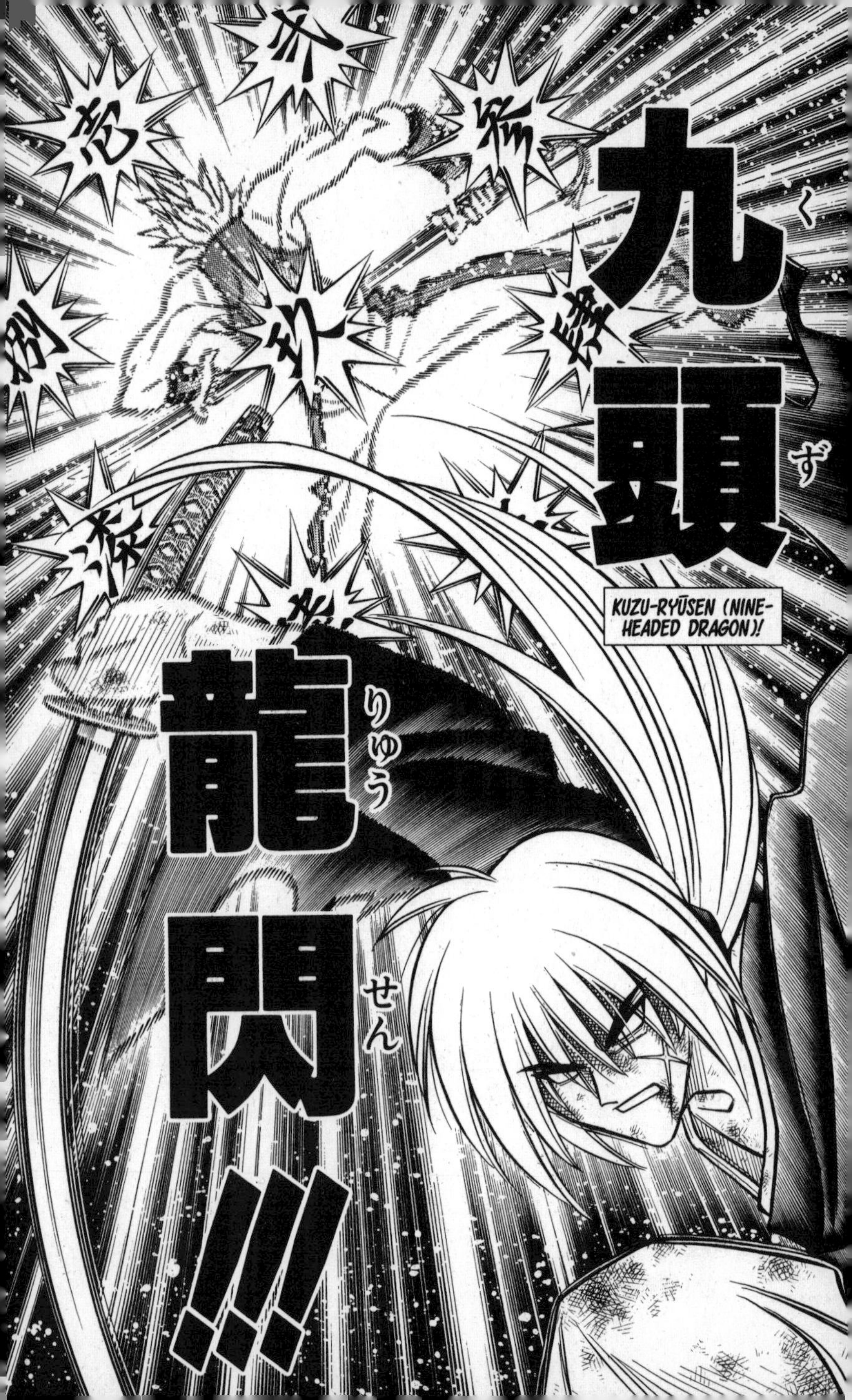
九頭龍閃!!!
KUZU-RYŪSEN (NINE-HEADED DRAGON)!

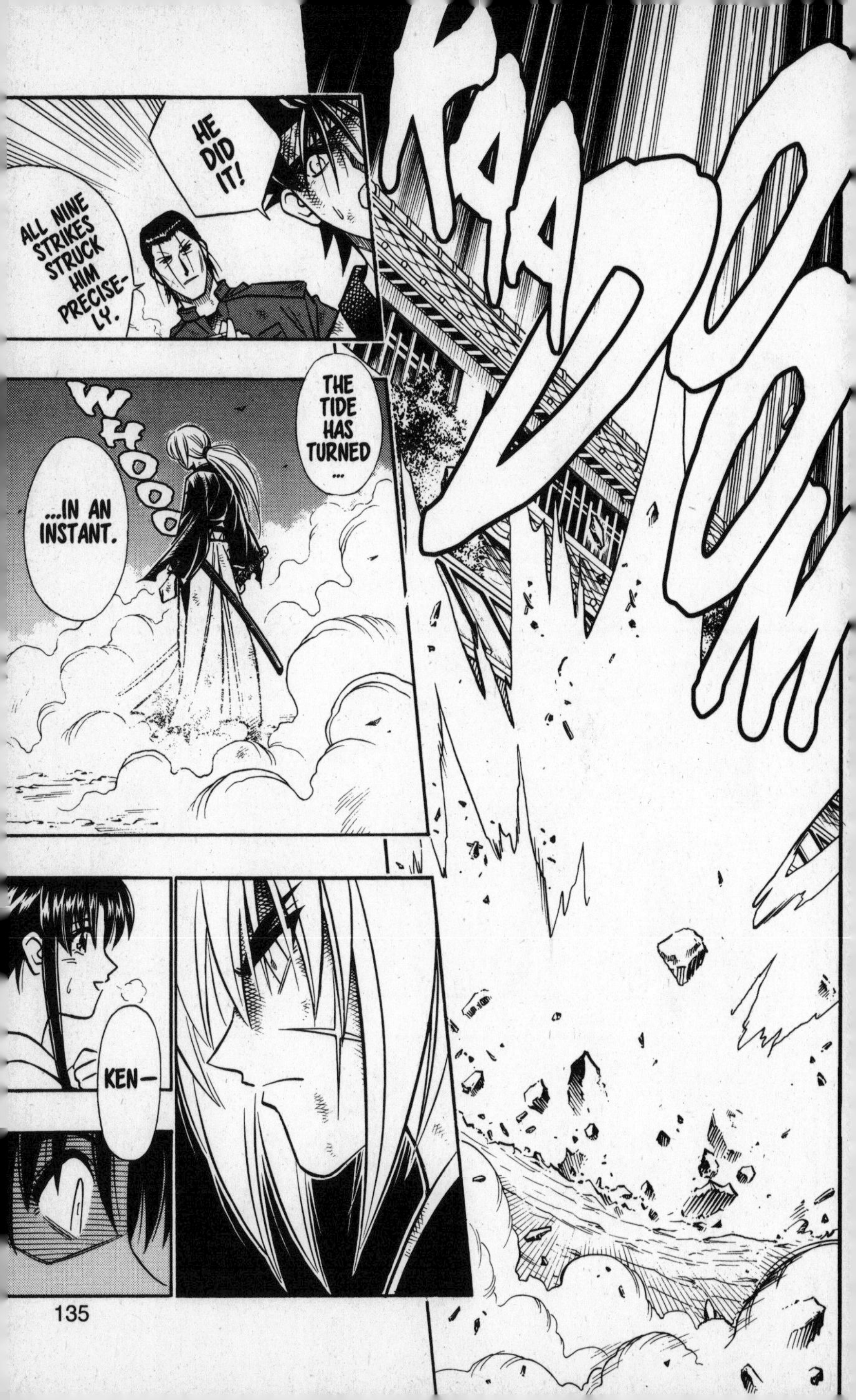
KADOOM
HE DID IT!
ALL NINE STRIKES STRUCK HIM PRECISE-LY.
THE TIDE HAS TURNED ...
WHOOO
...IN AN INSTANT.
KEN-

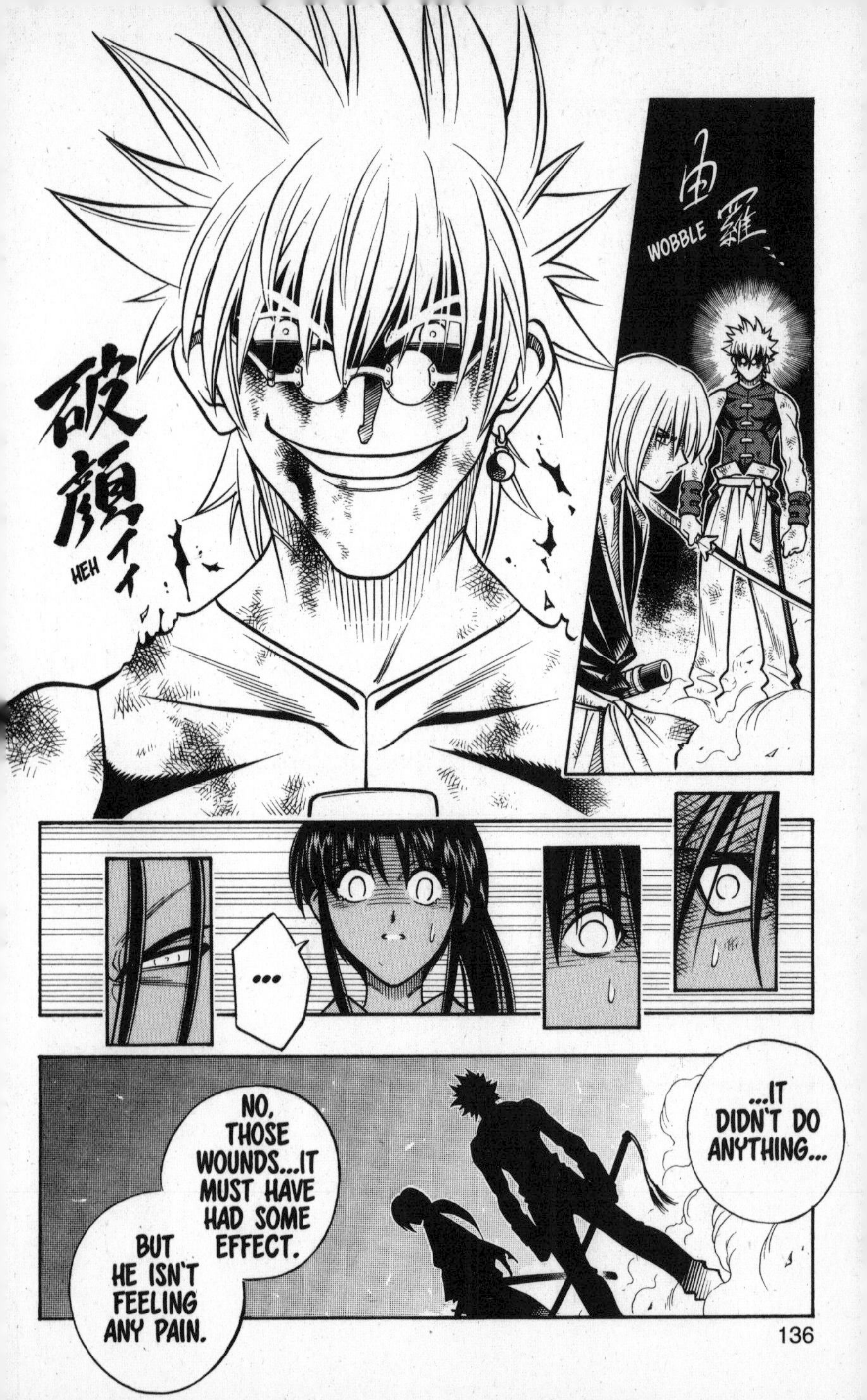
WOBBLE
HEH
...
...IT DIDN'T DO ANYTHING...
NO, THOSE WOUNDS...IT MUST HAVE HAD SOME EFFECT.
BUT HE ISN'T FEELING ANY PAIN.

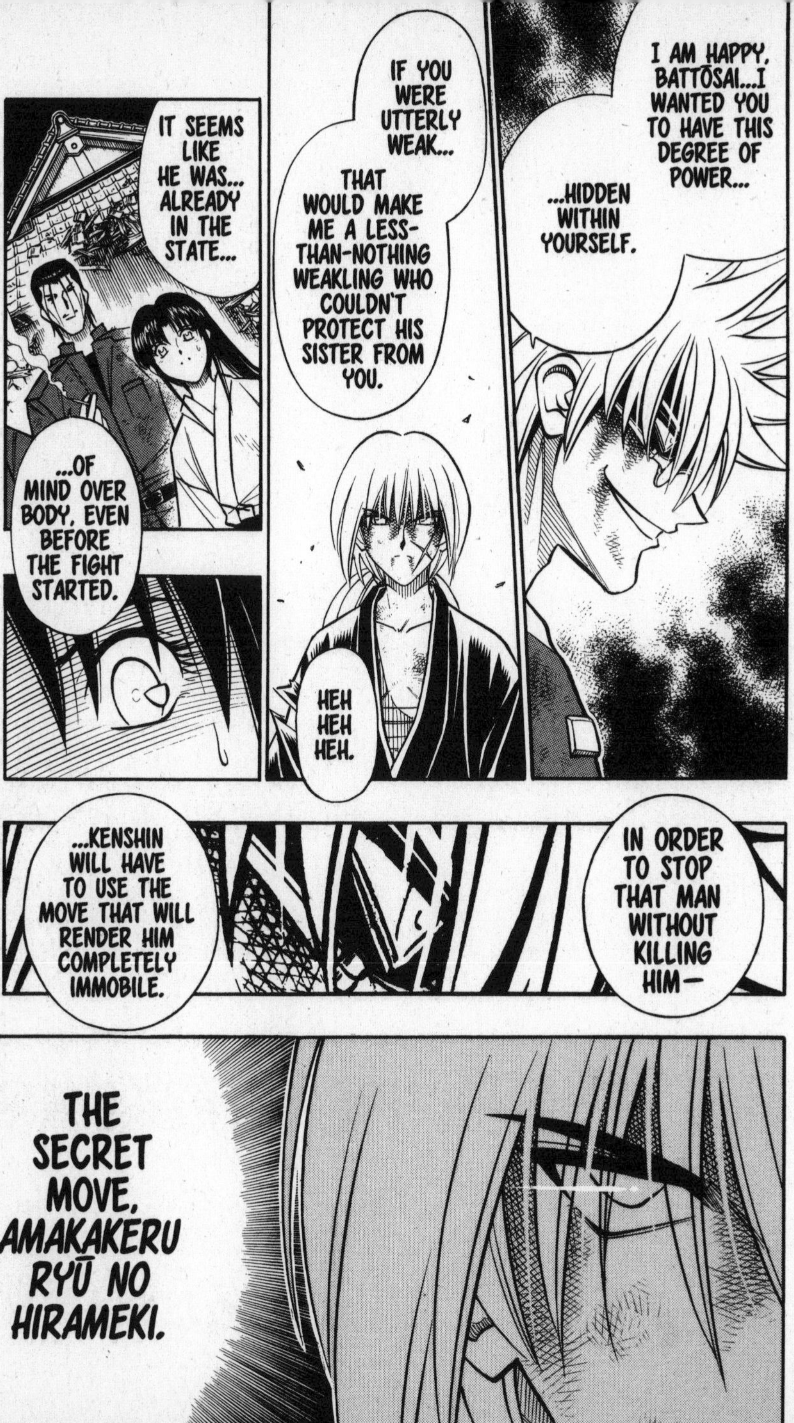
I AM HAPPY, BATTŌSAI...I WANTED YOU TO HAVE THIS DEGREE OF POWER...
...HIDDEN WITHIN YOURSELF.
IF YOU WERE UTTERLY WEAK...
THAT WOULD MAKE ME A LESS-THAN-NOTHING WEAKLING WHO COULDN'T PROTECT HIS SISTER FROM YOU.
HEH HEH HEH.
IT SEEMS LIKE HE WAS... ALREADY IN THE STATE...
...OF MIND OVER BODY, EVEN BEFORE THE FIGHT STARTED.
IN ORDER TO STOP THAT MAN WITHOUT KILLING HIM—
...KENSHIN WILL HAVE TO USE THE MOVE THAT WILL RENDER HIM COMPLETELY IMMOBILE.
THE SECRET MOVE, AMAKAKERU RYŪ NO HIRAMEKI.

Rurouni Kenshin

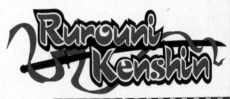

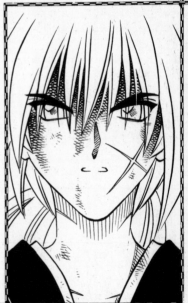

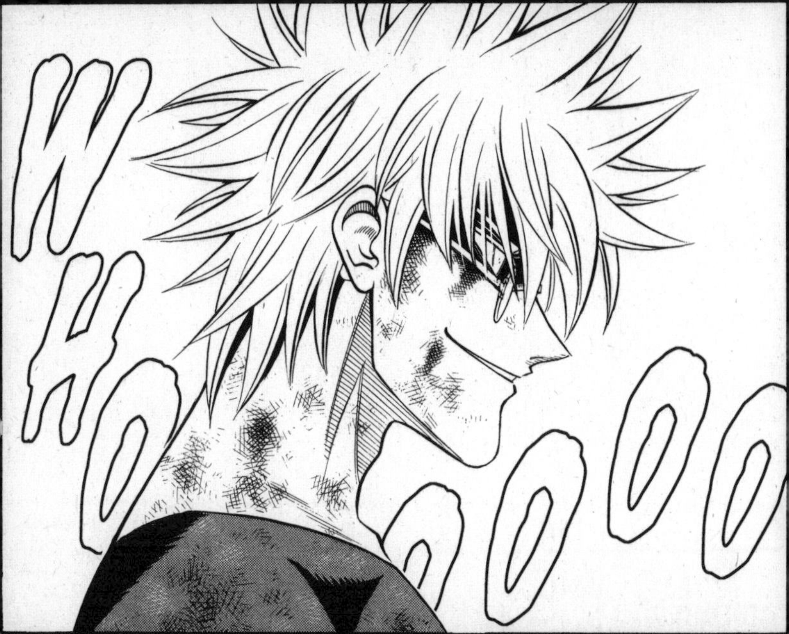
WHOOOOO

Act 204
Sin, Judgment, Acceptance

和月伸宏

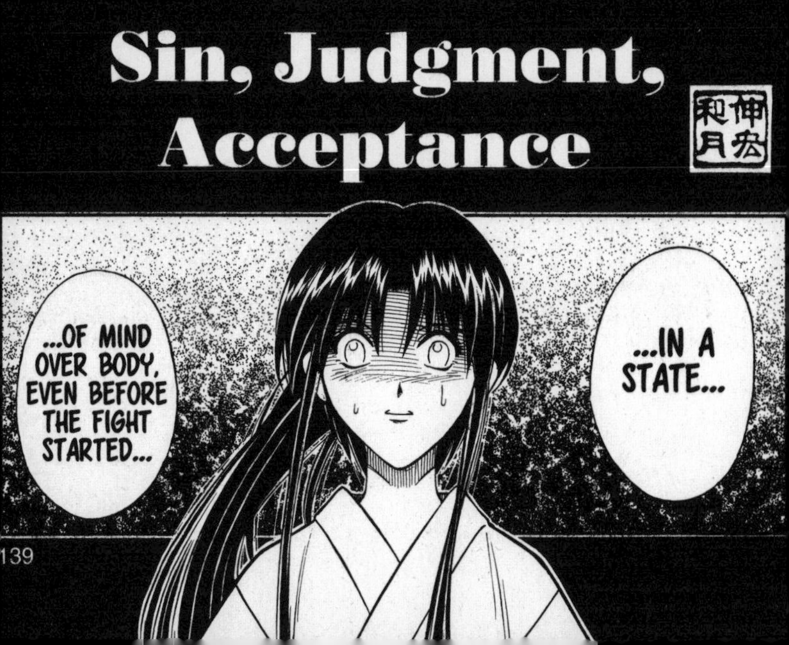
...IN A STATE...
...OF MIND OVER BODY, EVEN BEFORE THE FIGHT STARTED...

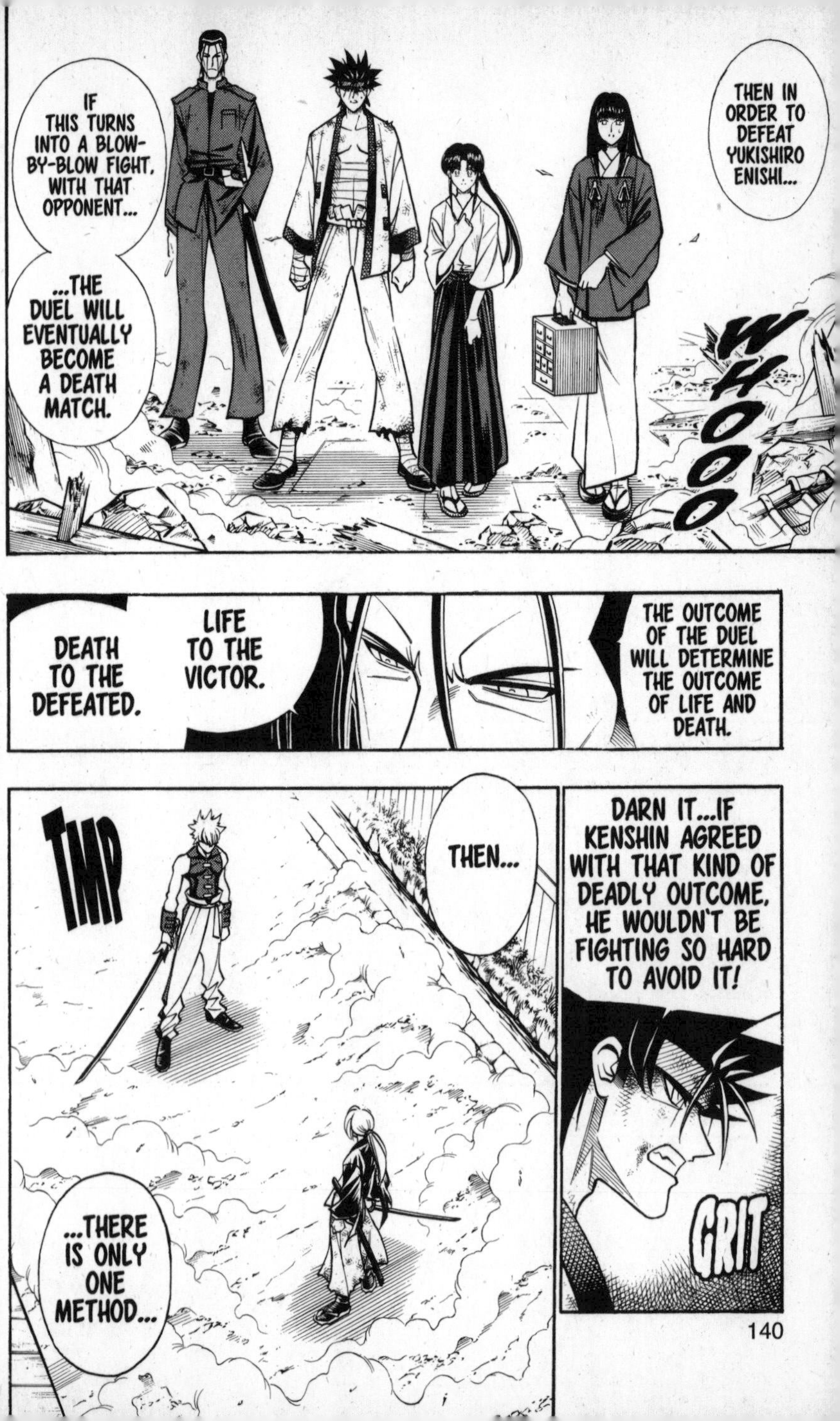

THEN IN ORDER TO DEFEAT YUKISHIRO ENISHI...
WHOOOO
IF THIS TURNS INTO A BLOW-BY-BLOW FIGHT, WITH THAT OPPONENT...
...THE DUEL WILL EVENTUALLY BECOME A DEATH MATCH.
THE OUTCOME OF THE DUEL WILL DETERMINE THE OUTCOME OF LIFE AND DEATH.
LIFE TO THE VICTOR.
DEATH TO THE DEFEATED.
DARN IT...IF KENSHIN AGREED WITH THAT KIND OF DEADLY OUTCOME, HE WOULDN'T BE FIGHTING SO HARD TO AVOID IT!
GRIT
THEN...
TMP
...THERE IS ONLY ONE METHOD...

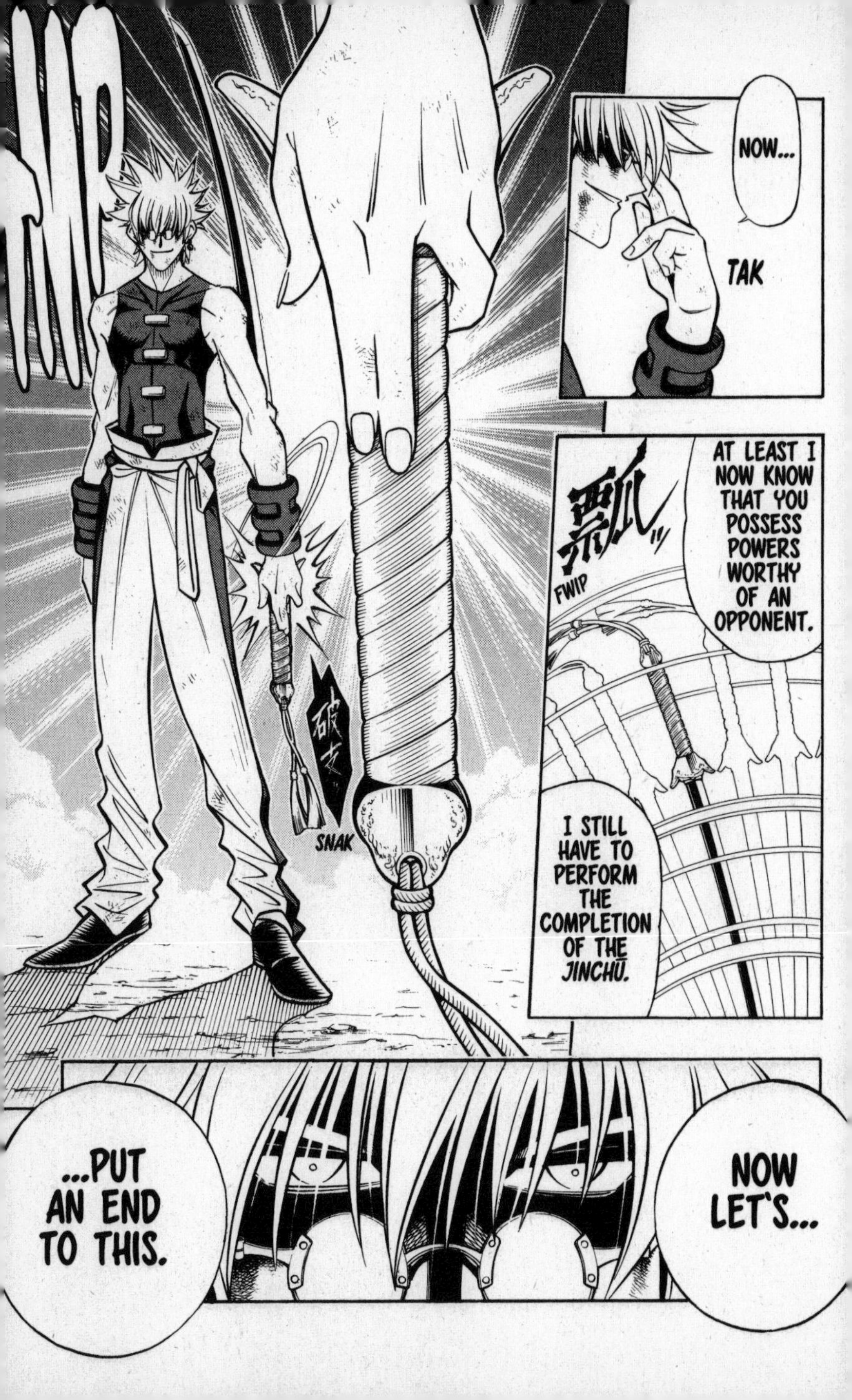
NOW...
TAK
AT LEAST I NOW KNOW THAT YOU POSSESS POWERS WORTHY OF AN OPPONENT.
FWIP
I STILL HAVE TO PERFORM THE COMPLETION OF THE JINCHŪ.
SNAK
NOW LET'S...
...PUT AN END TO THIS.

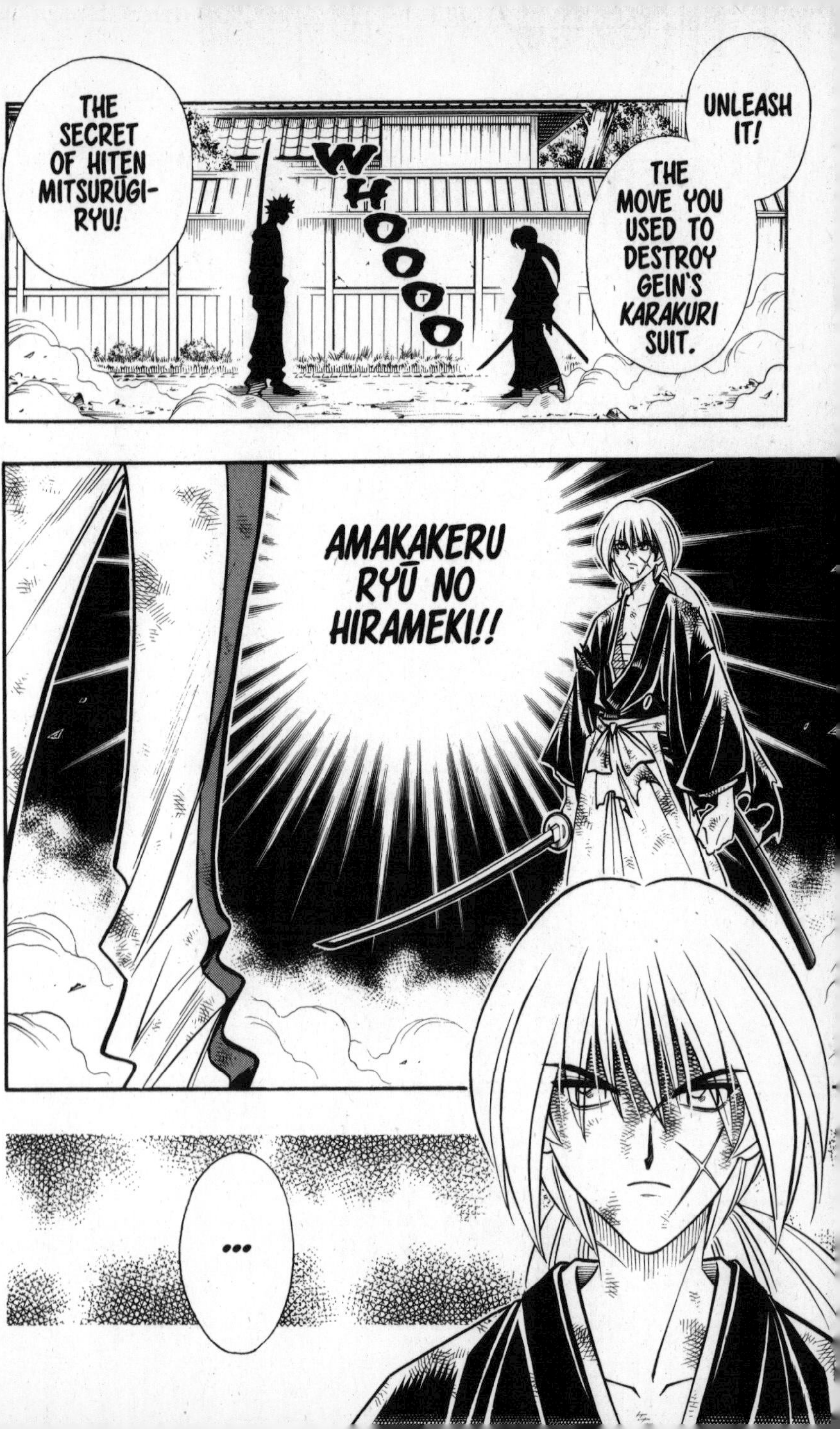
UNLEASH IT!
THE MOVE YOU USED TO DESTROY GEIN'S KARAKURI SUIT.
THE SECRET OF HITEN MITSURŪGI-RYU!
WHOOOO
AMAKAKERU RYŪ NO HIRAMEKI!!
...

READ THIS WAY

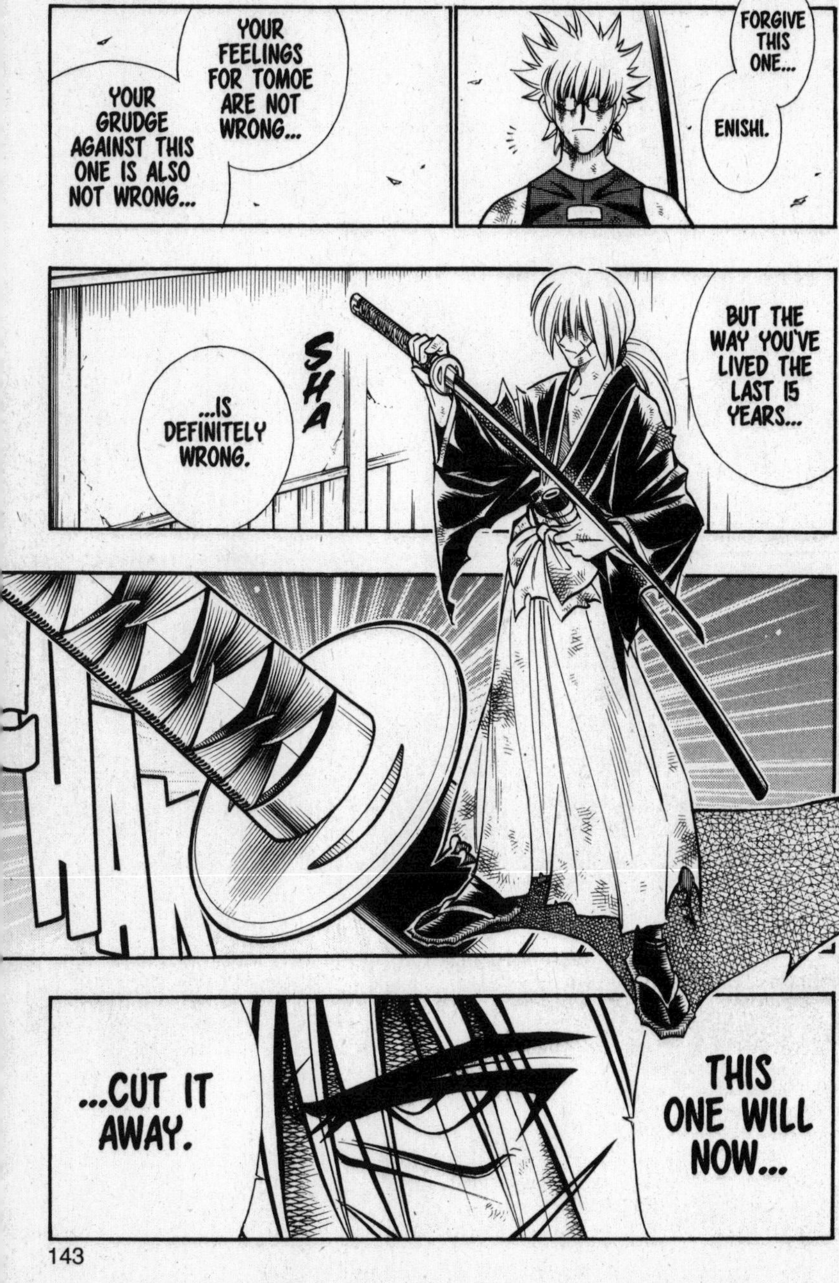
FORGIVE THIS ONE...
ENISHI.
YOUR FEELINGS FOR TOMOE ARE NOT WRONG...
YOUR GRUDGE AGAINST THIS ONE IS ALSO NOT WRONG...
BUT THE WAY YOU'VE LIVED THE LAST 15 YEARS...
...IS DEFINITELY WRONG.
SHA
THIS ONE WILL NOW...
...CUT IT AWAY.

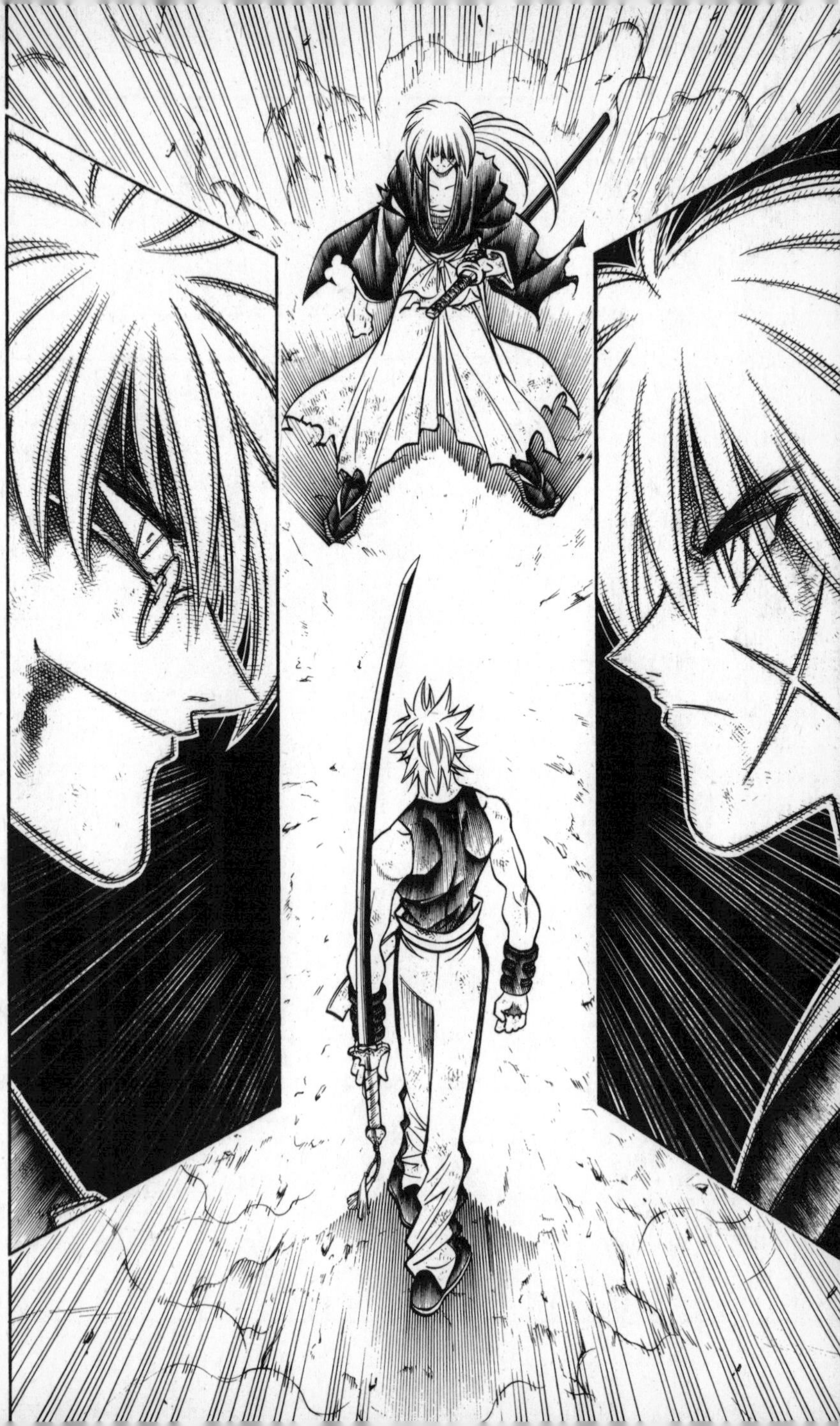

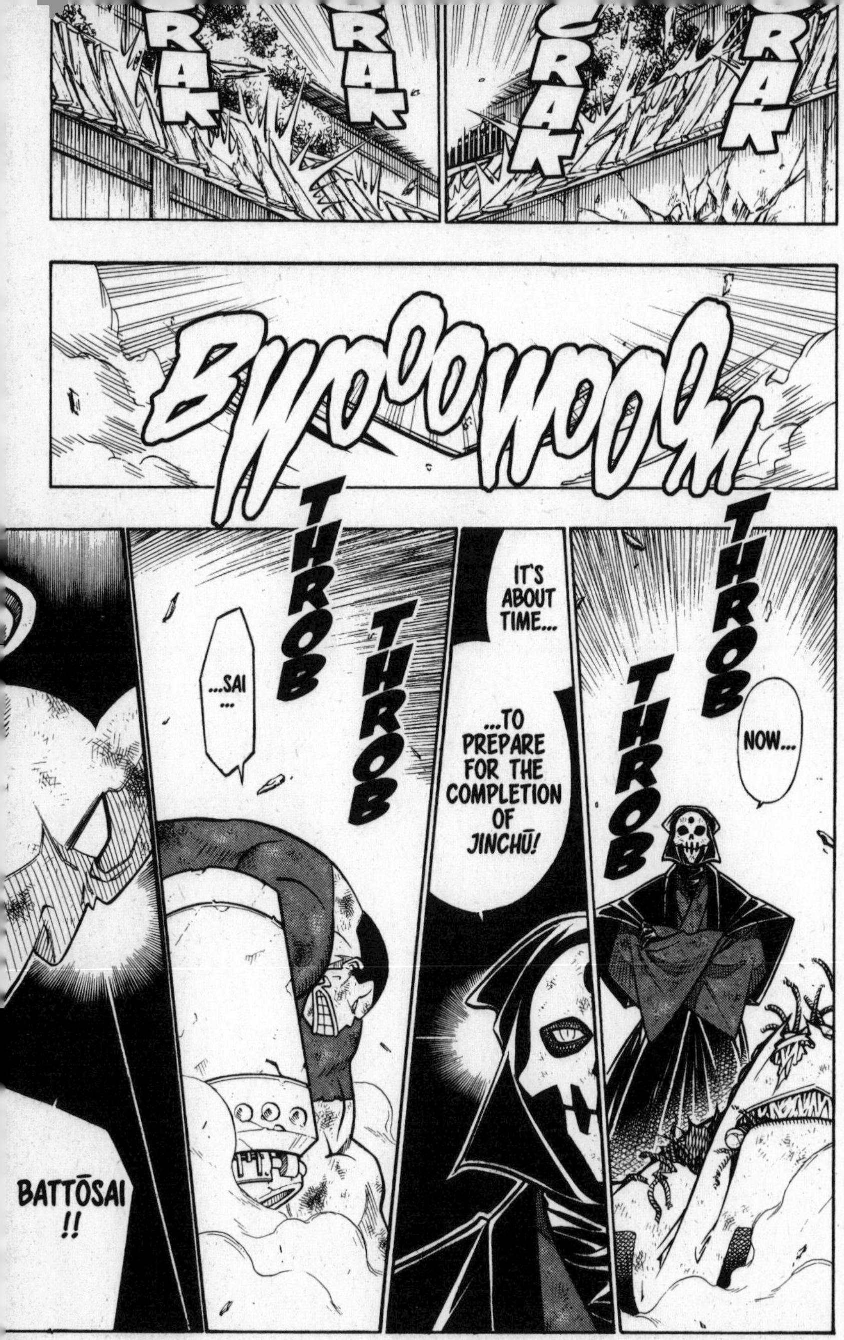
RAK
CRAK
RAK
RAK
BWOOOOOM
THROB
THROB
NOW...
IT'S ABOUT TIME...
...TO PREPARE FOR THE COMPLETION OF JINCHŪ!
THROB
THROB
...SAI ...
BATTŌSAI !!

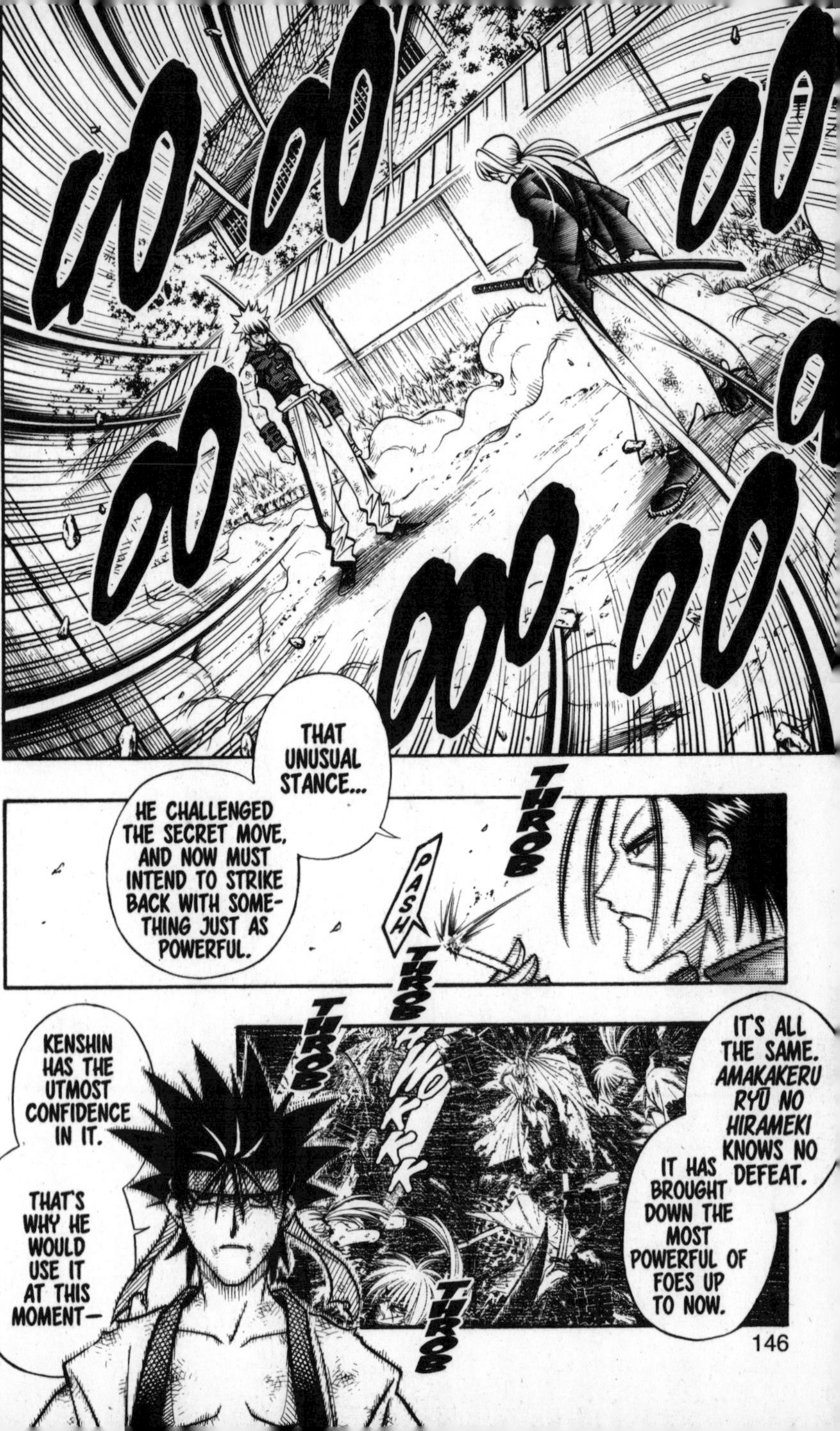
THROB
PASH
THROB
THAT UNUSUAL STANCE...
HE CHALLENGED THE SECRET MOVE, AND NOW MUST INTEND TO STRIKE BACK WITH SOME-THING JUST AS POWERFUL.
THROB
IT'S ALL THE SAME. AMAKAKERU RYŪ NO HIRAMEKI KNOWS NO DEFEAT.
IT HAS BROUGHT DOWN THE MOST POWERFUL OF FOES UP TO NOW.
THROB
KENSHIN HAS THE UTMOST CONFIDENCE IN IT.
THAT'S WHY HE WOULD USE IT AT THIS MOMENT—

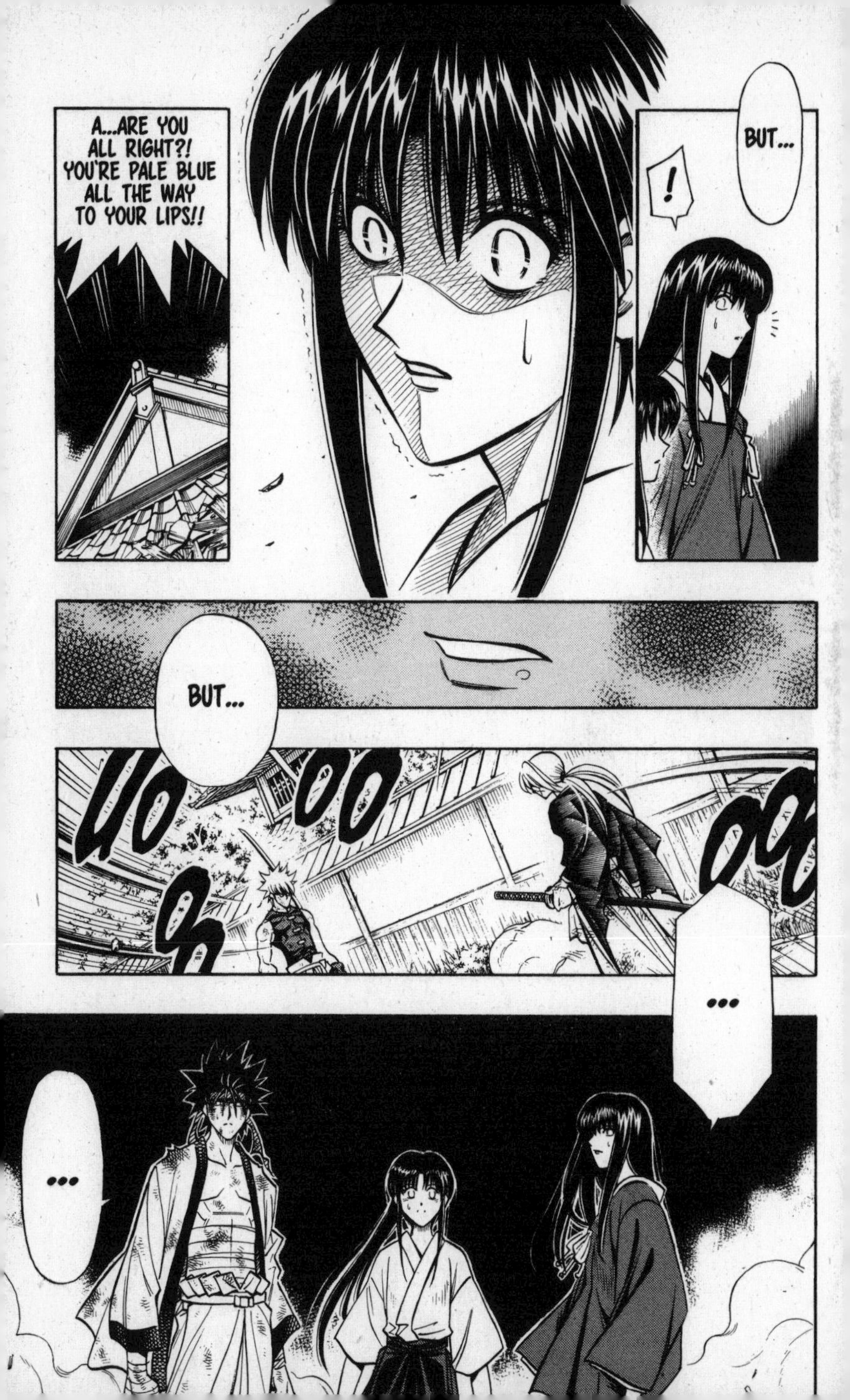
BUT...
!
A...ARE YOU ALL RIGHT?! YOU'RE PALE BLUE ALL THE WAY TO YOUR LIPS!!
BUT...
...
...

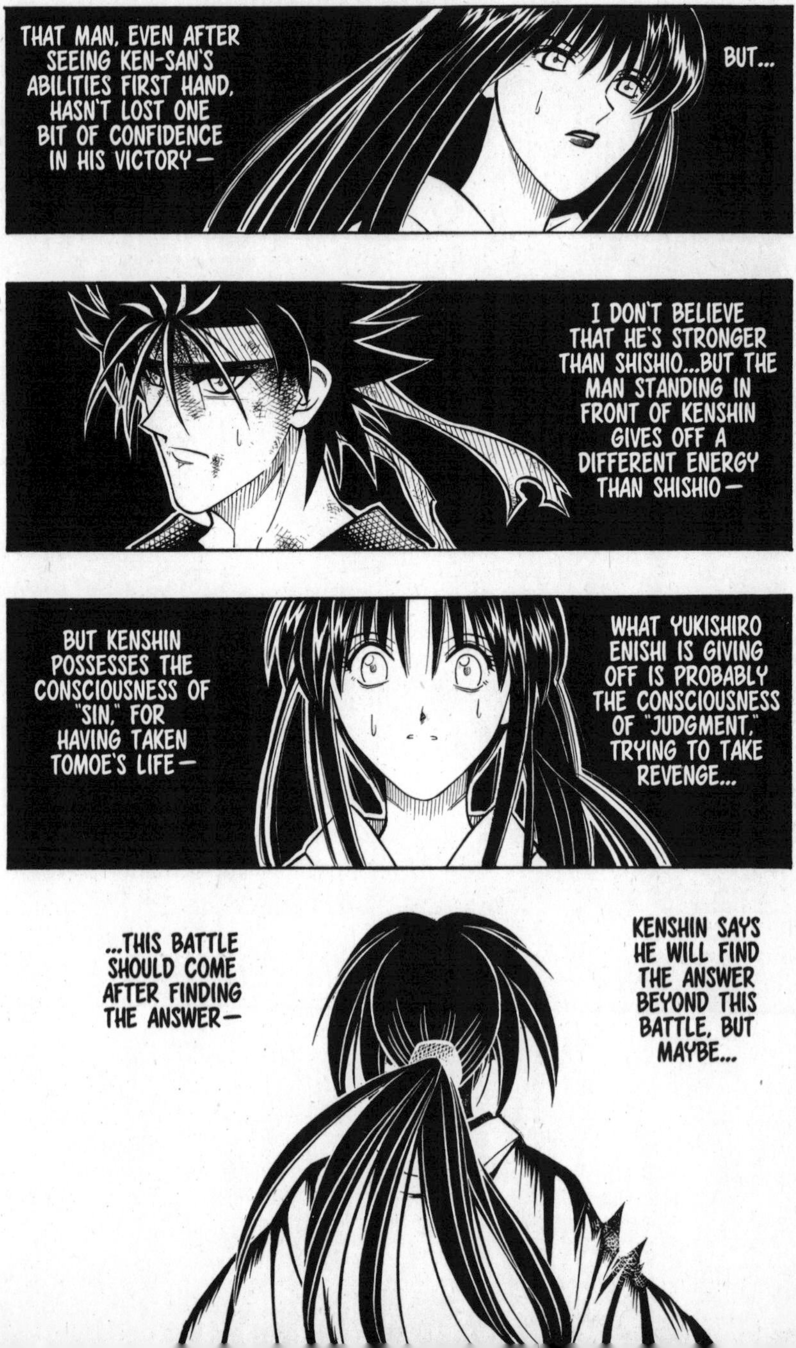
BUT...
THAT MAN, EVEN AFTER SEEING KEN-SAN'S ABILITIES FIRST HAND, HASN'T LOST ONE BIT OF CONFIDENCE IN HIS VICTORY—
I DON'T BELIEVE THAT HE'S STRONGER THAN SHISHIO...BUT THE MAN STANDING IN FRONT OF KENSHIN GIVES OFF A DIFFERENT ENERGY THAN SHISHIO—
WHAT YUKISHIRO ENISHI IS GIVING OFF IS PROBABLY THE CONSCIOUSNESS OF "JUDGMENT," TRYING TO TAKE REVENGE...
BUT KENSHIN POSSESSES THE CONSCIOUSNESS OF "SIN," FOR HAVING TAKEN TOMOE'S LIFE—
KENSHIN SAYS HE WILL FIND THE ANSWER BEYOND THIS BATTLE, BUT MAYBE...
...THIS BATTLE SHOULD COME AFTER FINDING THE ANSWER—

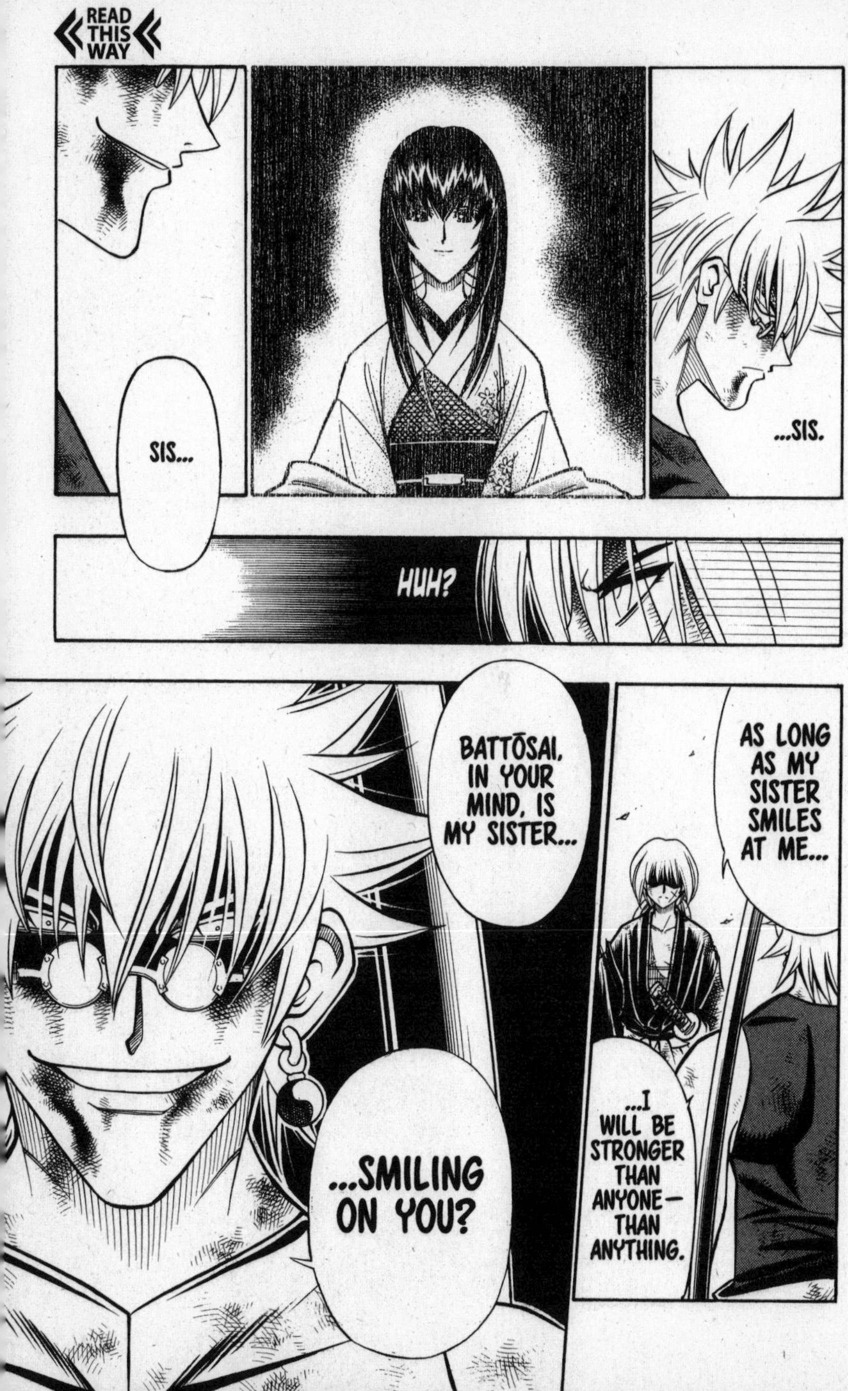
READ THIS WAY
...SIS.
SIS...
HUH?
AS LONG AS MY SISTER SMILES AT ME...
...I WILL BE STRONGER THAN ANYONE—THAN ANYTHING.
BATTŌSAI, IN YOUR MIND, IS MY SISTER...
...SMILING ON YOU?

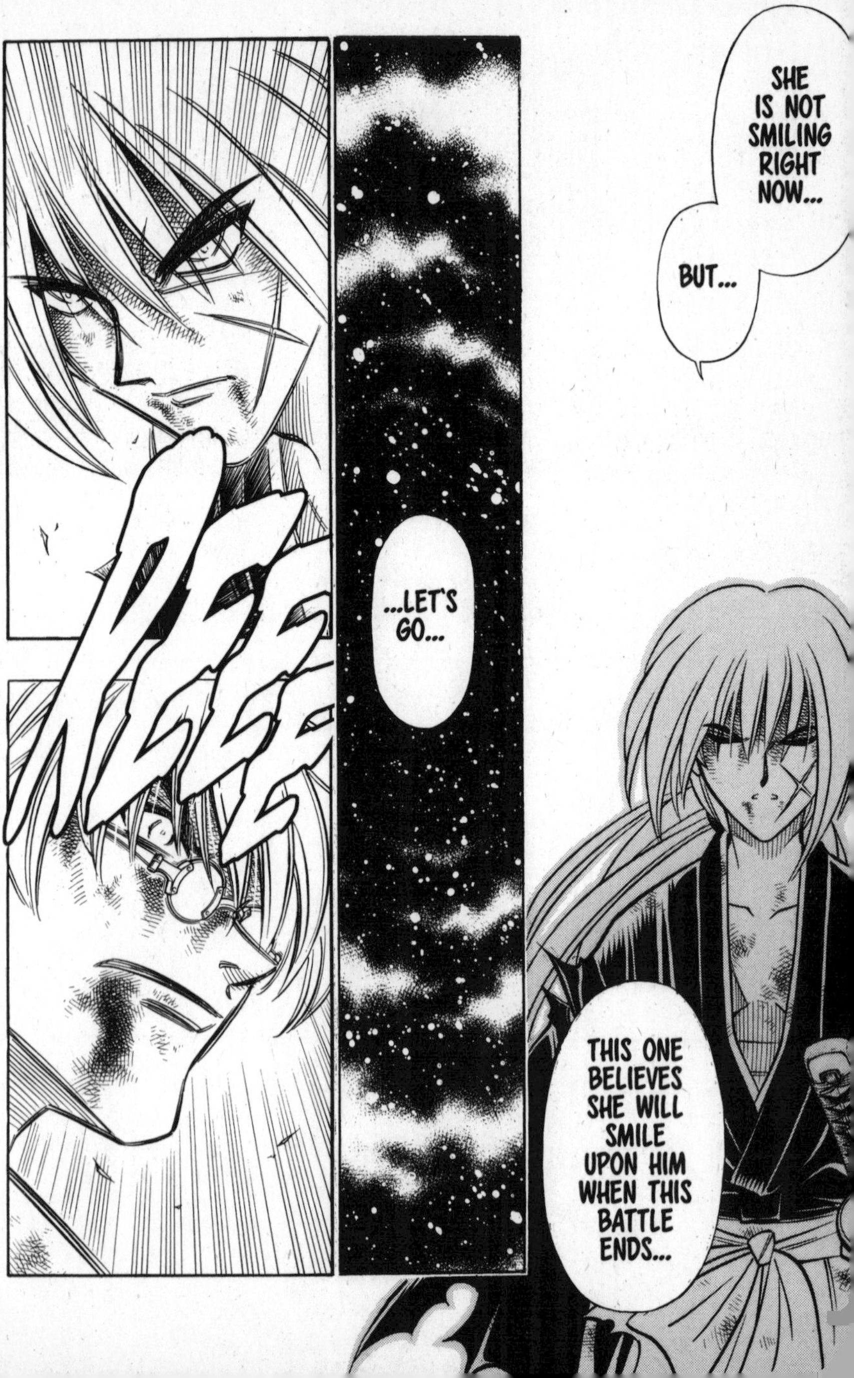
SHE IS NOT SMILING RIGHT NOW...
BUT...
THIS ONE BELIEVES SHE WILL SMILE UPON HIM WHEN THIS BATTLE ENDS...
...LET'S GO...

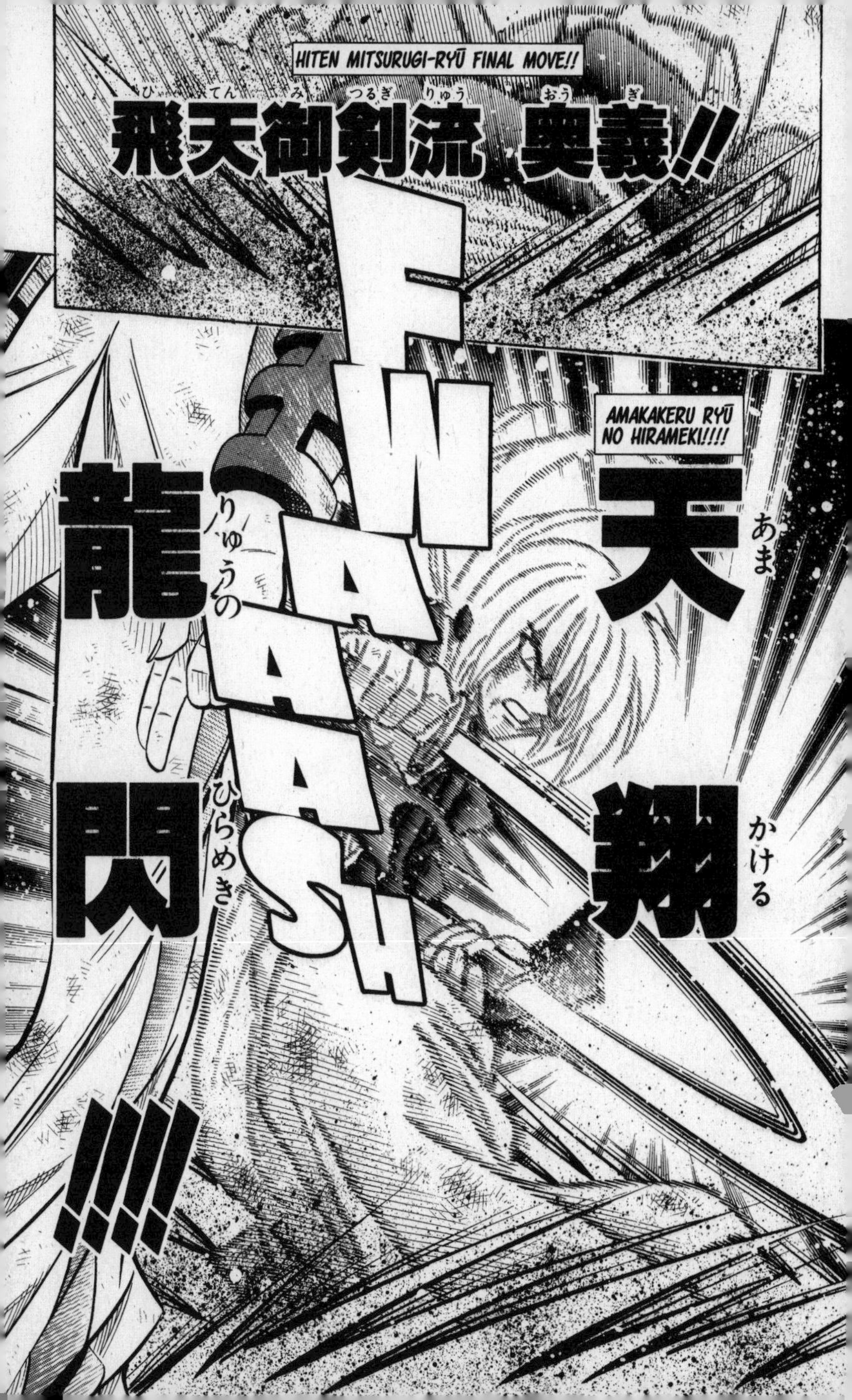
HITEN MITSURUGI-RYŪ FINAL MOVE!!
飛天御剣流 奥義!!
AMAKAKERU RYŪ NO HIRAMEKI!!!!
天翔龍閃!!!!
FWAAASH

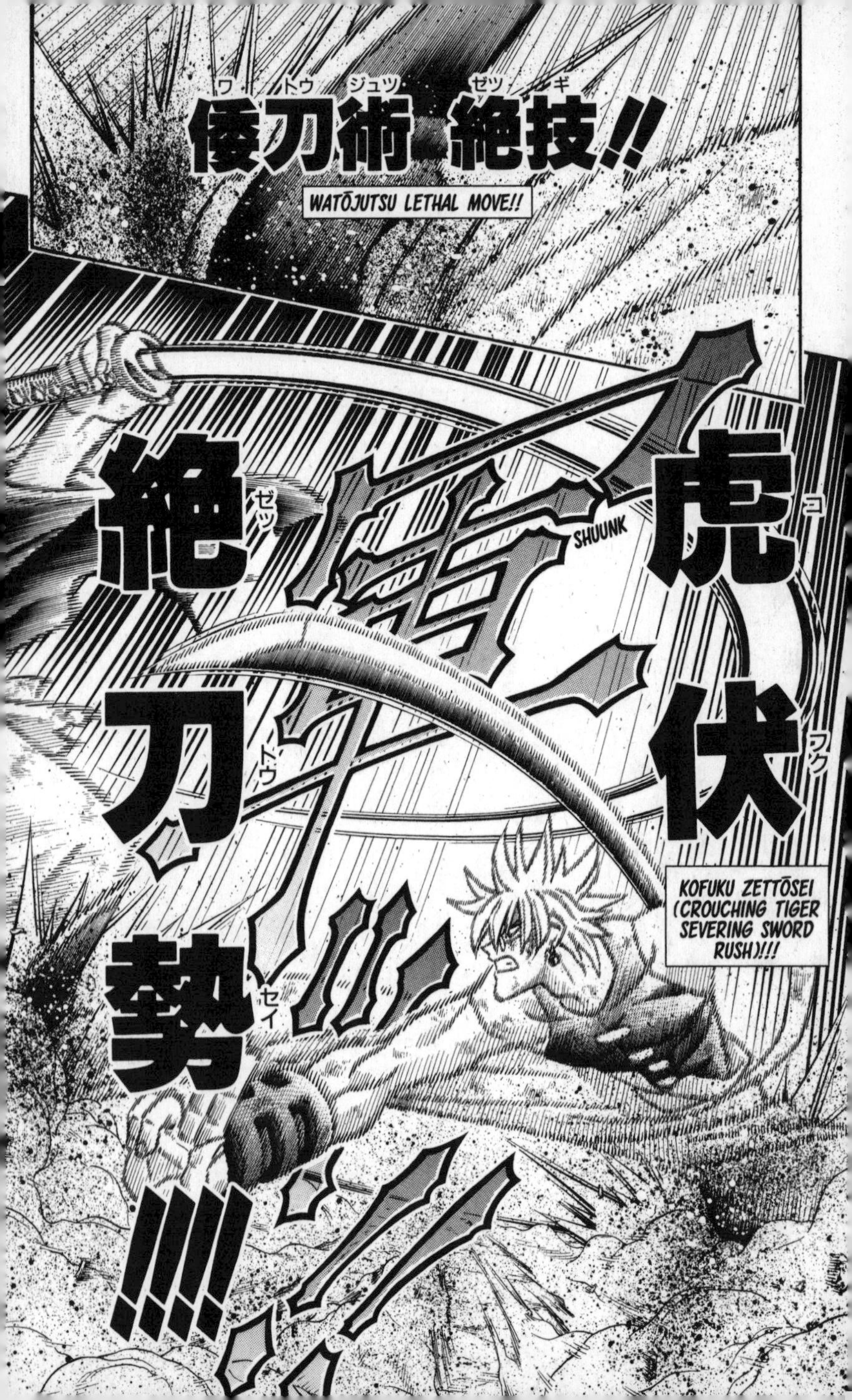
倭刀術 絶技!!
WATŌJUTSU LETHAL MOVE!!
虎伏絶刀勢!!!!
KOFUKU ZETTŌSEI (CROUCHING TIGER SEVERING SWORD RUSH)!!!
SHUUNK

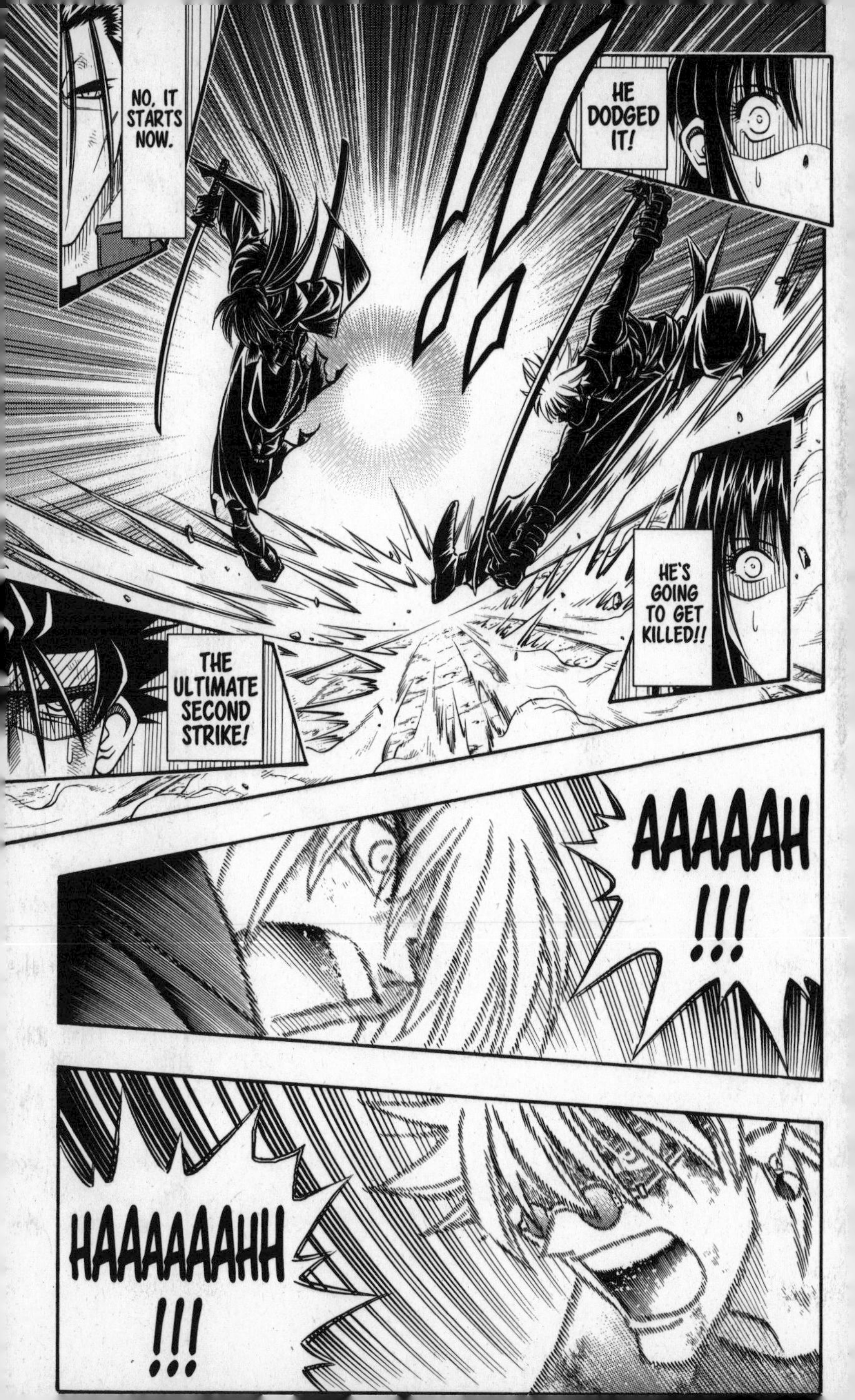
HE DODGED IT!
NO, IT STARTS NOW.
HE'S GOING TO GET KILLED!!
THE ULTIMATE SECOND STRIKE!
AAAAAH!!!
HAAAAAAHH!!!

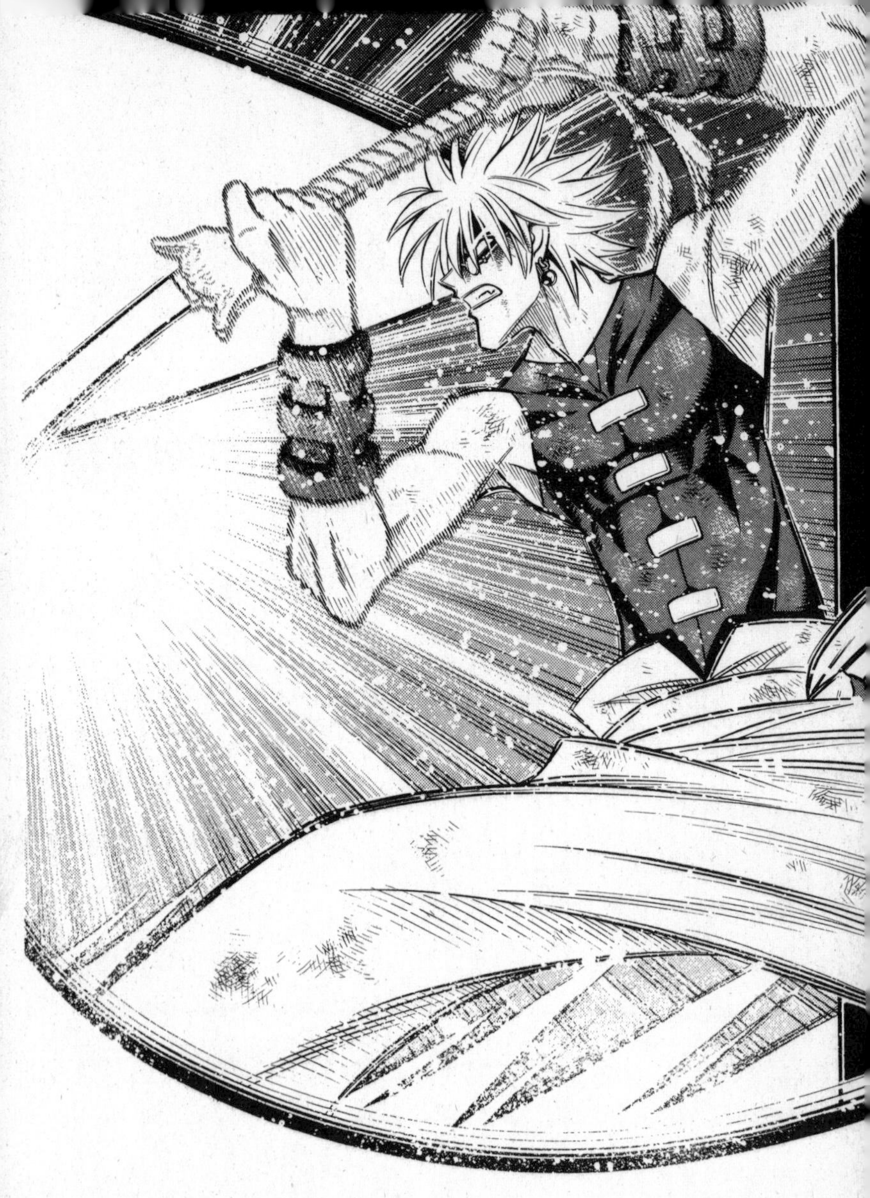

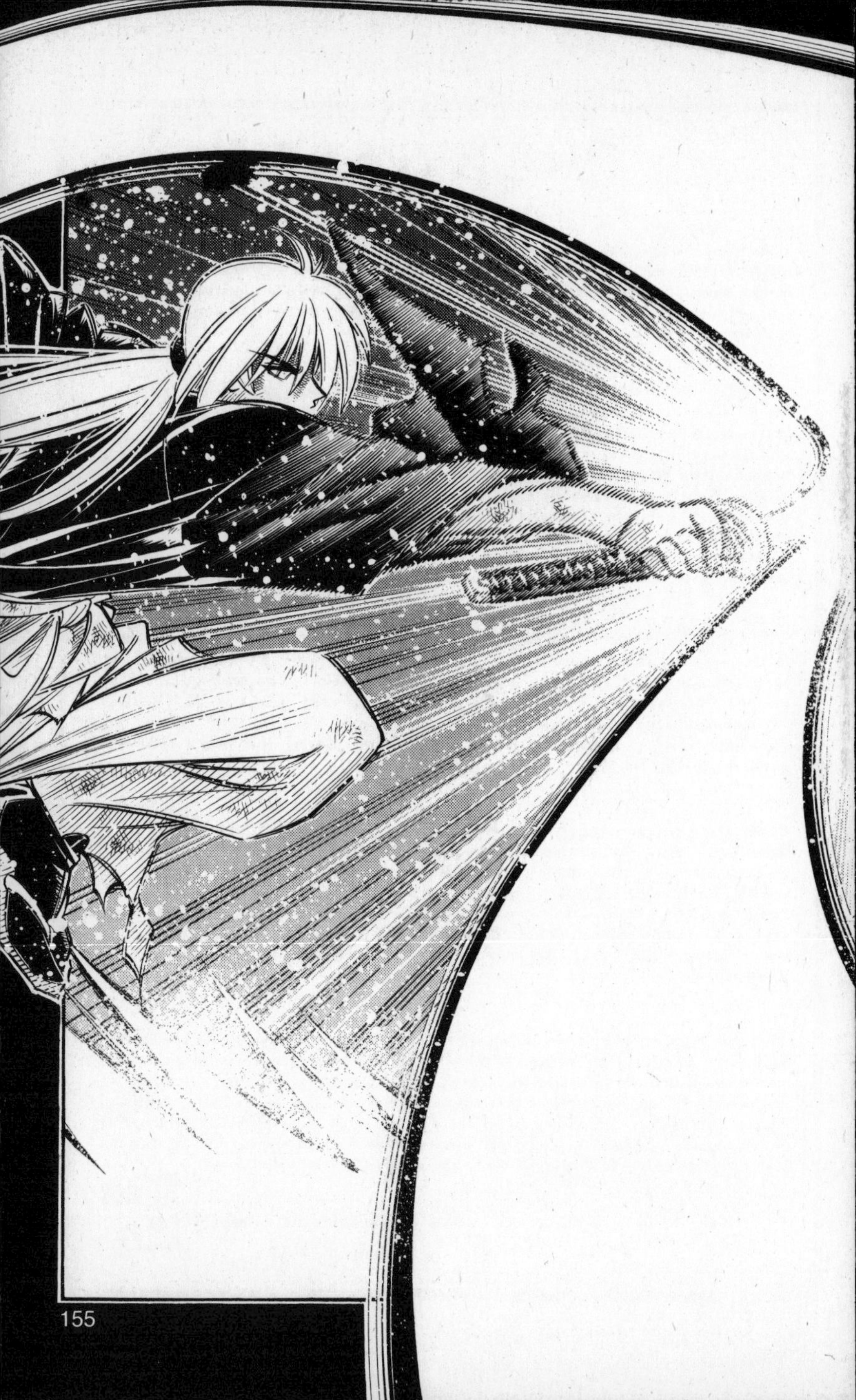

"FREE TALK"

Long time no see, this is Watsuki. In the transition from spring to summer, I felt sick and slept for a whole day. It seems like my energy level has fallen lower than I thought, so I said to myself, "I've gotta do something," in a Kansai accent. I've started by ordering the Ab○lex by mail order. I can't fall to illness for at least one more year!

While I wait for the Ab○lex, let's talk about figures and games. My recommendation for figures is the "X-Men Gift Pack 2". Last year's "Gift Pack 1" was worth crying for joy about, but this one is also magnificent. The characters that haven't been made into figures before, like the so-uncool Sunfire, and Banshee's first-appearance monkey face, are great. Please, Oh Mighty Toy Biz, release all X characters with the current action figure technology! I will be fine with a hundred-body kit the size of one tatami mat. Bring it on!! In terms of games, since I've been unable to make my once-a-week trip to the arcades due to the moving fiasco, I have completely stopped going to arcades. When someone says "And you call yourself a gamer!?" I point out that Watsuki is not a "Gamer," but a "manga artist who likes games." So take that. For Watsuki, "manga" is always the priority. But as I write this, it is close to the release of *Samurai Spirits 2, Asura Zanmaden* (SNK), so I am thinking of stopping by the arcades soon. I really hope a local arcade gets it this time, but we'll see... In terms of console games, I bought *Shiritsu Justice Gakuen* PS version (Capeom)" and played it with the assistants for only about one hour. I seriously have no time. By the way, I had some weird feelings for Akira. I might have fallen if it was 2D (3D up close is a bit harsh...).

Other than the previously mentioned, Watsuki also likes "dusk." The panoramic view from the new workplace nine floors up gives me a good feeling, and that alone makes it worth the move. On a very good day, I can see Mt. Fuji, and on a misty day it looks like I'm in London (though I have never been to London, or anywhere outside the country for that matter), giving off a good vibe. Getting energized with games and figures, and relaxing with the view. This seems to be the method of my self-control these days.

The last topic is, of course, manga. I have recently started to see the style and story design of my future works. I have written about the style before, so I'll omit that. In terms of the story, to put it simply, it's the "exciting anticipation" out of Thrill, Excitement, and Anticipation. You may think "What the heck?" But there is no better way to describe it with words. I'm sorry. Anyhow, those aspects will materialize way in the future, so now I will keep working at *Rurouni Kenshin* with all of my spirit.

See you in the next volume!

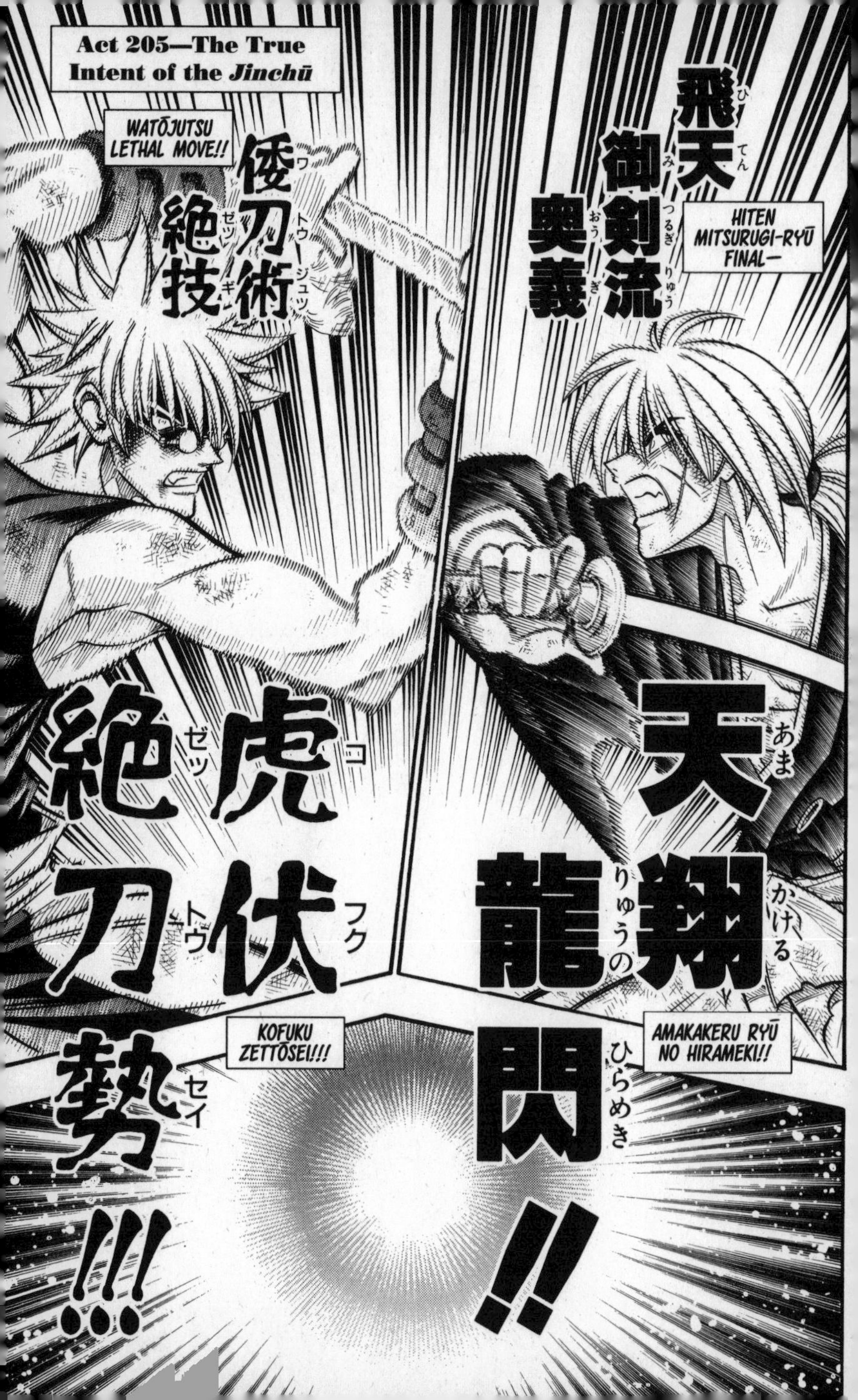
Act 205—The True Intent of the Jinchū
飛天御剣流奥義
HITEN MITSURUGI-RYŪ FINAL—
倭刀術絶技
WATŌJUTSU LETHAL MOVE!!
天翔龍閃!!
AMAKAKERU RYŪ NO HIRAMEKI!!
虎伏絶刀勢!!!
KOFUKU ZETTŌSEI!!!

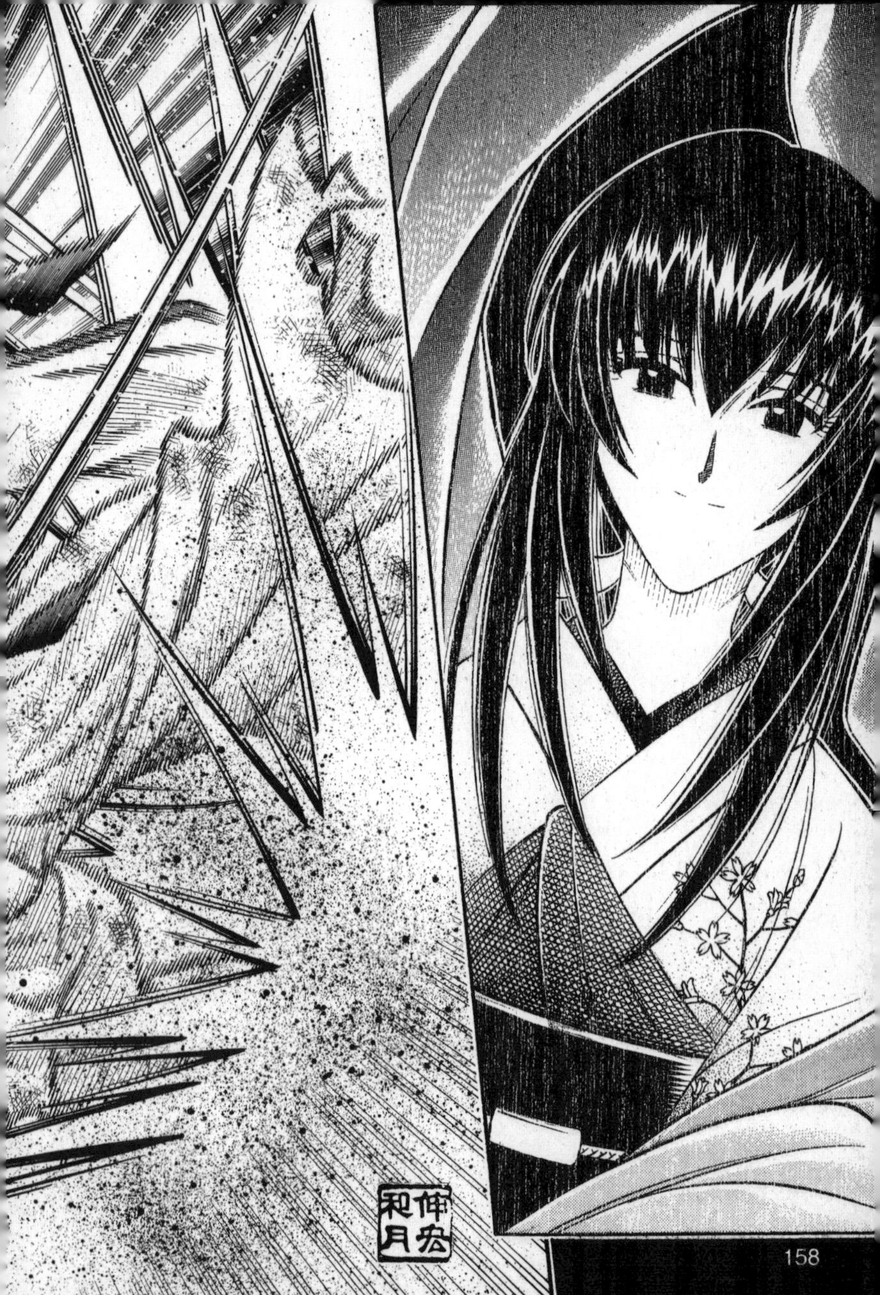

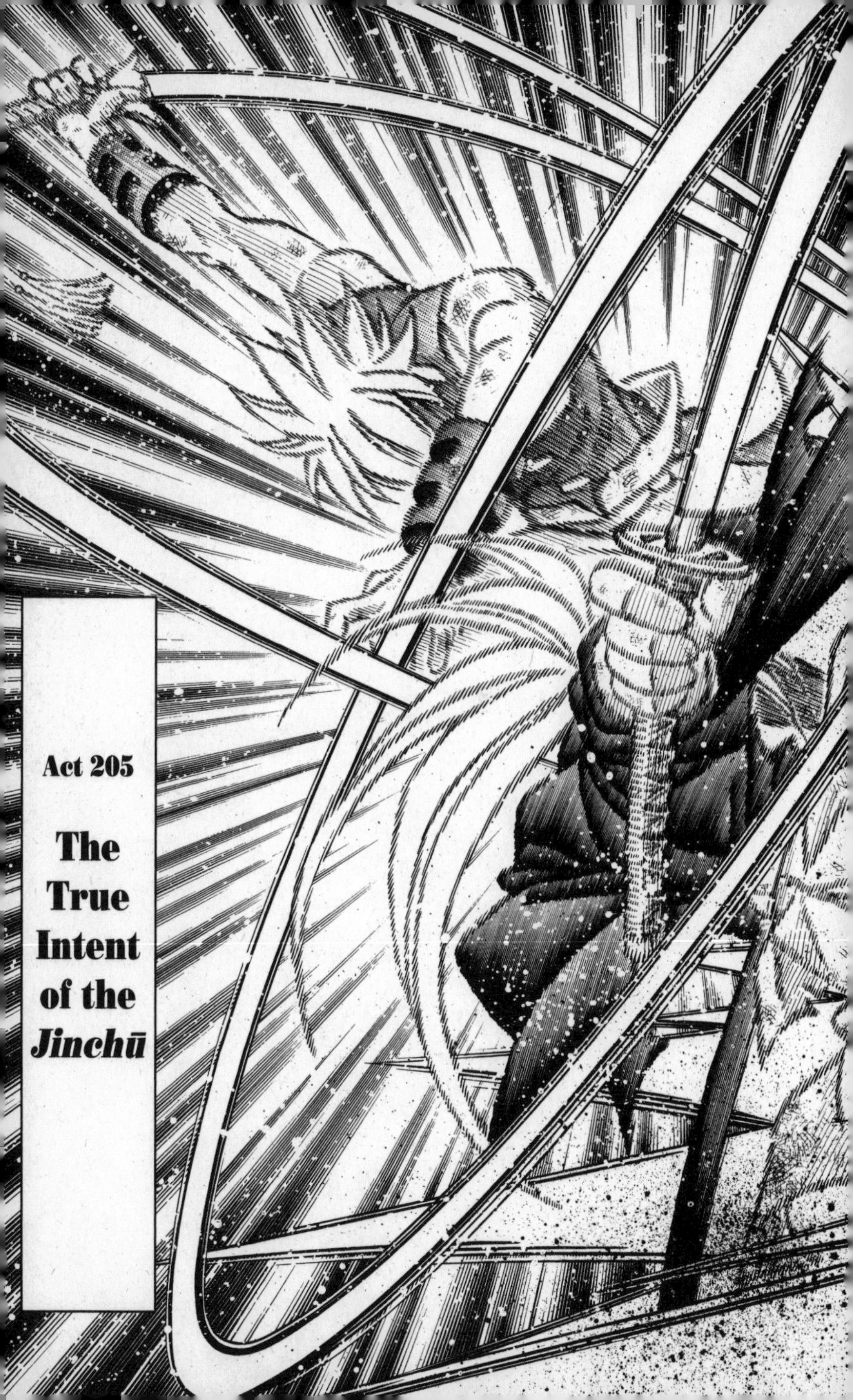
Act 205
The True Intent of the *Jinchū*

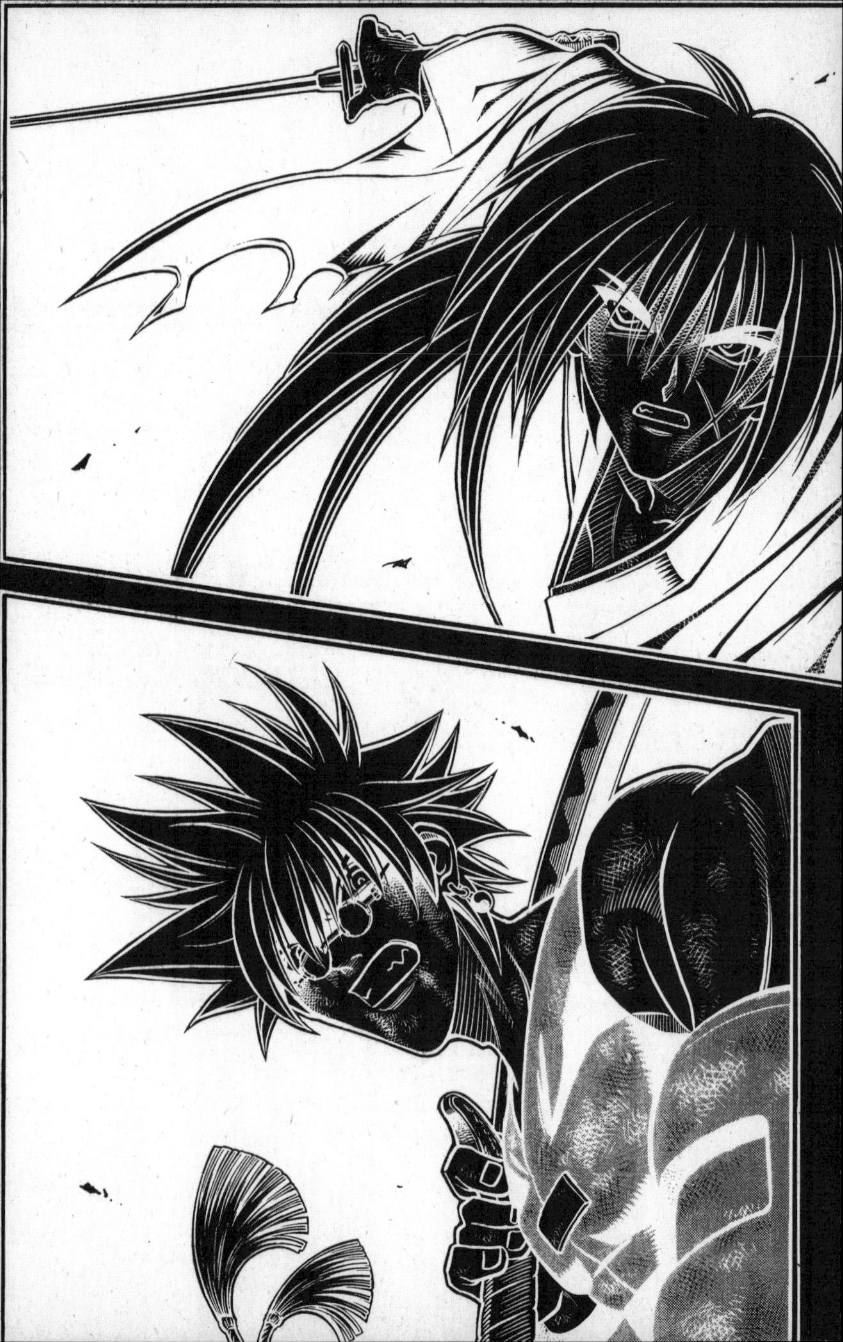

READ THIS WAY

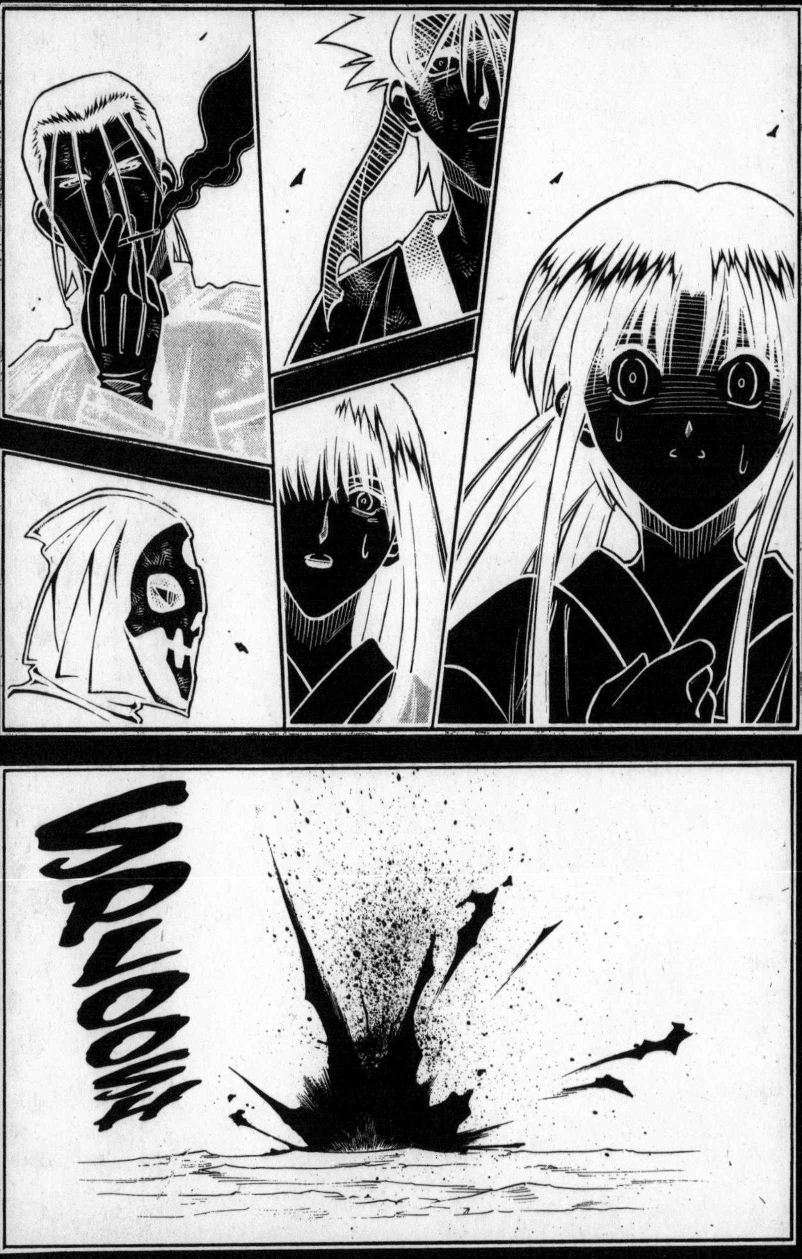
SPLOOM

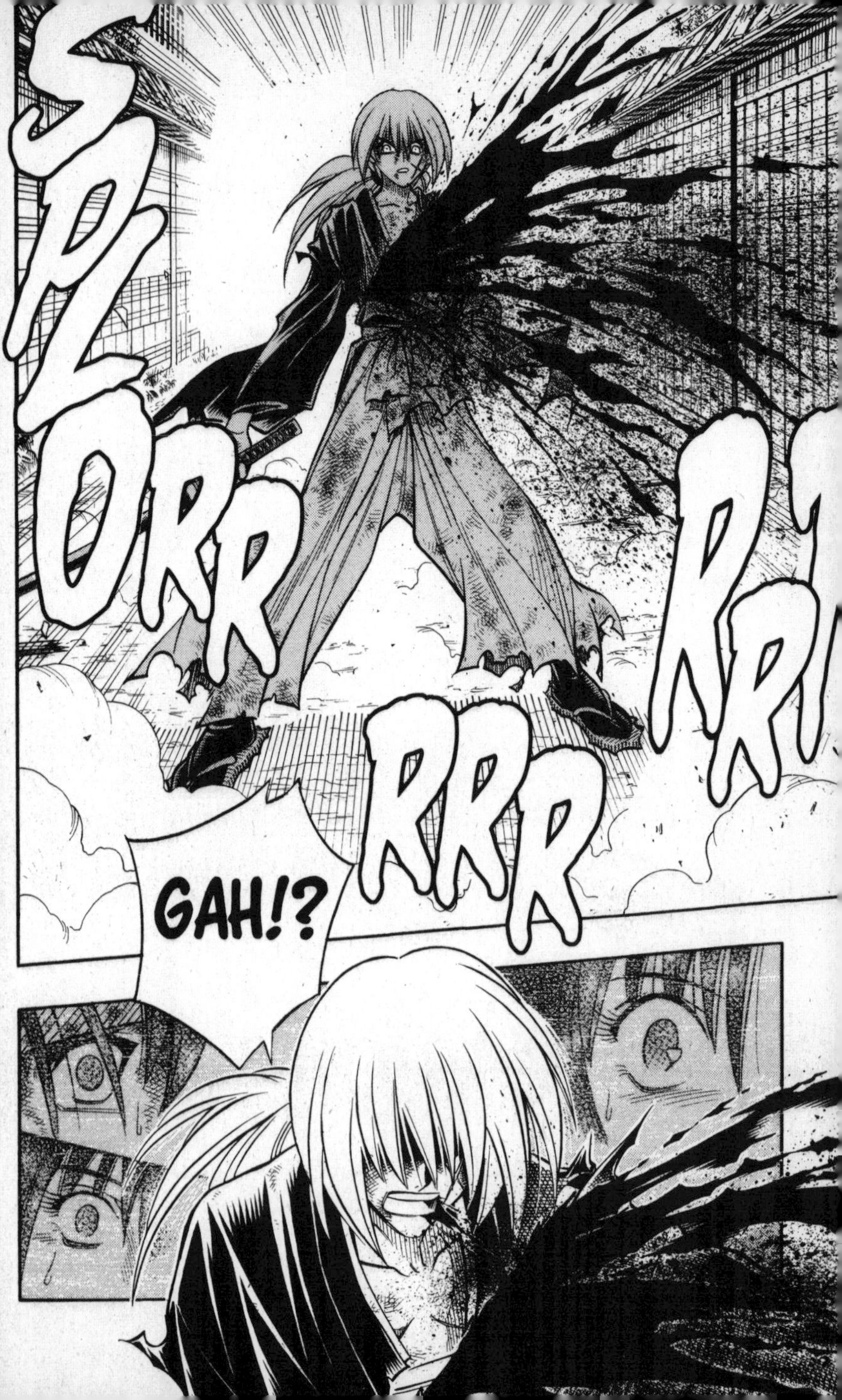
SPLORR
RRR
RRR
GAH!?

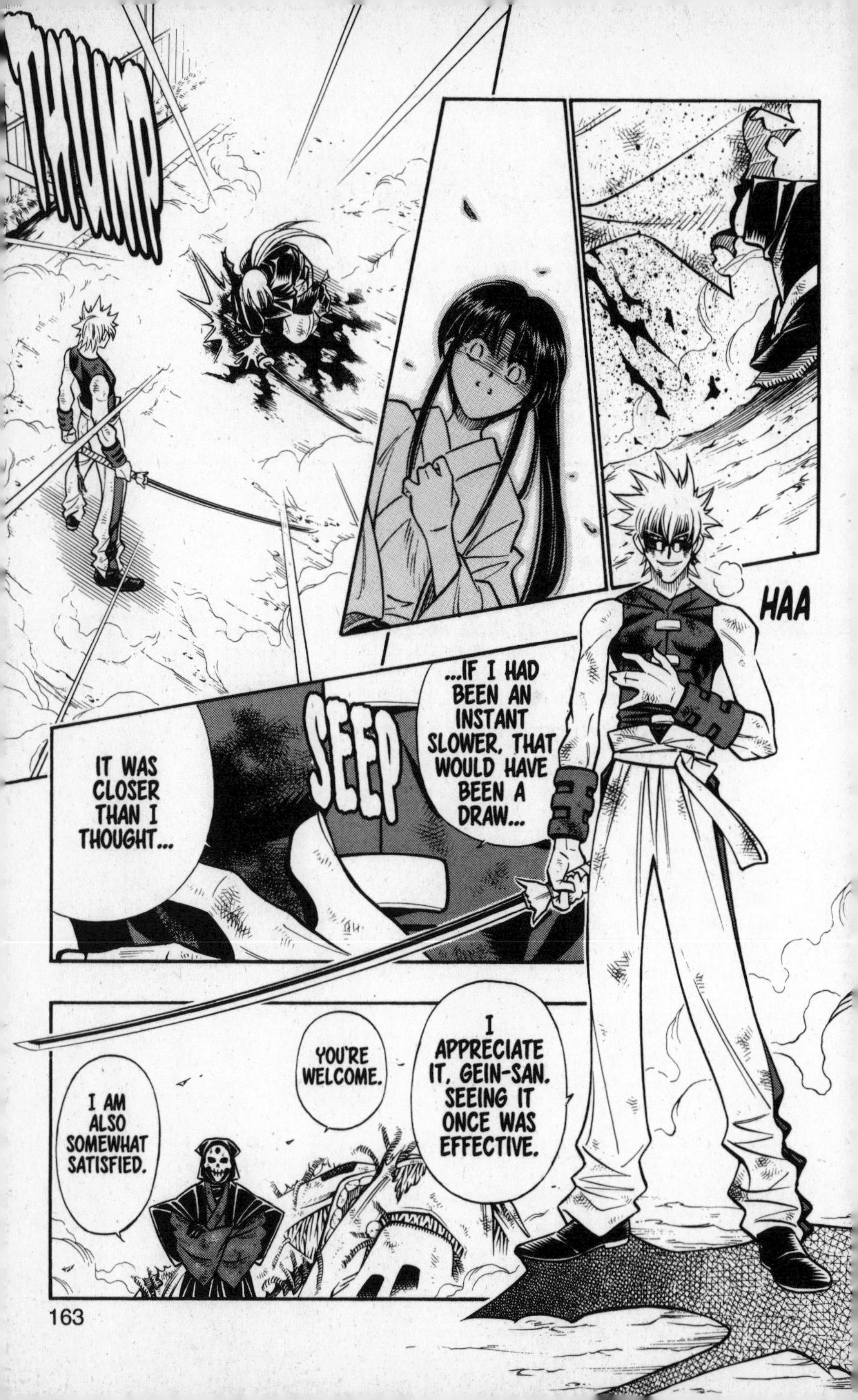
THUMP
HAA
...IF I HAD BEEN AN INSTANT SLOWER, THAT WOULD HAVE BEEN A DRAW...
SEEP
IT WAS CLOSER THAN I THOUGHT...
I APPRECIATE IT, GEIN-SAN. SEEING IT ONCE WAS EFFECTIVE.
YOU'RE WELCOME.
I AM ALSO SOMEWHAT SATISFIED.

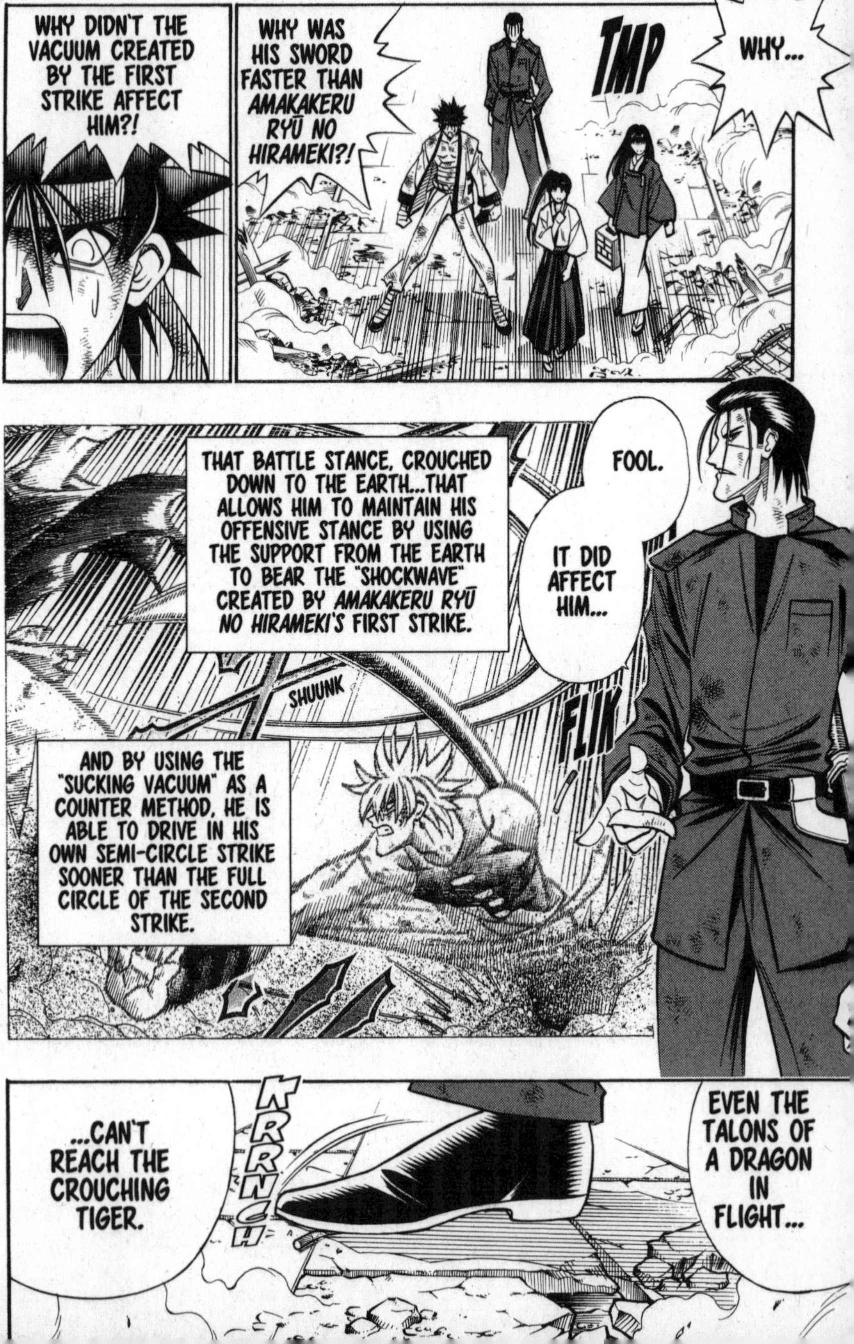
WHY...
TMP
WHY WAS HIS SWORD FASTER THAN *AMAKAKERU RYŪ NO HIRAMEKI*?!
WHY DIDN'T THE VACUUM CREATED BY THE FIRST STRIKE AFFECT HIM?!
FOOL.
IT DID AFFECT HIM...
THAT BATTLE STANCE, CROUCHED DOWN TO THE EARTH...THAT ALLOWS HIM TO MAINTAIN HIS OFFENSIVE STANCE BY USING THE SUPPORT FROM THE EARTH TO BEAR THE "SHOCKWAVE" CREATED BY *AMAKAKERU RYŪ NO HIRAMEKI*'S FIRST STRIKE.
FLIK
SHUUNK
AND BY USING THE "SUCKING VACUUM" AS A COUNTER METHOD, HE IS ABLE TO DRIVE IN HIS OWN SEMI-CIRCLE STRIKE SOONER THAN THE FULL CIRCLE OF THE SECOND STRIKE.
EVEN THE TALONS OF A DRAGON IN FLIGHT...
KRRNCH
...CAN'T REACH THE CROUCHING TIGER.

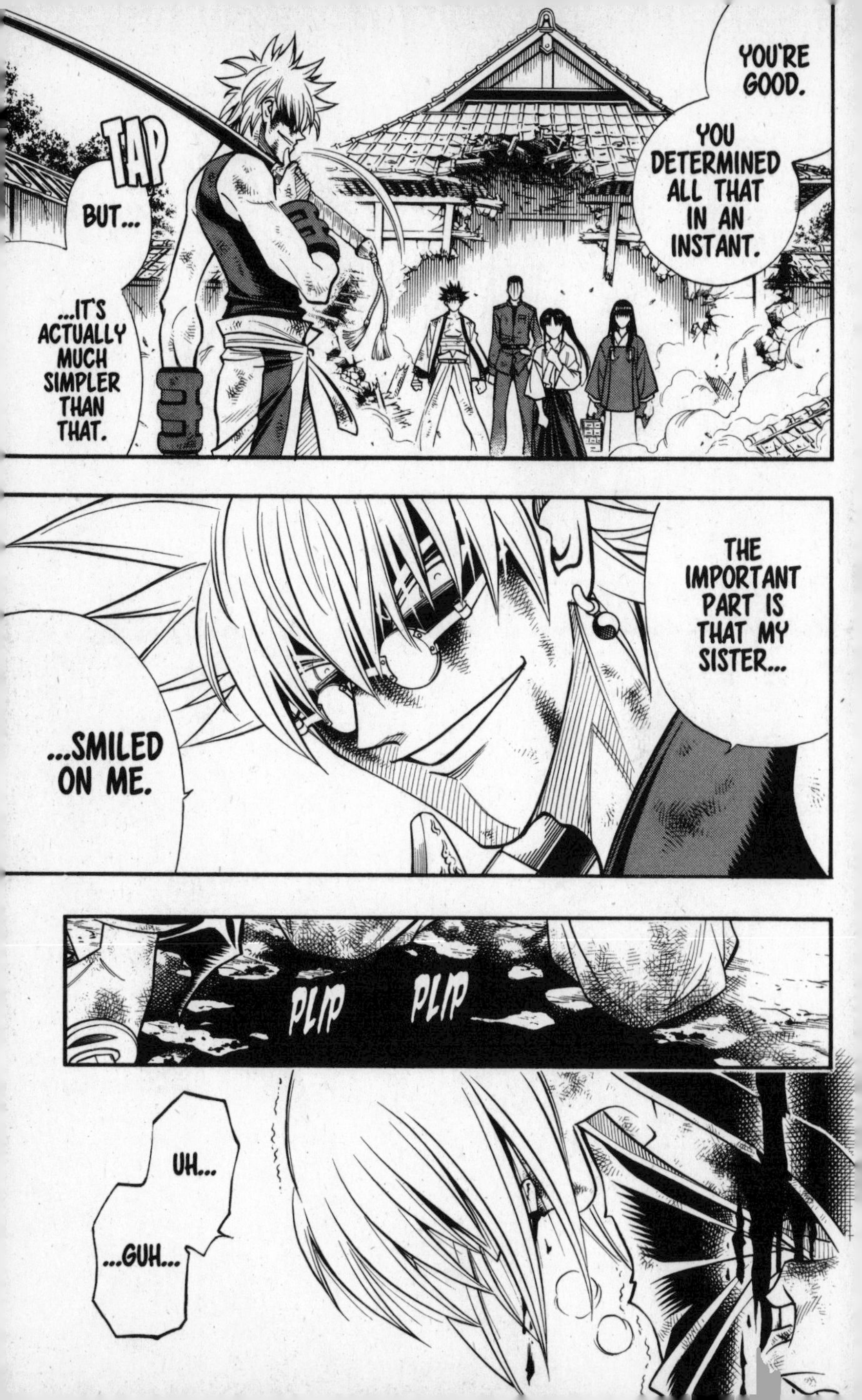
YOU'RE GOOD.
YOU DETERMINED ALL THAT IN AN INSTANT.
TAP
BUT...
...IT'S ACTUALLY MUCH SIMPLER THAN THAT.
THE IMPORTANT PART IS THAT MY SISTER...
...SMILED ON ME.
PLIP
PLIP
UH...
...GUH...

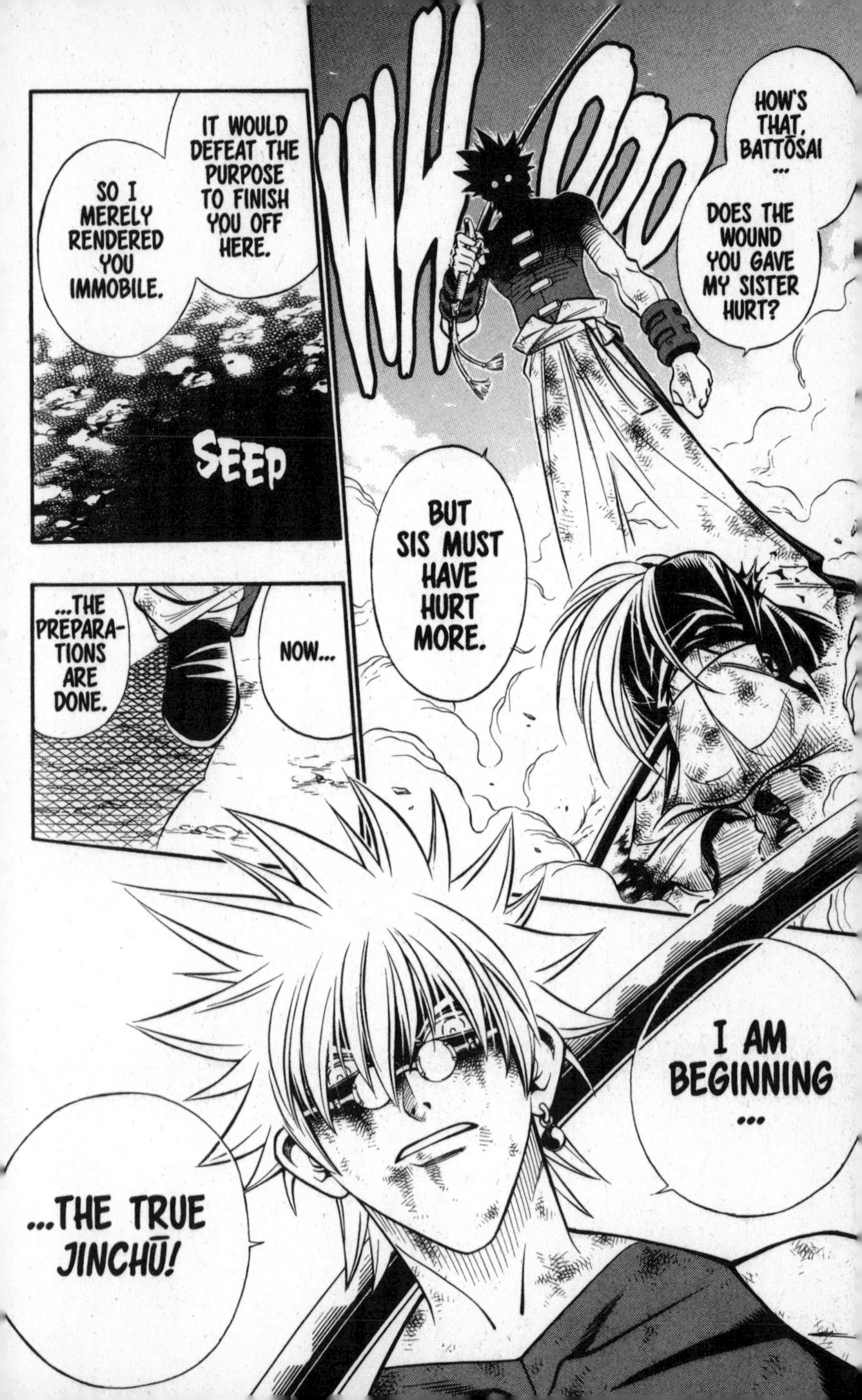
HOW'S THAT, BATTŌSAI ...
DOES THE WOUND YOU GAVE MY SISTER HURT?
WHOOO
BUT SIS MUST HAVE HURT MORE.
IT WOULD DEFEAT THE PURPOSE TO FINISH YOU OFF HERE.
SO I MERELY RENDERED YOU IMMOBILE.
SEEP
NOW...
...THE PREPARATIONS ARE DONE.
I AM BEGINNING ...
...THE TRUE JINCHŪ!

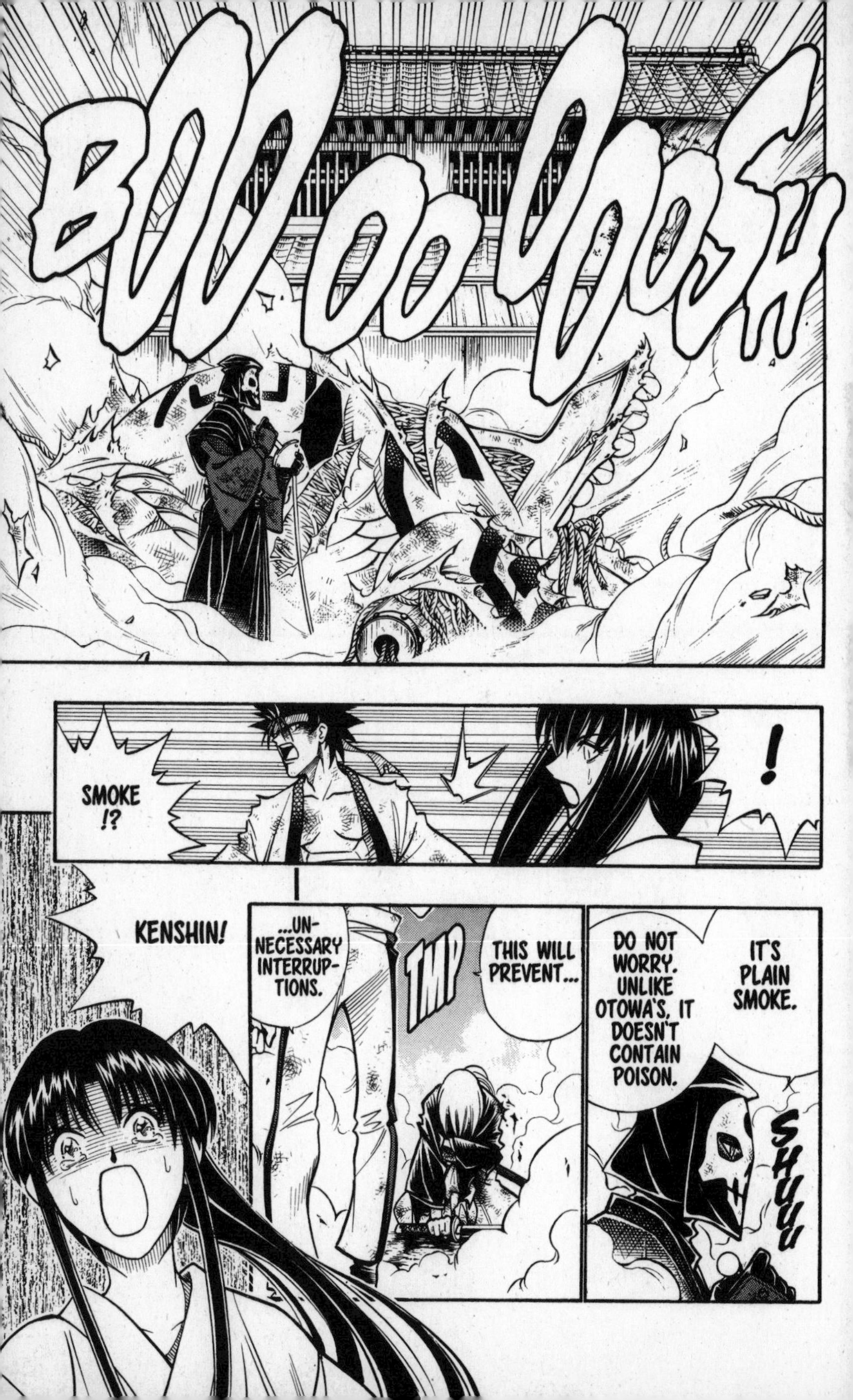
BOOOOOOSH
!
SMOKE !?
IT'S PLAIN SMOKE.
DO NOT WORRY. UNLIKE OTOWA'S, IT DOESN'T CONTAIN POISON.
SHUUU
THIS WILL PREVENT...
TMP
...UN-NECESSARY INTERRUP-TIONS.
KENSHIN!

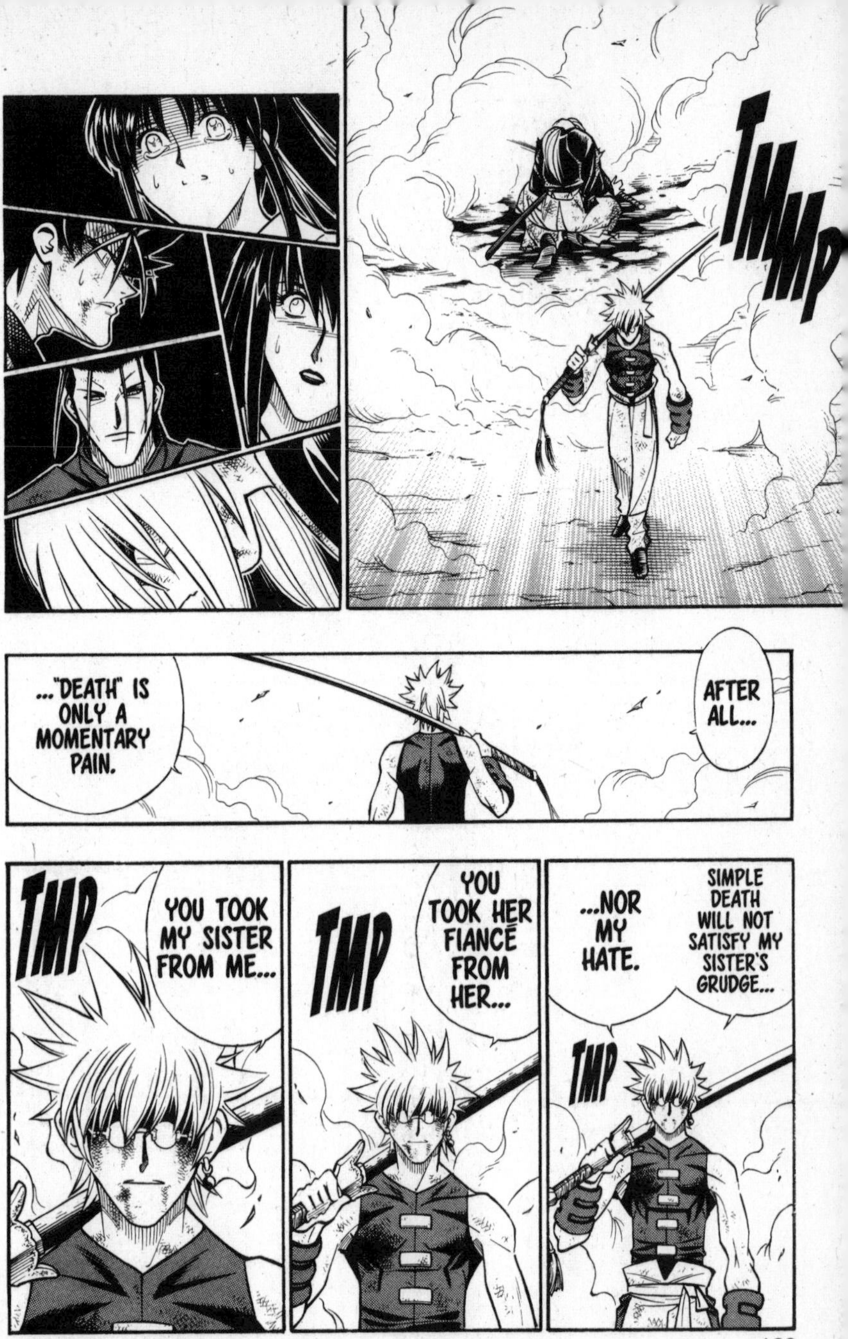
TMMP
AFTER ALL...
..."DEATH" IS ONLY A MOMENTARY PAIN.
SIMPLE DEATH WILL NOT SATISFY MY SISTER'S GRUDGE...
...NOR MY HATE.
TMP
YOU TOOK HER FIANCÉ FROM HER...
TMP
YOU TOOK MY SISTER FROM ME...
TMP

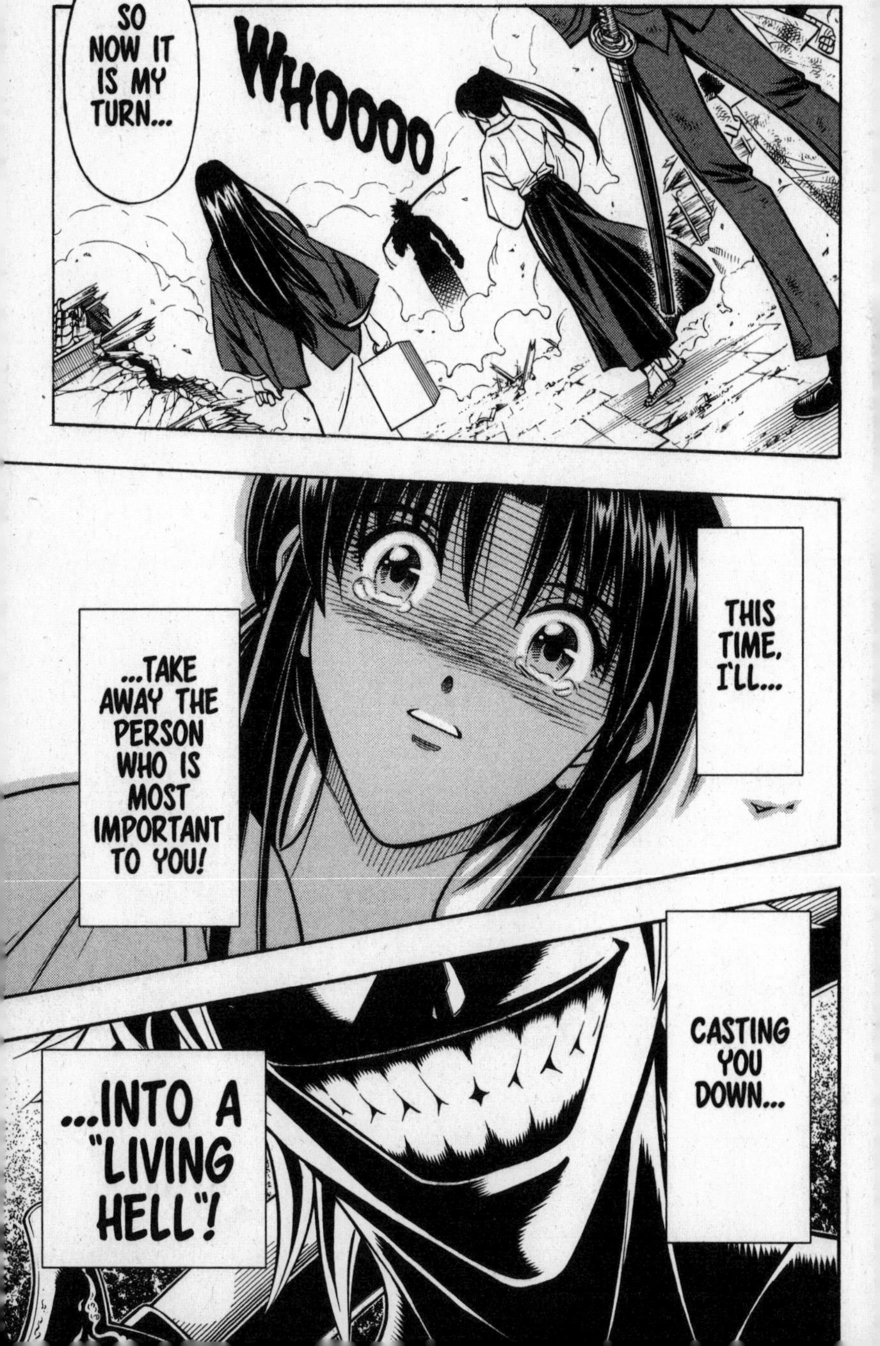
WHOOOO
SO NOW IT IS MY TURN...
THIS TIME, I'LL...
...TAKE AWAY THE PERSON WHO IS MOST IMPORTANT TO YOU!
CASTING YOU DOWN...
...INTO A "LIVING HELL"!

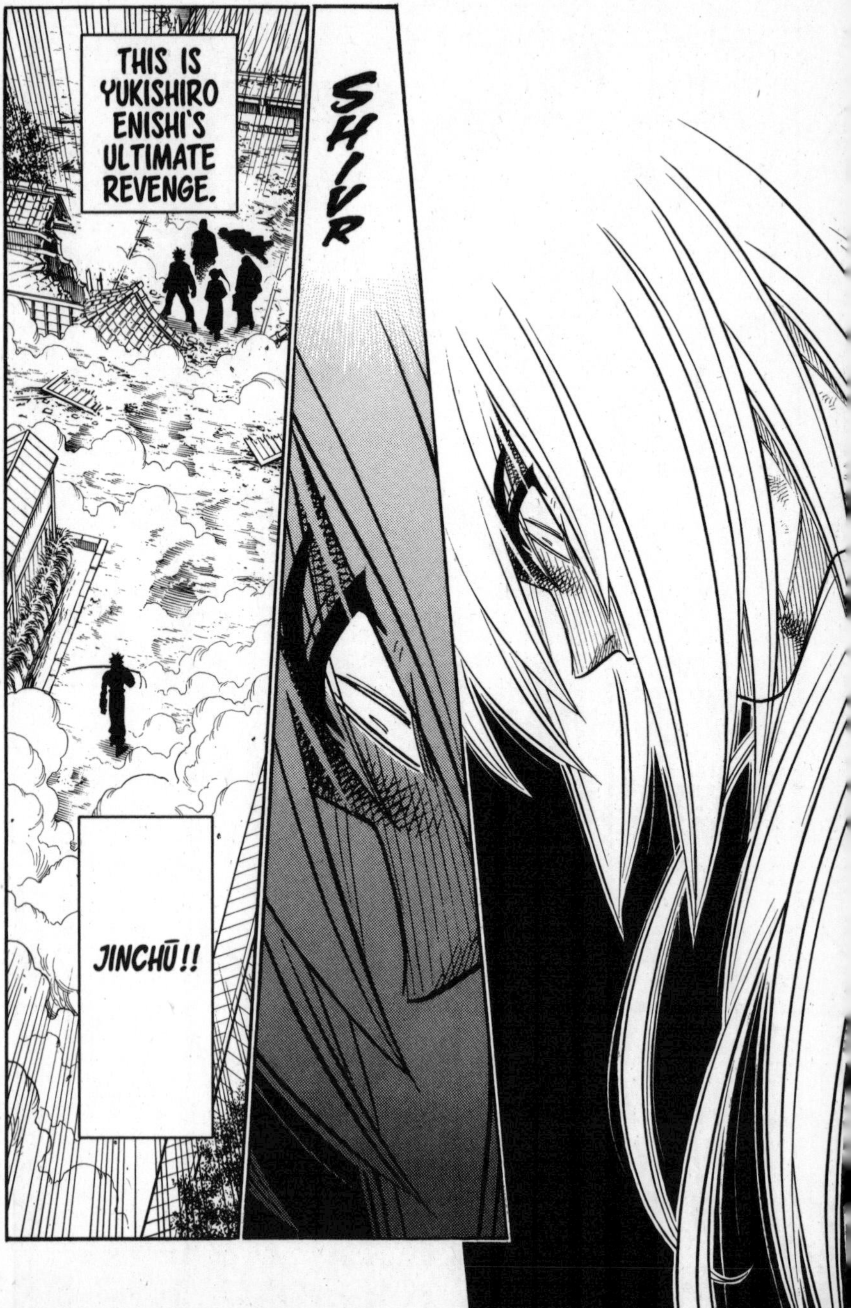
SHIVR
THIS IS YUKISHIRO ENISHI'S ULTIMATE REVENGE.
JINCHŪ!!

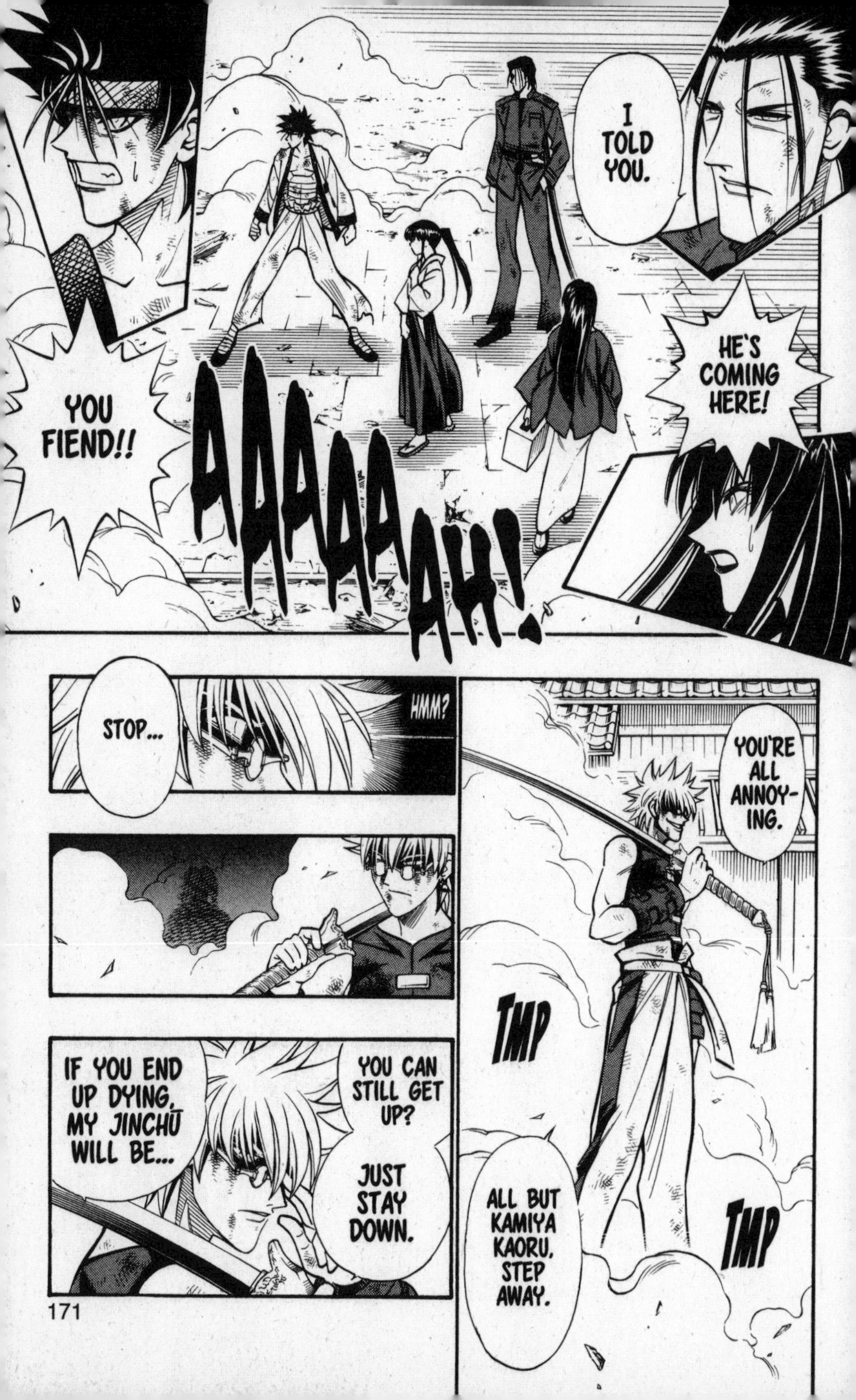
I TOLD YOU.
HE'S COMING HERE!
AAAAAAH!!
YOU FIEND!!
YOU'RE ALL ANNOY-ING.
TMP
TMP
ALL BUT KAMIYA KAORU, STEP AWAY.
HMM?
STOP...
YOU CAN STILL GET UP?
JUST STAY DOWN.
IF YOU END UP DYING, MY JINCHŪ WILL BE...

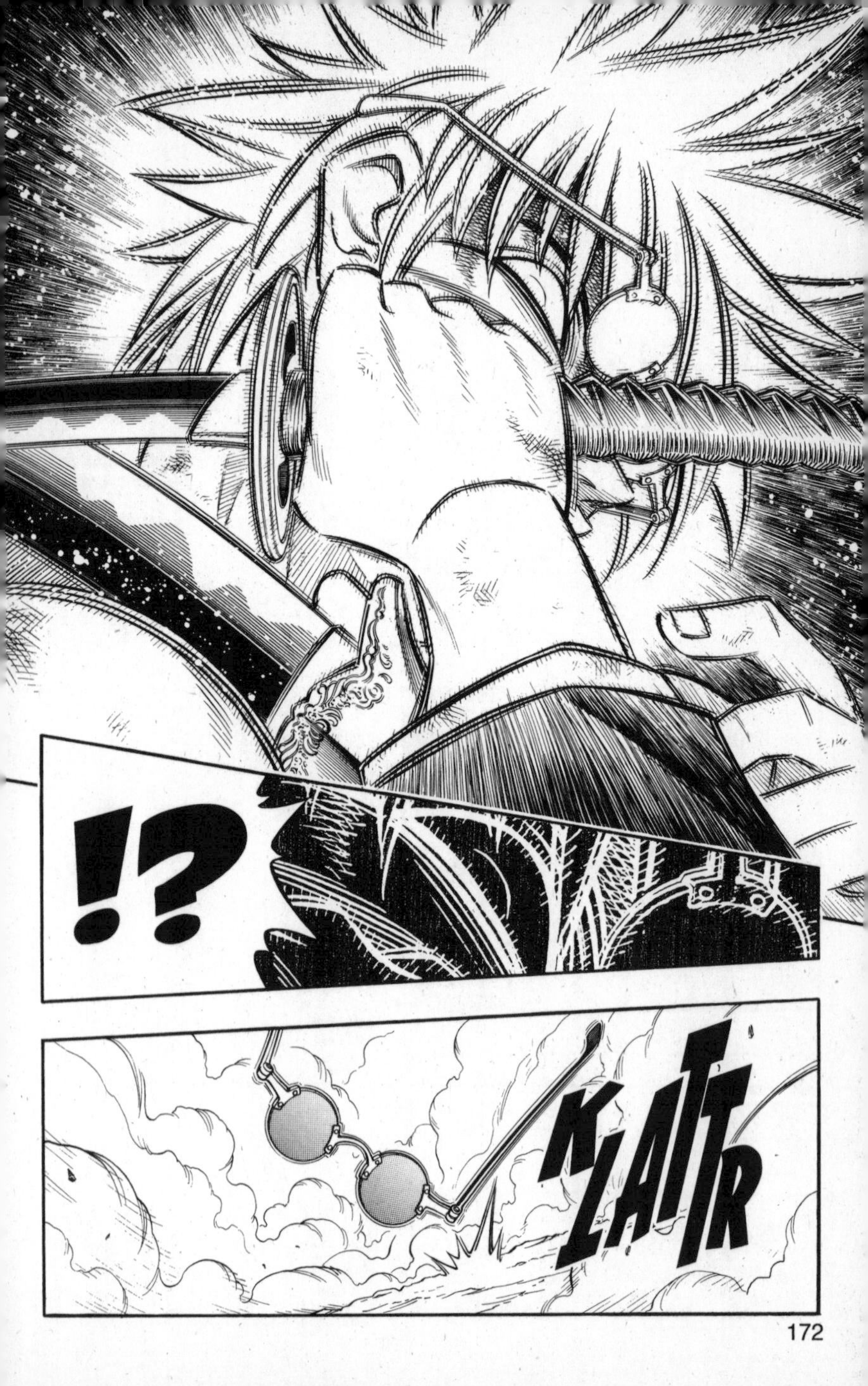
!?
KLATTR

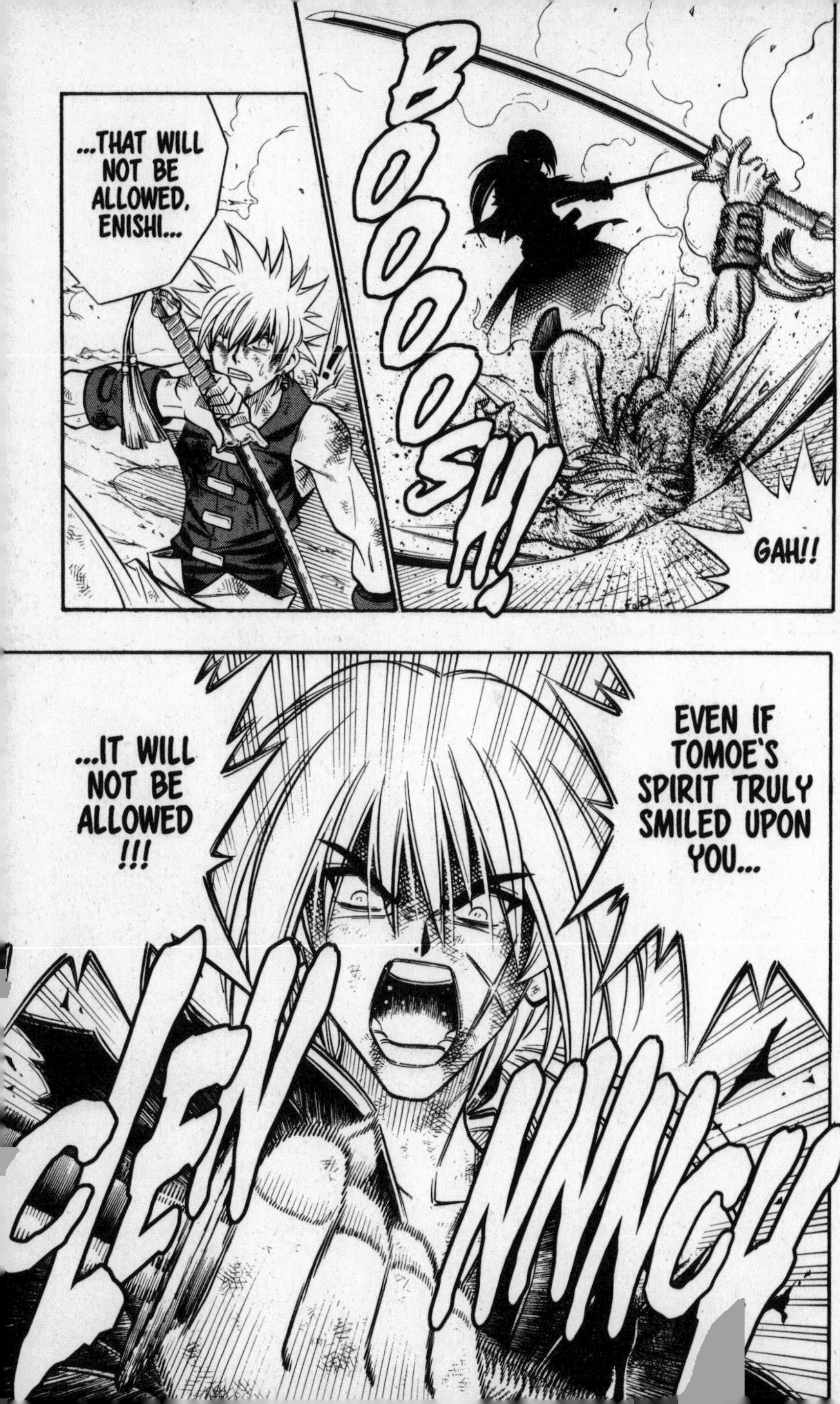
BOOOOOSH!!
GAH!!
...THAT WILL NOT BE ALLOWED, ENISHI...
!
EVEN IF TOMOE'S SPIRIT TRULY SMILED UPON YOU...
...IT WILL NOT BE ALLOWED !!!
CLENNNNCH!!

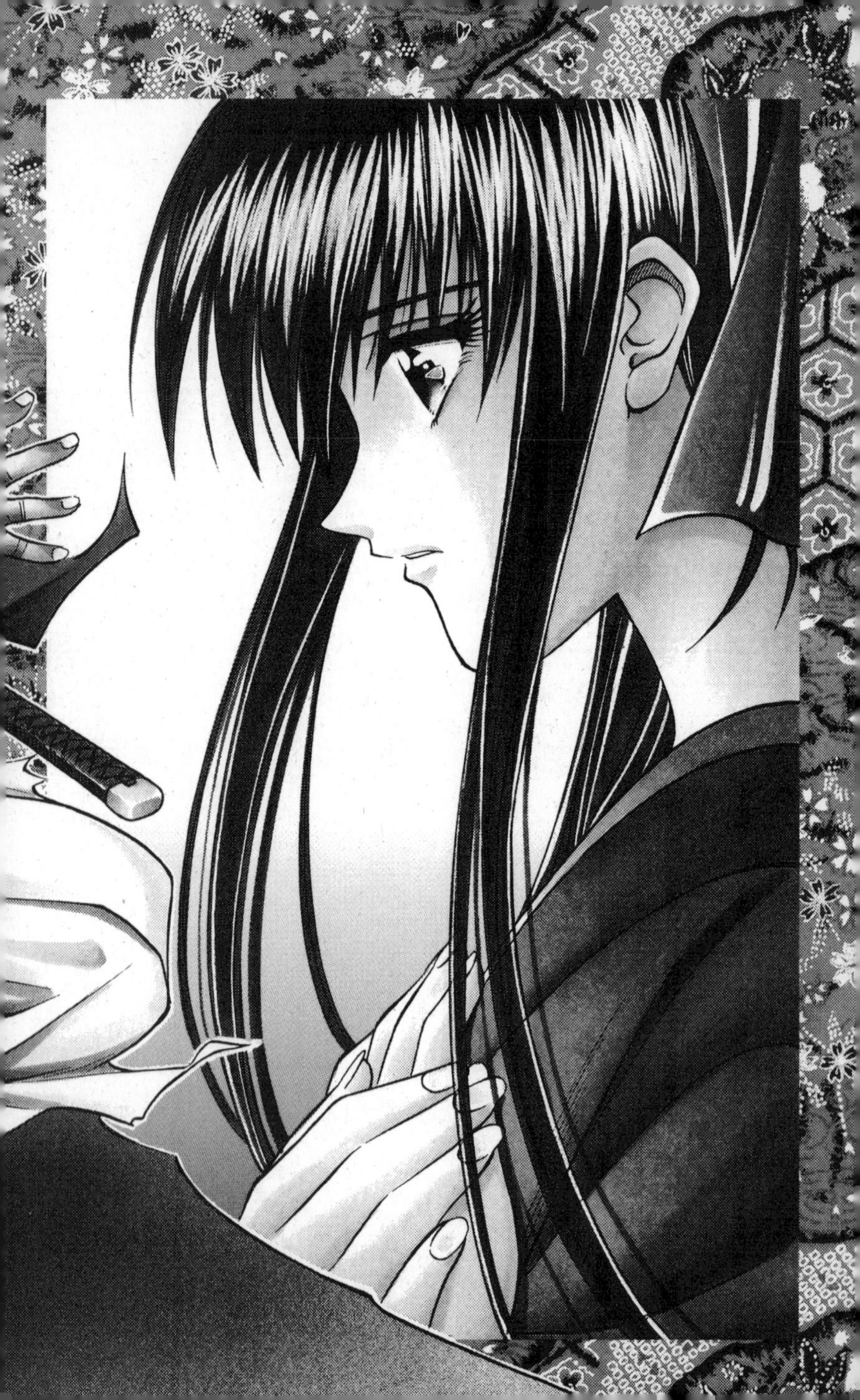

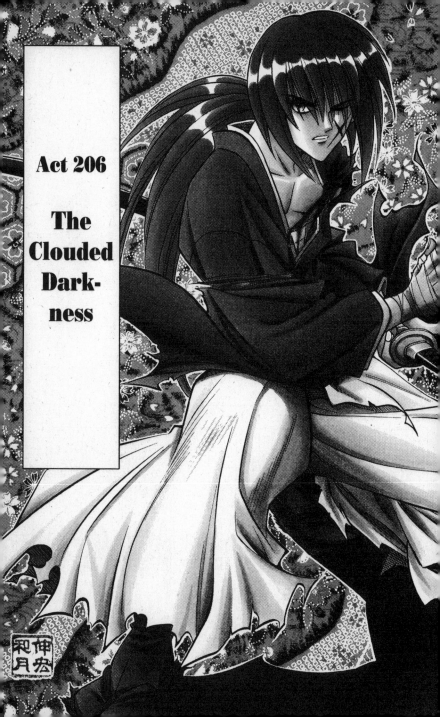

Act 206

The Clouded Dark- ness

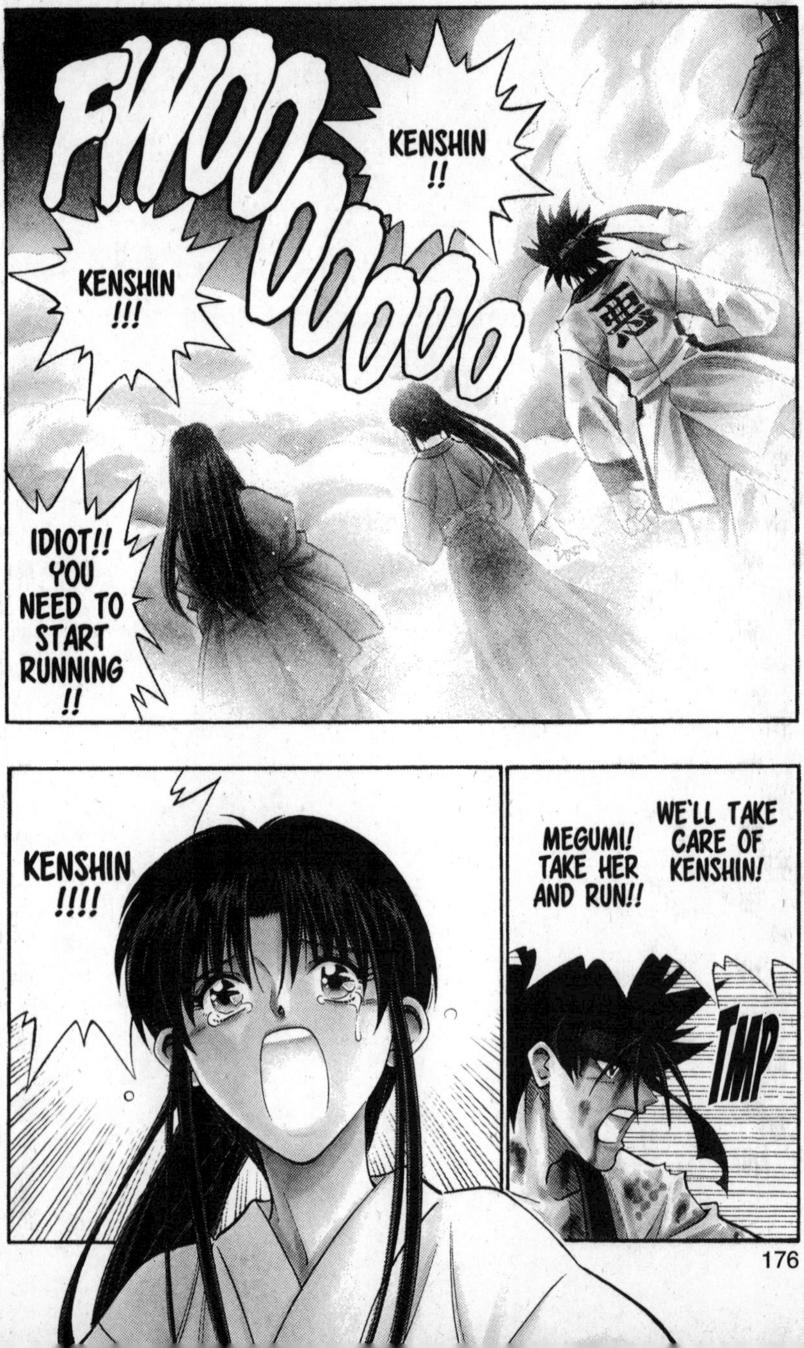
KENSHIN !!
FWOOOOOOOO
KENSHIN !!!
IDIOT!! YOU NEED TO START RUNNING !!
WE'LL TAKE CARE OF KENSHIN!
MEGUMI! TAKE HER AND RUN!!
TMP
KENSHIN !!!!

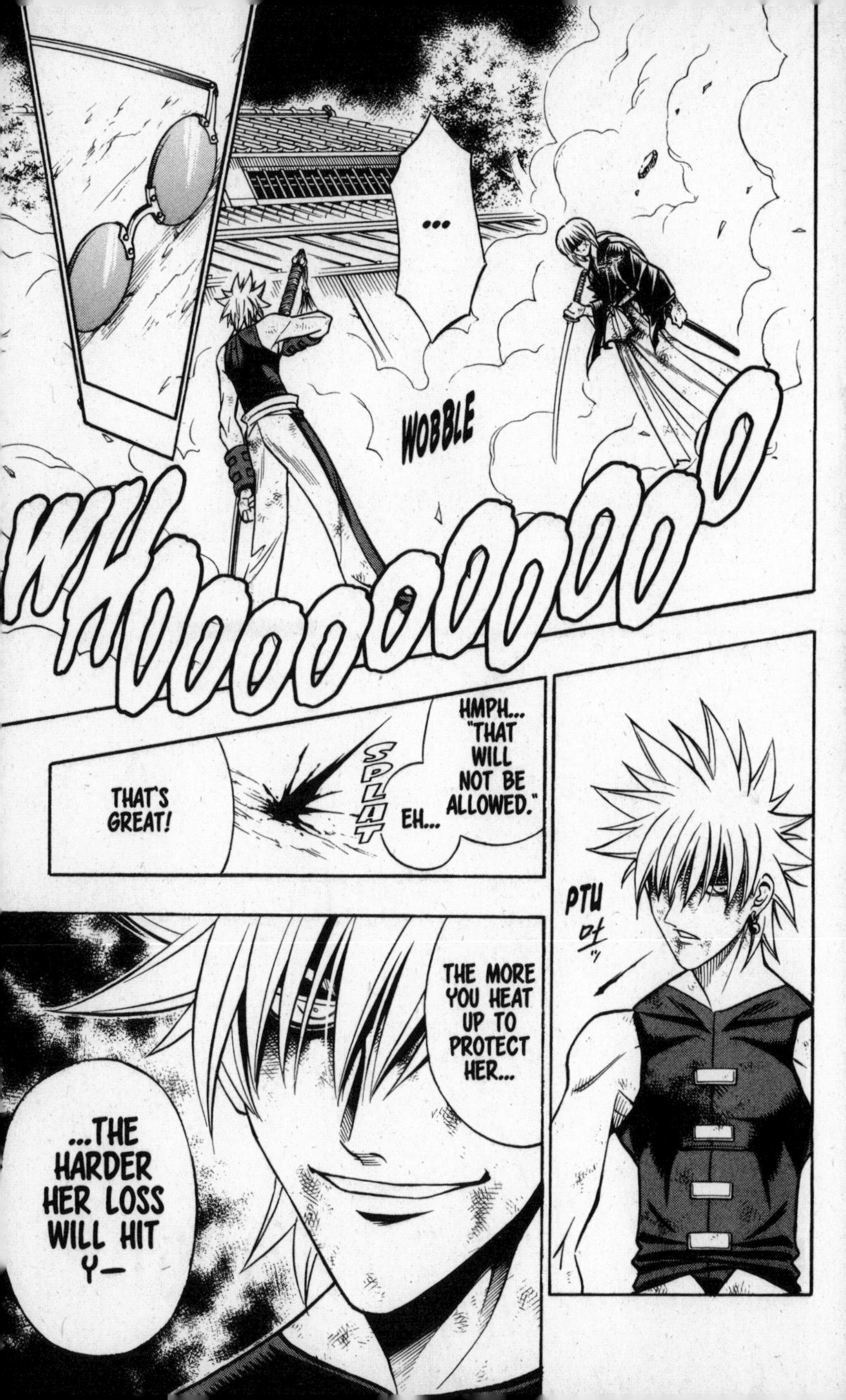
...
WOBBLE
WHOOOOOOOOOOOOO
PTU
HMPH... "THAT WILL NOT BE ALLOWED."
EH...
SPLAT
THAT'S GREAT!
THE MORE YOU HEAT UP TO PROTECT HER...
...THE HARDER HER LOSS WILL HIT Y—

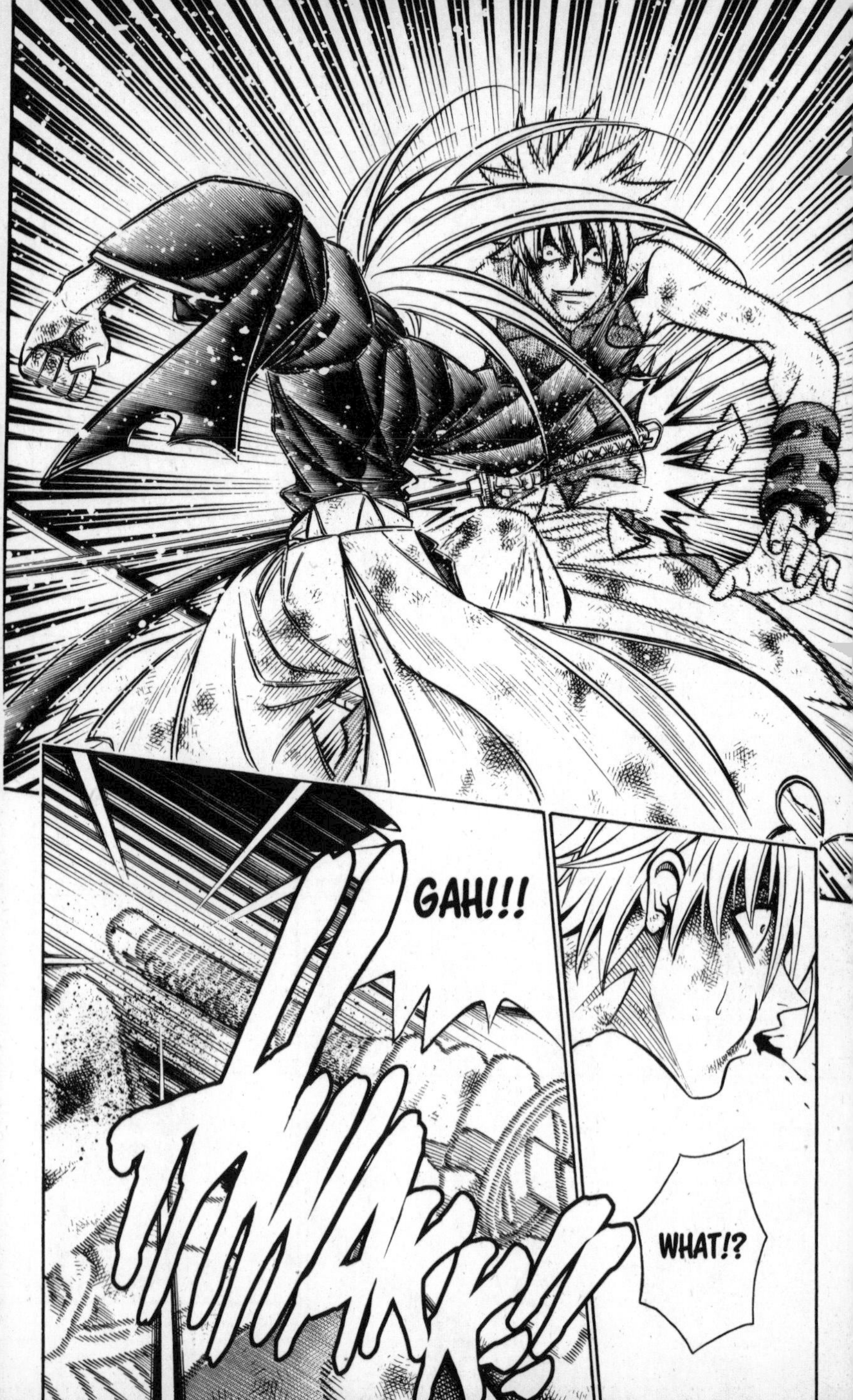
WHAT!?
GAH!!!

READ THIS WAY

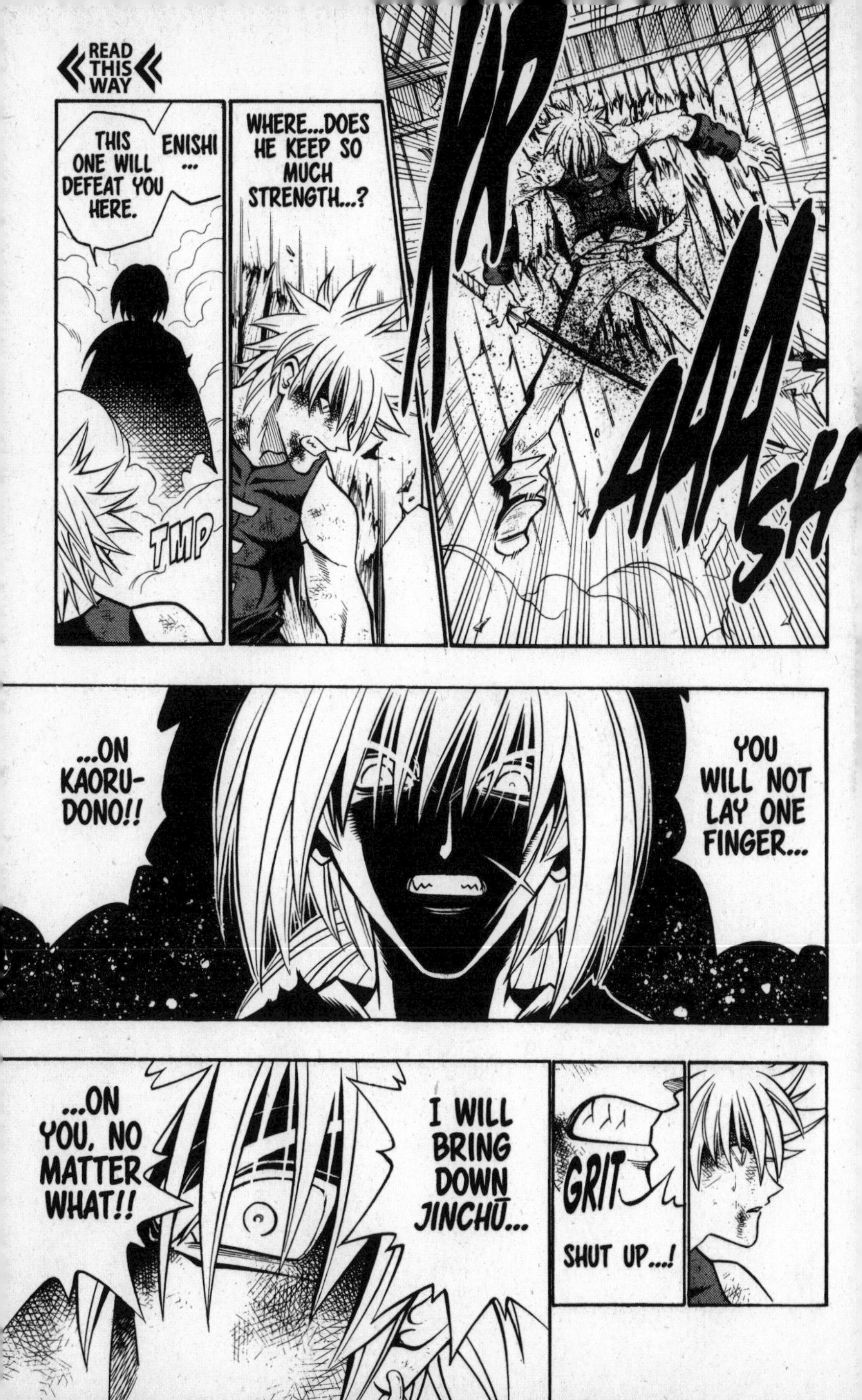

WHERE...DOES HE KEEP SO MUCH STRENGTH...?
ENISHI...
THIS ONE WILL DEFEAT YOU HERE.
TMP
YOU WILL NOT LAY ONE FINGER...
...ON KAORU-DONO!!
GRIT
SHUT UP...!
I WILL BRING DOWN JINCHŪ...
...ON YOU, NO MATTER WHAT!!

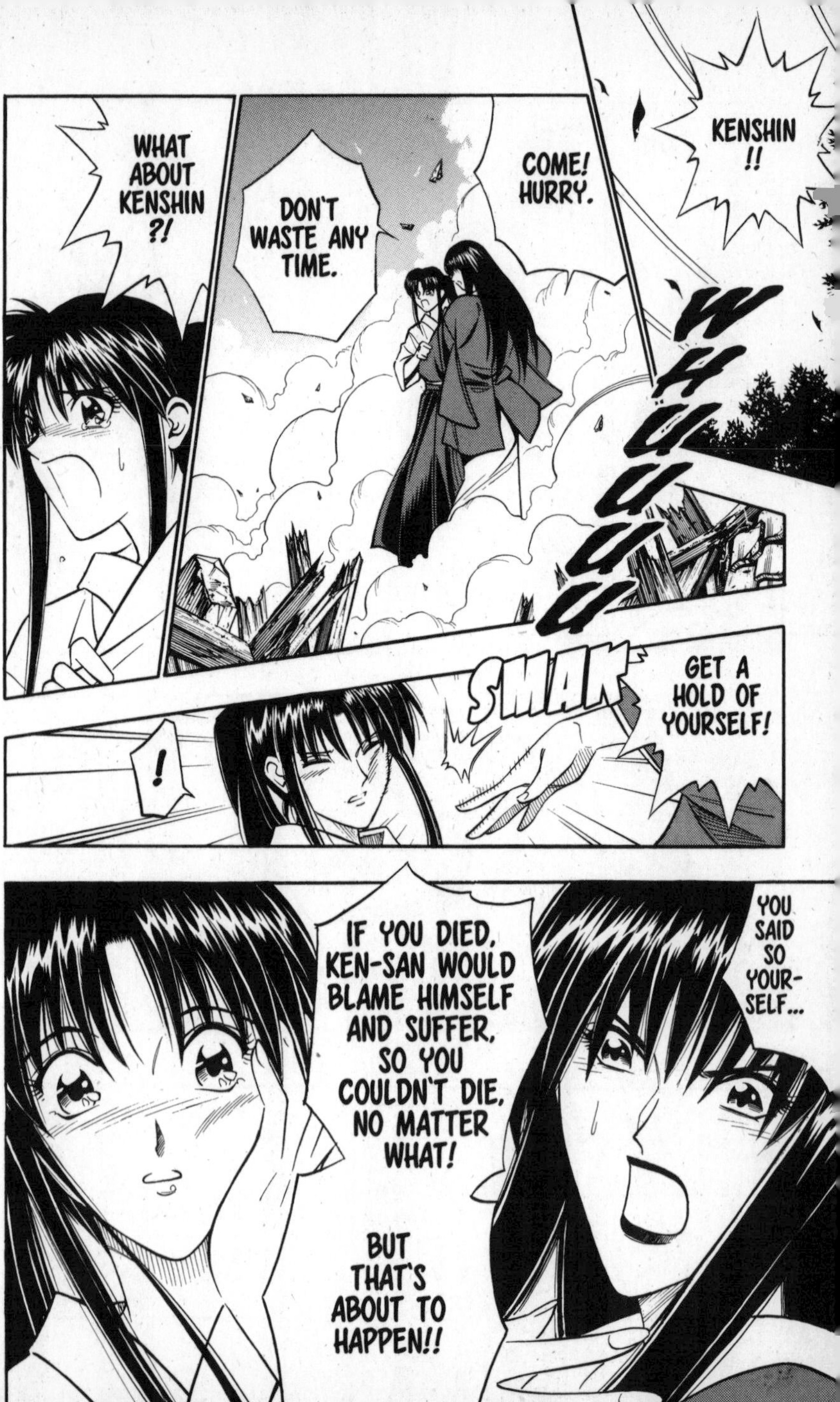
KENSHIN !!
WHUUUUUU
COME! HURRY.
DON'T WASTE ANY TIME.
WHAT ABOUT KENSHIN ?!
GET A HOLD OF YOURSELF!
SMAK
!
YOU SAID SO YOUR-SELF...
IF YOU DIED, KEN-SAN WOULD BLAME HIMSELF AND SUFFER, SO YOU COULDN'T DIE, NO MATTER WHAT!
BUT THAT'S ABOUT TO HAPPEN!!

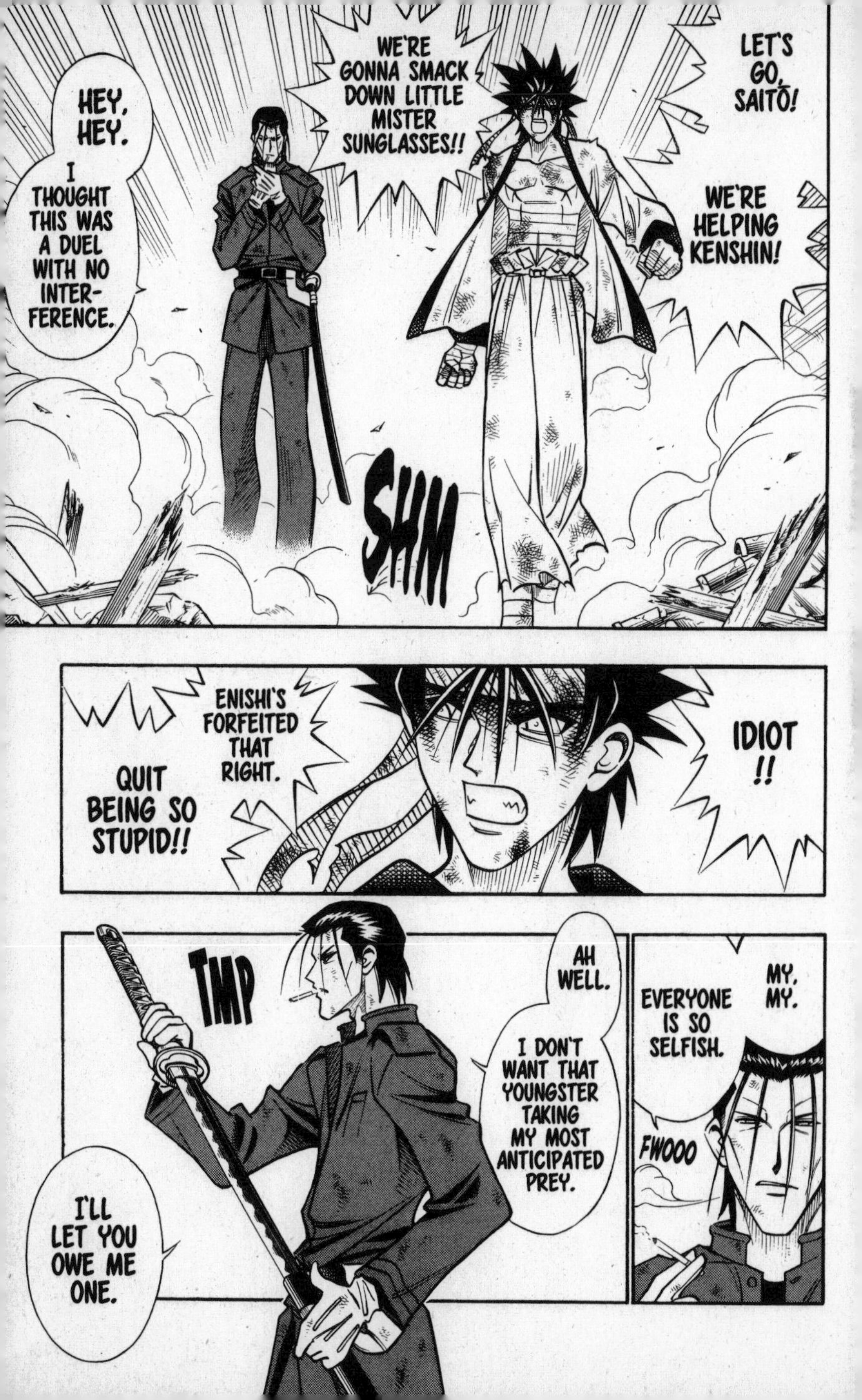
LET'S GO, SAITŌ!
WE'RE HELPING KENSHIN!
WE'RE GONNA SMACK DOWN LITTLE MISTER SUNGLASSES!!
SHM
HEY, HEY.
I THOUGHT THIS WAS A DUEL WITH NO INTER-FERENCE.
IDIOT!!
ENISHI'S FORFEITED THAT RIGHT.
QUIT BEING SO STUPID!!
MY, MY.
EVERYONE IS SO SELFISH.
FWOOO
AH WELL.
I DON'T WANT THAT YOUNGSTER TAKING MY MOST ANTICIPATED PREY.
TMP
I'LL LET YOU OWE ME ONE.

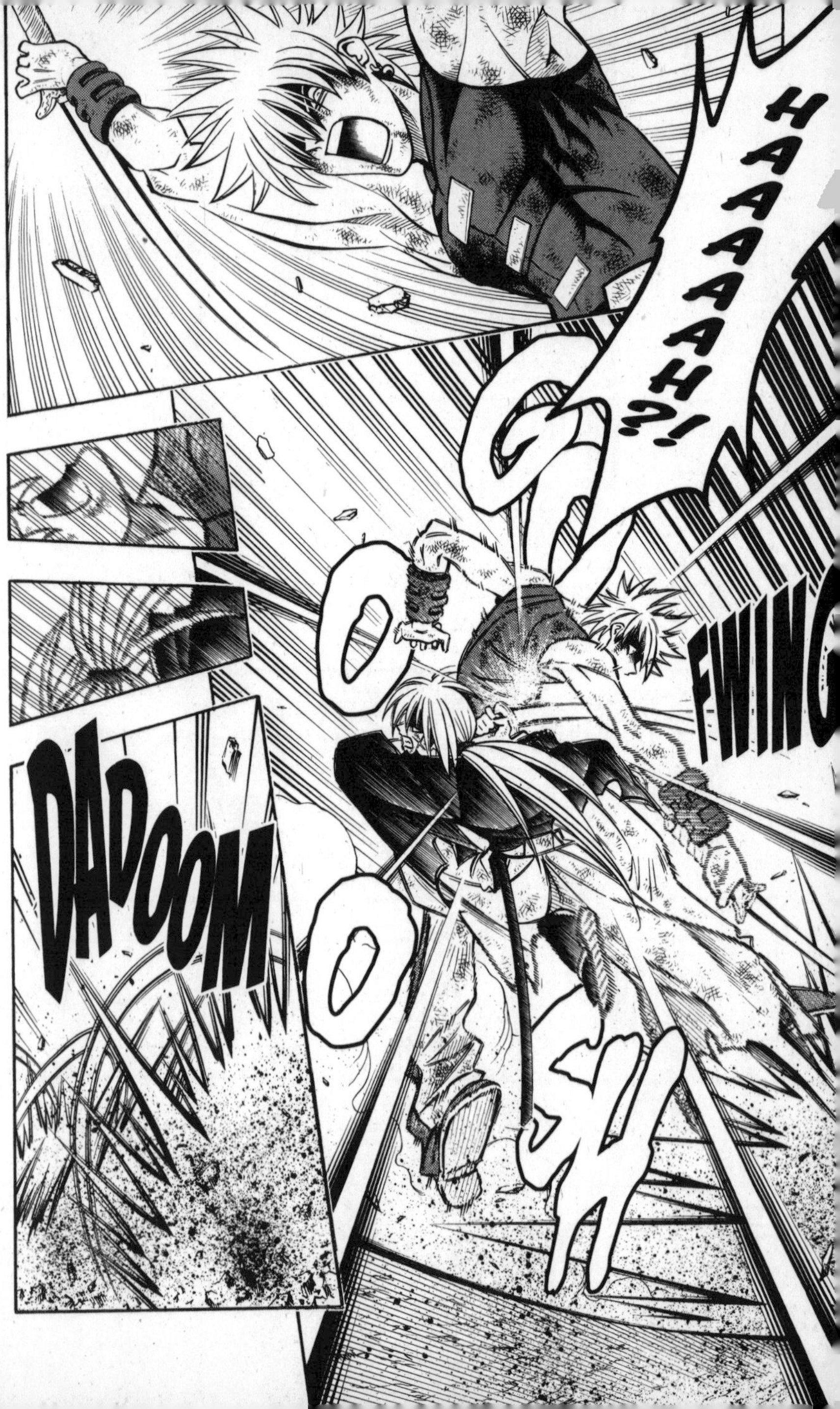
HAAAAAH?!
FWING
GOOSH
DADOOM

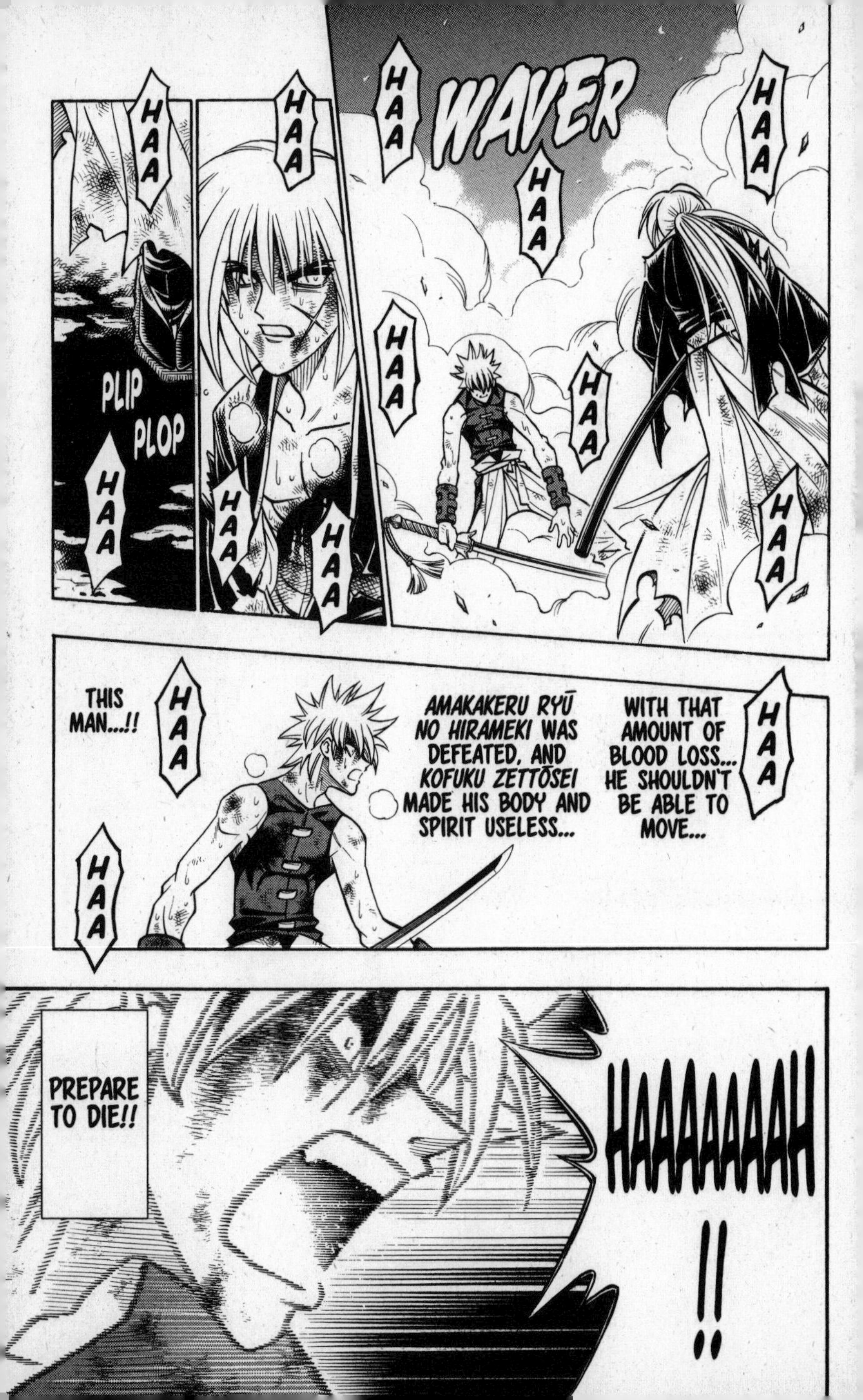
HAA
HAA
WAVER
HAA
HAA
HAA
HAA
HAA
HAA
HAA
HAA
HAA
PLIP
PLOP
HAA
HAA
WITH THAT AMOUNT OF BLOOD LOSS... HE SHOULDN'T BE ABLE TO MOVE...
AMAKAKERU RYŪ NO HIRAMEKI WAS DEFEATED, AND KOFUKU ZETTŌSEI MADE HIS BODY AND SPIRIT USELESS...
HAA
THIS MAN...!!
HAA
HAAAAAAH!!
PREPARE TO DIE!!

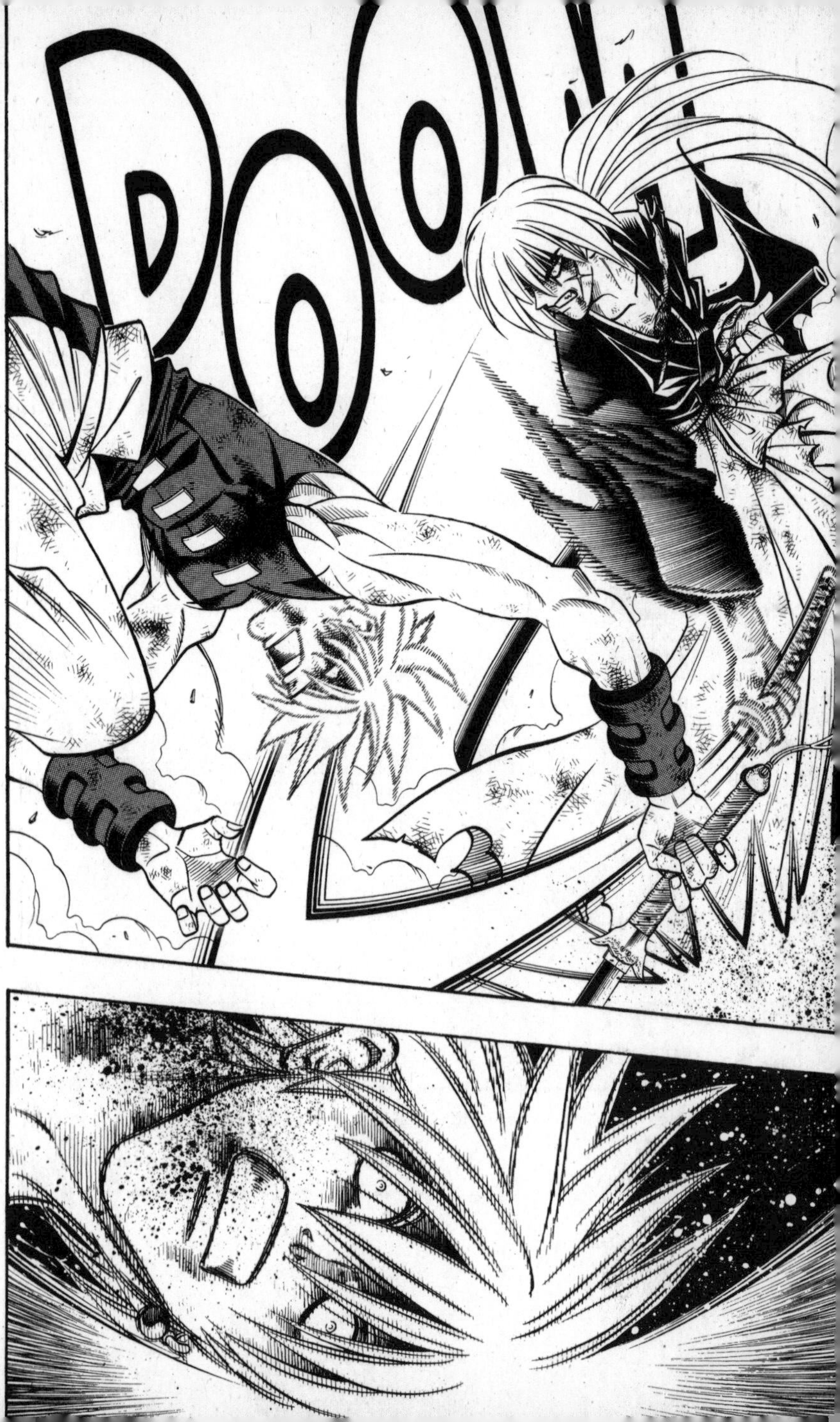
DOO!!

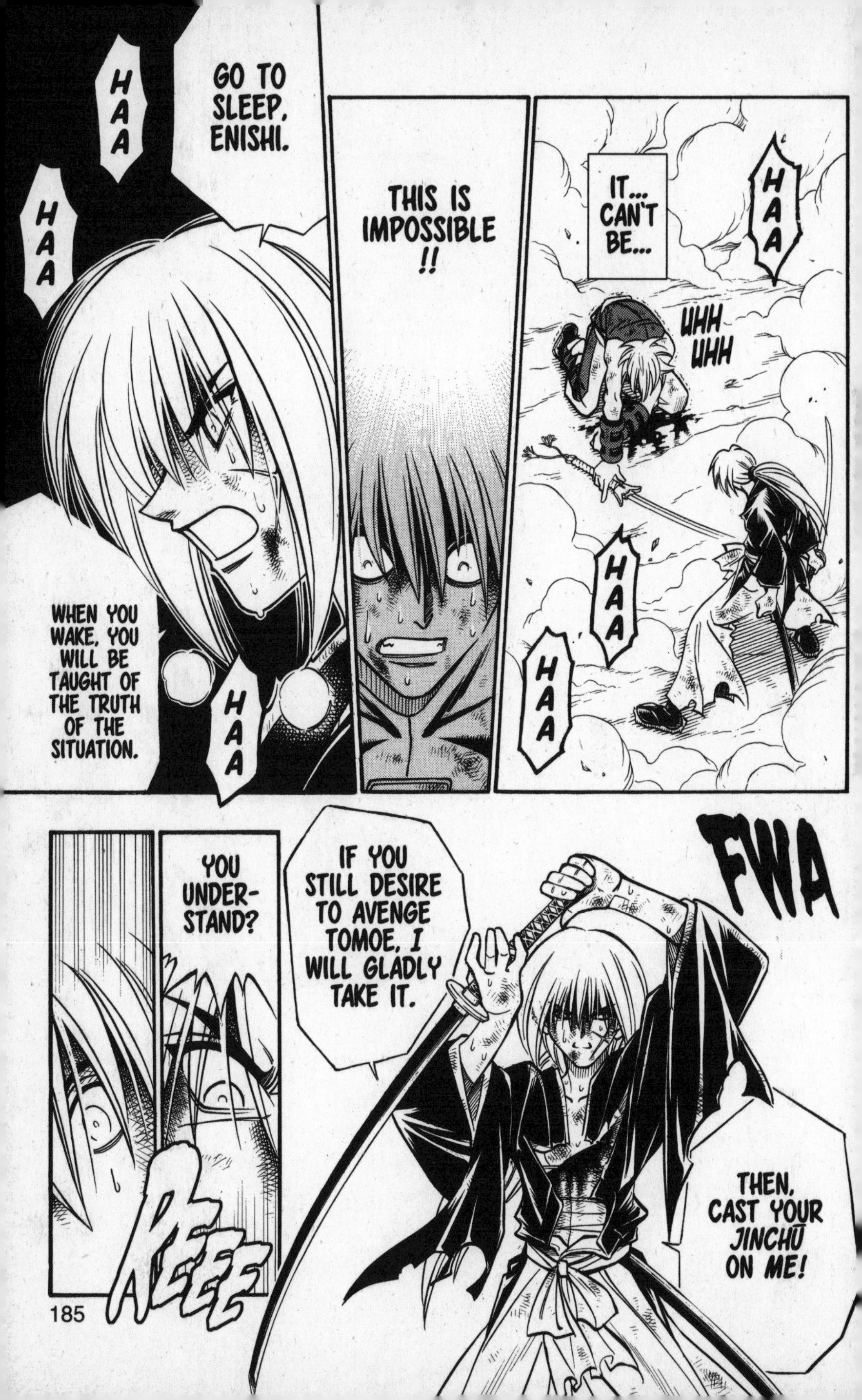
HAA
IT... CAN'T BE...
UHH UHH
HAA
HAA
THIS IS IMPOSSIBLE !!
GO TO SLEEP, ENISHI.
HAA
HAA
WHEN YOU WAKE, YOU WILL BE TAUGHT OF THE TRUTH OF THE SITUATION.
HAA
FWA
IF YOU STILL DESIRE TO AVENGE TOMOE, I WILL GLADLY TAKE IT.
THEN, CAST YOUR JINCHŪ ON ME!
YOU UNDER-STAND?

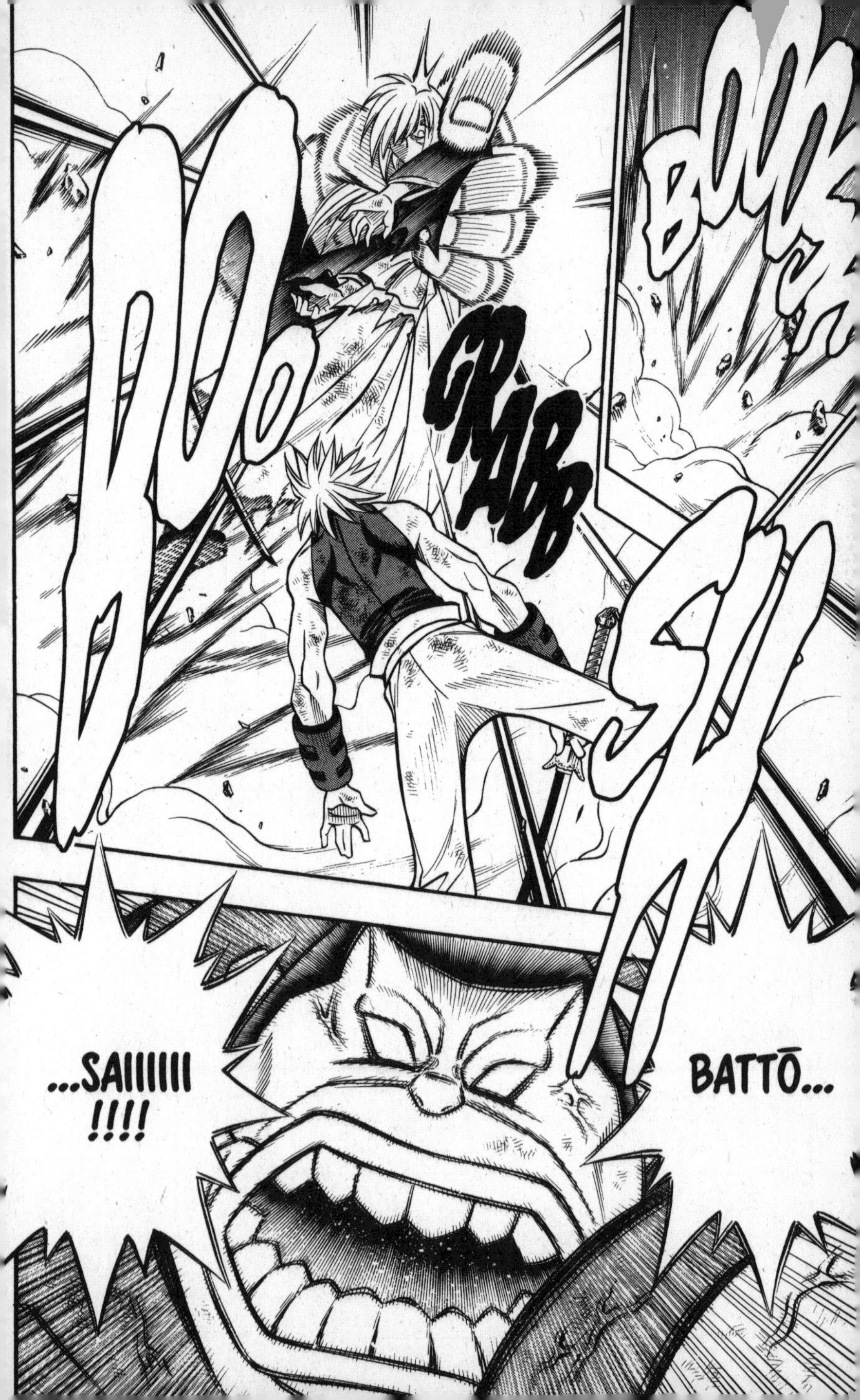
GRABB
BATTŌ...
...SAIIIIIII
!!!!

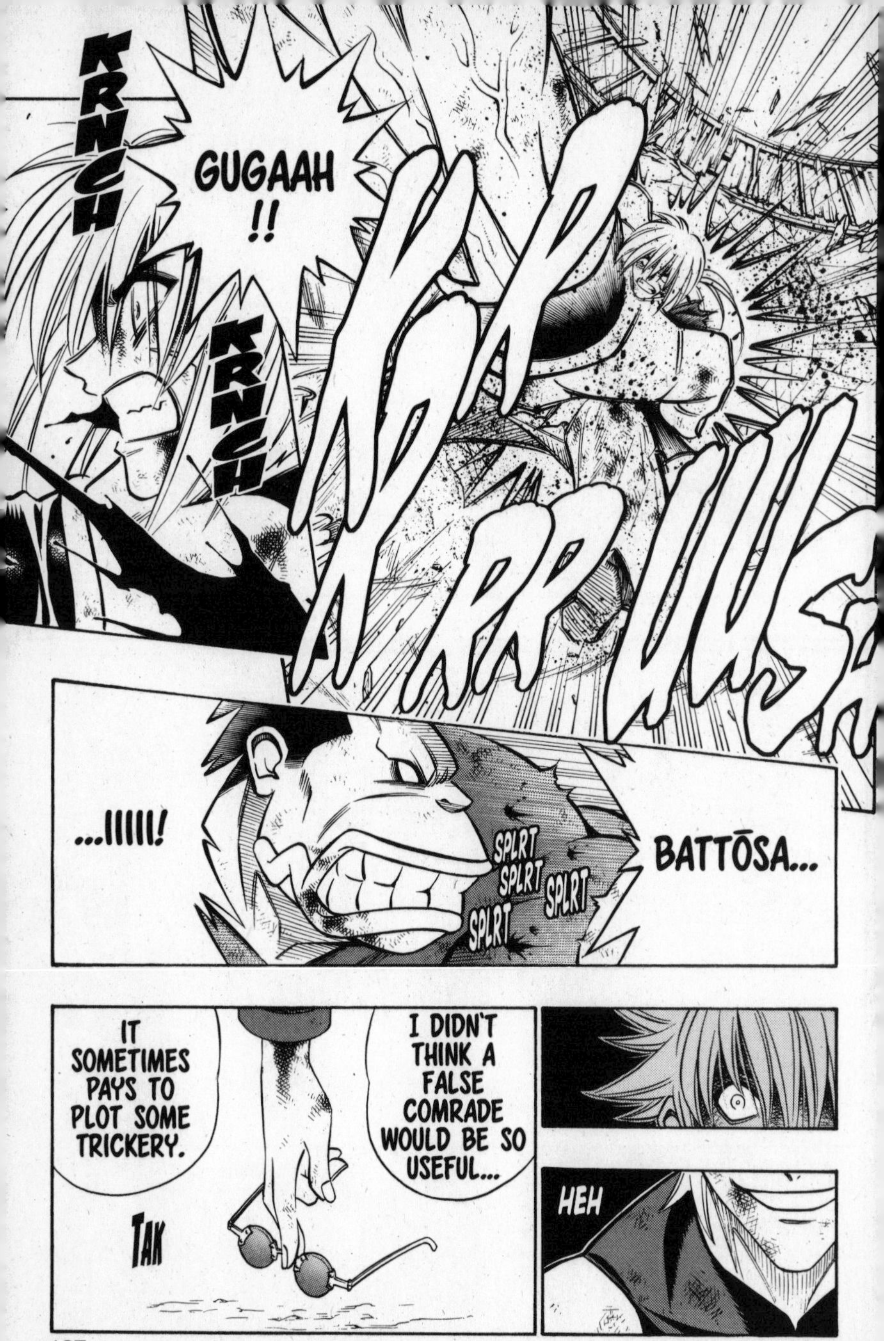
GUGAAH !!
KRNCH
KRNCH
BATTŌSA...
SPLRT
SPLRT
SPLRT
SPLRT
...IIIIII!
HEH
I DIDN'T THINK A FALSE COMRADE WOULD BE SO USEFUL...
IT SOMETIMES PAYS TO PLOT SOME TRICKERY.
TAK

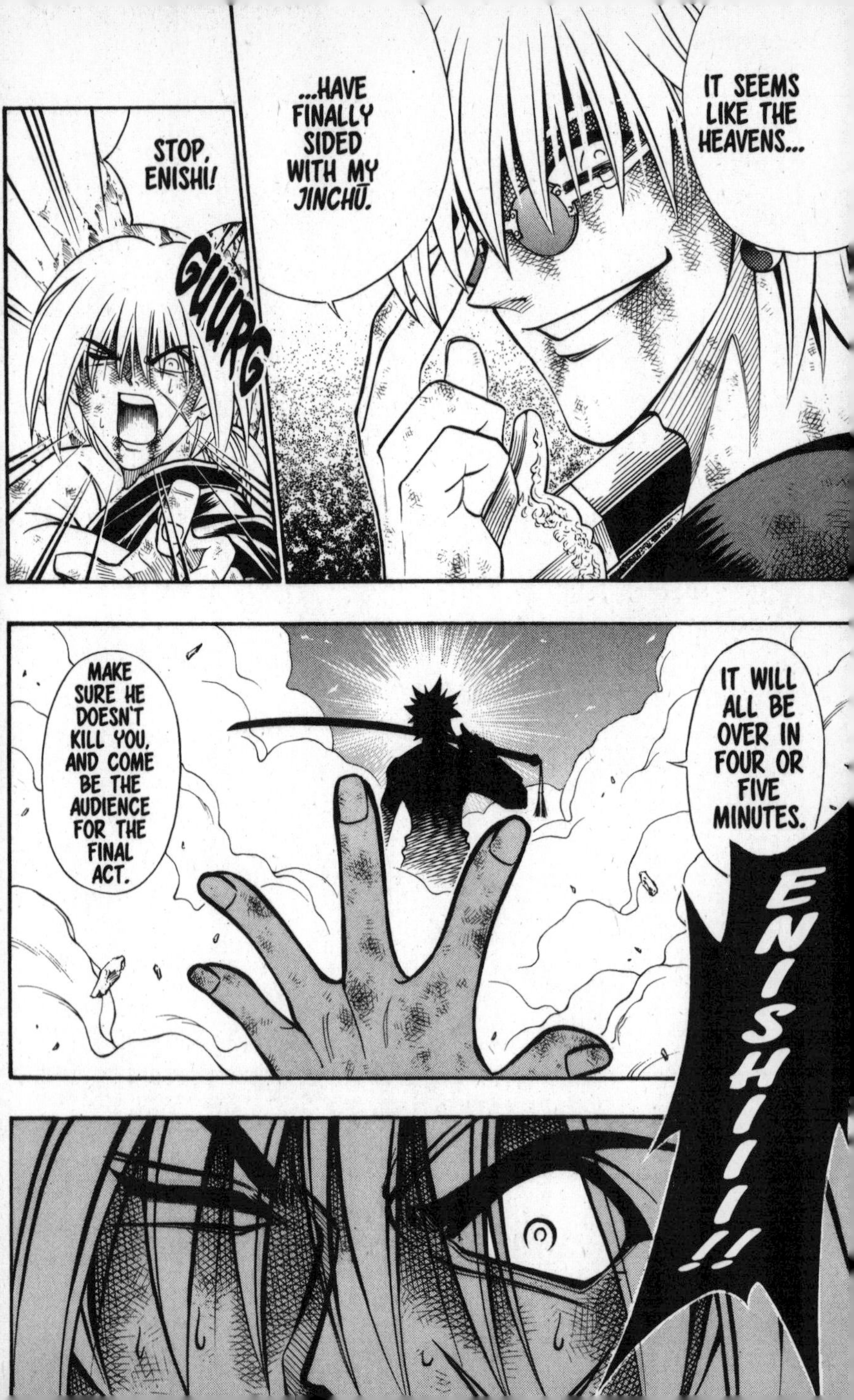
IT SEEMS LIKE THE HEAVENS...
...HAVE FINALLY SIDED WITH MY JINCHŪ.
STOP, ENISHI!
GUURG
IT WILL ALL BE OVER IN FOUR OR FIVE MINUTES.
MAKE SURE HE DOESN'T KILL YOU, AND COME BE THE AUDIENCE FOR THE FINAL ACT.
ENISHIIIII!!

READ THIS WAY

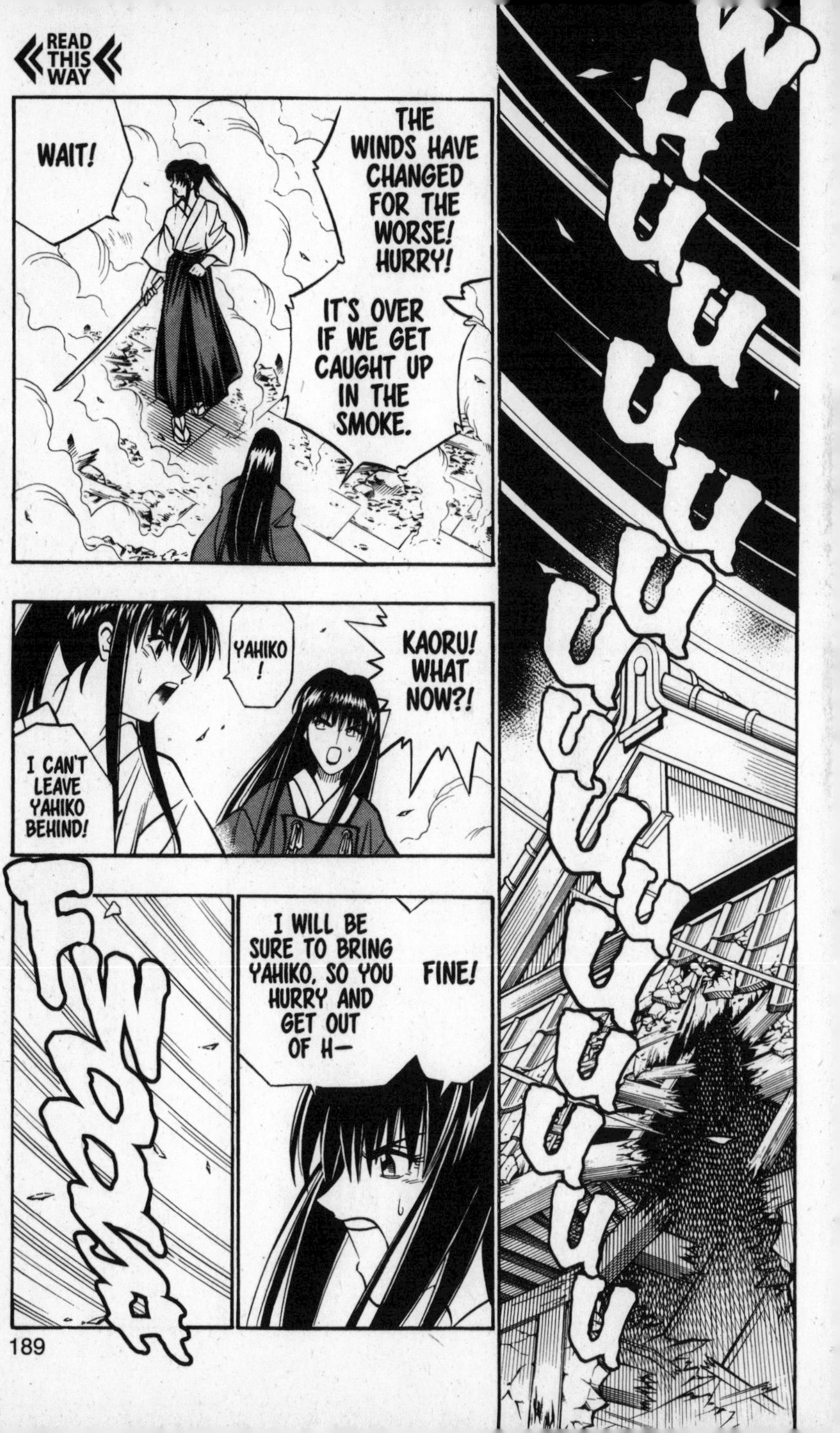
WHUUUUUUUUUUUUUUUU
THE WINDS HAVE CHANGED FOR THE WORSE! HURRY!
IT'S OVER IF WE GET CAUGHT UP IN THE SMOKE.
WAIT!
KAORU! WHAT NOW?!
YAHIKO!
I CAN'T LEAVE YAHIKO BEHIND!
FINE!
I WILL BE SURE TO BRING YAHIKO, SO YOU HURRY AND GET OUT OF H—

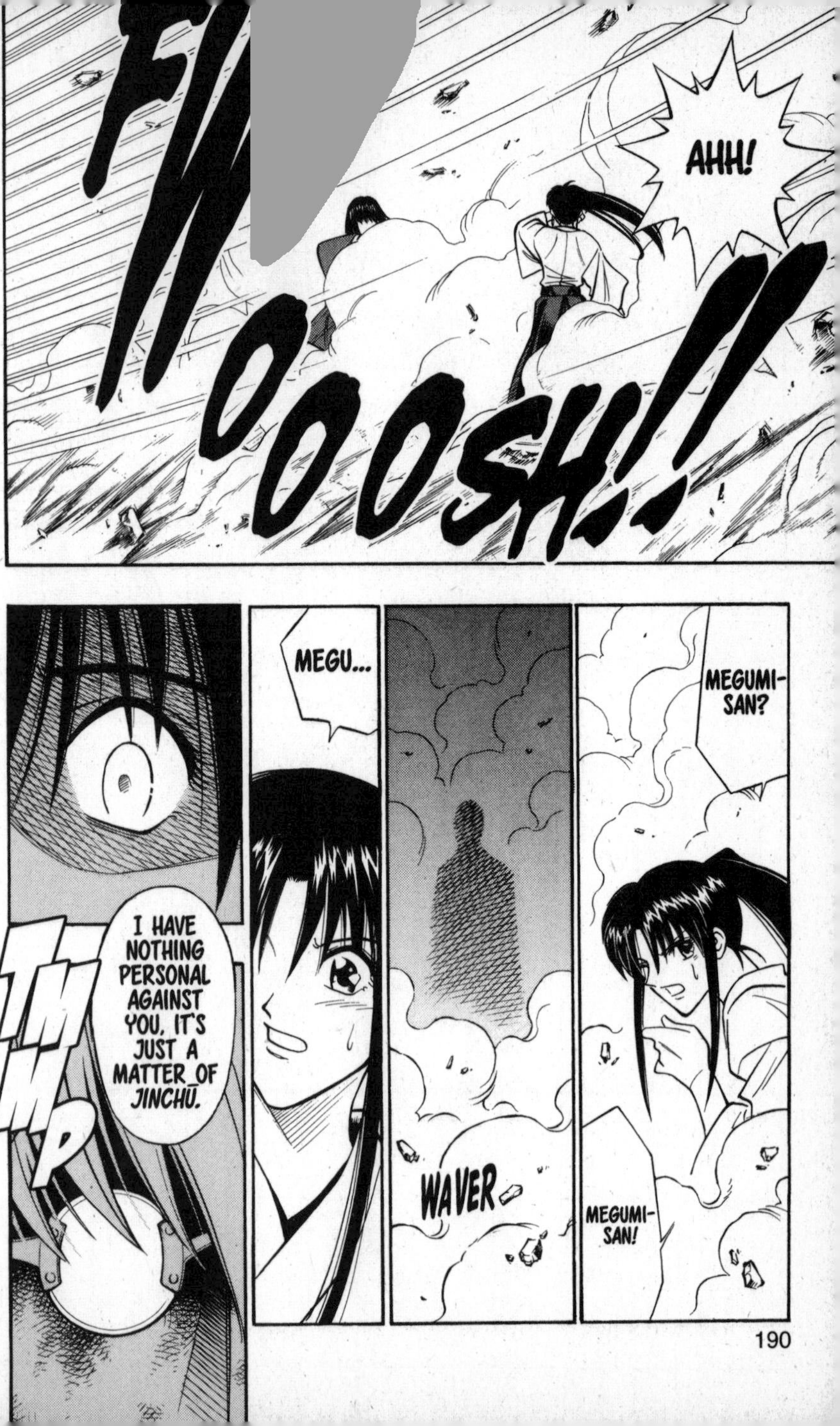
AHH!
FWOOOSH!!
MEGUMI-SAN?
MEGUMI-SAN!
WAVER
MEGU...
I HAVE NOTHING PERSONAL AGAINST YOU, IT'S JUST A MATTER OF JINCHŪ.
THMP

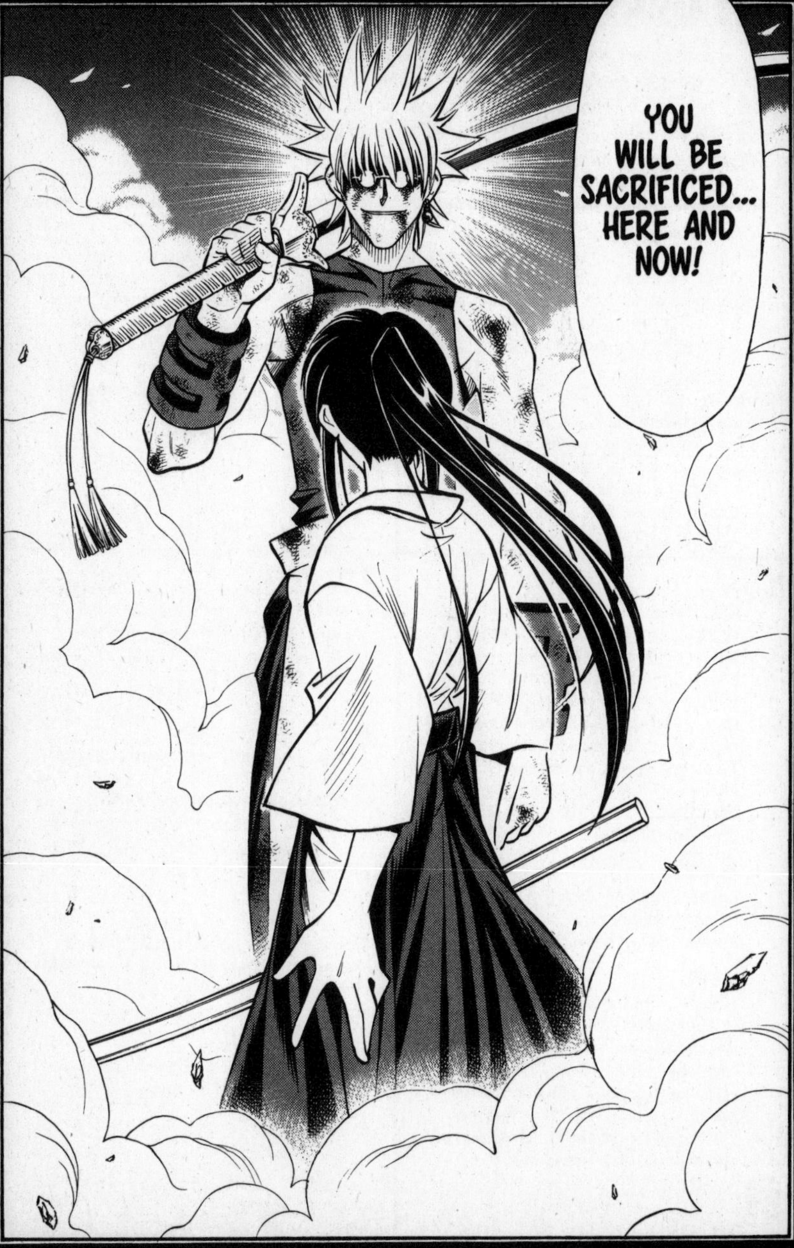
YOU WILL BE SACRIFICED... HERE AND NOW!

 To Be Continued in Vol. 24: The End of Dreams

GLOSSARY of the RESTORATION

A brief guide to select Japanese terms used in **Rurouni Kenshin**. *Note that, both here and within the story itself, all names are Japanese style—i.e., last or "family" name first, with personal or "given" name following. This is both because* **Kenshin** *is a "period" story, as well as to decrease confusion—if we were to take the example of Kenshin's* sakabatô *and "reverse" the format of the historically established assassin-name "Hitokiri Battôsai," for example, it would make little sense to then call him "Battôsai Himura."*

Hiten Mitsurugi-ryû
Kenshin's sword technique, used more for defense than offense. An "ancient style that pits one against many," it requires exceptional speed and agility to master.

hitokiri
An assassin. Famous swordsmen of the period were sometimes thus known to adopt "professional" names—**Kawakami Gensai**, for example, was also known as "Hitokiri Gensai."

Gatotsu
The signature move of Saitô Hajime, series creator Watsuki reportedly based his (fictional) version on an actual, historical, horizontal (or "flat") sword-technique. There are four "types" of **Gatotsu**: *Isshiki*, *Nishiki*, and *Sanshiki* (Variants One, Two and Three), as well as *Gatotsu Zeroshiki*—the final technique which doubles or even triples the power of the original thrust.

Ishin Shishi
Loyalist or pro-Imperialist **patriots** who fought to restore the Emperor to his ancient seat of power

jinchû
Hitokiri were fond of the word *tenchû*, or "judgment from the heavens," which expressed their belief that judgment lay in their hands. Enishi, on the other hand, calls his form of revenge **jinchû**, meaning that if the heavens won't cast judgment on Kenshin, he will with his own brand of justice.

Amakakeru Ryû no Hirameki
Lit., "Heavens-Bridging Dragon Spark" (as in spark of "inspiration," not "fire" or "flame"). Final or "succession" move of **Hiten Mitsurugi-ryû**, it incorporates everything Kenshin has been taught so far—including the overriding will to *live*. Also known as "Dragon Flight of Heaven."

Bakumatsu
Final, chaotic days of the Tokugawa regime

-chan
Honorific. Can be used either as a diminutive (e.g., with a small child— "Little Hanako or Kentarô"), or with those who are grown, to indicate affection ("My dear...").

-dono
Honorific. Even more respectful than **-san**; the effect in modern-day Japanese conversation would be along the lines of "Milord So-and-So." As used by Kenshin, it indicates both respect and humility.

Edo
Capital city of the **Tokugawa Bakufu**; renamed **Tokyo** ("Eastern Capital") after the Meiji Restoration

Himura Kenshin
Kenshin's "real" name, revealed to Kaoru only at her urging

-san

Honorific. Carries the meaning of "Mr.," "Ms.," "Miss," etc., but used more extensively in Japanese than its English equivalent (note that even an enemy may be addressed as "*-san*").

shôgun

Feudal military ruler of Japan

shôgunate

See *Tokugawa Bakufu*

"Swift Death to Evil!"

Although there is some debate on who originated the term (some say it was the personal slogan of Saitô Hajime; others hold it to be a more general motto of the Shinsengumi itself), a more liberal translation of *"Aku • Soku • Zan"* might be "Evil unto Evil"...where, in this case, the "evil" would be beheading, or death.

tachi

Tachi are longer and more curved than *uchigatana*, and used from horseback. They were worn attached to the belt, blade down.

Tokugawa Bakufu

Military feudal government which dominated Japan from 1603 to 1867

Tokyo

The renaming of "*Edo*" to "*Tokyo*" is a marker of the start of the *Meiji Restoration*

uchigatana

Also known as katana, *uchigatana* or "striking swords" had predecessors in the Heian period, and became standard for foot soldiers during the Nambokuchô period. Unlike *tachi*, the *uchigatana* is worn through the sash, edge up.

Zipangu

Japan was once one of the foremost mining countries of the world. Marco Polo heard rumors of this land of gold (Zipangu, Cipango) while in China, and it is through his writings about the marvelous golden country that Europe was introduced to Japan.

Kawakami Gensai

Real-life, historical inspiration for the character of *Himura Kenshin*

karakuri

Intricately constructed mechanized dolls or automatons, *karakuri* were in many ways the predecessors of Japan's modern mechanical robots and devices

kenjutsu

The art of fencing; swords arts; *kendô*

-kun

Honorific. Used in the modern day among male students, or those who grew up together, but another usage—the one you're more likely to find in *Rurouni Kenshin*—is the "superior-to-inferior" form, intended as a way to emphasize a difference in status or rank, as well as to indicate familiarity or affection.

Kyoto

Home of the Emperor and imperial court from A.D. 794 until shortly after the *Meiji Restoration* in 1868

Meiji Restoration

1853-1868; culminated in the collapse of the *Tokugawa Bakufu* and the restoration of imperial rule. So called after Emperor Meiji, whose chosen name was written with the characters for "culture and enlightenment."

rurouni

Wanderer, vagabond

sakabatô

Reversed-edge sword (the dull edge on the side the sharp should be, and vice versa); carried by Kenshin as a symbol of his resolution never to kill again

-sama

Honorific. The respectful equivalent of *-san*, *-sama* is used primarily in addressing persons of much higher rank than one's self...or, in a romantic sense, in addressing those upon whom one is crushing, wicked hard.

IN THE NEXT VOLUME...

With Kenshin incapacitated by an insensate Kujiranami, Enishi is afforded the opportunity he has long awaited to complete his unearthly *Jinchû*. Though Kenshin valiantly wields his *sakabatô* to atone for his past crimes and protect his friends' future, what will happen to that resolve if Kaoru dies? What good is a swordsman who can't even protect the ones he holds dearest? Those who reside at Kamiya Dojo find themselves at a dire crossroads in their journey, the outcome of which is frightfully uncertain.

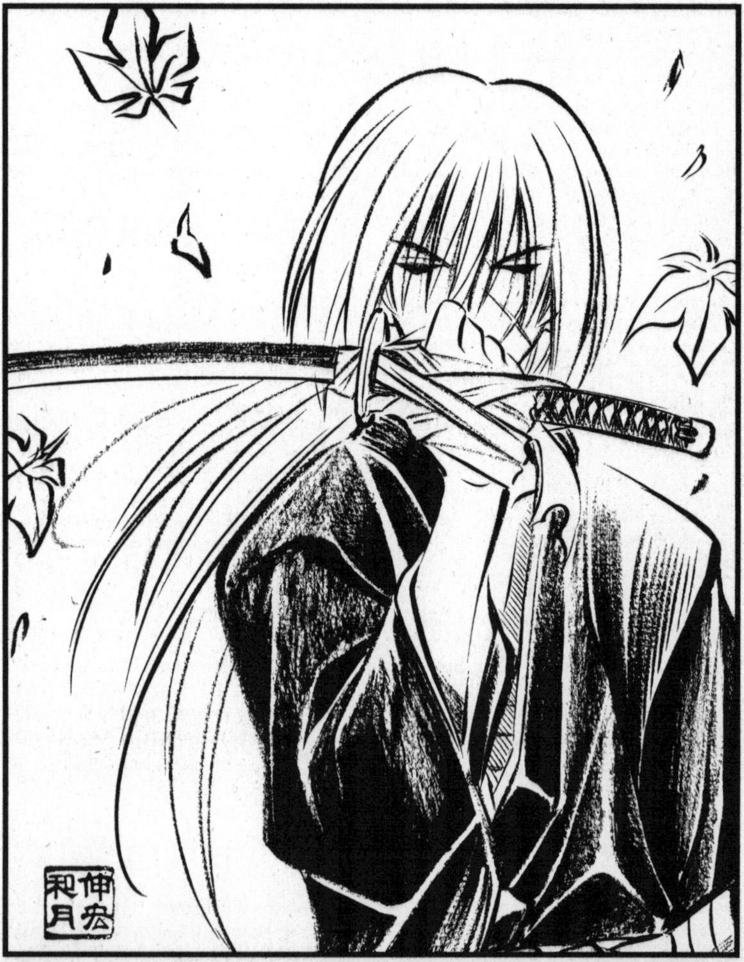

Available Now

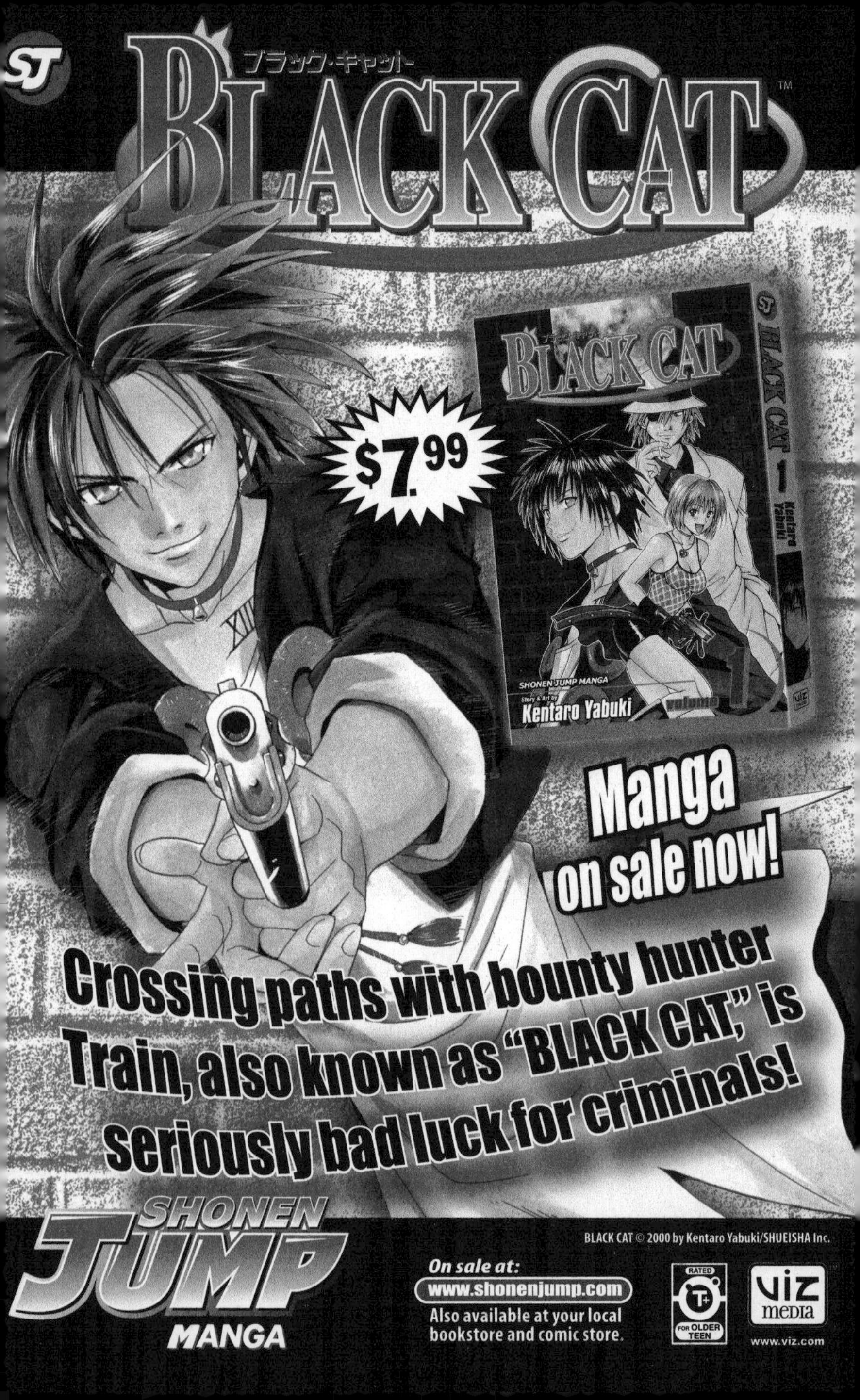

SJ
ブラック・キャット
BLACK CAT™
$7.99
SJ BLACK CAT 1 Kentaro Yabuki
BLACK CAT
SHONEN JUMP MANGA
Story & Art by
Kentaro Yabuki
volume
Manga on sale now!
Crossing paths with bounty hunter Train, also known as "BLACK CAT," is seriously bad luck for criminals!
SHONEN JUMP MANGA
BLACK CAT © 2000 by Kentaro Yabuki/SHUEISHA Inc.
On sale at:
www.shonenjump.com
Also available at your local bookstore and comic store.
RATED T+ FOR OLDER TEEN
viz media
www.viz.com

BLEACH
ブリーチ

By Tite Kubo, creator of _ZOMBIEPOWDER_.

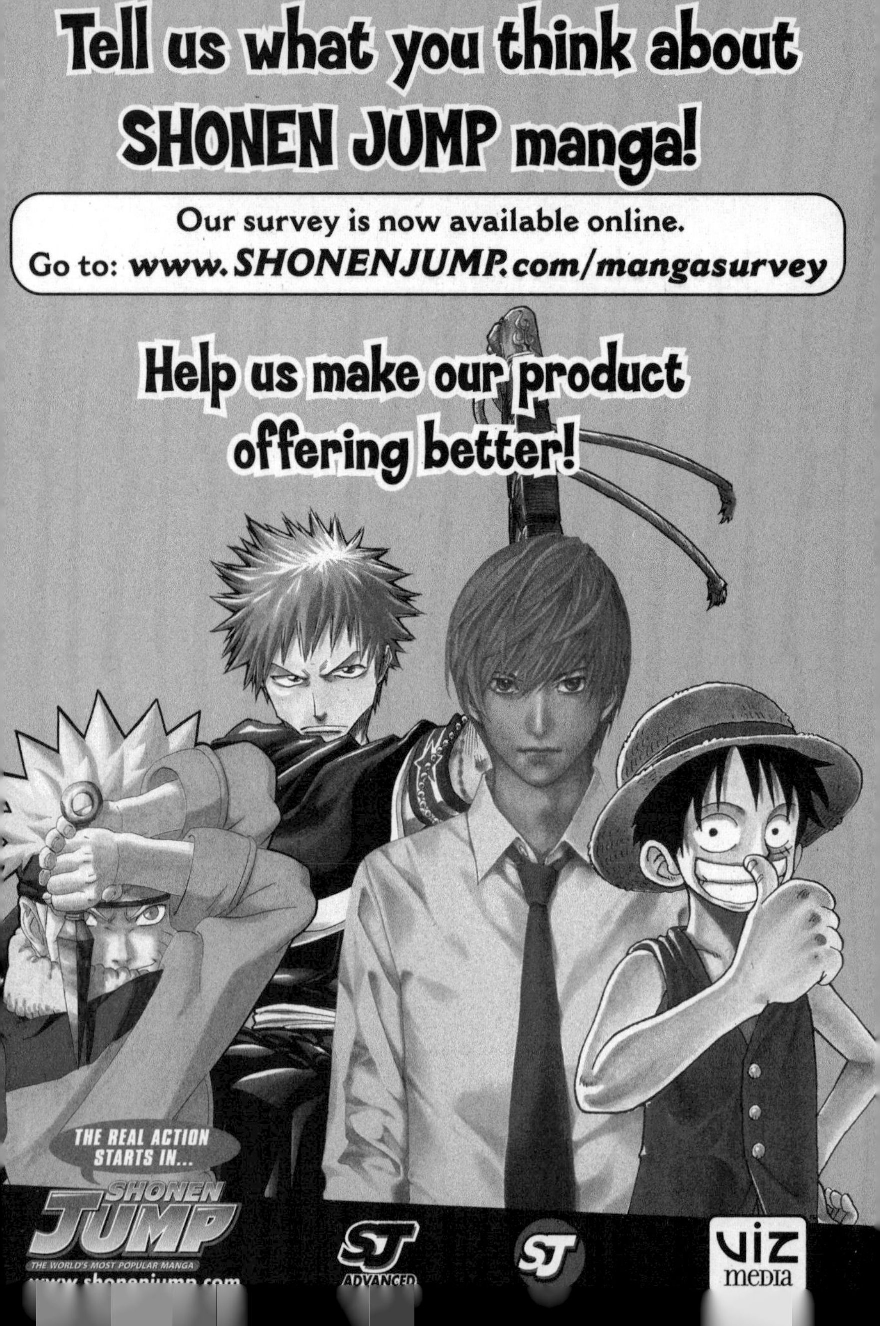
Tell us what you think about SHONEN JUMP manga!
Our survey is now available online.
Go to: www.SHONENJUMP.com/mangasurvey
Help us make our product offering better!
THE REAL ACTION STARTS IN...
SHONEN JUMP
THE WORLD'S MOST POPULAR MANGA
SJ ADVANCED
SJ
viz media